Haunted in the
New World

Jewish Literature and Culture
Series Editor, Alvin H. Rosenfeld

Haunted
in the
New World

JEWISH AMERICAN CULTURE FROM

CAHAN TO *THE GOLDBERGS*

Donald Weber

Indiana University Press

BLOOMINGTON AND INDIANAPOLIS

This book is a publication of

Indiana University Press
601 North Morton Street
Bloomington, IN 47404-3797 USA

http://iupress.indiana.edu

Telephone orders   800-842-6796
Fax orders   812-855-7931
Orders by e-mail   iuporder@indiana.edu

*The paper used in this publication meets the minimum
requirements of American National Standard for Information
Sciences—Permanence of Paper for Printed Library Materials,
ANSI Z39.48-1984.*

MANUFACTURED IN THE UNITED STATES OF AMERICA

Weber, Donald, date-
Haunted in the New World : Jewish American culture from Cahan to The Goldbergs /
Donald Weber.
p. cm. — (Jewish literature and culture)
Includes bibliographical references and index.
ISBN 0-253-34579-0 (cloth : alk. paper)
1. Jews—United States—Identity. 2. Jews—Cultural assimilation—United States.
3. Americanization. 4. American fiction—Jewish authors—History and criticism. 5. American
fiction—20th century—History and criticism. 6. Popular culture—Religious aspects—Judaism.
7. Jews in the performing arts—United States. 8. Jews in literature. 9. Emigration and
immigration—Psychological aspects. I. Title. II. Series.
E184.36.E84w53 2005
305.892'4073—dc22
2004023618
1   2   3   4   5   10   09   08   07   06   05

For Barbara, Jennie, and Daniel

The United States lured me not merely as a land of milk and honey, but also, and perhaps chiefly, as one of mystery, of fantastic experiences, of marvelous transformations. To leave my native place and to seek my fortune in that distant, weird world seemed to be just the kind of sensational adventure my heart was hankering for.

—David Levinsky

CONTENTS

ACKNOWLEDGMENTS

It gives me great pleasure to acknowledge the many friends, colleagues, and family who offered constant support and encouragement during the course of writing this book. They know how close to the heart this project has been. With deep gratitude, let me take this opportunity to thank them publicly.

As the book progressed, I was able to try out emerging ideas in a variety of academic settings. As a result, the study began to take shape under the pressure of a deadline. For their generous invitations to give a presentation or contribute to an essay collection I want to thank Joyce Antler, Andrew Bush, Jules Chametzky, Hasia Diner, Joel Foreman, Jim Hoberman, Michael P. Kramer, Jack Kugelmass, Jeffrey Shandler, Gerald Sorin, Steven Whitfield, Hana Wirth-Nesher, and Steve J. Zipperstein.

I also want to thank a number of funding agencies and research institutions for their support: the National Endowment for the Humanities; the Woodrow Wilson Center for International Scholars; the Lucius N. Littauer Foundation; the Institute of United States Studies, University of London; the Oxford Centre for Hebrew and Jewish Studies; and the Rothermere American Institute, Oxford. I am grateful as well to the staffs at a host of libraries who helped at various stages of my research: the George Arents Research Library for Special Collections, Syracuse University; the Museum of Television and Radio; the New York Public Library for the Performing Arts; the UCLA Film and Television Archive; the Margaret Herrick Library, Academy Foundation, National Academy of Motion Picture Arts and Sciences; the American Jewish Historical Society; the Museum of the City of New York; and the Jewish Museum. The Inter-library loan librarians at Mount Holyoke College—as always—proved crucial in locating hard to find materials.

Over the years I have drawn on the expertise of numerous friends and colleagues for their insights. For reading sections of the manuscript at various stages I owe a sizeable debt to Christopher Benfey, Sacvan Bercovitch, Joshua Brockman, Daniel Czitrom, Sander L. Gilman, Daniel Horowitz, Rudolf Janssens, Amy Kaplan, George Lipsitz, Max Novak, the late Michael Rogin, Jeffrey Rubin-Dorsky, Robert Shilkret, and Paul Staiti.

ACKNOWLEDGMENTS

At Indiana University Press I am especially grateful to Janet Rabino-wich for believing in the project. I also want to thank Alvin H. Rosenfeld for his support; I am honored to be included in his "Jewish Literature and Culture" series. To Joyce Rappaport, thanks for a masterful job of copyediting. To Rebecca Tolen and Jane Lyle, thanks for seeing the book through its various stages of preparation.

At Mount Holyoke, thanks to Andrew Lass, Sue Leduc, and Maryanne Aslo for helping me through the stressful final stages of manuscript prepa-ration. Thanks as well to Joan Davis for her superb indexing skills. And a special thanks to Penny Gill for supporting the project in its final stages. Above all, massive thanks to Donal O'Shea, the Dean of the Faculty, for his constant and generous support of my project.

A number of special, loving thank-yous:

To Jay Fliegelman, for over thirty years of crucial friendship.

To my extended Weber family, above all my Aunts Anne Gilbert, the late Bebe Mendelowitz, Frieda ("Tiny") Stolzberg, and all my uncles and cousins (especially Paul Mendelowitz), for your insights into (and perfor-mance of) the deeper meanings of Bronx Jewish life.

To my mother, Jessie Weber, for leavening my "Bronx" Jewish self with rich (and nourishing) doses of Cleveland *Yiddishkayt.*

To my father, Hyman Weber, legendary living room comic, for mak-ing me laugh until the milk ran through my nose, among other filial legacies.

To Barbara, for being my shrewdest reader for over thirty years.

To Jennie and Daniel, brilliant performers in the Weber tradition, for keeping the faith.

Thanks to the following university presses for permission to adapt the following previously published materials:

A version of Chapter 1 appeared as "Outsiders and Greenhorns: Christopher Newman in the Old World, David Levinsky in the New," *American Literature* 67 (1995): 725–45. Reprinted with permission of Duke University Press.

Portions of Chapter 3 appeared in "Accents of the Future: Jewish Popular Culture," in *The Cambridge Companion to Jewish American Litera-ture,* ed. Michael P. Kramer and Hana Wirth-Nesher (Cambridge: Cam-bridge University Press, 2003), 129–33.

Portions of Chapter 6 appeared in the following publications: "Mem-ory and Repression in Early Ethnic Television: The Example of Gertrude Berg and *The Goldbergs,*" in *The Other Fifties: Interrogating Midcentury American Icons,* ed. Joel Foreman (Urbana: University of Illinois Press,

1997), 144–67; "The Jewish-American World of Gertrude Berg: *The Goldbergs* on Radio and Television, 1930–1960," in *Talking Back: Images of Jewish Women in American Popular Culture,* ed. Joyce Antler (Hanover, N.H.: Brandeis University Press, 1998), 85–99, 262–65; "Goldberg Variations: The Achievements of Gertrude Berg," in *Entertaining America: Jews, Movies, and Broadcasting,* ed. J. Hoberman and Jeffrey Shandler (Princeton, N.J.: Princeton University Press, 2003), 113–23, 296–98.

Chapter 7 is adapted from "Manners and Morals, Civility and Barbarism: The Cultural Contexts of *Seize the Day,*" in *New Essays on Seize the Day,* ed. Michael P. Kramer (Cambridge: Cambridge University Press, 1998), 43–70.

The Epilogue is adapted from "Taking Jewish American Popular Culture Seriously: The Yinglish Worlds of Gertrude Berg, Milton Berle, and Mickey Katz," *Jewish Social Studies* 5 (Fall 1998/Winter 1999): 124–53.

Haunted in the
New World

INTRODUCTION

Adjusting to America

You will not be able to erase the old home from your heart. Your heart will be drawn elsewhere. And in your solitude, images will rise up and stare in your faces with eternal sorrow.[1]

—Abraham Cahan (1916)

During the early years of the last century, the immigrant-filled streets of lower Manhattan had become a vibrant scene of what social critics at the time called the drama of "Americanization." Invoked most often by genteel, native-born observers troubled by the arrival of so many "aliens" from distant shores, "Americanization" referred to a complicated process of social adaptation. For the staggering number of Jewish immigrants— well over a million by 1900—who began arriving in America from Eastern Europe in the late nineteenth century, the psychological–symbolic transition from raw "greenhorn"—or *greener*, as Jews fresh off the boat called themselves in self-mocking Yiddish—to grateful, if hesitant, New World citizens remains emblematic of the archetypal American story itself.[2] *Haunted in the New World* explores how modern Jewish American writers and makers of popular culture responded to the personal and collective challenge of adjusting to America, voicing their imaginative encounter in accents of resistance and celebration, irony and longing. In the process, this study reveals the shaping power of a range of core emotions—what psychologists call "affects"—for a deeper understanding of Jewish American expressive culture in the twentieth century.[3]

"Americanization is a spiritual thing," a writer in the *Saturday Evening Post* remarked in the summer of 1918, at the height of this mass migration to the New World.[4] For some immigrants, the process—really the pressures—of cultural adaptation proved exhilarating, resulting in the new arrivals' wholesale embrace of their host society. Indeed, for many who made the arduous journey in steerage, "America" loomed as redemptive ideal, an invitation to a new life in another "chosen land." In *They Who Knock at Our Gates* (1914), the immigrant writer Mary Antin offered an ardent patriotic response to a litany of nativist attacks, specifically, to E. A. Ross's defamatory *The Old World in the New* (1914), an appeal for New World racial purity that worried (among other things) about barbarian "Jewish invader[s]" from the East and their "certain ways and manners."[5] In reply, Antin associated the current migration-in-progress with the sacred history of the nation itself, a narrative that opened with huddled Pilgrims seeking freedom in the New World—an inheritance which, she felt, was continuing into the present. "The ghost of the Mayflower pilots every immigrant ship," she claimed, "and Ellis Island is another name for Plymouth Rock."[6] How could the latter-day heirs of the Pilgrims' spirit not embrace, with unalloyed gratitude, America's providential destiny as asylum for mankind? Even Anzia Yezierska, who along with Antin and Abraham Cahan was one of the great early twentieth-century Jewish writers, recognized the spiritual potential of New World inheritance, despite the constant struggle of her fictional "daughters of loneliness" to feel settled in this strange New World: "What, after all, is America, but the response to the demands of immigrants like me, seeking new worlds in which their spirits may be free to create beauty?" Yezierska asked, voicing the immigrant soul's yearning for America as symbol of self-reinvention. "Were not the Pilgrim Fathers immigrants demanding a new world in which they could be free to live higher lives?"[7]

Yet the rituals of *becoming*, the invitation to adopt New World ways— assenting to the nation's cultural ideals, political history, and traditions of "democratic" selfhood—could also prove daunting, even mysterious. For Horace Kallen, an important contemporary social critic who participated

[2]

in the urgent debates over the fate of arriving immigrants, the project of Americanization concealed latent dangers, especially for the immigrant psyche. In 1915, Kallen introduced the term *cultural pluralism*—an enabling mode of preserving distinctive "ethnic" identities—in response to the shrill nativist calls for complete assimilation on the part of aspiring "Americans." In time, Kallen recognized the emotional costs of such *oysgrinung* (the Yiddish phrase denoting the assimilative "out-greening" process itself) on the part of the country's would-be citizens. "Although he can swiftly change his clothes and his superficial manners, thus throwing off the external differences between himself and his new *milieu*," Kallen observed in 1924, "the conversion of habit and attitude [the "spiritual" aspect] are [*sic*] another story":

> In the new community [the immigrant's] old habits and attitudes do not obtain the old results, and the old results are no longer successful adjustments to the situation. The immigrant's personality suffers attrition and dislocation. He doesn't belong, and so, cannot find himself. Disjoined from the old ways and values and not yet at home in the new, he becomes demoralized.[8]

Dislocation; disjoined; demoralized. Such extreme, charged terms convey the unhinging potential latent in the passage to America, the unforeseen *baggage* not checked in steerage. Indeed, Kallen's analysis bespeaks the various ruptures, both spatial and psychological, afflicting the *unsettled* immigrant, unmoored in the wake of New World migration. Kallen's heartfelt litany highlights the burden—call it the ordeal—of Americanization: the immigrants' challenge to *locate* themselves, to construct a new home in the utterly un*heimisch* (un-home-like) America.

Abraham Cahan poignantly captures such New World disorientation in a 1916 editorial in the *Forward*, the famous Yiddish newspaper he founded in 1897 and that he edited well into the next century. Feeling himself politically adrift in the wake of various incidents of antisemitism at home and abroad (the Leo Frank case in Atlanta, continued pogroms in Tsarist Russia), Cahan sought some spiritual solace in the embrace of his adopted homeland. "We have to be Americans. . . .We shall love America and help to build America," Cahan implored his readers. But the editorial soon shifts into a different register, toward anxiety and lament, revealing the ambivalent underside of New World exuberance: "But you will not be able to erase the old home from your heart," Cahan cautioned. "The heart will be drawn elsewhere. And in your solitude, images will rise up and stare in your faces with eternal sorrow."[9]

In 1916 Cahan was in the middle of composing his classic novel of and John F. Kasson have described the fundamental shaping power of etiquette manuals, which emerged in response to the consolidation of bourgeois culture, especially in the more socially open late-nineteenth-century cities, filled with various migrants. According to Kasson, the veritable explosion of etiquette manuals by the end of the century signaled the anxious response of the Protestant establishment and its strategy of instating social control: "the fine points of manners could operate as another means of exclusion at the upper ranks of society, for much of urban middle-class life the cultivation of bourgeois manners served as an instrument of inclusion and socialization."[13]

At the same time, the rise of such manuals reflected the worried establishment's skewed perceptions of American social reality lurking on the "other" side; in Halttunen's description, "polite society imposed some order on a society of placeless, liminal people . . . it offered a haven from the dangers of life in a world of strangers."[14]

The strangers, however, were already knocking—"the visible alien at the gate," in nativist E. A. Ross's anxious phrase—seeking entrance.[15] For some Jewish immigrant artists, the codes of civility existed (indeed, *always* exist) to be decoded, unmasked and demystified as merely socially constructed, imposed styles of behavior, and not as descriptions of some "natural" social order. For others, the authority of America as cultural ideal could be truly unsettling; a wholesale embrace of imagined New World destiny might send the rejected self, seeking assimilation, reeling in psychic disarray. Such Jewish American dilemmas of contact and negotiation inform the case studies in cultural identification, disillusionment, and ambivalence presented in *Haunted in the New World*.

Again, from a wider perspective, such affective complexities, the result of the ordeal of assimilation, express what sociologist Zygmunt Bauman calls "the harrowing experience of ambivalence": the narrative of Jewish modernity itself.[16] For this story, I draw on Sander L. Gilman (especially his study of Jewish self-hatred), Zygmunt Bauman (especially his sociologies of modernity), and above all, on Norbert Elias, the great historian-sociologist of manners and civility. Taken together, their ways of reading the social dramas of assimilation have striking relevance for deciphering the inner journeys of Jewish American artists, especially in the twentieth century.

The compelling interpretive power of Elias issues from a profound recognition that the price of assimilation is often measured in a consuming self-consciousness that, depending on the situation, can be debilitating (just ask David Levinsky) or enabling, as in the overturning power of parody and mimicry (just ask the Marx Brothers). For Elias, displaced from his native Breslau and writing his masterpiece *The Civilizing Process* in England during the 1930s (published originally in German, it did not appear in English until 1978), the "phases of assimilation" that accompany the civilizing process expose those "aspiring outsider groups," seeking to rise in social status, to potential "deformations of consciousness and attitude." "Total assimilation to a higher established group succeeds only very exceptionally in one generation," Elias argued; indeed, the modern effort at "individual social advancement" leads, inevitably, to a "crossfire from all sides ["from below as from above"] to which individuals are exposed in their social rise."[17]

In less abstract language, Elias is describing what we now recognize as the potential dangers latent in the "outsider's" identification with an idealized cultural authority: the desire to imitate, to pass, to be accepted as a member of the society one esteems, and seeks acceptance by—a version, we might say, of the drama of Americanization.

The psychic strains of identification, however, often issue in betrayal—exposure—at the level of manners and civility, in the form of transgressive behavioral and bodily etiquette. In Elias's analysis, "The education, standards of living and fears of the rising groups and the upper class are in this phase still so different that the attempt to achieve the poise of the upper class leads in most cases to a peculiar falseness and incongruity of behavior which nevertheless conceals a genuine distress, a desire to escape the pressure from above and the sense of inferiority. And this shaping of the super ego on upper-class models also brings about in the rising class a specific form of shame and embarrassment."[18]

Thus shame, "the most Jewish of emotions" for Zygmunt Bauman, rises in the disjunctive space between *performance*—the art of maintaining "poise" before the gaze of the judging dominant culture—and exposure. So exposed, the performing (Jewish) self, seeking acceptance, collapses, revealing before one's own eyes an array of self-betraying, self-convicting behaviors.[19] Shame, we might say, haunts the territory of assimilation, ready to spring. It is, according to Silvan Tomkins, "the affect of indignity, of defeat, of transgression and of alienation." And self-hatred, the emotional residue of this complex social-psychological process, tends to flow in the wake of felt rejection, threatening to dissolve the newly vulnerable self into an abyss of unlovability.[20] The unforgiving "toxic" effect of shame and self-hatred leaves its self-lacerating marks everywhere on the Jewish American immigrant landscape; *Haunted in the New World* surveys its coordinates as it gauges its impact.

In the following series of case studies, I map the complex emotional landscape of modern Jewish American expression, ranging from chapters on early immigrant fiction and film (Abraham Cahan, Anzia Yezierska, and the various incarnations of the "Jazz Singer") to close readings of the major writers in the literary canon (Henry Roth and Saul Bellow), to an examination of two novels that explore the psycho-social dimensions of post-war antisemitism (Arthur Miller's *Focus* [1945] and Bellow's *The Victim* [1947]) to the world of popular culture—above all, the radio and television career of Gertrude Berg and her famous alter ego, "Molly Goldberg."

In an autobiographical Epilogue, I explore my own relation to the 1950s Bronx world of my comedian manqué father and his love for Jewish popular culture. In this respect, the last section of *Haunted in the New World* offers a personal meditation by a Jewish son on his "twice-removed" nostalgia: a nostalgia, it turns out, for his father's nostalgia. The late Irving Howe styled this sentimentalized stance toward the Jewish past, perhaps ungenerously, "unearned nostalgia"; lacking patience for the mindless "chic" celebrations of ethnicity during the ethnic "revival" of the 1970s, Howe railed against the cultural degradations of what Philip Roth's Nathan Zuckerman calls "that cheap middlebrow crap" mounted by shmaltzy Broadway musicals and vulgar Borscht Belt comics, schmearing their shameless punchlines with layers of Yiddish shmutz.[21]

In defense of nostalgia, I imaginatively return to the middle-class Bronx world that also loved that "crap," and account, in retrospect, for the local appeal of Jewish American popular culture during the fifties. What, I want to discover, were the particular claims on the extended Weber family, residing in second-generation comfort (the first apartment in the building, I'm told, to own a television) in the northeast Bronx, at 3031 Holland Avenue. Receptive to the core, why did they howl with delight at the vulgar antics of Uncle Miltie? (The short answer relates to the sweet insider pleasure of his shtick.) Why *did* the Bronx love "Molly Goldberg," along with Mickey Katz's Yinglish parodies? Why, after a serious heyday in the fifties, is Mickey Katz enjoying such a comeback? And, finally, why do I, devoted Jewish son that I am, feel such a profound need to revisit this sentimentalized territory of popular culture in the first place?

The answers, I suspect, have both intellectual and emotional coordinates, with roots driving deep into my Jewish self. The intellectual project involves exploring the expressive forms shaped by and in Jewish American modernity itself. "The assimilatory pressure, that trade mark of modern politics," observes Zygmunt Bauman, "cast the Jews in social contexts from which contradictions of modernity were most poignantly experienced and hence easier to scan, to comprehend and to theorize." Thus "Jewish contributions to modern culture," Bauman continues, "are better understood not as expressions of 'Jewish struggle with modernity,' but as by-products of 'modernity's struggle with itself.' "²² In this respect, *Haunted in the New World* examines the "by-products" and "side-effects" of twentieth-century Jewish American culture: the complex range of emotions stirred, dislodged by the imagination under the pressure of modernity itself.

And, on a more personal level, I suppose that *Haunted in the New World* represents my own shifting relation to Jewish memory, complicated by a son's profound nostalgia, inflected by ambivalence and embrace.²³ In the end, the effort to read deeply, to reach the emotional core of modern Jewish American culture, becomes a sign of love, a gesture of empathy, expressed through acts of interpretation.

1

OUTSIDER IN THE OLD WORLD,

GREENHORN IN THE NEW

Christopher Newman and David Levinsky

I have been in America almost three years. I came from Russia where I studied at a *yeshiva*. My parents were proud and happy at the thought that I would become a rabbi. But at the age of twenty I had to go to America. Before I left I gave my father my word that I would walk the righteous path and be good and pious. But America makes one forget everything.[1]

—Letter to the *Bintel Brief*, 1908

Americans in Europe are *outsiders*," the young Henry James observed in October 1878. His words appeared in an article titled "Americans Abroad," written for the *Nation* in response to Frederick Sheldon's stinging portrait of "The American Colony in France" in the same journal six months earlier.[2] Sheldon had caused a stir by describing the embarrassing poverty of manners displayed by Americans traveling in Europe. He had remarked upon their inability to fathom Old World styles of behavior or to decode the ambiguous signs of social convention that tended to baffle the forthright, plainspeaking, above all *innocent* American tourist. "The American traveller," Sheldon charged, "does not know his place in this complex society. . . . in his ignorance of custom and etiquette he will thrust himself even upon royalty, utterly unconscious of the disgust he is producing."[3]

Of course James was no apologist for the social and aesthetic advantages of the still raw, provincial American scene; after all, in 1879, a year after Sheldon's article, James would cause a cultural stir of his own by the satiric listing of those "items of high civilization . . . absent from the texture of American life" in his study of Hawthorne, a deeply personal meditation on literary and regional legacies, which he published on the threshold of his departure for Europe. [4] (James eventually left America in 1883 and did not return until 1904.) Arguing in defense of the American character abroad, James claimed that his native land could be understood only if the fundamental aspect of the country's history was appreciated: "We are the only great people of the civilized world," the young American author explained in 1878, "that is a pure democracy, and we are the only great people that is exclusively commercial."[5]

If in 1878 James seemed occupied by the question of American innocence, and thus felt compelled to soften the sting of Sheldon's acerbic critique, it may be because James's novel *The American* (1877) had just recently been serialized (June 1876–May 1877) in the *Atlantic Monthly*.[6] *The American* is concerned, above all, with the fate of its deeply democratic and conspicuously commercial hero, Christopher Newman, and his futile attempt, as it turns out, to read the mysterious signs of an unfathomable Europe and his failed quest to marry—and thereby save—the Bellegardes' Old World daughter, the incarnation of his New World romantic dream. *The American,* in my view, offers a provocative way of reading later Jewish American fiction, above all Abraham Cahan's classic *Rise of David Levinsky* (1917), if we reimagine James's famous "international theme" of New World "innocence" overwhelmed by Old World conspiracy as a *reverse* immigrant narrative. In this reading, Newman, "the great Western Barbarian"(68),[7] as Mrs. Tristam, James's representative of the self-conscious alienated American colony styles him, emerges as an American greenhorn in Paris, a New World pilgrim who cannot decode the archaic ways and generational layerings of the Old, embodied by the Bellegardes. In poignant contrast, we have the confessions of Cahan's bewildered, nostalgia-riven David Levinsky, the would-be Talmudic scholar turned rich industrialist who, despite his newly acquired wealth and social status, cannot find any happiness in the New. By setting James's *The American* in creative dialogue with *The Rise of David Levinsky,* I highlight a number of resonant, indeed overarching, themes that organize James's early comic novel as well as shape Cahan's canonical account of New World adjustment. In juxtaposing these two novels about migration and frustrated desire (among other things), I seek to begin mapping the emotional landscape of Jewish American literary and cultural expression in the twentieth century.

In his comic bumblings, Christopher Newman might have been satirized as a *greener* on the early twentieth-century Yiddish stage—a clownish, rough-mannered immigrant from the West seeking to negotiate a maze of custom, struggling to comprehend the arcane habits of the Bellegarde family and their codes of behavior occulted within layers of mystery. Despite his professed desire to abide by the "proper forms" of this Old World spectacle, Newman's lack, in the aristocratic eyes of the Bellegardes, of appropriate "foundations," his thin personal history, and above all his failures in etiquette, doom his ardent American quest. In this respect, Newman can be deemed an "outsider," in a modern, anthropological–sociological sense: an alien barred, literally, at the end, from the encircling "closed" society fashioned—indeed guarded by—the mysterious Bellegardes. Newman's misperceptions—misreadings of the entrenched barriers of Old World custom thwarting his happiness—generate the substantial comedy in the novel.[8]

In an early exchange between Newman and the sphinx-like, always sarcastic Madame de Bellegarde, for example, the family matriarch asks him, "What was your business?" Newman replies, "I have been in everything . . . At one time I sold leather; at one time I manufactured washtubs." In response, "Madame de Bellegarde made a little grimace. 'Leather? I don't like that. Wash-tubs are better. I prefer the smell of soap. I hope at least they made your fortune.'" *Greener* that he is, Newman misses the telling grimace, a physical reaction to his fluid democratic self—the sign of Madame de Bellegarde's *distaste* for the commercial—that will eventually grow into complete revulsion. As an American outsider, Newman behaves like a textbook example of Sheldon's innocent American abroad, unconscious of the "disgust" he produces. He tries heroically to remain steady in his romantic quest, but the Bellegardes' stylized manners, the Marquis's (the oldest son, in charge of family image and destiny) "polished aphorism[s]," his social power, derived from a self constructed "of forms and phrases and postures," keep Newman slipping and sliding, always off balance: "M. de Bellegarde made him feel as if he were standing barefooted on a marble floor."[9]

The plot of *The American* turns on Newman's reversal of fortune in his earnest quest: the Old World family's initial grudging assent to Newman's brief of marriage and the later perplexing withdrawal of their daughter from a New World alliance. As James renders it, Newman's social and political difficulties flow from his aura of American newness, his lack of "antecedents"; above all, the Bellegardes reject his status as "a commercial person."[10] Significantly, the language James summons to express the opposition between Newman's fluid social identity as an American and the Bellegardes' static, aristocratic position employs metaphors of ingestion and disgust. Thus, when exasperated over his frustrated romantic endeavors Newman confesses to his fellow expatriate, Mrs. Tristam, about the prickly Marquis—"There's a man I can't swallow, mix the drink as I will"—we overhear the novel's core rhetorical strategy, its virtual structure of feeling. Within the novel's affective boundaries, neither side can tolerate—literally stomach—the other. Disgusted by the presence of Newman, in whose reflection as potential brother-in-law the Marquis internally grimaces, the Marquis outwardly evinces a "conscious ironical smile," another telling sign that the socially naïve Newman fails to note. Thus, beneath the novel's apparent surface of civility and manners, there rages a raw battle of will, destiny, and desire. Indeed, in his free-floating innocence, James tells us that Newman is "constantly forgetting himself, and indulging in an unlimited amount of irresponsible inquiry and conjecture"; the Marquis, on the other hand, "never forgot himself for an instant." Not surprisingly, then, Newman can't fathom that in his presence the Marquis "was holding his breath so as not to inhale the odour of democracy."[11]

Thus Newman wanders into—or, as a barbarian outsider, invades the closed gates of the Bellegardes, unconscious of his grating effect on their monarchist sensibilities, unaware that his commercial identity and democratic aspect—the "essence" of his Americanness stink in their Old World nostrils. To be sure, at key moments he recognizes that his initially successful courtship of Claire makes the family gag. Approaching the elderly Marquise, who "looked at him fixedly, without moving," Newman "said to himself, that her daughter had been announcing her engagement, and that the old lady found the morsel hard to swallow."[12] But in general, Newman remains oblivious to his mounting incivilities, his improper social etiquette. Eventually his lack of deeper understanding of the Bellegarde worship of surface and civility proves fatal, for their royalist attitudes compel the family, despite their poverty, to choose unalloyed heredity and honor rather than the suspect smell of commerce embodied in and emanating from Christopher Newman.[13]

To distill the drama of *The American,* the gaffe that frustrates Newman's romantic design occurs at the height of his self-assurance. Having received the family's tacit consent to marry, Newman commits the unforgivable sin of proclaiming his victory. "Now that his prize was gained," James writes, Newman "felt a peculiar desire that his triumph be manifest." Yet his motivation, as James renders it, is complex. In reality, Newman is profoundly irritated by the Bellegardes' reticence with respect to the engagement; theirs was "but a limited resonance" in response to his "victory," and Newman itches (as James puts it) to "break all windows." Why does he possess a "somewhat aggressive impulse to promulgate his felicity"? is James's fairly dense description of Newman's mental state. "He wanted," as James explains in a key passage, "for once to make the heads of the house of Bellegarde *feel* him."[14] Newman, that is, seeks some sign, not simply that he is accepted by Claire, but that he has gained a social status recognized, indeed *legitimated*, by the ancient Bellegardes.

But a public display of Newman's imagined or dreamed incorporation proves—once again—hard for the family to swallow. When Newman decides to throw a huge engagement party for himself—after announcing, with obvious pride, that he has already telegraphed the news of his marriage to various American cities, much to the Marquise's chagrin—his intemperate action forces the Bellegardes into hastily sponsoring their own. Madame de Bellegarde "had no idea whatsoever of giving a fete," her younger son and Newman's confidante Valentin explains to the American, "but finding it the only issue from your proposal [Newman's party], she looked straight at the dose—excuse the expression—and bolted it, as you saw, without winking."[15]

Newman's behavior at the family's reception, as many critics have pointed out, prompts the sudden reversal in his romantic fortunes. In a fatal breach of etiquette, Newman escorts the Bellegarde matriarch "across the floor," "walk[ing] [her] through the rooms" of the large reception. Riven with deep embarrassment by the humiliating parade before her own people, the Marquise separates herself from Newman, saying, "with measured softness," " 'this is enough, sir.' " Heady with his apparent victory (the defeat of desiccated Old World nobility by the democratic–commercial self), Newman remains, nevertheless, unconscious of the scene of profound shame he has occasioned. " 'I feel quite like one of the family,' " he announces, without irony, feeling he has at last been *tolerated*, and thus *incorporated* into the family.[16] What he cannot fathom is how this public ordeal overturns the secretive, immobile, inert Bellegardes; by setting the Marquise "in motion" before all the eyes of the monarchist world, Newman fatally releases—as he unconsciously fulfills—his own aggressive desires, expressed by this act of supreme incivility. His indelible "greenhornness"—he is, after all, an immigrant alienated in the Old World—

makes his suit for Claire intolerable to the intolerant Bellegardes. " 'They really couldn't endure you any longer,' " a shrewd Mrs. Tristam again explains to Newman, in despair over his abrupt change of fortune. " 'It was your commercial quality in the abstract they couldn't swallow.' "[17]

Of course *The American* contains other rich themes—of power and its embodiment, of gender politics, of arcane French political history.[18] From the perspective outlined above, the language of ingestion and disgust emerges as central to James's imagination of the "American" as "outsider," a New World alien *expelled* from Europe.[19] At the same time, the novel's core rhetoric of incorporation and expulsion anticipates the unsettling tones of early twentieth-century debate over the fate of constantly arriving immigrants, mainly from Eastern and Southern Europe, to the New World's shores. Could they be "Americanized"—"melted" and "stirred"—into the nation? After almost thirty years of self-imposed exile, James himself witnessed—with varying degrees of dismay, perplexity, and wonder—the new American world of arriving immigrants. Visiting Ellis Island in 1904, he registered his deeply personal response to the impact of New World migration:

> The impression of Ellis Island, in fine, would be . . . a chapter by itself. . . . It is a drama that goes on, without a pause, day by day and year by year, this visible act of ingurgitation on the part of our body politic and social, and constituting really an appeal to amazement beyond that of any sword-swallowing or fire-swallowing of the circus. The wonder that one couldn't keep down was the thought that these two or three hours of one's own chance vision of the business were but as one tick or two of the mighty clock, the clock that never, never stops—least of all when it strikes, for a sign of so much winding-up, some louder hour of our national fate than usual. I think indeed that the simplest account of the action of Ellis Island on the spirit of any sensitive citizen who may have happened to "look in" is that he comes back from his visit not at all the same person that he went. He has eaten of the tree of knowledge, and the taste will be forever in his mouth.[20]

James's experience of "terrible little Ellis Island" amounted to a fall into history—into the future of America—a descent that left him feeling like an outsider in his own homeland. What so startled James was the sense that the "aliens" now residing in his old New York were *already* comfortable in their New World surroundings. "Foreign as they may be," James observed, "newly inducted as they might be, they were *at home,* really more at home, at the end of their few weeks or months or their year or two, than they had ever in their lives been before."[21]

and become a mere, elementary, grasping animal."[26] The meaning of "the Jewish fire," with its sources, resonances, and vicissitudes, is the overarching subject of Jewish American expression through the 1920s.

Above all else, *The Rise of David Levinsky* charts the arc of repression, self-hatred, and denial in the immigrant psyche. Having arrived in what Cahan terms "a topsy turvy country,"[27] Levinsky quickly discovers that decoding the conventions of style and manners is the only way to project, or even to know the self. If Christopher Newman is at ease with his American manners—as evidenced by his instinctive habit of stretching his long legs while sitting, which is James's emblem of his hero's native expansiveness—Levinsky, like Howells's Lapham—who is something of a Vermont greenhorn himself in civilized Boston—remains forever anxious about his social position. Levinsky is always ashamed, for example, of what he calls, disparagingly, his "Talmudic gesticulating"; he can't seem to keep his hands still while talking, an embarrassing vestige of his orthodox past. It is "a habit," he confesses, "that worried me like a physical defect. . . . It was so distressingly un-American. I struggled hard against it. I had made efforts to speak with my hands in my pockets; I had devised other means for keeping them from participating in my speech. All of no avail. I still gesticulate a great deal, though much less than I used to."[28]

But the struggle to be "American" generates its own distresses and deformations, instilling in Levinsky a constant dread of exposure as a "greenhorn." As a result, he continuously polices himself, guarding against behaviors that might betray the self he wishes would disappear. On a train with fellow Jewish salesmen hurtling through the Midwest, Levinsky meets the self-mocking Loeb, who tells jokes at Levinsky's expense. The encounter produces a series of self-lacerating injunctions and nervous self-questionings that reveal the dynamic of denial latent in the immigrant ordeal of Americanization: " 'Don't be excited' "; " 'Speak in a calm, low voice as these Americans do' "; " 'Had I talked too much?' "; " 'Had I made a nuisance of myself?' "[29] In these sad expressions of self-consciousness, shame, and self-hatred, we overhear the desolation—and dissolution—of a ghetto subject. Indeed, shame rises as the palpable affect summoned to fill the void that follows the out-greening, socializing process of Americanization itself.

For the most part, David Levinsky appears marginally conscious of either the source or controlling power of his affliction. He wonders at the "salacious banter" of Joe, the man who early on schooled him in the garment trade, one of whose "favorite pranks was to burlesque some synagogue chant from the solemn service of the Days of Awe, with disgustingly coarse Yiddish in place of the Hebrew of the prayer"[30]—a mode of survival, or revenge, by means of the deflating, overturning power of parody. But David is psychologically unable and imaginatively un-equipped to mediate the problem of cultural hyphenation. He can't trans-late, or displace, the pain of self-laceration into comedy routines—like Joe's subversive "banter"—nor, like Jack Robin (né Jakie Rabinowitz, the cantor's son, in Samson Raphaelson's short story "The Day of Atonement" [1922] and later, in *The Jazz Singer* [1927]) can he express his anguished hyphenate condition through song. And as for radical politics as a mode of salvation, especially after 1905, in his spiritual progress from worker to boss Levinsky loses all empathy for the working classes, unlike the life-long socialist Cahan. And finally, Levinsky cannot re-center himself even through marriage and family life.

While Levinsky claims to want a home, and at times even yearns for his old shtetl of Antomir,[31] the spectacle of the "strictly orthodox," "old-fashioned," yet middle-class Jewish style of the Kaplans, to whose daughter Fanny he is for a time engaged, only fills David with scorn. The Kaplans' huge front parlor is "depressingly out of keeping with its sense of home. It had pink-and-gold furniture and a heavy bright carpet, all of which had a forbidding effect. It was as though the chairs and the sofa had been placed there, not for use, but for storage. Nor was there enough furniture to give the room an air of being inhabited, the six pink-and-gold pieces and the marble-topped center-table losing themselves in spaces full of gaudy deso-lation."[32] Levinsky's "American" tastes are here offended by the "gaudy," parvenu style of the Kaplans; a newly Americanized gentleman, he cannot tolerate their bad furniture manners.

Indeed, the issue of manners becomes quite important during a Pass-over seder where, this time, David can't endure the family's banal dinner conversation. Sampling Mrs. Kaplan's Passover matzoh balls, the would-be son-in-law exclaims, "They have the genuine Antomir taste to them." "He likes everything that smells of Antomir,"[33] pious *alrightnik* Mrs. Kap-lan incorrectly surmises about her guest. David's gastronomic nostalgia, though, masks his bad faith. As it turns out, the problem with the Kaplans is that they remind him—in smell and behavior—of the world he has labored to forget. Like the Marquis de Bellegarde, who is offended by Christopher Newman's democratic odor, Levinsky can't tolerate the bad taste of the Kaplans. His disgust reflects not only cultural snobbery, but also the authorizing power of the world to which he imagines he owes allegiance: "civilized" America. (In the case of the Marquis, it is allegiance to the genealogical weight of French Catholic monarchy.) And that hege-monic power compels him to interpret the "barbarians" in *his* midst as aliens or greenhorns. "I was ambitious to be a cultured man 'in the European way,' " Levinsky reflects in a key meditation. "There was an odd con-fusion of ideas in my mind. . . . I had the notion that to 'become an Ameri-can' was the only tangible form of becoming a man of culture (for did I not regard the most refined and learned European as a 'greenhorn'?)."[34]

Levinsky's overarching self-hatred thus triggers a tortured reaction between the desired ideal self, reflected in and by the dominant culture, and his inner, socially marginal "descent" identity (in the sense defined by Werner Sollors), which appears to tarnish, by its very presence, the ide-alized world in which he seeks acceptance. When James's Marquis looks in Newman's mirror, he sees only the looming apocalypse of a fading aristo-cratic family unmoored—unsettled—by the boorish American's lack of proper antecedents; the Kaplans loom as unsavory "Jewish" types for Levinsky because at some buried level he recognizes himself in them. Levinsky's disgust is thus stirred by the shame of reawakened, dislodged memories; the Marquis's disgust issues from the anxiety he feels upon gazing into the dreadful commercial future signified by "the New/man."

Thus, when the seder chicken is finally served, David catches Fanny ("my intended wife," he calls her) eating "voraciously, biting lustily and chewing with gusto. The sight of it," the more refined would-be suitor reflects, "jarred on me somewhat, but I overruled myself." The word over-ruled suggests Levinsky's struggle to embrace the heimisch Fanny, despite his culturally conditioned revulsion. As if Fanny's raw table manners weren't enough—and they do prove fatal to the romance—David is next forced to watch the Kaplans' son Rubie "gesticulate and sway backward and forward as I used to," displaying, at his father's request, his prowess at Talmud. Although David tells himself that the nostalgic sight of true learn-ing "deeply affected" him, his reaction betrays his abject bad faith.[35] In truth, Rubie's gesticulations summon the anxiety-inducing image of David's own Old World behaviors, under repression. In the end, the en-counter with the Kaplans highlights Levinsky's conflicted self and cul-tural predicament: the compulsion to shake off Old World ways and the longing—however forced or fabricated and compelled by the void gener-ated by the dominant culture—for the recuperation of the (imagined) homelike place that was Antomir.

David Levinsky's New World, American journey, then, is ultimately static. He moves from one unsatisfying "Episode of a Lonely Life"—the title of the novel's last section—to another. Cahan parallels the Passover table scene when Levinsky later attends the seder of the Yiddish poet Tevkin, whose secularized children laugh at his uncharacteristic attempt to recover the ritual aspects of the meal. Wrapping himself in a "white shroud" (like his father before him), Tevkin's gesture bespeaks the effort to recapture a felt sense of lost piety, but his faith-keeping act brings only ridicule from the rising generation. " 'Father looks like a Catholic priest,' " a freethinking son remarks, sensing the (unconscious) mimicry embodied in the father's actions; " 'Don't say that, Emil,' " Levinsky immediately retorts, telling us how "I rebuked him." But inherited piety, however faithfully re-enacted, pales in comparison with the attenuating, draining powers of the American ideology to which the poet also adheres. " 'This is the Fourth of July of our unhappy people,' " he announces, in a comical appropriation of the host country's sacred history Cahan wished to satirize. But every gesture at recovery of ritual faith and memory only highlights the absorptive Americanizing agency of the dominant culture.[36]

At the end of *The Rise of David Levinsky*, David returns, tellingly, to the originating scene of both his personal liberation and social anxiety, the gentile restaurant, a site of cultural empowerment as well as trauma in much early twentieth-century ethnic literature and film. Levinsky now recalls what he terms his "first baptism of dismay as a patron of a high-class restaurant" (*baptism* is the key word, suggesting an immersion into the civilizing rituals of the host culture). Earlier, he was intimidated, terrified by the place where he must meet a Mr. Eaton, "a full-blooded Anglo Saxon of New England origin."[37]

> The immense restaurant, with its high, frescoed ceiling, the dazzling whiteness of its rows and rows of table-cloths, the crowd of well-dressed customers, the glint and rattle of knives and forks, the subdued tones of the orchestra, and the imposing black and-white figures of the waiters struck terror into my Antomir heart. The bill of fare was, of course, Chinese to me, though I made a pretense of reading it. The words swam before me. . . . The worst part of it all was that I had not the least idea of what I was to say or do. The occasion seemed to call for a sort of table manners which were beyond the resources . . . of a poor novice like myself.[38]

This is Levinsky's worst nightmare: the exposure of his "Antomir" self before the judging gaze of waiters, emblems of the civilized world he finds overwhelming yet part of the domain he dreams of conquering. In this early, self-conscious stage, squirming before a figure of imagined authority, he can mask his shame only by cracking jokes "at [his] own expense"— the costs of shame, we might say, are measured in self-mockery—and by deferring to Mr. Eaton, who mercifully shows David the *greener* how to behave: "Not only did he do the ordering, explaining things to me when

2

GASTRONOMIC NOSTALGIA

Anzia Yezierska

I think that table manners are the beginning of all culture.[1]
—Anzia Yezierska

Manners, and table manners in particular, are no laughing matter.[2]
—Margaret Visser

In a famous essay on *The Rise of David Levinsky,* the critic Isaac Rosenfeld articulated some of the key themes of early Jewish American fiction. Levinsky's problem, as Rosenfeld recognized in 1952, was "a core of permanent dissatisfaction" in his identity as "the Diaspora Man"—an unmoored self whose "constant longing . . . for the conditions of his past confirms him in an unchanging spirit." The more Levinsky tries to sate the "hunger," expressed by a vague "yearning for fulfillment," the more his character is tormented by the general insubstantiality of his success. Thus the indelible "core" of "dissatisfaction . . . become[s] an organic habit"; he remains driven both by a need to "preserve" the hunger (Rosenfeld's crucial—and often quoted—observation), for it shapes his identity (*without* the yearning and dissatisfaction he would cease to exist) and by a desire to hunger no more, to be relieved of the burdens of exile.[3] In this respect, *Levinsky* is Cahan's profound portrait of modern Jewish homelessness; not even the promised land of America can provide a *heimisch*, homelike resting place for the wandering migrant soul, haunted in the New World.

The early immigrant author Anzia Yezierska did not fashion as fully conceived or psychologically as rich a character as Cahan's Levinsky. In her two collections of stories and four novels, however, she did evoke in powerful ways the emotional costs of Americanization upon her vivid assortment of Old World mothers, New World daughters, and other-worldly fathers who people her tales of the Lower East Side. If Levinsky is afflicted by gnawing unfocused hunger, Yezierska *literalizes* that hunger, making ethnic foodways, and with it, the ordeal of table manners, the site of the struggle between generations. Thus Yezierska's imagination of "hunger" is expressive of how she understood, indeed, how she interrogated, the meaning of immigrant experience itself.[4]

As both Mary F. Dearborn and Yezierska's daughter Louise Levitas Henriksen have observed, the most important interval in Yezierska's career as an emerging writer was her brief but intense association with the philosopher-education theorist John Dewey, whose seminar at Teachers' College in 1916 Yezierska attended, and for whose sociological project among the Russian-Polish Jews of Philadelphia she worked as translator. Dewey, it appears, was overwhelmed by her energy and presence (he was fifty-eight, and she was thirty-five at the time); "to know her," recalls Henriksen, "was to be close to an emotional volcano, always ready to erupt."[5] Dewey responded to Yezierska's fiery nature with heated love poetry of his own, and although by 1916 Yezierska had already been married twice, and had even studied acting, it seems that she did not—or could not—respond physically to Dewey's infatuation. "Yezierska believed in sexual freedom," Dearborn notes, "but—in Deweyan terms—she believed with the head rather than the heart. . . . She seems to have enjoyed the idea of being a femme fatale [her first novel, published in 1922, was titled *Salome of the Tenements*] . . . but she was never very good with the follow-through."[6]

Whatever the biographical truth of this romantic tale of cultural border crossing may be, the "affair" with Dewey became the foundational scene for Yezierska, the primal episode she reworked over and again in her fiction: the encounter between a yearning ghetto "Jewess" and a "reserved" Puritan professor whose aloof manner is disrupted by the "volcanic" Old

World, embodied in the immigrant dreamer herself. In turn, the WASP figure in Yezierska helps distill the raw, unalloyed energy of her heroines, offering a higher cultural ideal for the hungry hearts who fill her fictional canvas. "Inside the ruin of my thwarted life," the narrator of "Soap and Water" confesses—one of Yezierska's earliest stories, written under the inspiration of Dewey and printed in *The New Republic* in 1917 at his own behest—"the *unlived* visionary immigrant hungered and thirsted for America" (emphasis in original).[7]

Like David Levinsky, then, Yezierska's heroines seek an America in the image of their ghetto desires; and like Cahan's Americanized hero, whose "rise" enables the ethnic artist to critique both the dominant and marginal cultures he straddles, the journey out, beyond Delancey Street or (in some stories) the return to the Lower East Side, allows Yezierska to question both the claims of traditional folkways, along with the material and spiritual promises of Americanization itself. The tension between the old and the new, emotion and composure, "raw" ethnic and pedigreed WASP, is her ultimate subject, and its forms of literary presentation are shaped—again, like Cahan's—by a rhetoric of appetite, of shame and disgust, and above all, of ethnic foodways.

Virtually all of Yezierska's themes are sounded in the opening two stories of her first collection, *Hungry Hearts* (1920). "Wings" and "Hunger" are companion tales that follow the fortunes of Shenah Pessah, who is infatuated with "John Barnes," the Dewey-like sociology professor (or perhaps a composite character drawn from the Philadelphia project) doing local research for a thesis on the "Educational Problems of the Russian Jews."[8] In her fiction, Yezierska always satirizes these voyeuristic, mannered social scientists, vehemently rejecting their dry abstractions, their habit of objectifying subjects, and above all their limited powers of imagination. ("Frank Baker," another college sociologist in "Children of Loneliness" [1923] utters "only smooth platitudes," to the distress of college girl Rachel Ravinsky, who can't tolerate his insipid observations of East Side life.)[9] Yet even as they become more fully drawn, more complicated—like the Dewey stand-ins "John Manning" in *Salome of the Tenements* (1922) and "Henry Scott" of *All I Could Never Be* (1932) (in this case Yezierska incorporated actual lines from Dewey's love poetry in the text)—the immigrant dreamer remains obsessed with the world of cool manners and elegant style that she attributes to the privileged cultural position of her authentically American lover. College people may be "icebergs of convention" once they are forced to rub up against Delancey Street, but from within her raucous ghetto house of greenhorn manners, Shenah can only hear "the music of his [John Barnes's] voice" and gaze in fascination "at his clothes—the loose tweeds, the pongee shirt, a bit open at the neck."[10] ("Arthur Hellman," the wealthy and correct socialite in *Arrogant Beggar* [1927] is "cool, calm, perfect" in the imagination of Adele Lindner, Shenah's fictional sister.)[11] Beyond his smooth voice and casually perfect ensemble, it is Barnes's "irresistible presence" that "seizes [Shenah's] soul. It was as though the god of her inmost longing had suddenly taken shape in human form and lifted her in mid-air."[12]

The plot of "Wings" flows from Shenah's effort to conjure a new self for Barnes through surface transformation. "My whole life hangs on how I'll look in his eyes," she declares, so she proceeds to pawn her mother's hand-stuffed feather bed ("the last memory from Russia," she confesses to the pawnbroker) in order to "lift myself out of my greenhorn rags."[13] (This plot receives fuller treatment in *Salome.*) Seeing her decked out in new clothes that "voice the desire of her innermost self"—a straw hat trimmed "with cherries so red, so luscious, that they cried out to her, 'Bite me!' " and (with rich irony) a green dress of the "crispest organdie" (its bright color reminds her of Russia), Barnes, after touring with Shenah around the Lower East Side, embraces her, murmuring "poor little immigrant!" as her "soul swoon[s] in ecstasy as he drew her toward him." Of course Barnes leaves Shenah in the thrall of hope and desire, but in the end she resolves that she must "show him you're a person. . . . By day and by night, you got to push, push yourself up till you get him and can look him in his face eye to eye" (note the rhetoric of shame and the personal summons to overcome it). Inspired (not enraged) by his unkind behavior, Shenah receives the closest Yezierska approaches to an epiphany, as "a wistful serenity crept over her": "After all," she consoles herself, in the wake of freshly acquired self-knowledge, "he done for you more than you could do for him. You owe it to him the deepest, the highest he waked up in you. He opened the wings of your soul."[14]

Thus Yezierska's first portrait of the Jewess–Wasp boundary crossing issues in gentile flight. Barnes's behavior, we assume, stems either from pity or condescension toward Shenah's American striving; he can't distinguish his rising romantic sentiment from his dry, case study mentality. For her part, Shenah gains, we presume, a new, more confident self—and self-esteem; she vows to meet the John Barneses of this world without shame, eye to eye. Shenah builds on this empowering insight in the next story of *Hungry Hearts,* titled "Hunger." In this case, though, the Barnes figure is replaced by his immigrant alter ego, the only partially Americanized Sam Arkin, who makes the fatal mistake of wooing his imagined bride of his Old World youth (to borrow the title of Charles Chesnutt's great turn-of-the-century story of black acculturation) by escorting her to

"Levy's Cafe" and ordering, "with a flourish," "herring and onions for two" without considering that his dream girl might have different (New World) tastes. Let me quote their wonderful—and revealing—restaurant exchange in full:

> "Here is it." He led her in and over to a corner table. "Chopped herring and onions for two," he ordered with a flourish.
> "Ain't there some American eating on the card?" interposed Shenah Pessah.
> He laughed indulgently. "If I lived in America for a hundred years I couldn't get used to the American eating. What can make the mouth so water like the taste and the smell from herring and onions?"
> "There's something in me—I can't help—that so quickly takes on to the American taste. It's as if my outside skin only was Russian; the heart in me is for everything of the new world—even the eating."
> "Nu, I got nothing to complain against America. I just don't like the American eating, but I like the American dollar. Look only on me!" He expanded his chest. "I came to America a ragged nothing—and—see—" He exhibited a bank book in four figures, gesticulating grandly.[15]

As we might expect, Shenah does not envision a future linked with Sam and his gesticulating "four figure" bank book. The incarnation of the American success story, he nonetheless displays "neglected teeth, [and] thick, red lips"; in this sense, Sam functions like Gitelson for Levinsky, an embarrassing emblem of the world from which Shenah feels alienated—a powerful contrast to John Barnes, whom Yezierska styles "the Other one" (*Him and him only* I want," Shenah declares [emphasis in original]). Bewildered and stunned by her rejection, Sam sinks "prostrate" to the ground, from where he is instructed in the meaning of immigrant hunger: "'Sam Arkin! . . . All that you suffer I have suffered, and must go on suffering. I see no end. But only—there is something—a hope—a help out—it lifts me on top of my hungry body—the hunger to make myself a person that can't be crushed by nothing or nobody—the life higher!'"[16]

In her most compelling stories, Yezierska's imagination seems fired by the spectacle of greenhorns like Shenah and Sam in awkward transition—or more often, like the shrill Old World mother in the prize-winning story "The Fat of the Land" (1919)—trapped between two worlds, floating in liminal suspension. The ordeal of Americanization *is* dangerous,[17] in Yezierska's rendering, for it can devolve into a narrow angle of vision (emergent parvenu that he is, Sam can only see the bank book he waves before his eyes); at the same time, because her self is unsettled, on the threshold of unmooring, Shenah can appreciate the spiritual "life higher" held out by the new country (does she unconsciously echo Whitman in preaching to the materially inclined Sam?) that invites her soul to create "a person who'll yet ring in America."[18] Shenah, that is, sees beyond the limiting vision of Sam to embrace the spiritual potential of the New World, a readiness which explains the attraction of the Dewey/Emersonian figure for Yezierska's hungry visionaries.

In "To the Stars," collected in *Children of Loneliness* (1923), the young Sophie Sapinsky dreams of a writing career while she labors as cook over a "steaming stove" "stew[ing] the same *tsimmis*, fry[ing] the same *blintzes*, stuff[ing] the same *miltz*" [animal intestine] day after day. However, she is encouraged in her true calling by college President Irvine. Self-conscious about her "immigrant English" as a proper vehicle for literary expression, she seeks his help (his "long education," she calls it) in "fixing" her ungrammatical prose:

> "Fix it up?" he protested. "There are things in life bigger than rules of grammar. The thing that makes art live and stand out throughout the ages is sincerity. Unfortunately, Education robs many of us of the power to give spontaneously, as mother earth gives, as the child gives. You have poured out not a part, but the whole of yourself. That's why it can't be measured by any of the prescribed standards It's uniquely you." Her face lighted with joy at his understanding.
>
> "I never knew why I hated to be Americanized. I was always burning to dig out the thoughts from my own mind.
>
> "Yes, your power lies in that you are yourself. Your message is that of your people, and it is all the stronger because you are not a so-called assimilated immigrant.
>
> Ach! Just to hear such talk! It was like the realization of a power in life itself to hold her up and carry her to the heights.[19]

Sophie's deep knowledge echoes Randolph Bourne's contemporaneous vision of American society enriched with hyphenate citizens refusing to melt, or be melted. In her way, Shenah resists one potential result of the Americanizing process by rejecting Sam's crass *alrightnik* mentality, but she also rejects the foodways that, extending Irvine's logic, make her "unique." "American eating," that is, *absorbs* discrete ethnic identity.

If in his Emersonian office President Irvine helps Sophie to embrace the real self sounding in the immigrant accents of her prose, the immigrant, in turn, instructs the American academic how to reach the people. Listening to his prophetic, yet impenetrably abstract, vision of a democratic "new school" ("The new school," educational theorist Irvine announces, "must aim to make up to the disinherited masses by conscious instruction, by the development of personal power for the loss of external opportunities consequent upon the passing of our pioneer days"—Was

An abject Jetta Goudal as Sonya and an aloof Godfrey Tearle as Manning in *Salome of the Tenements* (1925), Famous Players-Lasky Corp. Courtesy of the Academy of Motion Picture Arts and Sciences.

Why is Sonya driven to possess Manning? In part, it is because of his "low voice of cultural constraint," and in part because he willingly participates in the allegorizing, self-abstracting behavior characteristic of Yezierska's immigrant heroines. " 'You have the burning fire of the Russian Jew in you, while I am motivated by a sickly conscience, trying to heal itself by the application of cold logic and cold cash.' " (Not surprisingly, in response to Manning's interpretation, Sonya confesses, " 'Why, you make me feel so natural, I could go on talking to you forever like you were a no-body.' ")[24] Each character, that is, is attracted to the exotic aspect of the other: Manning, "the product of generations of Puritans," is overwhelmed by the "suppressed avalanche" of feelings unleashed in Sonya by the free air of the New World (recall Yezierska's "volcanic" character), while Sonya is taken by Manning's prematurely grey hair ("a cloud of white light, adding the final touch of divinity to [his] luminous features") and, more important, by his identification with *her own* struggle to break from the weight of tradition. If Sonya fashions herself as "the ache of unvoiced dreams . . . the unlived lives of generations," Manning rebukes himself (with language that could be borrowed from William Carlos Williams's contemporaneous 1925 study of American origins *In the American Grain*) as "a puritan whose fathers were afraid to trust experience."[25]

It is Manning's Dewey–Emersonian struggle—at least initially, in Sonya's eyes—to overturn tradition, to reform, through philanthropy and settlement work, the arid culture "his people" have established that an-swers to the deep longing in Sonya to elevate her "race." (At one point, Manning sounds like Emerson in "The American Scholar," speaking of "our colleges" as "temples of Moloch into which youth is poured to come out stamped and moulded in the old forms.")[26] The problem, however, is that in Yezierska's vision of ethnic–WASP border crossing, the lines mark-ing boundaries of language and cultural difference remain fixed, untrans-ferable, and untranslatable. For all their mutual recognition of a shared reforming zeal, Sonya and Manning ultimately misread each other, both in the gestures of sexual desire, which spurs Sonya's rage and eventual flight, and in the forms of *mannered* social behavior—above all, as reflected in etiquette—which ultimately thwart Sonya's dreams of acculturation.

To put it more simply, after her marriage Sonya is made to feel *like an immigrant*, an intolerable social identity in light of her effort to construct a new American self from, in her own estimation, sordid ghetto origins. In a kind of flashback taken from her childhood, we learn that as a little girl Sonya refused to wear "shoe-strings" instead of ribbons in her hair, even though her family was poor. " 'When I begin school,' " she announces to her parents, " 'I got to have a red silk hair ribbon like the American children. . . . I ain't no immigrant. I ain't going to stand for shoe-strings on my hair.' "[27] This stubborn declaration defines her innermost desire as it locates the germ of self-hatred born of perceived cultural difference. What drives Sonya is less a humanitarian vision of the ghetto uplifted than a private dream of personal fulfillment based on the unquestioned authority of the dominant culture. " 'I only wish I could be like them,' " she tells Manning, in reference to the extreme self-consciousness she feels "in their company," where her self-image as "a wild savage in a dressed-up parlor of make believes" releases a trembling scorn: " 'Every gesture I make, every word I say is a shock to their lady-like nerves.' "[28]

Sonya's dilemma results from her inability to step outside the cultural drama of Americanization in which she is embedded; she can't recognize, or feel, the inauthentic mode of selfhood that Manning represents. Infatuated with his winning "low voice of cultural restraint"—recall that what stirs, and spurs Gatsby in his romantic quest is Daisy's alluring voice, which sounds like "money"—she can only hear the "low" registers, which soften the rebellious outbursts of her youth ("I ain't no immigrant"), not the more ominous tones of cultural "restraint"—the altar of manners to which Manning (and *his* world) worships. Gazing transfixed at the copy of the Mona Lisa over Manning's desk, Sonya reads "generations of self-control" in the enigmatic face (a portrait of "the eternal ancestress of Manning and his kind"). At this point, Sonya begins to feel the throb of her Lower East Side past; "her happiness was double-edged," Yezierska observes; "In her zeal for the new gods she felt the wound that had been left in tearing away from the old."[29] That wound—the sensitive, shame-ridden greenhorn self defended by theatricality, buried in repression—throbs again during the post-wedding party celebration, when Sonya is reminded, like Levinsky in the upscale restaurant, of her inescapable immigrant self. And *un*like Newman at the Bellegarde ball, Sonya rediscovers the strict, socially defining boundaries of etiquette and social class that distinguish the territory she longed for from the world she had sought, despite the pain of separation, to escape.

As a kind of prelude (or segue) to that fatal celebration, Yezierska provides a number of brief but telling portraits of Sonya the newlywed, including that of an already discontented bride troubled by her husband's perverse (in her view) attention to his *Atlantic Monthly,* which he scans on the train ride back to the city. In truth, Manning buries himself in the magazine because Sonya has (we're told) embarrassed him by her "overdemonstrativeness in a public train"; for her part, Sonya links the surprising cooling of conjugal passion with the dry magazine itself: " 'How can he read those lifeless words of the high brows?' " she asks herself. (Question: Why, immediately after winning her genteel husband, can't Sonya admire Manning's taste in literature? Answer: For all her idealization of the dominant culture, she is secretly repelled by its reserved tones, above all its dead language. Manning, after all, is decidedly not a type of "man thinking," Emerson's ideal of the American Scholar. Looking up from the *Monthly,* he "beam[s]," " 'So we're going to our real home! . . . Five generations of

brides have come to the room in my town house which will be ours.' "[30]
Rather than lifting her out, into the realm of pure spiritual possibility,
Manning, in very *un*-Emersonian fashion, wishes to bury Sonya under
layers of family tradition. Earlier, he had been taken with her raw energy,
moved by her poignant ignorance; indeed, Manning sensed his own salvation from stagnant Protestant inhibition in her very being. Then he had
asked himself, "What manner of antecedents had passed down to her such
resistless power that transcended her lack of schooling? . . . Who are you?
What are you?" In this (condescending) phase, he seems like an optimistic,
or at least a more openminded Marquis de Bellegarde, curious, if not ultimately smitten by Sonya's lack of a past. The problem of antecedents looms
more ominously after the marriage, however, as Yezierska charts Sonya's
journey into the deadening, socially proper world of the Mannings.[31]

The signs of Sonya's exile among the genteel are highlighted, as they
tend to be in Jewish American literature, at table. Famished after the long
train ride, she enters the dining room and attempts to break through the
crust of dinner table formality by "instinctively," Yezierska informs us,
announcing the extent of her hunger: " 'I'm so starved I could eat up the
shells of the oysters and all!' " (Sonya has evidently come a long way from
the world of blintzes and tsimmis). She then

> reached for the largest fork and hungrily lifted an oyster to her lips. The
> masked-face butler silently, but significantly, placed the correct fork in
> front of her. The blood rushed to her cheeks. She glanced at Manning,
> then down at her plate, shamed and confused. Her first impulse was to
> throw the correct fork after the butler, who had retreated behind his
> screen in the pantry. But she only bit her lip and forced back her tears.[32]

Without the example of a kindly Mr. Eaton, who helped ease Levinsky
through the mysteries of table etiquette, demonstrating proper oyster fork
technique, Sonya feels the weight of shame and judgment; but she must,
somehow, repress the rage: the impulse to hurl the fork bespeaks the
seething underside of shame. What Sonya loses in appetite, however, she
gains in an acute sense of smell, for in the upper reaches of the Manning
mansion she registers a palpable "oppressive bigness, the stifling tapestries
and smell of old, old things" (recall Levinsky's snobby repulsion at the
Kaplans' gaudy newness). In the nose of the Old World, Christopher
Newman reeks of democracy; in Yezierska the new American world gives
off a stifling stuffiness, a smell redolent of weighty generations and their
refined table manners. Indeed, when she accuses Manning, " 'You don't
want my people. You never loved me for, me, myself. You only love dead

traditions. Your only religion is your family pride,' "[33] Sonya herself arrives at a version of Newman's sharp insight into the Bellegarde's unbending resolution to maintain the family's sacred history, at all costs.

Sonya's plight—and it is to an extent Levinsky's dilemma as well—is that she has no enabling "religion," no intrinsic code of behavior or structure of beliefs to help negotiate the journey out of the ghetto. It is clear that Sonya refuses the identity and status of "immigrant," but the idealized world of Manning, once possessed, leaves her feeling hungry and unloved. Yezierska portrays Sonya's complete alienation during the reception for the newlyweds, which ends in disaster.

Looking on in anguish at her old neighbor Mrs. Peltz (a vivid Lower East Side character imported from other Yezierska short stories), whose helpless—and hopeless—efforts at eating a large leaf of lettuce with "a queer small fork" ("in desperation" Mrs. Peltz eventually "grabbed the leaf with her fingers and stuffed it into her mouth"), Sonya herself tries to illustrate more "civilized" table manners by "nervously and none too successfully . . . roll[ing] a lettuce leaf on a fork as a demonstration." When it comes to genteel social convention, we note, Sonya's talents as actress, her theatrical style, fail her; confronted by the ultimate test of the social status she craves, her unformed manners betray her indelible greenhorn roots. The experience is apocalyptic; "when Mrs. Peltz began pouring out her tea in a saucer in the regular East Side fashion, Sonya's nerves began to snap inside of her." But instead of acknowledging the rising disgust as she witnesses Yezierska's version of the return of the repressed (as Levinsky does before the spectacle of out-of-place Gitelson in the Waldorf dining room), Sonya flees the scene "unobserved." If the psychological "aim" of shame is invisibility and the itch to forget, then Sonya's behavior is expressive of the ordeal of shame on the immigrant self, the *unsettling* reaction to displacement and uprootedness—figured in the sign of flawed table manners and the revelation of gauche greenhorn styles in general.[34]

Sonya survives the ordeal; she is able to resist the attendant leveling of the self that follows in the wake of shame. Indeed, her resistance to humiliation results in an empowering angle of vision: no longer feeling the claims and authority of Manning as husband, Sonya can now see through the false ideology of proper forms that demand she "make [her]self a parrot of words and a monkey of manners"; she can now hear "the echo of a language that had no meaning for her." Thus the failed marriage between representative American and representative immigrant exposes the impossibility of "trying to find a common language"—the utopian linguistic–cultural ideal of native-hyphenate bonding of Yezierska's New World heroines. "We do not mix our circles,"[35] Manning explains at one point to Sonya, a declaration that reverberates with the anxious tones of inviolability, and the nativist's need to construct self-enclosed spheres against the threat of ethnic pollution. As she is an immigrant like Christopher Newman, who learns to his dismay about the impassable boundaries circling the Bellegardes's closed society, Sonya senses at the end that the warm ethnic habit of unfettered emotionality is chilled by "the winter coldness of a sterile race," her native openness and animated temper are thwarted by "the invulnerable thickness of this New England Puritan" (recall Nick Carroway's description of Tom and Daisy as "unbreakable"). Above all, Sonya's journey (again, like Newman's—and perhaps like Gatsby's as well) ends in "a dark, impenetrable void that none of her ardor could pierce."[36]

Salome of the Tenements concludes with Sonya's partial return downtown, to the Lower East Side, in the form of her more appropriate (as it turns out) lover, Jacques Hollins (né Jackie Solomon). The haute couture designer has loved Sonya all along (" 'It's because I know everything about you that I love you,' " he admits), for he recognizes in her theatrical style and yearning for beauty his own deepest self. These long-withheld feelings turn out to be mutual on Sonya's part—she hears music play when he confesses his love—and the novel abruptly ends (Yezierska had difficulty with the conclusions of all her major works) with the couple heading off to Paris ("with your eyes," Jacques affirms, "I'll see Paris for the first time"), the self-created immigrant entrepreneurs presumably ready to conquer the (old) world of high fashion in a reverse migration to the center of European style.[37]

Salome of the Tenements thus turns out to be a cautionary tale about the dangers of cultural boundary crossing. Ethnic and American styles, manners, and languages don't mix in Yezierska's narrative of immigrant striving—the immigrant self cannot be melted, cannot be absorbed in the pure (if tasteless) soup of Manning genealogy. Still, as her characters tend to discover, the more homelike ghetto cannot easily be recovered either, no matter how much the pain of its loss is assuaged by nostalgic return.

The great figure for such geographic and psychic immobilization is Hannah Breineh of "The Fat of the Land" (1919), a woman caught between the dry, uptown civility of her successful children with whom she lives and in whose presence she induces shame, and the discomfort she feels upon revisiting Delancey Street and Mrs. Peltz (who later appears in *Salome*), who keeps the faith in the old neighborhood. Hannah Breineh's uprooting is complete, her alienation absolute. Nothing feels homelike on Riverside Drive, where she is "forced to eat in the public dining room" or else sneak her meals out of sight in the kitchen. Nor is her presence appreciated. As in so many examples of Jewish American immigrant expression, children wish their parents would disappear. " 'God knows how I've tried to civilize her,' " Hannah's daughter Fanny complains, " 'but Delancey Street sticks out from every inch of her. Whenever she opens her mouth, I'm done for.' "[38] "The Fat of the Land," however, doesn't fully explore the sources and implications of generational shame as powerfully as the immigrant cinema; instead, it voices Hannah Breineh's liminal plight. Trapped along socially deadening *alrightniks'* row, she remains "starved out for a piece of real eating" in an unsustaining environment; like Sam Arkin, yet sadly without the youth and strength of ambition, she "can't swallow down their American eating." All Hannah Breineh can do is laugh the bitter laugh of irony, a perspective born of an historical consciousness of generations unavailable to her Americanized children. " 'Why should my children shame themselves from me? From where did they get the stuff to work themselves up in the world? . . . It is I, who never had a chance to be a person, who gave [them] the fire. . . .' "[39] This key insight sounds as if it comes from the other side of the generational chasm; beyond adjusting to America, Hannah Breineh recognizes that filial rejection and the shame of exposure are the true, if bitter, fruits of this new land.

The dialectic between flight and nostalgia continues as the enabling creative tension in Yezierska's next two novels, *Bread Givers* (1925) and *Arrogant Beggar* (1927). By critical consensus, *Bread Givers* stands out as Yezierska's most important work, in part because in it she alters the site of conflict from the *ur*-story of gentile–ethnic relations to the matter of Jewish family life and religious authority in general, and in part because the story of Sara Smolinsky's (the book's narrator and heroine) journey out allows Yezierska to survey and critique the various options—or lack of options—available for the second generation in the 1920s. In each novel, the meaning of homecoming lies at the center, serving as the challenge and enigma of historical and personal identity-seeking resolutions. What are the claims of the past? of filial obligation? On what moral and political foundations can the self negotiate the American scene? These questions continue to trouble Yezierska's characters, who must struggle—along with their creator—to extract a measure of stability out of the fluid, betwixt-and-between New World.

Much has been written about *Bread Givers* during the recent revival of Yezierska's reputation. In Sara's challenge to her father's rigid and selfish devotion to faith, in her ability to see through and therefore avoid the various cautionary tales offered by her sisters' unfulfilling marriages (perversely brokered according to Old World tradition by Reb Smolinsky), in her enmity toward patriarchal authority in general (after her mother dies she refuses to have her only blue suit ripped, in defiance of Jewish mourning rituals), and in her emerging self-consciousness (which enables her to reject a self-centered suitor like Max Goldstein, despite the self-esteem his attention bestows)—in all these striking transformations, Sara arrives as a proto-feminist, a young woman whose hard-won clarity of vision saves her from her sisters' unhappy matrimonial fates.

Interestingly, Sara's resisting power flows from her identification with the ideology of personal freedom that she ascribes to the American Way; she appropriates New World ideology to authorize her bid for liberty. In answer to her father's invocation of biblical law about "how only through a man has a woman an existence," Sara dissents, " 'It's a new life now. In America, women don't need men to boss them' "; and when in livid response the father charges her with blasphemy for her rebellion, she rejoins, " 'I'm going to live my own life. Nobody can stop me. I'm not from the old country. I'm American!' " The authority of America thus sustains Sara; it feeds her in the way that every character in *Bread Givers* has some form of personal faith to draw on. Reb Smolinsky is literally sustained in his ancient faith, while his wife, who laments the lack of food on the table, is nourished by her rich memories of shtetl life (Sara's mother, that is, feeds on nostalgia); in contrast, sister Masha devours the popular fashion magazines, from which she constructs a self that feeds on the male gaze ("And these melting looks in men's eyes were like something to eat and something to drink to her").[40]

For the most part, Yezierska focuses on Sara's hunger, which is translated as a desire for education to match her yearning for ghetto liberation. The vision of an emancipated self is shaped at a small New England college, where Sara marvels at the "neat finished quietness of their tailored suits," the "spick-and-span cleanliness" of her fellow students, "their fingernails so white and pink," "the hollering clean" of the men, the collective "plain beautifulness"—in short, the authorizing auras, the refined tastes and antiseptic smells of the genteel world.[41] Her cultural passage reaches a symbolic conclusion during a train ride home, when, as a newly minted teacher at ease and confident with her acquisition of American habits and postures, she sits in the Pullman's restaurant car to enjoy (we gather) her first American meal:

> How grand it felt to lean back in my chair, a person among people, and order anything I wanted from the menu. No more herring and pickle over dry bread, I ordered chops and spinach and salad. As I spread out my white, ironed napkin on my lap, I thought of the time only four years before, when I pinched pieces out of the loaf, and wiped my mouth with a corner of a newspaper and threw it under the seat.[42]

If table manners are linked, in Yezierska's symbolic anthropology, with the onset of civilization, then to be seated "at ease" in the new Zion of an American dining car, like "a person among people," announces Sara's New World arrival. Here is Shenah Pessah's dream of "American eating" come true: selfhood as a function of foodways, identity through sanctioned etiquette.

Did Yezierska in her own mind embrace Sara's mode of arrival? Did she, too, equate the achieved self with the acquisition of perceived New World manners and the rejection of Orchard Street herring? The conclusion to *Bread Givers* only partially addresses these issues, but it suggests that at some level the pull of heredity had to be acknowledged, that the aching wound of separation felt by Sonya trapped in the sterile Manning mansion needs the salve of memory. The problematic ending of *Bread Givers*—Sara's apparent capitulation to her father's authority—raises the question of Yezierska's stance toward her children of loneliness, her relation to the world of the Fathers in general.

According to Henriksen, *Bread Givers* is a deeply autobiographical book, and writing it helped Yezierska realize "a growing power in recreating her past and understanding it better. . . . The writing freed her." The act of critical reconstruction also led her to visit her father soon after the novel was published, a reunion that, she reports in her 1950 autobiography, *Red Ribbon on a White Horse,* turned out badly. In art, however, Sara arrives at what Henriksen calls "a tenuous truce" with Reb Smolinsky, after she is moved by the pathetic image of him peddling chewing gum on Grand Street.[43] She is persuaded on this matter by Hugo Seelig, her school principal and fiancé, who urges Sara to take her father home. Seelig is a version of Jacques Hollins as a teacher, except that he is intellectually curious about the forgotten world of the rabbis and wishes to reconnect through learning Hebrew. When they first meet, Hugo asks Sara, tellingly, "in a low voice," " 'What do you remember of Poland?' " to which she answers, " 'Nothing—nothing at all. Back of me, it's like black night.' " Hugo's repression is less absolute, for he can "remember a little"; he can still recover shards of history and the sounds and smells of village life. It is this "memorial" office that distinguishes him from the other men in the novel, for Hugo's fragmentary but vivid memories let him see the unbreachable bonds that link father and daughter, an insight that Sara, too, will gain: " 'After all,' " he explains, " 'it's from him that you got the iron for the fight you had to make to be what you are now.' " This insight, we might say, is the Hannah Breineh "revelation" that finally softens Sara's adamant rejection; it is her recognition—Yezierska describes Sara's gesture of reconciliation at the very end as "unconscious"—of filial ties, of her father as the source of "the fire, the passion, to push myself up from the dirt."[44]

Still, the concluding tones of *Bread Givers* ring ominously. Reb Smolinsky agrees to live with the couple (he will teach Hugo Hebrew). " 'Our home will be the richer if your father comes with us,' " Hugo says. Sara "laugh[s] at his easy enthusiasm." Whether this is the laugh of the knowing ironist born of the ravages of traditional Jewish family life, Yezierska does not say. Children of loneliness, Hugo and Sara may be able to renegotiate their relation to the past through nostalgia (when leaving the Reb at prayer, they "lingered for the mere music of the fading chant"), but as they walk away, Sara feels "Hugo's grip tighten[ing] on my arm" and the palpable "shadow" of the past hovering over her.[45] In the end, Yezierska leaves the question of Sara's future, a future haunted by more recent memories she can't consign into the black night of repression, unresolved.

Arrogant Beggar (1927), Yezierska's next novel, once more begins with the gritty world of the Lower East Side and its impact on Adele Lindner, a variation of Sara without the weight of family to rebel against. Adele is less intellectually ambitious than Sara; she is more like Sonya (also without parents to swerve from) in her desire for acceptance by genteel society. In the opening pages, Adele seeks liberation from "the smells from the fish store below" as well as from the advice of surrogate ghetto mothers who earnestly counsel, " 'A taste from my gefulte fish will make you forget your troubles.' "[46] Adele's "troubles," of course, relate to the smell and taste of gefilte fish itself; like other Yezierska daughters, she is in gastronomic flight from the world of ethnic foodways. Even her would-be tenement lover Shlomoth repulses her, with his "gushing response" to her invitation to visit. Adele writes him after she has settled in "Hellman House," a school for the training of domestic servants (from where she hopes to launch her dreams). When this unappealing vestige of the old neighborhood appears with flowers, "He jerked out his hand to grasp mine. What a hand! The damp skin clinging to my fingers felt like a limp fish wriggling against my palm. Not to hurt his feelings, I twisted my mouth into a smile."[47] Shlomoth's schlemiel awkwardness and his fishy residue harden Adele in her rejection of her origins. But she eventually discovers that barriers of class and taste guard the social gates that she hopes one day to pass through.

A sister to Salome, Adele confesses to "a fire inside me that could cook and clean its way into the hearts of people just as if I were an actress on the stage."[48] *Arrogant Beggar* follows Adele's growth in self-knowledge from that false theatrical—and vocational—consciousness to a recognition of the degradations of domestic service ideology and her eventual discovery of a true calling, as salon-proprietress to the immigrant avant-garde of the Lower East Side. Significantly, Adele's change of heart, a shift in her cultural stance, inaugurates a larger transformation in both her culinary and historical imagination.

Adele's progress toward disillusionment is highlighted by a number of social and psychological jolts, most dramatically illustrated in a scene of rejection and ensuing shame. Gushing with enthusiasm for the staid Mrs. Hellman (the socialite-philanthropist who runs Hellman House), bursting with gratitude for the chance to climb out of an imagined swamp of ghetto filth, Adele embraces her, kissing Mrs. Hellman on the cheek. Shockingly, Mrs. Hellman responds with a gesture of disgust; wiping the kiss away from her face, she is repulsed (we assume) by the potential of lower-class contamination. Adele is indeed stunned at this unfeeling act, and struggles with the rage that surfaces in her recognition of the condescension and ethnic-class prejudices expressed by the woman she once idealized. She now tears up a speech intended to praise the vision of Hellman House before its gathering of trustees ("I thought the world was a desert of landladies," she had written initially) and instead launches into a bitter denunciation of the suffocating world of Hellman House and of her earlier naïve self: "'I hate this Home. I hate myself for living here. . . . I hate every damned bit of kindness you've ever done me. I'm poisoned—poisoned with the hurts, the insults I suffered in this beastly place."[49]

Unhoused from this toxic environment, Adele wanders once more through the Lower East Side desert in search of physical and spiritual nourishment. Ironically, in light of her rejection of all things tainted with a fishy aspect (including Shlomoth), Adele drifts into a *dairy* restaurant where she is surrounded by the sounds and smells of the ethnic foodways from which she had earlier sought relief. Cries of "*Gefulte fish!*," "*Borscht* and cheese *blintzes!*," and "Chopped herring and onions!" ring out from waiters demanding their orders be filled. The remaining plot of *Arrogant Beggar* charts Adele's return to the scene of her original revulsion and her efforts at starting over. She takes a job as a dishwasher at the restaurant ("With gritted teeth, I plunged my hand into the scummy water and began to wash"—her "baptism," we gather, into the repulsive ethnic element) where she is befriended by an old woman, Muhmenkeh, who functions as both surrogate mother and representative of the Old World.[50]

Her transformation begins when she witnesses a scene of ethnic bonding between women, the selfless gift of "a thick slice of hot fried herring and onion, sizzling in its own fat" brought over by Muhmenkeh's neighbor ("A woman with hips like pillows," Adele wickedly observes). The three feast together in what Muhmenkeh calls a "*sooda*"—Yiddish for festive meal, thus revisiting through language and ritual the Old World traditions effaced in crossing over. Muhmenkeh's facility with Yiddish is clearly a positive quality in the novel; it bequeaths her the power to withstand the alienation that afflicts the rising generation. Touched by the display of affection and solidarity through food, and joining hungrily in the makeshift celebration, Adele experiences a palpable psychological shift. Her imagination of the street is overturned, and her formerly negative perspective has been altered: "A sudden clearness came to me. I felt close to all things living." A revived appetite for herring and onions signals, it would seem, a new relation to the Lower East Side; alive with ethnic potential, it becomes a fluid social field to be reshaped rather than an oppressive landscape to be escaped. Declaring her self virtually reborn, a witness to "a new wonder over the old streets," Adele draws on her domestic training to open a coffee house, which soon becomes a popular gallery for displaying new artists as well as a local literary salon.[51]

Significantly, Adele *creates* her New World "space," in the sense, perhaps, of D. W. Winnicott's "transitional" or "potential" space, by blending her American cooking-and-cleaning training with "authentic" Old World ambience, in effect reconstructing the "homelike" through foodways, along with an animated atmosphere. When the Russian-Polish émigré pianist, and Adele's alter ego, Jean Rachmansky, samples the fare, he is transported:

> He ate and drank. "But this is Poland, this *kuchen* [cake]." He smiled as he looked about the room. "This place feels European. It makes me think of the *krechma* [tavern] where my father used to play."

But nostalgia, no matter how warm or caressing, cannot soothe the ache of uprootedness. Nor can a Sheneh Pessah-like relish for American eating resolve the enigma of New World identity.[52]

In *Arrogant Beggar,* Yezierska thus tempers nostalgia through the figures of Adele and Jean, immigrant children who *translate* their hazy Old World memories into art—Adele though recovering *krechma* ambience and baking authentic *kuchen,* Jean through the shtetl-bred feelings he brings to the piano. In this respect, Jean (a more interesting but too briefly limned type of Jackie Solomon before he changes his name to "Jacques Hollins"), who plays "Ancient Hebrew melodies, folk tunes" with "chords that struck at the very roots of their [his salon audience] long-forgotten past . . . [their] memories of homeland," performs, in a therapeutic sense, the work of delayed, unfinished, or even unacknowledged mourning for his fellow emigrants who are feeling lost and bewildered in the distinctively *unheimisch* new land.[53] And by transubstantiating *kuchen* into "Poland" (for Jean, *kuchen* literally *embody* his homeland), Adele carves out—by marketing tradition?—an alternate identity *unavailable* to either Shenah Pessah, Rachel Ravinsky (the daughter caught in liminal anguish in "Children of Loneliness"), or Hannah Breineh's embarrassed uptown progeny. Significantly, at the end of *Arrogant Beggar* Adele becomes both dutiful daughter—she feels herself adopted by Muhmenkeh, her implicit instructor in home cooking, in telling contrast to, say, Mr. Eaton, who tutors Levinsky in table manners—and faith-keeping grandmother. After Muhmenkeh dies, Adele offers herself as the familial touchstone for Muhmenkeh's newly arrived granddaughter. By reclaiming the past, by acknowledging her particular office in the New World—to help ease the pain of uprootedness for the rising generation—Yezierska's heroine—virtually the only one among her cohort—is released from the scars and burdens of loneliness.

Yezierska herself, however, could not have emulated Adele's example, for *her* story involved escape from the cooking classes at Teachers' College and domestic science indoctrination at the Clara de Hirsch home. After 1920, she became a literary celebrity, courted by Hollywood, designated the symbolic voice, speaking on behalf of the immigrant. Yet through the 1920s, Yezierska could only, it appears, visit and revisit—except in *Bread Givers*—the scene of ethnic-WASP encounter to retell the ultimate failure of the utopian potential of such a union. "Her fascination with the gulf separating the immigrant from native-born American turned into an obsession,"[54] writes Mary Dearborn, and in *All I Could Never Be* (1932) Yezierska rehearsed its inevitable trajectories for the last time, in this case offering perhaps the closest transcription of the John Dewey episode we have. Indeed, early drafts of the novel reveal that Yezierska inserted Dewey's name in the text; only later (and only at the insistence of a close friend) was the character's name changed to "Henry Scott." But the "matter" of John Dewey, once the inspiration for her early tales about the comedy and sadness of the dream of acculturation, by 1932 seems exhausted; at the edge of almost twenty years of silence and obscurity (in 1950 Yezierska did resurface with her "autobiography," *Red Ribbon on a White Horse*), the thinly disguised protagonist of *All I Could Never Be* seems utterly lost, in search of new sources of creativity. In light of recent biographical studies, which describe Yezierska's numerous apartment relocations in and around New York City and beyond, it seems clear that she wandered in continuous exile, in search, it appears, of a "home" she could no longer recover, not even in art.[55]

Two powerful vignettes form the Prologue to *All I Could Never Be,* and they establish the complex psychology of the aspiring writer whose career the novel eventually traces. The first depicts Fanya as a young girl in the old country, sent by her indigent mother to rich relatives in Warsaw, who feed her each time and then send her home with money. On one visit, Fanya's happiness in feeling part of the family is shattered when her cousin discovers lice in her beautiful but now contaminated hair. Immediately expelled from the family, "the condemned child" (as Yezierska's narrator calls her) is delivered to the train station by the servant; in a description of Fanya's way home, Yezierska powerfully expresses the character's emotions:

> Fanya remained tensely silent. Lips drawn into a tight line. Eyes grimly staring ahead. The little face was drained of all color. The features rigidly set, hard as stone. Not a whimper escaped her. But inside the coach, out of sight of her outraged relatives and the scornful servant, the tension broke. Hiding herself in a corner—alone—apart, moans of grief burst from the depths of her shame.[56]

This episode of wrenching shame and unlovability is followed by a second, "founding" anecdote, the story of Fanya's social gaffe after she has shared Thanksgiving dinner on Sutton Place (a real "American" meal) with the Farnsworth family (Fanya meets Miss Farnsworth while working behind the counter in a department store). It turns out that this genteel family is "a little taken aback by" Fanya's "unrestrained show of emotion" in their home, followed by her effusive thank-you note to proper Mrs. Farnsworth in the form of a gushing poem: "Madonna! Mother-spirit / . . . Let me warm my lost, homeless heart on your breast / I'm so cold, so starved, so maddened with loneliness." Such raw honesty, however, only begets silence, a rejection that the open, earnest immigrant counter girl can only begin to understand as yet another soul-rivening episode of shame: "Slowly the bitterness of being ignored seeped through her flesh. She had humbled herself, exposed the famine of her soul to strangers. In her loneliness—her social famine—she had mistaken a little friendliness, a gesture of politeness, for personal response."[57]

In *All I Could Never Be* it is never absolutely clear how these scenes of shame and repressed rage, which are announced in the Prologue, are meant to establish Fanya's character, to "explain," during the course of the novel, her journey from the disillusioning Dewey-type encounter (treated in detail) to Fanya's sojourn in California, and finally to the pastoral countryside of Vermont where, at the very end, Fanya is shunned even by the local, reticent Yankees. To be sure, Yezierska's portrait of Henry Scott/ Dewey, the symbol of "all" Fanya "could never be," as "otherworldly," with "quieting hands" and with a "fragrance of something higher and finer than any man of her own race" reverberates with rich potential as a portrait of the various incarnations of this archetypal character.[58] Enlarging the deepest meanings Dewey held for her, Yezierska now describes how Scott, who happens to speak Dewey's actual words in places of the text, confers upon Fanya "a place in history"—a key phrase that registers Dewey's office as the one who shaped and clarified the unfocused and unformed immigrant volatility of his student; Henry possesses what Yezierska calls the "disciplined energy" of the Pilgrims.[59]

At the same time, we learn in more profound ways how the Emersonian-philosopher-immigrant conjunction enables each to mediate the constraining forms that impede true vision. Walking with Henry along the Lower East Side, Fanya is moved at her own change of heart and insight: "He had made me see through the dirt and the poverty into their hearts, until the ghetto rose before her, as a city set on a high hill whose light could not be hid." And Scott, himself "caught up by her voice," begins to see the Lower East Side in transformed ways as well: "'I should never have seen your people as I've seen them tonight, if not for you.' "[60]

But the utopian possibilities inherent in gentile–Jewish merging come to nothing, after Scott's single expression of sexual desire goes unresponded (to recall, again, that Fanya/Yezierska wasn't able to "follow through" with the original affair because Dewey loomed as a vague reminder of her own awesome, Old World father).[61] After that lost opportunity, the balance of *All I Could Never Be* unravels into a series of minor epiphanies, sudden revelations that resonate only in light of Yezierska's cumulative work. For example, Fanya gains a new awareness about the complex dynamic of self-hatred and repression through the agency of Helena Hoffman (a friend who observes the sacred Day of Atonement): "'How could I have forgotten the Day of Atonement?'" Fanya asks in bewilderment,

> "All these years I have gone about a little bit ashamed of my manners, my background. I was so eager to acquire from the Gentiles their low voices, their calm, their poise, that I lost what I had—what I was."[62]

A profound discovery, to be sure, but a subject that the novel never explores. And as for the "serene, aloof" Henry Scott, who, as with Dewey's ungenerous behavior toward Yezierska in real life, ignores the gift of Fanya's published first book, it begins to dawn on Fanya, "in a revealing flash," how wide the "gulf [is] between them—how immeasurably far apart they were—had always been."[63]

In the end, though, Yezierska cannot resolve the cultural conflict that haunts each of her characters, for despite a fleeting recognition of her own "weakness," Fanya resists the impulse of return, even though she is moved by the sound of a ghetto rabbi chanting over Chanukah lights. Instead, the Epilogue unaccountably opens in the Vermont countryside (here Yezierska is drawing directly on personal history, but without any clear design), where we learn that Fanya now feels "her attempt to return to the ghetto had been blind and absurd" (an interval not portrayed in the novel, however).[64] *All I Could Never Be* loses focus at this point, devolving into a rambling, bizarre narrative that critics even in Yezierska's own time found strange. Fanya settles in a picturesque New England town in order to write. She takes in a traveling hobo whom no one in the community will put up for the night; in the novel's last lines it is intimated that Fanya sleeps with her visitor: "Without looking at each other, they read each other's essences and flowed together in understanding." Fellow Russian "exiles in strange lands," they are "suddenly granted a vision of home" in Vermont.[65]

The difficulty that Yezierska had with *All I Could Never Be* (after its critical failure in 1932, she rarely published again and lapsed into virtual obscurity) bespeaks the larger problem she faced as an ethnic artist: how to construct a self able to mediate the raw emotions of shame and rage depicted in the Prologue; how to fashion, that is, a character capable of standing, if not aloof from the constraints of the dominant culture, then at least creatively marginal to the cultural conditions that generate a debilitating self-hatred and crippling bad faith. Does Fanya choose to "get even" (to use a familiar phrase) with the WASPs of "Arlington" by sleeping with the stranger "Mr. Pavlowich" (or is she merely responding empathically to a fellow "hungry heart"?); can she summon her ethnic difference to expose—or subvert, or parody—the emotional reticence of "Dewey" and thus overturn the weight of mannered generations that stifle expression?

Moving back and forth, in attraction and revulsion between the imagined world of the gentiles and the just as abstracted world of the ghetto, Yezierska's heroines—and perhaps Yezierska herself—remain sadly trapped, in much the same way that Cahan's Levinsky is trapped. "In his pursuit of whatever he considers pleasurable and good," Isaac Rosenfeld understood fifty years ago about the complex nature of David Levinsky's character—and I would argue most of Yezierska's as well—Levinsky "seeks to return to his yearning as much as he does to escape it."[66]

From this perspective, Yezierska's children of loneliness are driven by a dialectic of hunger: first, for the "American eating," metaphorically inscribed in the cool civilized emotionlessness of "Dewey," and then by a return to Old World foodways as yet another ineffectual mode of identity,

According to most scholars, popular culture enacts a subculture's deepest desires, fears, and longings. In early twentieth-century America, popular culture enabled the work of Americanization as it provided opportunities—expressive outlets—for cultural dissent, giving audiences the choice, say, of remaining outside the American consensus, or of nationalistic assent, inviting them to celebrate their status as New World citizens. During the early decades, Jewish artists appropriated the existing popular media to address the emotional concerns of their audiences; in the process they helped shape—indeed invented—a vision of the country designed to help negotiate the often bewildering, *alien* landscape (external and internal) in which the immigrants found themselves.

In this respect, Jewish American popular culture sounds everywhere with what Henry James nervously characterized as the "accent of the future"—the grafting of immigrant speech onto English—a new "American" tone that he associated with the realm of the popular. Amidst the intense café culture of the Lower East Side James glimpsed—with patrician disquiet—a hungry, vibrant audience, ready to consume. Indeed, this uneasy guardian of "civilized" American speech recognized in the linguistic energy of the urban masses "the germ of a 'public.'" Returning to his homeland (transformed by immigration) at the turn of the new century James encountered an emerging audience, the noisy incarnation of "a new thing under the sun." In their own creative response to newness, the immigrants indelibly altered the American tone. [2]

The originating site for much of Jewish American popular culture was, of course, the Lower East Side itself. If that legendary region now resides, nostalgically, only in memory—although, as Hasia Diner has shown, in the last twenty-five years a rich "memory culture" industry has sprung up in the forms of walking tours, tenement museums, and the marketing of symbolic ethnicity itself[3]—in the early twentieth century the Lower East Side housed a vibrant scene of nickelodeons, Yiddish theaters, literary cafes, and, above all, an audience receptive to new forms of entertainment. The demographics are well known. Between 1880 and 1924, New York's Jewish population grew dramatically, from 80,000 to 1,250,000, with an estimated five million Jews passing through Ellis Island during this interval.[4] The sheer volume of migration helped nourish a lively street culture, generating a powerful urban energy that was manifested in people's desires to engage the New World, indeed, to dream of self reinvention.

"The streets are crucial," Irving Howe noted in his study of immigrant culture, *World of Our Fathers* (1976); "[f]orming each day a great fair of Jewish life, they became the training ground for Jewish actors, comics, and singers."[5] Similarly, Alfred Kazin claimed that "the positive creative role of the Jew as modern American . . . was in the first years of this century being prepared not in the universities . . . but in the vaudeville theaters, music halls, and burlesque houses where the pent-up eagerness of penniless immigrant youngsters met the raw urban scene on its own terms."[6] Early popular entertainers like Al Jolson and Fannie Brice imbibed the urgent dynamism of the streets. According to the contemporary pop-culture critic Gilbert Seldes, their performances were "surcharged with vital energy," expressive of what he termed, in the early 1920s, "the daemonic" in American theater.[7]

Why was the creative encounter between America and immigrant so potentially explosive? For Seldes, the answer had to do with what we now term cultural *difference*: with the perception—both by the official, "dominant" culture and by the artists themselves—of Jewish entertainers as *other*. "It is noteworthy," Seldes observed of Jolson and Brice early in their careers, "that these two stars bring something to America which America lacks and loves—they are, I suppose, two of our most popular entertainers—and that both are racially out of the dominant caste. Possibly this accounts for their fine carelessness about our superstitions of politeness and gentility. . . . within these bounds Jolson and Brice go farther, go with more contempt for artificial notions of propriety, than anyone else."[8]

It may be difficult, in our own time, to recover the electricity of a tireless Jolson in concert at the Winter Garden Theater ("You ain't heard nothin' yet!" was his signature expression, refusing to let his audience go home) or the "insider pleasure" of hearing Fannie Brice perform dialect routines like "Mrs. Cohen at the Beach" (1927) or Yiddish-inflected songs like "I'm an Indian" (1921); we may even consider the "fine carelessness" of their "art" less than brilliant. For Seldes, their status as ethnic outsiders enabled figures like Jolson and Brice to transgress boundaries of civility, at least for the implied genteel audiences who could afford to attend shows at the Winter Garden and Ziegfield theaters. For the large immigrant population and (especially) their children still living, through the 1920s and 1930s, on the Lower East Side, Yiddish theater and the movies were the preferred modes of entertainment. In these venues—either live on stages along Second Avenue (where most of the Yiddish theaters were located) or on screen (movie houses were initially concentrated in ethnic neighborhoods)[9]—audiences watched their deepest anxieties and desires enacted, literally displayed before their eyes. Rescreening early immigrant cinema enables us, some eighty years later, to fathom the ordeal, the emotional costs of Americanization. The films continue to speak to us, not merely as sentimental artifacts indulging our own needy nostalgia, but rather as texts that open up a world where the claims of memory, the rawness of generational struggle, the rivening impact of shame remain palpable, alive. In this respect, immigrant movies depict the combustible reaction of street vs. home, English vs. Yiddish (or "potato Yiddish," as the less than perfect rhetoric of *shund* (trashy) theater was derisively styled), of "civilized" America and the nation's linguistically mongrel future. Out of that exhilarating encounter much popular culture in America was forged.

At the beginning of the 1920s, movies drew heavily on existing literary materials, often adapting short stories from popular magazines or translating plays from the Yiddish theater directly to the screen. There is a rich history of this "primitive" immigrant cinema, helpfully catalogued by scholars of early American film like Lester D. Friedman, Patricia Erens, and Kevin Brownlow. Only a few very early examples of the films survive; the extant titles suggest that brief comedies, on the order of "The Cohens and the Kellys"—a series of silent features chronicling the comedy of deeply stereotypic ethnic families negotiating the New World as they also learn to overcome the superficial differences between them—along with historical spectacles, melodramas, and historical movies based on recent history ("pogrom" films, in Erens's taxonomy) dominated the movie houses through the mid-1920s.[10]

Among the most important directors in the silent era was Edward Sloman, who between 1922 and 1928 made five features, including *His People* (1925) and *Surrender* (1927)—both of which survive—and *We Americans* (1928). As an impressive example of silent immigrant cinema, *His People,* based on the short story "The Jew" by Isadore Bernstein, stands out for the intensity of its acting and the resonance of its depiction of the Jewish family undergoing Americanization. The film vividly refracts these core dilemmas, which in *His People* concern a pious father and his two sons, an ungrateful yet favored son who seeks an *alrightnik* lifestyle away from his grimy Lower East Side origins, and a faithful yet unappreciated son who boxes professionally under an Irish name, "Battling Rooney." Looking back forty years later, Sloman recalled his own warm feelings for *His People:* "This is my favorite film . . . because it was such a sure-fire picture. I knew when I started that it was going to be a great hit."[11]

His People remains powerful because of Rudolph Shildkraut's—a star of German theater who emigrated to Hollywood in the early twenties— and Rosa Rosanova's tour de force performances as Papa and Mama Cominsky, the struggling Old World couple on Delancey Street, helpless before their lawyer-son Morris's acculturating, New World desires. In particular, Rosanova—who made a career playing Jewish mothers, starring in the screen adaptation of Anzia Yezierska's *Hungry Hearts* (1922) and Frank Capra's *The Younger Generation* (1929), which was based on a Fannie

"And you say I'm not your father?" Morris shamed by his father's arrival at an uptown dinner party in *His People* (1925). Courtesy of Universal Studios Licensing LLLP.

Hurst story and, later, Broadway play (see below)—emerges as the veritable incarnation of the mournful, long-suffering, yet ultimately strong Jewish matriarch.

The plot of *His People* turns on shame-ridden Morris's almost fatal denial of his father: while dining uptown, with his upscale fiancée's refined family, Morris (now renamed "Maurice") refuses to recognize his slovenly dressed downtown Jew of a father, who has surfaced on *alrightnik* row in search of his son—an unbidden figure who represents for Morris the embarrassing greenhorn self, under repression. Earlier, at the threshold of Morris's leave-taking, father and son kiss tenderly on the lips, a remarkably affecting image, symbolic of the son's undeniable claims of affiliation, despite the ruptures caused by filial shame. "Remember, Morris," the emotional Old World father tells his departing son, "we always have on

Jessel (1925), then by the classic film (1927) and then through a variety of subsequent radio, film, and television adaptations (notably by Jolson himself on the Lux Radio Theatre, broadcast on June 2, 1947, followed by Danny Thomas in 1952 and Jerry Lewis in 1959). *The Jazz Singer's* "plot" continued, at least through 1980 with Neil Diamond's schmaltzy remake, to speak directly to "American Jewish," and no doubt to more general "ethnic" audiences.[15] In its "deep structure," the jazz singer enacts—as it measures—the psychological and familial costs (in the words of Diamond's hit tune), of the process of "coming to America."

As a way of locating the figure of Jolson, both in *The Jazz Singer* and in early twentieth-century immigrant culture in general, listen to the following exchange toward the end of Yezierska's *All I Could Never Be* (1932), a vignette that highlights the appeal of constructing a new self in the fluid world of immigrant-saturated New York. In one of her phases, Fanya works as a waitress in a "Sixth Avenue Restaurant," where she serves a customer whose hearty appetite and electric aura bespeak a decidedly new tone, the distinctive accent of popular culture:

> "Miss! Can you wait on me quick—please! A young man's vibrant voice called. "I'm starved. Haven't eaten or slept in twenty-four hours."
>
> Fanya turned, her swift glance taking in the buoyant brightness of the young face.
>
> "What will you have?"
>
> "Ham and eggs."
>
> When she came back with his order, she found him smiling to himself like a man in love. Joy radiated from his eyes. The very air was alive with his life. He gulped down his food in huge mouthfuls, and talked as he ate.
>
> "Rehearsing my play on Broadway. It's going great."[16]

In this charged instant, Fanya briefly rubs against another universe, the unkosher realm of show business, where the matter of table manners and genteel etiquette, of "low voices" and Protestant restraint pale before the elemental hunger and driving desire generated by the excitement— invitation—of life on the stage itself.

For some reason Yezierska chose not to explore the cultural meanings of this charismatic Broadway character.[17] Yet we can follow his progress in the Warner Brothers film version of *The Jazz Singer* (1927). By examining the figure of Jolson—especially his animated body language—in this movie about the conflict between religious tradition and the allure of the street, we can witness the striking transformation of Levinsky's gesticulating hands—behavior that stirred shame and the itch to repress in the self-conscious greenhorn—into the perpetual motion of Al Jolson, driven in response to some inner dynamo. In the early twenties, before the film was made, Gilbert Seldes registered the "nervous energy," the "vital energy," the "spasmodic energy," the "electrical energy" of vaudeville entertainers like Jolson, Eddie Cantor, and Fannie Brice. Jolson *embodied* the rhythms of city life, incarnating the new world of popular culture—an alternate "religion" that displaced, as it appropriated, the faith of the fathers.[18]

Before we turn to the figure of Jolson, however, it is important to trace briefly the permutations of the jazz singer idea, from short story to play to film. The American origins of the jazz singer begin with a young Samson Raphaelson, who, after being riveted by a Jolson performance at the University of Illinois in 1917 (where Raphaelson had been a student) decided to write a story about "Jakie Rabinowitz," scion of ten generations of cantors, who must choose between the promise of commercial success on stage (he "was no ordinary singer of ragtime") as "Jack Robin," and his deep historical obligation to follow in the cantorial line. Recalling Jolson's performance in a later article, Raphaelson reports the singer's unforgettable "emotion" on stage, "his velocity, the amazing fluidity"—kinetic qualities that somehow stirred in Raphaelson's mind the image (really, the feeling) of Jolson as cantor; above all, he sensed that Jolson radiated "the emotion of a cantor," the holy singer of religious praise.[19]

In the subsequent short story "The Day of Atonement" (1922), the tension between generations turns as much on the sacrilege of Jack's "jazz" singing as on the threat of his intermarrying. At a moment of truth, Jack explains to his mother, in answer to her hope that "if a *Yiddisher* boy marries a *Goyisher* girl . . . she could be learned to buy *Kosher* meat and to have two kinds of dishes, for *Fleischige* and for *Milchige*" (this exchange, which voices the orthodox anxiety about the taboo of mixing meat and dairy, does not appear in either the play or movie), how he can't imagine keeping a kosher home with Amy (his wife-to-be) because "I was brought up that way, ma, and I've been unhappy all my life." Hungry to assimilate, Jack wants to shed the irksome dietary laws of *kashrut* and thus "be happy like Amy is." Overhearing this blasphemy, the shocked cantor rises from his book, and with "eyes blazing . . . pointing a shaking finger at Jack," orders him out of the house. (In the subsequent film, the young Jack leaves home after he is beaten by his father for the transgression of singing in a Lower East Side saloon.) At the end of the story, Jack is at the threshold of Broadway success; but hearing of his father's death returns to the synagogue, dons his father's *talis* (prayer shawl), and rebonds with the affective world he had sought to deny. The synagogue, and its worn but evocative furnishings "called," Raphaelson explains, "to something surging and powerful in him, something which made his whole life since his boyhood seem blurred and unreal."[20]

That "something" turns out to be the *defining*, to recall Alter Brody's stringent critique of Yezierska, power of religious piety, the claims of "descent," which, Werner Sollors argues, locate "ethnic" identity in terms of genealogy and familial heritage. Those claims, we are meant to understand, release Jack from his *inauthentic* identity as jazz singer. The filial return also dislodges Jack's buried Jewish heart. "In his heart you're a good boy," his mother repeats. In the end, with "his dark eyes afire," "swathed in the folds of a great black-striped linen *Talis*," we witness how the act of faith-keeping observance brings a kind of resolution to the ambiguity of hyphenate identity. By contrast, in Raphaelson's opening description, Jack appears "draped in perfectly fitting suits of Anglo-Saxon severity"—a stylistic nod to the authority of the dominant culture that cannot mask the pain behind his "black eyes [which] were restless, cynical, and without joy."[21]

Still, it is not apparent how Jack's restless energy and cynical stance will enable him to readjust to Orchard Street, the old world to which he literally and spiritually returns in "The Day of Atonement."[22] But Raphaelson's brief sketch is not concerned with the dilemmas of homecoming; instead, we watch the first jazz singer discover his true calling by chanting the *Kol Nidre*, the prayer of renunciation, in place of his father. In fulfilling his deeper "descent" identity—or does it mysteriously claim him, as passive inheritor?—Jack exchanges the "chaotic, crassly unreal" experience of the street and Broadway for the "orderly nobility" (Raphaelson's judgmental language is telling) affiliated with the world of his father(s). Such renunciation, the story seems to suggest, rekindles ancient spiritual fires as it confers "authentic" selfhood.[23]

Three years later, in 1925, Raphaelson translated "The Day of Atonement" into a play starring George Jessel as Jack Robin. As in the original story, Jack at the end honors the historical legacy of five (no longer ten) generations of Rabinowitz cantors by replacing his father at the High Holiday altar—but not before Raphaelson draws out in richer ways the theme (undeveloped in the story) of tonal and emotional blurrings in the creative interaction of jazz rhythms and prayer. Jack's self is now characterized by "an engaging combination of wistfulness and impudence" (in Raphaelson's stage direction) as the "note of his personality," but we never quite gain a glimpse of the so-called impudence. Instead of that streetwise style, we're told that when he faces the moral authority of his father, Jack's buoyant stance of "bravado . . . glibness . . . [and] flippant smartness" is reduced to "a feeble echo"; he can only recover an "authentic" (my quotation marks) expressive mode when singing jazz songs like "Red Hot Mama," which, Raphaelson's direction informs us, he delivers "with rich plaintiveness."[24]

Jack returns home after five years, seeking his parents' blessing—"to have your love again" is how he explains it during an anxious moment of parental—fatherly—recrimination. " 'What kind of life are you living?' " his father thunders, asking the cosmic question of the rising generation born in America. In partial answer, this incarnation of *The Jazz Singer* explores the religious—cultural struggle within Jack, who "wants to be a part of America," as he explains to Mary, his love interest (there's no talk of marriage in the play) yet not be banished from home. In one scene, probably the strongest in the play, Jack tries to explain that his "dirty music from the sidewalk," as the cantor styles his apostate son's debased world, draws out the emotional strains of Jewish liturgy:

> You're right, papa. . . . You did teach me to sing songs of prayer. And I sang them here for you. But when I got out on the street with the other kids, I found myself singing the same songs they sang. And they're very much alike,—our songs—and the street songs.
>
> Well, listen—[*He sings "Ain Kelohenu," a Hebrew prayer tune. He sings four bars of it, swiftly, with feeling. And then, suddenly, to exactly the same tune and with exactly the same plaintiveness but with a new rhythm and shaking the shoulders, he sings a popular song*] . . . I just got them mixed, Papa—See?[25]

Cantor Rabinowitz, however, is not persuaded by the son's emotional performance. He can't hear the shared tones that blur the music of the street with that of the temple; like the transgression of mixing meat and milk, purity of tonal boundary must be acknowledged and maintained.

The drama of *The Jazz Singer*, the play, centers on Jack's moral and spiritual crisis of faith: will he perform opening night on Broadway (in this version, as in the movie, he is about to make it as a star) or will he chant the sacred *Kol Nidre* in place of his ailing father? In Raphaelson's resolution, the beckoning but unkosher realms of Broadway and Mary Dale are (again) powerless against the pull of tradition. Despite Harry Lee's (Jack's producer) secular argument to mother Sara that Jack "ran away from all this"—meaning religious orthodoxy—and that his singing in the synagogue would be an act of bad faith ("I want the boy to be true to himself," he explains); and despite Mary's appeal, again to Sara, that she "found him. . . . I helped him to realize his own powers" (another version of the host culture—immigrant, Dewey—Yezierska story); and, finally, despite Jack's own self-doubts and bitterness over the choice itself (during

Cantor Rabinowitz enraged by his son's rejection of tradition.
Staged publicity photo for the Broadway production of *The Jazz
Singer*. Courtesy of the Billy Rose Theatre Collection, The New
York Public Library for the Performing Arts, Astor, Lenox and
Tilden Foundations.

this charged moment the stage direction reads that Jack is "*On the point of
collapse. His voice is bitter, sardonic in defeat*")—despite all appeals to his
secular self, when he hears the news of his father's death, he is instantly
transformed. "I thought I could get away from Cantors!" he sobs, feeling
the accusing eyes of God rebuke his soul.[26]

In the end, Jack defines himself according to the authorizing weight of
the fathers, rather than according to popular culture. "I'm the son of my
father, Mamma. I'm a Cantor, see? . . . I'm Cantor Rabinowitz!" Jack utters
this declaration, we are told, not in self-mockery but "*strong in the power
of decision.*" In the end, too, he acknowledges the claims of memory
against the repressions of Americanization: "What a little boy learns, he

George Jessel wrapped in the folds of tradition at the end of *The Jazz Singer*. Courtesy of the Billy Rose Theatre Collection, The New York Public Library for the Performing Arts, Astor, Lenox and Tilden Foundations.

never forgets." Jack's last spoken words in the play, "Goodbye, Mary," suggest a kind of individual renunciation as the self-anointed cantor prepares to sing the famous prayer of collective renunciation, with which the play closes.[27] Thus the original story and expanded play both end on a note of filial duty and a shunning—albeit anguished, in the case of the drama—of insubstantial secular temptation.

The film version of *The Jazz Singer* had a complicated pre-production history. The Warner Brothers, especially Harry, sought the film rights to the play early on, and originally signed its star George Jessel to play Jack Robin.[28] But the Warners reneged on their contract because, according to Jessel, he protested the radical revision planned for the movie, which concludes not with the cantor's son at prayer but with the jazz singer returning in triumph on the stage. A more compelling explanation—or conjecture—about the replacement of Jessel with Al Jolson is Neal Gabler's, who surmises that Jessel, "a strident professional Jew," was, in effect, deemed "too Jewish" for the "assimilationist fable" the Warners had in mind.[29] In this respect, Al Jolson, the son of adamantly Old World Rabbi Moshe Yoelson, was virtually playing himself in the movie, perhaps reenacting scenes from his own life. "Al and I had been absorbed by American customs, American freedom of thought, and the American way of life," Jolson's older brother recalled; "My father still dwelt in the consciousness of the strict, orthodox teachings of the old world."[30]

The Jazz Singer vividly portrays the chasm separating the generations in its opening tableaux, which alternate between the Rabinowitz home on the eve of the Day of Atonement, with Sara cooking up a storm, and scenes of young Jakie singing and dancing in a local saloon. Yudelson, the neighborhood *kibbitzer*, who for some reason is guzzling beer in the same place as the sacred time approaches, discovers Jakie's transgression, and immediately runs back to the cantor to report the tragic news. The cantor himself rushes out into the street—the only time he is seen outside his home, except when he is singing in the adjacent synagogue—and drags the boy back. The mother tries to mediate in the ensuing verbal battle. She tries to intervene, to appeal to her husband, but the opposing clash of temperaments and beliefs proves unresolvable; she is thrust away as Jake is beaten, an apostate son absorbed by popular culture (the buttons he wears on his shirt amount to a badge of street allegiance), hopelessly fallen in the unforgiving eyes of patriarchy.[31]

With much pain and longing, Jakie leaves home (making good on his threat to flee if beaten), taking a portrait of his mother as a memorial to his (already) past life. Distracted by the summons of the holy hour, the cantor departs for synagogue, where we hear, in ironic counterpoint to Jakie's exaggerated belting out of "My Gal Sal," the lyrically sweet singing of *Kol Nidre*. As the first act of *The Jazz Singer* comes to an end, we watch the figure of Cantor Rabinowitz as he performs his holy and historic office. Standing piously erect in his holy white garb, with his hands lovingly supporting a prayer book, he sways gently up and down to the rhythms of restrained supplication.

The next segment introduces the mature Jack Robin, the aspiring jazz singer. It is a crucial sequence in the movie, for Jolson's initial appearance, in light of the cultural themes of manners, civility, and foodways that shape so much early twentieth-century Jewish American expression, is an absolutely charged moment. In a setting not found in either the story or play, the movie adaptation—by Alfred Cohn, a well-known Hollywood scenarist who also wrote the screenplay for *His People*—shifts the action across the country, from Orchard Street to "Coffee Dan's" in San Francisco, an "underground" joint where Jack and his friend Buster (played by William Demarest, who twenty years later played "Jolson's" manager in *The Jolson Story* [1946]) go to, as Buster says in a fragment of dialogue not used in the movie, "bum a feed off" Buster's friend, who works as the "impresario" at Coffee Dan's.[32] There are many resonant aural and visual symbols in this original segue that prove crucial for a reading of *The Jazz Singer,* and for American ethnic expression in general.

The first symbol applies to the music that accompanies—and thus comments on—the action. We move in counterpoint from *Kol Nidre* to fifteen bars of the jaunty "Hop Skip," as it is called in the original musical score to the film, a lively tune that keys the "jazzy" atmosphere of Coffee Dan's. During this interlude, the camera brings us face to face with plate after plate of ham and eggs; in one instance we see a high stack of them, in another we see a tight close up—the spectacle of ham and eggs is thus literally *shoved* in our face. Next, a screen card announcing Al Jolson's "entrance" as Jack Robin is accompanied by eight bars of "Mammy," Jolson's signature song from his vaudeville and concert performances—the musical theme, that is, identifies Jolson as the country's leading popular artist (as opposed to "Jack Robin's" own obscurity). At the same time, "Mammy" signals the movie's trajectory, for in his last performance Jack/Jolson sings "Mammy" in blackface before his mother in a fascinating epilogue appended to the original script, a tacked-on ending that appalled Raphaelson after the premiere and troubled Jessel. And to complicate the resonances of "Mammy" as Jolson's musical sign even further, after Jolson's own mother died when he was eight, she remained, according to his biographer, "his leading lady—the unacknowledged mistress of his private life and his stage career."[33] His continuous mourning thus sheds light on why the most evocative, emotionally charged scenes in *The Jazz Singer* occur between Jolson and the actress Eugenie Besserer, who plays his screen mother. In J. Hoberman's acute formulation, they constitute "a psychodramatic re-enactment of Jolson's youth."[34]

The musical score now returns to "Hop Skip" (for a long thirty-one bars) and we finally see Jack/Jolson. According to Cohn's original script,

"Jack and Buster are eating heartily with all the gusto that characterizes a healthy appetite that has been whetted by lengthy fasting"[35] (note the ironic allusion to the obligatory fasting of Yom Kippur). On screen, however, we witness the spectacle of what Seldes meant by Jolson's legendary energy. "Whatever he does," Seldes remarked, Jolson does at the highest possible pressure. . . . He cannot underplay anything, he lacks restraint."[36] Absorbed by the figure of Jack at Coffee Dan's, we gaze at the utterly kinetic Jolson scarfing down ham and eggs, eating, chewing, pumping his elbows, swaying in time to the music; in a kind of rhythmic euphoria, the music itself is driving to the core of his being: Jolson simply can't sit still.

Jack, we are meant to understand, is in his true element, a raucous scene of democratic American eating: not the high-mannered gestures of "civilized" etiquette required, say, in Levinsky's Waldorf, but the unself-conscious world of popular culture in which the imposed structure of manners is overturned by pure uninhibited appetite. Accordingly, when Jack leaves the table for the microphone, Buster grabs food off Jack's plate and talks with food in his mouth; such incivilities go unnoticed in this fluid environment, the leveling world of show business. In vivid contrast to Levinsky's fork anxiety and unsettling fear of waiters, Jack's lively, animated table manners reflect his unembarrassed—recall that Raphaelson's key word for Jack is *impudence*—relation to American "low" culture.

Ignorant of that "other" world and its "civilized" pretensions, Jack attacks the plate of ham and eggs, eating the American traife with relish, reveling in the unkosher sign of his absorption in American (food)ways. Thus what he eats, how he eats, and where he eats register his unconflicted arrival in the world beyond Orchard Street. If Yezierska's heroines remain caught between wanting a taste of the "American eating" and the *heimisch* foodways of the Old World, the movie revision of *The Jazz Singer,* by adding the spectacle of Jolson eating ham and eggs with relish at Coffee Dan's, images the immigrant son in the full glory of his incorporation of America, a figure for the open, tolerant society he seeks to join and eventually conquer.

The ham and eggs interlude is quickly followed by Jolson's—Jolson "is always Jolson," Seldes recognized, no matter what stage character he was playing—first two songs, an emotional rendition of "Dirty Hands, Dirty Face" (partially authored by Jolson, by the way), about a father's love for his street urchin son—the song is interesting, in light of the movie's plot, for it voices the dream of generational conciliation—and a tour de force performance of "Toot, Toot Tootsie." Requesting that the band "give it to 'em hard and heavy" (Jolson calls the bandleader "Lou"—he's speaking to his real life musical director, Lou Silvers), he launches into an undulating, flowing array of syncopated body movements, sexy in any cultural moment, urging on the band with phantom shrieks of "get hot!" whistling during the break with a brilliant demonstration of fluttering fingers in non-stop, blurry motion. After watching this startling performance, we can begin to understand why Seldes reacted to Jolson's "galvanic little figure, leaping and shouting" to describe what he called the "daemonic" in the American theater.[37] Here, I believe, we see the reversal—or, better, the creative adaptation—of Levinsky's gesticulating hand anxiety, the physical complement to his fork anxiety. If Levinsky buries his hands to mask his shame, Jolson is *shameless* in his unfettered swayings and grindings; if Levinsky is repulsed by the Talmudic gesturings of his old (world) self under repression, Jolson is *unbuttoned* in his New World body language. Indeed, Jolson whistles like he eats ham and eggs (and later, in a famous ad-libbed "talking" scene with his mother, he plays the piano like he eats), with authentic gusto for the taste of popular culture.

Thus the first imaging of Jolson in *The Jazz Singer* places him in his own familiar sphere as the country's foremost entertainer; at the same time, it uncannily recalls the thematics of foodways and civility that structure the fictional imagination of Cahan and Yezierska. It recovers that shaping rhetoric, however, only to overcome it, in order to exorcise those core affects that haunt the immigrant self—the cultural self-hatred and shame that immobilize (as we have seen) David Levinsky in his unalleviated hunger and longing. The weight of tradition and the authority of imagined New World manners—arguably Yezierska's and Cahan's ultimate theme— appear invisible, indeed impotent, in the liminal world of Coffee Dan's. Only in that creative space can the jazz singer, in transition from tradition to celebrity, declare himself licensed to eat—and sing—what and how he pleases.[38]

Yet the movie's internal drama of generational and religious conflict, played out in the figure of Jack (and, perhaps, as an uncanny recapitulation of Jolson's own biography), conveys considerable anguish and pathos, in the tradition of immigrant cinema. For example, when Jack is drawn to a Chicago concert hall to hear the famous Cantor Rosenblatt sing "Yarzeit" (a prayer for the dead), the experience conjures the haunting memory of his own father, and implicitly dislodges the son's filial guilt. In this powerful scene, the real-life cantor Yossele Rosenblatt's hands remain utterly still during the performance; they remain suspended, above his waist, at the level where a prayer book might be held. Ultimately, however, *The Jazz Singer* resolves the "intractable problem" of Judaism in America "painlessly," by letting Jack Robin fulfill his filial burden *and* garner worldly success.[39] Unlike Levinsky, "Jolson takes his Americanness for granted," observes J. Hoberman;[40] and that seemingly unworried stance dramatizes the psychic and cultural distance separating *The Rise of David Levinsky* and *The Jazz Singer.* Still, the movie's fantastic, appended ending—Jolson singing "Mammy" to his "mother" at the actual Winter Garden Theater, with "The Jazz Singer" emblazoned on the marquee—only highlights the fabricated aspect of Hollywood's dream factory. Only in America can cantors' sons keep faith with the past *and* be a star on Broadway.

In real life, however, Jolson appears to have been as aimlessly driven, as generally unsatisfied, as ultimately alone (in his will he gave most of his fortune to organizations, not to family or longstanding friends), and universally disliked as David Levinsky.[41] Each New World striver searched endlessly, without peace, to replace a lost mother. If their lives ended in sadness, it may be because the hunger generated by the immigrant desire—recall Isaac Rosenfeld's insight concerning New World "hunger"—to incorporate the fruits of America can never really be sated, for New World fare will always remain, at some level, tasteless, bitter, insubstantial.

The ordeal of Americanization remained a core theme in early American cinema through the end of the 1920s. Perhaps its most powerful representation is Frank Capra's half silent, half talkie *The Younger Generation,* made in 1929 for Harry Cohn's newly formed Columbia Pictures. The film was based on a now obscure play by Fannie Hurst called *It Is to Laugh,* which opened and quickly closed on Broadway in December 1927. The play was itself based on an earlier Hurst story, "The Gold in Fish," which appeared in the popular *Hearst's International and Cosmopolitan* magazine for August 1925.[42] In addition, the screenwriter for *The Younger Generation* was Sonia Levien—the scriptwriter on the film version of Yezierska's *Hungry Hearts*—and it starred Rosa Rosanova as Mama Goldfish (also the Jewish mother in *His People*); Jean Hersholt as Papa Goldfish; Jacob Krantz as the son, Morris; and Lina Basquette as the daughter, "Birdie," who was Sam Warner's widow.

In *The Younger Generation,* Capra concentrates on the figure of the mannered, self-conscious Morris Goldfish and his quest for an untainted and—like his jazz age contemporary, Jay Gatsby—self-invented new name which, he believes, will enable him to rise in the world of antique dealers on Fifth Avenue. Where Mama Goldfish in Hurst's original story is bewildered by the son's declaration of a new family name ("Maurice Fish"), in the film Rosanova acts like a mediator (similar to the mother in *The Jazz Singer*) between son and family, an apologist for his parvenu desires. Embracing the son's material ambition, Mama Goldfish appears dolled up in sequins and beads, a Yiddish New World flapper whose disjunctive styles—heavily accented Old World voice, swanky New World dress—display the conflict at the heart of the movie: the attractions of making it set against the familiar, organic world of the Lower East Side from where, as a result of the son's quest for social recognition, the family has been uprooted.[43]

As this still compelling movie unfolds, we observe that to split the name *Goldfish* in two, to take, in effect, a "fish" out of water, as Birdie, and eventually her mother understand, is to commit a cultural severing fatal for emotional and familial health. As a result of his name change, Morris is imaged as utterly alone, emotionally inert, without a prospect of a family (unlike Birdie, who marries a tin pan alley song writer and has a child). Indeed, Capra contrasts Morris's static aloneness with the old world father's animated communal spirit—only on the Lower East Side, where he can be both a *macher* and a comedian, does Papa Goldfish feel himself alive, in his true element.

In Hurst's original story, Birdie is cast as the agent of "return," soothing her ailing father through nostalgia, by recalling their previous, happier life on Delancey Street. "The Gold in Fish" ends with Birdie and Mama Goldfish taking the subway uptown, to the Bronx—by implication, to the new Lower East Side.[44] The movie, however, bears down hard on the fate of Morris. His mother rejects his invitation, saying, "I want you to forget everything" (she even turns down the son's offer to travel with him to Paris for Coney Island!) and returns with Birdie to the East Side. In the end, alone in his empty *alrightnik* mansion, chilled by a lack of family, Morris wraps himself before a fireplace in a shawl, which uncannily resembles first a *talis*, and ultimately a burial shroud.

The Younger Generation thus incorporates many of the central themes of early Jewish American popular culture. Significantly, Frank Capra, the film's young Italian American director, was, at some level, also drawing on his own immigrant story: the second-generation narrative of repression and denial, of the son seeking to forget the parents' old world ways and the (inevitable) residues of estrangement and entrapment, which come with the dangerous territory of Americanization itself. Seventeen years after *The Younger Generation*, Capra set in *It's a Wonderful Life* in the shtetl of Bedford Falls, transforming its idealized world of endlessly postponed—or denied—desire for escape into a celebration of family and community. If Morris Goldfish ends up cold and alone, a cautionary tale of Americanization, then Jimmy Stewart's George Baily is warmly surrounded on Christmas eve by family and friends, at the threshold of a new life. Capra explored the tension between familial and communal constraint—the dark underside of Capra's (immigrant?) vision of American life—earlier in *The Younger Generation*. Morris remains, in Neal Gabler's nice formulation, a "prisoner of assimilation."[45] In the end, Capra's *Younger Generation* richly portrays how the Jewish immigrant story could inspire the imagination of the young Italian-American film director. Indeed, Capra recognized the perhaps unresolvable dilemmas of Americanization: in himself, in the first generation of Hollywood moguls, who sought to repress all vestiges of "Jewishness" in their public dream visions of America, and perhaps for the vast majority of his audience cramming movie theaters along Second Avenue and other urban centers as well.[46]

Early immigrant cinema therefore projected New World desires as well as cautionary tales for audience consumption, in some instances—as in *The Younger Generation*—incorporating both in the same film. Alongside mainstream cinema in America, there also existed an extensive artistic universe of Yiddish filmmaking, whose writers, directors, and stars occasionally crossed over into Hollywood. For the most part, however, the celluloid world that was conjured in Yiddish cinema inhabited a parallel but separate sphere. Yet in a few cases, the Yiddish cinema offered— implicitly and explicitly—telling commentaries on the social, psychological, and political issues inscribed in more widely distributed films. Two major examples of Yiddish cinema that explore—as they comment on—the tonic themes of early immigrant cinema are *The Cantor's Son* (1937), which was the Yiddish cinema's direct response to *The Jazz Singer*, and Maurice Schwartz and Sidney Goldin's film version of *Uncle Moses* (1932), based on the 1918 novel by Sholem Asch and Schwartz's legendary stage version, performed on Second Avenue (by the early 1930s Schwartz was considered the greatest living actor of the Yiddish theater). Viewed together they respond in striking ways to the core issues that preoccupied immigrant cinema throughout the 1920s.

In the Warner Brothers version, the exemplary story of Jakie Rabinowitz ends in filiality and secular success—the cantor's son remains dutiful and becomes a star. In *The Cantor's Son*—an "anti-*Jazz Singer*," in J. Hoberman's view[47]—the son returns to the familiar—and spiritually sustaining—world of the shtetl and decides to stay. For all the material and romantic appeal of Jewish New York, the claims of memory overturn the allure of the New World. As a disillusioned character in *The Cantor's Son* cautions about the mythic expectations associated with the New World, "America is not America."[48]

The Cantor's Son, which opened on Christmas Eve in 1937, remains a testament to the powerful role of nostalgia in Jewish American popular culture. It features the legendary cantor-turned-movie-star Moishe Oysher (making his film debut) who, in the role of Saul (Shloyme) Reichman forsakes his family and hometown Belz as a young boy, lured by a troupe of traveling actors and the promise of freedom that their untraditional way of life represents. The scene quickly shifts to Jewish New York, where Saul is "discovered" by Helen, a popular singer (played, incidentally, by Oysher's real-life wife, Florence Weiss) and is eventually made into a star by a local radio mogul. The highlight of the movie is their gorgeous rendition of the Jewish classic, "Mayn Shtetele Belz"—a song about memories of homeland and family—delivered in a richly harmonized duet.

Who is this popular singing idol named Saul Reichman? Where does he belong? Where does his Jewish heart truly reside? Like Jake Robin (né Rabinowitz), Saul continues to feel, to *hear* the weight and melodies of generations of cantors; unlike Jack, however, he still remembers the sounds and the emotional *feel* of his beloved Belz; above all he recalls the taste of nourishing soup, offered years ago by his shtetl sweetheart, to whom he vows his everlasting love. As in Cahan and Yezierska, but with different outcomes, Old World foodways possess the residual power to dislodge repressed ethnic identity. Returning to Belz for his parents' fiftieth wedding anniversary, Saul reclaims his "descent" identity as cantor of the community, despite the appeals of his Americanized girlfriend, who realizes, sadly, that her mere material American world is no match for the implicit "authenticity" and community offered by *heimische* Belz.

The Cantor's Son thus projects the shtetl as an ideal world, an imaginary landscape where—in 1937—Yiddish-speaking audiences could nostalgically return, if only in the movie house in the Bronx. (Ironically, the film was shot closer to their American homes, in the green fields of New Jersey.) "Our boy didn't forget he's a Jew," the cantor's mother ecstatically announces. It may be that by 1937, most Jewish mothers, long uprooted from little towns like Belz, could no longer assume the same filial yearning on the part of their own sons. "Belz," that is, could only be remembered in popular song. In this respect, *The Cantor's Son*, like most popular culture, expresses a collective longing, highlighting in the process the disjunction between reality and desire, collective fantasy and the bitter facts of Americanization. Summoning nostalgia to salve the ache of their audience's New World condition, the Yiddish cinema's answer to *The Jazz Singer* sought, through a large dose of sentimentality, to arrest an imagined narrative of declension: *The Cantor's Son* thus rewrites the *ur*-immigrant story of Jews seeking an inauthentic, assimilated new life in America, offering an utterly fantastic vision of reverse pilgrimage (we should all sail for Poland in 1937?) as a poignant countervision to New World debasement.[49]

The Yiddish film version of *Uncle Moses* also explores the fate of New World transplantation, but in more complex ways. In his astonishing performance, Maurice Schwartz embodies the figure of Moses, the boorish shtetl butcher from Kusmin turned wealthy clothing manufacturer in

4

HAUNTED IN THE NEW WORLD

Henry Roth

In food there should be some trust.[1]
—*Call It Sleep*

Well before Henry Roth died in 1995 at the age of eighty-nine, living in relative obscurity in Albuquerque, New Mexico, in exile from his Lower East Side homeland, the story of his "blocked" career as a novelist had become the stuff of legend. After publishing *Call It Sleep* in 1934, when Roth was, astonishingly, still in his twenties, he found himself unable to continue writing fiction. Like a number of American authors who came of age in the charged political atmosphere of the 1930s, Roth joined the Communist Party in 1933, just before *Call It Sleep* appeared. But his altered allegiance—exchanging a Joycean aesthetic for a proletarian vision of art, as demanded by the Party—proved fatal for his literary imagination. As Roth explained to various interviewers over the years, "as soon as I grappled with commitment, I became immobilized. . . . Allegiance once deeply inhaled was as lethal as carbon monoxide, and as inseparable from fancy's bloodstream."[2]

In light of the legend, it was not surprising that the publication, beginning in 1994, of *Mercy of a Rude Stream,* a tetralogy of novels that continues the saga of Roth's coming of age in early twentieth-century New York, should have been met with celebration and wonder. After all, it was itself miraculous that Roth, who was afflicted with a severe case of rheumatoid arthritis in his fingers, could even physically generate thousands of manuscript pages; and it was even more wondrous that Roth, deep into his seventies and eighties, could somehow recover the vanished world of his Harlem youth, indeed could render in still vivid images his memories of immigrant family life, the territory that had indelibly shaped his own coming of age *two* generations earlier. Pecking away at his computer (named "Ecclesias," and with whom Roth engages in therapy-like dialogue), an aging "Ira Stigman"—the voice identified as the author of these memory narratives, and the name given to the adolescent hero of *Mercy*—revisits the past in a brutally honest act of remembrance and reinterpretation. *Mercy* is a "work deliberately hybrid and unfixed," observes Mary Gordon,[3] by an aging author-in-exile trying to fathom the psychologically complex younger man who, only a few years removed from a cold-water Harlem tenement, came to write the masterpiece *Call It Sleep.*

The voice we hear throughout *Mercy of a Rude Stream* is, of course, that of Roth himself; but these garrulous volumes only manage to convey, as the critic James Wood points out, "the loose flow of memory";[4] they no longer possess the lyrical intensity, or what Marshall Berman nicely terms the "visionary gleam," of *Call It Sleep.*[5] That first incandescent novel continues to loom in Roth's mind, a still mysterious *fact* of creation: "The writing of the one novel had gone so deep, he would be forever after haunted by the experience. Some metaphoric vein of precious ore he had struck within the psyche—and he could never ignore, never forget it, do what he might. . . . Some vein of a rare lode of perception he had been fortunate enough to strike within the spirit, a lode he had exposed, kept radiating beyond his control."[6]

In this respect, Roth remained forever haunted by the achievement of *Call It Sleep;* he continued, that is, to be obsessed by the memory of displacement from the organic, safely enclosing world of the Lower East Side, the rich imaginative vein of immigrant family life he had mined as a young writer starting out in the thirties. For it was *as a result* of the experience of displacement, the trauma of being "unhoused" in the year 1914 from Ninth Street and Avenue D to the more multicultural neighborhood of East 119th Street in Jewish-Irish-Italian Harlem, that Roth invariably attributed his famous literary "blockage." "I felt at home there," Roth admits, speaking about his early childhood on the East Side in the second volume of *Mercy of a Rude Stream*, subtitled *A Diving Rock on the Hudson*, "shored and stayed by tenets I imagined inhered in the nature of things."[7] As a memorial to that vanished place and time, Roth kept an enlarged photo of the Lower East Side hanging on the wall behind his desk in Albuquerque—a nostalgic image that, perhaps, helped soothe the ache of his New Mexican diaspora.[8]

Reading through the installments of *Mercy of a Rude Stream*, we follow Ira Stigman's journey from working-class immigrant son to budding Greenwich Village literary modernist. At the end of the last volume, *Requiem for Harlem*, Ira packs up his East Harlem room, as he is in a hurry to move downtown, to live with his mentor–lover Edith Welles. We are thus invited to read his narrative autobiographically, as young Henry Roth's own story of deliverance. Indeed, Roth's vision of his raw younger self revisits the core themes of immigrant imagination as expressed in early film, as well as in the fiction of Abraham Cahan and Anzia Yezierska.

The six-year-old David of *Call It Sleep* is haunted by specters of darkness surrounding his slowly expanding world; from his very first hours in America, he is terrified by the looming threat of violence embodied in his tyrannical father, who is himself bent by New World existence. In fact, virtually every character in Roth feels preyed upon—by memory, by guilt, and by shame linked to transgressive desire, almost always associated with sex; and each searching soul seeks some mode of salving comfort—at times through nostalgia, or through foodways, or, in the famous case of David, via the spiritual light of faith—as a mode of survival. From the moment of their arrival in the New World, Roth's emigrants seem burdened with personal baggage, weighed down by the remnants and residues of their Old World lives. Roth himself harbored rich but complicated memories of the Lower East Side—*his* literary-symbolic baggage—for sixty years; that world anchored him to, yet ultimately tangled him up in, the past. Over half a century later, it remains the site of his deepest guilt as well as the source of his most brilliant art.

As a way into Roth's vision of immigrant New York, and the Jewish American world he conjures in *Call It Sleep*, let me begin with the figure of young Ira Stigman, uprooted from Ninth Street and Avenue D, transplanted to the "borderline" community of East Harlem, encountering his newly arrived relatives from the old country. Older than David—but lacking the boy's rich childhood consciousness of wonder and fear—nearing the age of bar mitzvah, Ira begins to feel a deep disgust with the Jewish world he inhabits after the recent "invasion" of his mother's extended family to the new neighborhood. Ira, as the narrator tells us,

> thought the new relatives . . . would be somehow charmingly, magically, bountifully pre-Americanized. Instead—they were greenhorns! Greenhorns with uncouth, lopsided and outlandish gestures. . . . greenhorns engaged in all manner of talk too incomprehensible for him to understand, speaking "thick" Yiddish, without any English to leaven it. . . . The newcomers' crudity and grimace, their green and carious teeth, the sense of oppressive orthodoxy under Zaida's sway—how they rushed to the sink at his behest to rinse their mouths in salt water—their totally alien behavior combined to produce in Ira a sense of unutterable chagrin and disappointment.[9]

Looking back, Ira/Roth now begins to recognize the cultural dynamic that drove his shame-ridden, ungenerous "first repudiation of his own kith and kin"; if he hadn't been compelled to leave the Lower East Side, he feels, in retrospect, that he would have been better prepared to accept the "un-American" behaviors that are on uncomfortable *public* display by the members of his own tribe. But in light of his victimization in his new school, as (at least in the elder narrator's memory) the focus of "Irish derision"—"the object of taunts and Jew-baiting: target of spitballs, rubberbands, blackboard erasers and pieces of chalk"—Ira can only internalize the self-hatred stirred in the antisemitic crucible of his East Harlem junior high.[10]

Looking back in 1977, Roth considered the shaping impact that antisemitic stereotypes had on him while he was growing up. "The importance in my development of being a Jew," he explained in an important interview, "lay precisely in the length I went to, or the efforts I made, to escape the stigma of being Jewish."[11] Thus Roth's "Ira Stigman," at the beginning of *Mercy of a Rude Stream,* carries the shameful burden of his ethnic stigmata, which he projects (in the psychoanalytic sense) onto his greenhorn relatives, whose crude "Jewish" antics and ill-mannered gesticulations the chagrined boy wishes would disappear. A textbook case of cultural self-hatred, Ira uncritically incorporates the mark of shame as the sign of his alien (Jewish) identity: he feels helpless before the (imagined) judging gaze of Irish-dominated East Harlem.

In this respect, Ira's way of feeling recalls the various *ur*-scenes of early Jewish American expression, which explored as one of its major themes the social and psychological impact of self-hatred—and its attendant New World affect, shame—in the would-be golden land of America. As discussed in earlier chapters, in the classic plot of immigrant fiction and film, Americanizing children reject the older generation and their *greener* ways. Ira's personality thus resonates with the familiar accents of contemporaneous Jewish American culture, ca. 1922–29: he is kith and kin to Anzia Yezierska's shame-ridden children of loneliness; to Edward Sloman's Morris (a.k.a "Maurice") Cominsky, denying his ragged but loving father; to Frank Capra's Morris Goldfish, who tries to split the gold from the fish, thus isolating himself from family. These conflicted second-generation Jewish sons and daughters are imaged in reactionary flight from home, unsure as to what alternate vision of the self they seek, or, in fact, what possible mode of New World identity beckons beyond the ethnic nest.

In this respect, too, Roth's Ira resembles a younger version of David Levinsky, who is worried about exposing his boorish "Jewish" manners before the ridiculing gaze of "poised" gentiles. Ira's own nostalgic equivalent to Levinsky's Antomir shtetl is, of course, the sacred landscape of memory, the *heimisch* world he associates with Avenue D. Unlike Levinsky, however, despite a number of odd jobs that introduce him to the possibilities of advancement in the New World, Roth's Ira rejects what he considers the crass middle-class business ethic as a way of locating himself—and therefore of rising—in America.

Until he is prepared to take literal flight, however, Ira remains mired in a noxious web of self-hatred; he is caught, to recall Norbert Elias's suggestive notion of psychic-social "crossfire," in an hierarchical system of cultural distinction, a psychological–social destiny that *compels* the Americanizing self, chagrined by greenhorn display, to value genteel "refinement" over a "Jewishness" judged declassé. During the ordeal of his bar mitzvah, for example, Ira can only worry about the "Yiddish din within *goyish* hearing" at the family celebration back on East 119th Street. He's embarrassed by "barbaric" Jewish noise invading the high-toned, civilized ears of the gentiles. As for the claims of religious identity itself, Ira can only rail against its felt constraints: "the Bar Mitzvah brought the realization he was only a Jew because he *had* to be a Jew; he hated being a Jew; he didn't want to be one, saw no virtue in being one; and realized he was caught, imprisoned in an identity from which there was no chance of his ever freeing himself. . . . Becoming a Jew, becoming a man, a member of the community was a sick mockery, became a sick memory."[12]

In all honesty, it is not perfectly clear how the retrospective, older "Ira," in dialogue with his computer-therapist/confessor "Ecclesias," interprets this youthful, shame-ridden self. In a scene involving Jewish foodways, explored in *A Diving Rock on the Hudson,* Ira tosses a salami sandwich away, out of fear that its strong smells "would outrage the delicate palates" of the "well-bred ladies" he is joining on a picnic. "Redolence of salami, garlic redolence . . . the more he sniffed the paper bag, the more worried he became, the more the contents assaulted and alarmed his nostrils. Jewish immigrant boor, he was certain to be judged, slum, Jewish boor." Looking back, the older Roth/Ira is now "remorseful" over this telling incident, and chides his younger self: "how wrong, how distorted, was your view of refinement."[13] But Ira cannot reach—as does, say, Gitl, in Cahan's short novel *Yekl* (1896)—such an ironic perspective regarding the politics of civility in the immigrant culture of the 1920s; instead, he continues to rattle the cage of his prison house of self-hatred, seeking escape. His salvation appears initially in the form of Larry Walker, his acculturated, artsy Jewish friend who lives in peace with his family uptown, in the more spacious, new suburban middle-class neighborhoods of the Bronx. Ira is attracted to Larry's apparently polished style, his "gentle [gentile?] gaze," his "good taste," and above all his "refinement." Interestingly, Ira's experience with the Walker household recalls the almost primal WASP-immigrant scene found in virtually every Yezierska novel: the cross-cultural encounter between fiery downtown Jewesses and cool, uptown civility. (In this respect, it's fitting that at first Ira believes that Larry's smooth aura of social refinement marks him as a gentile. Larry is a Jewish version of the charismatic Leo Dugovka, who in *Call It Sleep* charms David with his filial and gustatory freedom.) Preparing himself for dinner at the Walkers, Ira's worried, self-monitoring interior monologue might have been uttered by David Levinsky in a fit of restaurant anxiety:

> Next Friday evening at Larry's home. Jesus, try to eat right when you sit down at their table. It's gonna be high-toned. Don't *chompkeh,* Ira admonished himself, the way pop always rebuked you for doing. Don't gobble, gulp, smack your lips, suck your teeth. Should he say to Larry before they went to his house, "Look, I'm a *fresser.* Do you know what that is?" Larry had already seen how Ira ate in the lunchroom. . . . Ira drilled manners into his head.[14]

Why, looking back after almost sixty years, did Roth need to highlight what he describes, in one of the numerous journal-like reflections in *Mercy,* as "young Ira's deplorable table manners, his eating habits, his jerky, ravenous, noisy, chomp-chomp, despite efforts to deport himself with restraint, with a little decorum"?[15] What, we might ask, sixty years later, is *eating* Roth?

To eat ravenously, to "chomp"/chew noisily (as the verb "to *fress*" is translated in the Yiddish glossary appended to *A Diving Rock*)[16] amounts to *Roth*'s deepest imaging—at the level of symbolic behavior—of Ira's innate *Jewish* self, for Ira is a greenhorn despite (to spite?) himself. Through-out *Mercy of a Rude Stream,* Ira is rendered as a creature of pure appetite, a figure itching to transgress various spheres of social decorum, from table manners to codes of civilized student behavior to (as we eventually dis-cover) perhaps the most sacred taboo of family life. As the novel opens, Ira has been expelled from Stuyvesant High School for stealing fountain pens—"their acquisition," Roth explains, "conferred on Ira something akin to freedom, a new kind of freedom." But "his stealing of fountain pens [was] only part of the forbidden he felt within himself," Roth/Ira observes in the present, "only part of the corroding evil."[17] The shocking revelation of *Mercy of a Rude Stream,* however, is Ira's confession of having committed incest at age fourteen with his younger sister, Minnie: and this is the dark, unutterable, guilty secret of his life.

According to Allegra Goodman, the revelation of incest in the Stigman family romance can, perhaps, begin to explain Roth's sixty-year writer's "block." For an author whose career was built on mining the ore of child-hood memories, Roth "came to a place where he bit down into the truth. And the truth about his life as a young man was hard and unacceptable and even unprintable. . . . he could not even speak of it, and so his narrative stopped."[18] Within the plot of *Mercy of a Rude Stream,* Ira's insatiable desire for his sister—and later, his brutal relations with his simpleminded cousin Stella (most of the plot of the final volume, *Requiem for Harlem,* concerns Stella's false pregnancy and Ira's anxiety about the disclosure of their affair, and his eventual lover Edith Welles's help in arranging for an abortion)—are, more or less, self-absorbed behaviors symptomatic of Ira's "arrested" sexual development (exchanging motherlove for the "safer" sisterlove) and his warped sexual imagination in general. In *Call It Sleep,* David is forced to "play bad," locked in the dark cupboard, with Annie, the sexually curious, older girl who lives upstairs; in *Mercy of a Rude Stream,* Ira is obsessed with playing bad (a pathology resulting from David's early sexual trauma?), yet his sin exacts relatively little by way of moral or spiritual contrition—or even growth in consciousness—despite the emotional release offered by "Roth's" stunning confession. "The fate of Ira's sister," Mary Gordon acidly observes, "and the effect on her of years of incestuous coupling, never trouble her tormented brother. . . . He never worries about his sister."[19]

Ira doesn't appear troubled or worried about committing incest at every opportunity; this is because his "mind," as Roth/Ira explains, "was steeped in foulness, pickled in it."[20] Earlier, we witnessed a milder act of foulness in Ira's rebuke of his bad-mannered greenhorn relatives; Ira, we might say, is pickled in the nasty brine of self-hatred. In *Requiem for Harlem,* the foulness takes on a more complicated form because of Ira's *need* to be in touch with what Roth calls his "inner turbulence."[21] This foulness is nourished by the "craziness," the "*tsuris*" of Stigman family life—"I'm outta your *tsuris*,"[22] Ira, on the threshold of flight from East Harlem, yells at his helpless mother (the use of intimate Yiddish seems important, and is voiced, perhaps, as Ira's final revenge). In his impulse to escape that cloying atmosphere, he seeks to imbibe the cool sophistication and quiet gentility surrounding Edith Welles and the heady literary world she presides over downtown, in the Village.

By the end of Roth's/Ira's journey, Edith emerges as the object—and symbol—of his imagined new life. (Edith is modeled on Roth's real life literary and sexual mentor, the N.Y.U. English professor Eda Lou Walton.) Only Edith, it seems, truly recognizes Ira's artistic potential. From "what she had found hidden in his mind," she knows that he is indeed "rich in words":

> He didn't know how to be polite, but he knew words; he was rich in words, a millionaire that way, a gentleman of great estate: words un-bounded. . . . That's what Ira felt Edith Welles was probing for when she looked into his eyes with her round, unwavering, solemn ones: words. Words, tameless and teeming, headlong.[23]

In this respect, the overarching action of *Mercy of a Rude Stream* recalls, again, the core plot of Yezierska: the saga of the poorly educated but soulful immigrant hungering for recognition and inspiration (with "Jew-ish" hunger absolving the social sin of bad table manners) offered by an empathic gentile who represents, indeed *embodies*, American culture. For Yezierska, the template for this figure is John Dewey; for Roth it is Eda Lou Walton, to whom he dedicated *Call It Sleep*. At the end of the *Mercy* series, Roth implicitly explains how he ("Ira") arrived as a literary artist, and at what personal cost. "He had Edith, now. . . . She had opened up for him – oh cut out the smut at long last– a vibrant, new vision, vision of libera-tion, of independence, vision. . . . She kindled pride, self-esteem. She had faith, she said, in his literary potential."[24]

In all honesty, there is scant evidence in *Mercy of a Rude Stream* to suggest how Ira Stigman, a freshman at City College and winner of a prize-winning college essay on pipe fitting, will now go on to draft, just ten years later, a Joycean-inspired, visionary narrative of immigrant Jewish life. The last sentences of *Requiem for Harlem* ring with profound ironies, as Ira holds on tightly to his bundle of personal effects ("his cold fingers still aching") and boards an express train bound for the Village and a new life: "Strait was the route, and strait rails—the IRT swerved, squealing on the tracks of the long curve westward as it repaired downtown and the hell out of Harlem."[25]

course, far from "strait"; and the "rails" that *he* explores in *Call It Sleep* hold the promise of salvation. David inhabits a richly aural, multilinguistic ethnoscape whose various "ethnic" accents Roth's "Ira Stigman" has, by contrast, only begun to fathom, let alone learned how to interpret.

Above all else, *Call It Sleep* is a novel about the ordeal of New World adjustment told through the story of how an immigrant family manages to survive its uneasy reunion in America. The encounter, filled with ominous portents, begins unhappily, in the shadow of the Statue of Liberty, on the deck of the ship Peter Stuyvesant. While the immigrants surrounding them exhibit extreme displays of emotion—"Jews wept, jabbered, almost put each other's eyes out with the recklessness of their darting gestures"—Albert and his newly arrived wife Genya (who holds the bewildered child David tightly to her bosom) stand "silent, apart; the man staring with aloof, offended eyes grimly down at the water," their meeting deemed "untypical" in the eyes of the Prologue's distanced but clearly knowing narrator.[26]

As voyeurs to this couple's general misery, we witness the husband's unhinged rage, his "harsh voice," his "wrathful glare," the "choked" "snarl" as he hurls his infant son's polka-dot ribboned hat overboard, into the sea. Roth translates the parents' exchange (for they speak to each other in Yiddish):

> "Albert!" his wife caught her breath. "How could you?"
> "I could!" he rapped out. "You should have left it behind!" His teeth clicked, and he glared about the deck.[27]

This foundational scene captures the charged ambiguity at the heart of Schearl family drama, the essence of the tortured emotional dynamic among father, wife, and terrified son. What, we might ask, is the "it" that Genya "should have left behind"? Is it David's silly hat that, in his father's paranoid eyes, calls attention to *Albert*? Or is "it" David himself, whose very presence releases Albert's wrath? What has so deeply "offended" Albert?

It will take virtually all 441 pages of *Call It Sleep* for Roth to resolve these ambiguities. Significantly, the source of Albert's wrath has less to do with his external, vocational encounter with America (his various jobs, from typesetter to milkman) than with the psychological baggage that weighs him down *in* the New World. Albert's ordeal of Americanization is intensely personal; its story opens with the loosening of repressed history, in the form of David, whose living presence conjures for the father the archaic murderous danger embodied in the figure of sons.

Thus Albert, we might say, is "choked" and continuously haunted by the Old World. Indeed, he is obsessed by the memory of the guilty scene of watching, immobilized, while his father was fatally gored by a bull. He is also consumed—pathologically—by the question of David's paternity. "Poisoned by a guess,"[28] Albert calculates that David may not be his. Albert's New World affects, his paranoia and smoldering rage, are, in effect, New World symptoms with roots in pre-migration trauma, in the residual guilt of a tortured man who thinks himself capable of parricide.

Genya, too, is haunted by the past, by the memory of an affair with a gentile church organist in her Polish village, which resulted in her exile from her family and shtetl. By beginning with such radically imagined characters, *Call It Sleep* consciously resists the sentimentalized stereotypes found in much early twentieth-century Jewish American fiction and film. As Ruth Wisse explains, Genya "is not the typical immigrant mother, nor the embodiment of Jewish old-country virtues, but an outcast." Already "banished by their families, David's parents live like fugitives within the great immigrant community, a self-imprisoning family that is divided against itself by suspicion and guilt."[29]

It is left for David to construct a haven of stability in a psychic and physical landscape that harbors his two primary fears: the dark and his father. As *Call It Sleep* unfolds, David journeys out, with anxiety and trepidation, beyond the familiar, safe tenement apartment presided over by his mother to the unknown city streets, an alien territory where different languages are spoken and strange foods consumed: a dangerous world where one can easily get "losted." He'd prefer always to stay at home, "[b]rooding, engrossed in his thoughts," playing with a box of old calendar leaves and his collection of obscure street trinkets. David likes things that are "worn and old"; he is a boy of rich sensibility afflicted with unnamed longing for "A world somewhere, somewhere else." Hearing the street song "Waltuh, Waltuh, Wiuhlflowuh," about a little boy who "lived in Europe," makes David sigh, makes him relax; it "filled [him] with a warm, nostalgic mournfulness."[30]

Above all else, David is consumed by the hypnotic physical presence of his mother; he can't stop looking at her. At some level, Genya senses her son's (sexual) obsession. " 'The way you watch me,' she said with a laugh, 'makes me feel as if I were performing black magic. It's only dishes I'm washing.' " Asking "slyly" whether David would like a little sister or brother, David replies, "soberly," "no." Genya "teases" in response, " 'It would be better for you, if you had. . . . It would give you something else to look at beside your mother.' "[31]

Because of the pleasure he feels in the act of watching, David can't tolerate other people staring at his mother (his chronic scopophilia accounts for the rage he feels after his friends' vivid description of his mother's naked body, which occurs later in *Call It Sleep*), especially Joe Luter, Albert's would-be friend who has his own designs on Genya. Luter's sexually charged staring startles a jealous David into self-consciousness: "For the first time, David was aware of how her flesh, confined by the skirt, formed separate molds against it. He felt suddenly bewildered, struggling with something in his mind that would not become a thought."[32]

The figure of Genya is crucial in this respect, for she looms in the male imagination of *Call It Sleep* as an object of fantasy—of unconscious oedipal desire in David's bewildered longing; as the incarnation of an Old World *gentile* peasant women in Luter's nostalgia-inflected lust; as symbol of sexual betrayal and rebuke in Albert's guilt-ridden paranoia. Interestingly, in the case of Luter, Roth depicts yet another example of cultural haunting, but in this instance with the aim of New World seduction. Inflamed with sexual longing, Luter attempts to woo Genya under the sign of nostalgia. In a brilliantly ironic exchange, Luter indirectly intuits a deep, dangerous truth about Genya, which she deflects via a bad-faith demurral, seizing the part of wholesome Old World Jewess:

LUTER: "I remember the peasant wenches . . . One never sees the like here. It's scanty soil from what one sees of it in Brooklyn and its women are spare. But in Sorvik they grew like oaks. They had blond hair, their eyes blazed. And when they smiled with their white teeth and blue eyes, who could resist them? It was enough to set your blood on fire. The men [i.e., gentile men] never dazzled you that way?"
GENYA: "No, I never paid much attention to them."
LUTER: "Well, you wouldn't—you were a good Jewish daughter. . . . You know . . . the only woman I know who reminds me of those girls, is you."
GENYA: "Me? I'm only a good Jewish daughter."
LUTER: "I am not accusing you of anything else, but never since I have been in America have I seen a woman that so reminded me of them. Their lips were so full, so ripe, as if to be kissed."
GENYA: "God knows, there must be enough Austrian peasants even in this land. If Jews were let in, surely no one would bar the Slovaks."
LUTER: "Yes, I suppose so. I have seen a few of them, but none I cared much about."
GENYA: "You better look about a little more then."[33]

In this startling conversation, filled with sexual innuendo, we gain rich insight into the complexities of Genya's character, above all about how she uses sharp wit and irony as a mode of defense, indeed as a mode of New World survival. Unknowingly, Luter presses the still raw spot of Genya's secret history, an Old World story of gentile infatuation and ultimate betrayal on the part of a would-be "good Jewish daughter" (an irony about which at this point David and readers of *Call It Sleep* remain, of course, unaware). The contradiction does not appear to be lost on Genya herself, however; she draws on the aggressive style of Jewish humor to slip through Luter's trap with (to my ears at least) a self-deprecating, wise-ass crack: "If Jews were let in, surely no one would bar the Slovaks." Of course Luter can't fully appreciate Genya's wickedness; nor can he register the sting of Genya's final rejection. Only David can intuit his mother's indirect messages, playing *his* part as the child who suddenly hates ice cream and is ready for bed, in order to protect his mother from Luter's advances. " 'Let's forget about him,' " Genya advises David; " 'We won't even tell father he came, will we?' " " 'No,' " replies the son, entering his mother's conspiracy of silence.[34]

David's relationship with his mother runs far deeper than the intimacies associated with conspiracy. Genya assuages David's inchoate fears—of death, of the dark, of the darkness of death—and protects him from Albert's abject wrath. At key moments, Roth represents Genya's unconditional motherlove symbolically, in the form of foodways. When he finds himself lost in the city and searches for the name of his street, David eases his rising anxiety by chanting, in a revealing stream-of-consciousness style, a litany of his favorite dishes, his private fantasy of what returning home "tastes" like:

> Milk-supper, maybe, when he got upstairs. Sour cream, yum! Break pieces of bread into it. Sour cream with farmer-cheese. Mmm! Sour cream with eggs. Sour cream with what else? Borscht . . . Strawberries . . . Radishes . . . Bananas . . . Borscht, strawberries, radishes, bananas. Borscht, strawberries, apples and strudel. No. They didn't eat with sour cream. Sour. Cream. Sour. Cream. Like it, like it, like it. I—like—it. . . . How far was it still?[35]

This interior monologue casts David's act of summoning *milchig* desires as a way of negotiating the bewildering street, of avoiding the remembered threat of cellars ("Hate it! Wish there were houses without cellars"), and above all of fending off the terrors of the dark with its "hordes of nightmare."[36] Sweetly recalled "dairy" dishes ("like it, like it, like it") can transport David into his mother's arms—really, into her magic kitchen—where he imagines himself, at last, eating in peace.

As it turns out, the symbology of ethnic foodways emerges as a powerful structuring motif in *Call It Sleep*. "As long as I can get you to eat," Genya confesses to David, "I feel safe."[37] Indeed, even Albert finds in

Genya's kitchen a safe haven in a hostile world. After leaving his typesetter's job, he becomes a milkman, driving a horsedrawn milk cart around the Lower East Side. This shift makes the cosmically gruff father softer in his nervous son's eyes: "His brusqueness now was infinitely less dangerous to those around him." Devouring Genya's corn-meal with home made strawberry preserves after work elicits a rare "grunt" of satisfaction in Albert, along with an uncharacteristic note of feeling: " 'This is what I ate,' he smeared the deep, red jam on the corn-meal, 'when I was a boy.' " For a brief moment, the meal transports Albert into the realm of nostalgia; for David, the confession enhances his knowledge of Schearl family history (a modest but clear prelude to his stronger curiosity to discover the meaning of his mother's past sexual life in the old country): "this was one of the few facts that [he] had ever learnt of his father's boyhood."[38]

As he grows in consciousness, David continues to consume, to imbibe—at the level of imagination—the different worlds in which he finds himself. At home, staring at his mother's Sabbath preparations, David is aware of the transition from secular to sacred time, from the darkness symbolic of death (he's begun to understand the cosmic meaning of the funeral procession he'd witnessed earlier, in the street) to holy light in the form of flaming Sabbath candles. As his mother mimes the required religious gestures in lighting the candles (she has, after all, already confessed to a "pretend piety" to her son), "The match rasped on the sandpaper, flared up, making David aware of how dark it had become." "With a little, deprecating laugh, his mother stood before the candles, and bowing her head before them, murmured through the hands she spread before her face the ancient prayer for the Sabbath. . . . The hushed hour, the hour of tawny beatitude."[39]

Genya's self-mocking, ironic sensibility (along with feeding her son, this is *her* way of coping in America) refuses to embrace the awesome meaning of Sabbath light, but David is receptive to it; indeed, he seeks to experience the truth that the light of "faith" appears to embody. The core "action" of *Call It Sleep* charts David's yearning to be transported by an overturning experience that Roth represents as mystical. The child seeks, ultimately, the power embodied in the "light" so that he might overcome the two traumas that continue to haunt him, the dark and his father.

In Roth's own iconoclastic rendering, the light that can transform is not to be found in religious doctrine, but rather in the city streets themselves. Thus the brilliant comedy-satire of dialect and languages in the section of *Call It Sleep* that follows David's progress in *cheder* during—significantly—the onset of Passover, the Jewish holiday of memory and deliverance. The raw Yinglish dialect of the wise-ass street kids (" 'Aaa!

Phuh!' Yitzchuck spat out in a whisper, 'De lousy Hagaddah again!' ";
" 'Kent'cha tuck Englitch?' ")[40] disrupts the formal Hebrew fluencies of the
ritual Four Questions, thus mocking Reb Pankower's hapless efforts at
offering religious education in the New World.

Only David is receptive and alert to the sacred texts that swirl in
his brain (he quickly memorizes entire passages, including the famous
Passover song about the killing of the goat, to the astonishment of Reb
Pankower). He is especially curious about the biblical passage describing
Isaiah and the application of burning "angel coal" on the prophet's lips, in
an act of purification. With his literalizing, childish logic, David considers
the larger import of the story. What does it mean, David wonders, to
possess a "dirty mouth"?[41]

In one of the most important scenes in *Call It Sleep,* David offers his
own "commentary" while he listens to the Hebrew teacher narrate the
story of Isaiah and the angel:

> "But when Isaiah saw the Almighty in His majesty and His terrible
> light—Woe is me! he cried, What shall I do! I am lost!" The rabbi seized
> his skull-cap and crumpled it. "I, common man, have seen the Almighty,
> I, unclean one have seen him! Behold, my lips are unclean and I live in a
> land unclean—for the Jews at that time were sinful—"
>
> —Clean? Light? Wonder if—? Wish I could ask him why the Jews
> were dirty. What did they do? Better not! Get mad. Where? (Furtively,
> while the rabbi still spoke David leaned over and stole a glance at the
> number of the page.) On sixty-eight. After, maybe, can ask. On page
> sixty-eight. That blue book—Gee! it's God.[42]

At this key moment in *Call It Sleep,* Roth deepens the core themes of the
novel. David is profoundly stirred by the biblical story of sin and the
cleansing light of God's redemption, with the dirt being burned away by
the "fiery coal" applied by an angel holding "tongs" to the prophet's lips.
(In the theatrical gesture with his yarmulke, Reb Pankower appears stirred
as well.) He is moved beyond childlike curiosity because the parable of
Isaiah speaks to him on different levels—to David's other-worldly, latent
imagination as religious mystic, in search of salvation, and to his real, this-
wordly condition, as a frightened Jewish son, "losted" on streets, living in
an "unclean" America filled with palpable terror and temptation.

Throughout *Call It Sleep,* Roth represents David's journey toward
consciousness as a continuing struggle to determine the holy—"kadosh,
kadosh, kadosh," in the famous repetition of the Hebrew liturgy—from
"traife," the unclean. At first, David searches for the holy at home (the
light from his mother's Sabbath candles emits a spiritual glow); later, he

determines the source of God's light in the rabbi's text (specifically, "on page sixty-eight").[43] For Roth, however, the realm of the holy ultimately lies beyond home and school; as *Call It Sleep* reveals, spiritual light is contained, and has the potential to be released, *at the level of the street,* in the sheer transforming power of the modern city.

David receives intimations of the power of urban light in two brief scenes at the center of the novel. The first takes place at the edge of the East River. After observing the Passover ritual of the burning of leavened crumbs ("chumitz") in a wooden spoon—the last purifying act before the holiday of remembrance begins—David performs his own makeshift version of the gathering and burning away of "sin"/"dirt" while sitting along the river:

> A live, golden flame awoke; wood and cardboard caught, and in a few minutes the whole tindery mound was ablaze. Content yet strangely nostalgic, he crouched down beside the fire and watched the first tiny bead of flame run up the raveled threads of the rag that bound feather and spoon together. . . .
>
> —No more chumitz. All burned black. See God, I was good? Now only white Matzohs are left. Can go. Don't sit on the edge of the dock, mama says. It frightens her. It don't frighten me.[44]

While sitting at the edge of the water, watching the bridges spanning the East River, following the masts of ships moving along the current, a tugboat "yoked" to a barge, observing a cloud "shear[ing] the sunlight," David undergoes what can only be called a religious experience, "complete and dazzling." "His eyes dazzled. . . . His lids grew heavy. . . . And He was." The moment, Roth tells us, is "hypnotic": the cleansing of David's (imagined) "dirty" soul followed by the birth of a city poet-dreamer (a cousin to Joyce's young Dublin artist). As a result of his vision, "Sin melted into light."[45]

David's overturning experience at the river's edge joins a continuum of similar moments of complex epiphanies. These key episodes shape *Call It Sleep* as they map, in effect, David's journey from anxiety over darkness and death to light and safety (the safety of light?). Roughly awakened from his East River reverie by a tugboat sailor who is worried that the boy will "throw a belly-w'opper!" over the edge, David sits unable to move, "terrified, rigid." "Twice he sighed and with such depth as though he had been weeping for hours."[46]

What are the deeper meanings behind David's "sigh"? Why does he feel "strangely nostalgic" at the extinguishing of the *chumitz,* leading to this interval of stirred, of stimulated consciousness? The act of sighing, we might say, brings David home, specifically to the *memory* of home and the intensely private world he and his mother share.[47] To help ease her son's anxiety about the dark and death, Genya relates a richly enigmatic yet profoundly moving *Old World* story that her grandmother once told her. Beyond David's full comprehension, the parable concerns the grandmother's fierce independence (like her granddaughter, she only pretended to be pious), her refusal to behave according to her high social station in the community, and above all her eventual softening when confronted by the inevitable facts of aging and death. As granddaughter and grandmother walked in the woods, this revelation registered deeply, at the level of the body, leading to a recognition at the level of the soul. In Genya's telling, "And just as we were about to go in she sighed so that she shivered—deep—the way one sighs just before sleep."[48]

David can't fathom completely the deepest meanings of his mother's narrative (although it's clear that she identifies with her grandmother, whose Old World story she packed with her in steerage to America), but his mother's rich telling, conveyed through "the last supple huskiness of her voice," induces a "dreamlike fugitive sadness . . . in his heart," a type of nostalgia that links him intimately with his mother's emotional life. "If only the air were always this way," David dreams to himself, "and he always here along with his mother. He was near her now. He was part of her. . . . When she lifted the stove lid, the rosy glow that stained her wide brow warmed his own body as well. He was near her. He was part of her ["their intimacy, their identity"]. Oh, it was good being here. He watched her every movement hungrily."[49]

In light of his profound motherlove, can we speak of David's "strangely nostalgic" epiphany at the river's edge, expressed in and by his own act of sighing deeply, as an uncanny experience related to the fantasy of Genya's figure, highlighted in the glow of kitchen light? David, that is, *associates* light with his mother (including the image of the "gleaming [Sabbath] kitchen," which immediately follows Genya's story about her grandmother):[50] Kitchen light = mother's light = spiritual light in his associative mind. Thus, at some primal level David links the purifying fire that burns away the sinful *chumitz* with his own unconscious longing. David hungers for his mother; his "strangely nostalgic" longing, released by his infatuation with light, is, in effect, a screen memory masking oedipal desire.

By the end of "The Coal" section of *Call It Sleep*, David has encountered light, and has witnessed its power in a variety of locations. In one

instance, he is accosted by an Irish street gang led by "Pedey," whose litany
of "g'wan!'s" (in a later volume of *Mercy*, Roth vividly remembers Pedey's
"side-mouthed Irish way" of speech)[51]—forces David to insert a makeshift
sword made of zinc into the crack between the street car tracks. Pedey,
along with the rest of his tough guy crew, compels David by enticing him
with the promise of a spectacle:

> "Now we're gonna show yiz de magic."
> "Waid'll ye sees it." . . .
> "Yea, better'n movin' pitchiz!." . . .
> "Ye'll see all de movies in the woil! An' vawderville too! G'wan. . . .[52]

David obeys, out of fear, as well as out of curiosity. Roth describes the
scene of insertion in patently sexual terms. Holding the sword to the track,
at first David "fumbled, then finding the slot at last, [it] rasped part way
down the wide grinning lips like a tongue in an iron mouth. He stepped
back. From open fingers, the blade plunged into darkness." [53]

The sword's thrust issues in "Power! . . . power, gigantic, fetterless,
thudded into day! And light, unleashed, terrific light, bellowed out of the
iron lips."[54] David is terrified at the light's intensity, and runs through the
streets, to the *cheder*, in search of the light's origins, which he believes are
found in the story of Isaiah, the angel, and the dirt-cleansing coal. Bursting into the classroom, obsessed with the meaning of the light, he asks Reb
Pankower—whose first impulse is to beat David ("before David could
budge, the rabbi's heavy hands had fallen on his neck and he was being
dragged toward the cat-o-nine on the floor") to find him the "Isaiah"
place in the Bible. Reb Pankower can only laugh—hysterically, in shame-
inducing ridicule—at David's question. " 'Fool!' " the teacher admonishes,
" 'Go beat your head on a wall! God's light is not between car-tracks.' "[55]

David's response to Reb Pankower's rebuke is crucial. In a key passage,
we learn of his emergent (internal) power to resist the helpless fear he feels
at home, in the figure of his brutal father, and his growing ability to negotiate the threatening world of the street, embodied by cellars and closets,
and the metaphysical terror they inspire: "Ashamed, yet immensely relieved, David stood mute, eyes staring at the floor. The rabbi didn't know
as he knew what the light was, what it meant, what it had done to him. But
he would reveal no more. It was enough that the light had saved him from
being whipped."[56]

Only David has the capacity to appreciate the meaning of the "light"
generated by his brave thrust into the dark, in the salvific space between
the car tracks. Even the Irish gang has only a "secular" conception of the

light, linked to "megic," the power that projects movies, and the spectacle of popular culture in general (of course, for Al Jolson's Jewish generation, popular culture as a mode of being had more or less replaced the light of religious faith); and as for Reb Pankower, his warped obsession with the sacred text makes him blind to the "empowering" aspect of David's street vision. In contrast to Pedey and Reb Pankower, David discovers the liberating potential of urban-generated light. In a moment of intense revelation, David feels the power of a light that saves one from a whipping, delivers one from a father's unaccountable wrath. By the end of "The Coal" section, David incorporates this empowering light; he carries it within. As a result the world appears safer:

> "Inside my head. Better is inside. Can carry it. Funny! Ain't so dark anymore. Ain't even scared. Remember how I was? Way long ago? Scared. Used to run bing-bang-biff. Hee! Hee! Funny I was. I'm big now. Can go up alone. Can go up slow, slow, slow as I like. Can even stand here and don't even care. . . .
> —Funny. Still can see it. There. And over there. And over in the corner where it's real dark. It sticks inside all the time, gee, can't never be scared. Never. Never. Never . . .
> —Fo-o-urth floor. All off! Gee, happy I'm!
> He sighed.[57]

We are witness, at this moment, to the implicit birth of David, the Jewish American artist as a *very* young man. He can now look back on his life, not with nostalgic mourning, but rather with retrospective irony, at the comic self that had once been scared by the dark. Indeed, by playing with language he can seize the liberating potential of memory; by making a joke he can resist the enervating "mournful nostalgia" that seized him in the past, *by* the past. Instead of running upstairs in terror, he can play the role of the street conductor, in control of his destination, perhaps even his destiny. David's sigh now bespeaks comfort and release rather than signifying the shudder that follows hours of weeping.

David's journey toward a more complicated consciousness continues in *Call It Sleep* in the form of his encounter with alternate worlds, which are really worldviews. As it turns out, one zone in which the passage to New World redemption finds rich expression involves the matter of foodways. An emerging walker in the city, David is especially alert to the exotic fare hanging from store windows. While he is listening to the drone of Hebrew in *cheder,* the biblical prohibition against eating unkosher food prompts the following meditation:

And Moses said you mustn't . . . mustn't eat in the traife butcher store. Don't like it anyway. Big brown bags hang down from the hooks. Ham. And all kinds of grey wurst with like marbles in 'em. Peeuh! And chickens without feathers in boxes, and little bunnies in that store on First Avenue by the elevated. In a wooden cage with lettuce, and rocks, they eat too, on those stands. Rocks all colors. They bust 'em open with a knife and shake out ketchup on the snot inside. Yich! and long, black, skinny snakes. Peeuh! Goyim eat everything . . .[58]

David's innocent, disgusted reaction to the spectacle of *traife* clams and eels on display feeds Roth's substantial comedy of gentile vs. Jewish foodways. The satire (if that's an appropriate way of describing David's demystifying, "kosher" point of view) of "goyim eat everything" links David's way of seeing to the ironizing New World perspective found in the supremely comic figure of Aunt Bertha, with whom David forms an immediate attachment. Audacious and "ready-tongued," Aunt Bertha is a greenhorn with attitude. Not surprisingly, her sharp wit, her refusal to bend to New World conditions, her total lack of nostalgia, and her delight in verbal playfulness drive her brother-in-law Albert crazy. " 'You see I'm one who doesn't yearn for the homeland,' " she announces.[59] Indeed, Aunt Bertha "takes" immediately to American possibilities. A New World comedienne in the making, Bertha's wise-assness and pleasure in social and linguistic disjunctions look forward to the "red hot mamas" of stage and vaudeville. Bertha is ready, unabashedly, to *consume* America, on its own terms. An *alrightnik* obsessed with making it into the middle class, she ends up, appropriately enough, running a candy store further uptown.

Aunt Bertha helps open David to worlds beyond his downtown turf (their trip to the Metropolitan Museum of Art amounts to an hilarious attempt at gaining some "high" culture); as he grows in consciousness—especially after struggling to decipher the blend of hushed Yiddish and obscure Polish words with which his mother confesses the secret of her gentile, church "orghaneest" lover to her sister, a story that proves apocalyptic for David and the family—he becomes less apprehensive, indeed even more curious about other ways of being, and, as it turns out, ways of eating.

The character who figures—unknowingly—in David's quest for freedom is an older, blond-haired, blue-eyed Polish boy named Leo Dugovka, who (like his mother's Old World gentile lover) "dazzles" David with his charismatic presence. "There was a glamour about him." David is immediately attracted to Leo, for he represents everything that David is not: Leo has no father; he swims fearlessly in the East River; he eats anything, at any time ("'I eats w'en I wants tuh'"). David is especially impressed by the declaration of Leo's "antinomian" eating habits:

DAVID: "'So who gives yuh to eat?'"
LEO: "'I takes it myself?'"
DAVID: "'Gee!' David breathed in the enormous freedom."[60]

In a tour de force of comic dialect art, Roth draws on Leo's *consuming* knowledge of multicultural foodways to expand David's gastronomic horizons, letting him taste a world beyond sour cream. Listen, for example, to Leo's spiel on bread: "'An' I et ev'y kind 'o bread dey is,' Leo continued proudly. 'Aitalian bread-sticks, Dutch pummernickel, Jew rye—even watchuh call 'em, matziz, matches—' He snickered. 'Dey're nuttin but big crackers—D'ja ever eat real spigeddi?'"[61] David, however, is more curious about the religious icons affixed to the wall in Leo's apartment; he immediately senses, feels their emotional power. He is especially absorbed by the figure of the crucifix and the painting of "Jesus an' de Sacred Heart," an image of Jesus "pointing at his breast in which the red heart (not his "bowels," as David had originally thought) was exposed and luminous."[62] Enamored of Leo's world, David seeks to emulate his new friend's apparent "self reliance," above all his mastery over his neighborhood.[63]

The interlude with Leo quickens the pace of *Call It Sleep*, enabling Roth to gather the novel's major themes into a truly stunning crescendo, achieving a whirlwind of dramatic action, internal and external. David himself seems in constant motion, his legs churning across the city streets, gliding on the single roller skate—a bribe in the form of a gift from Leo, whose substantial appetite is aroused by the news that David's Aunt Bertha runs a candy store nearby with her two available stepdaughters: "'I like Jew-goils!'"[64] he announces—an uncanny allusion to Ira Stigman's own sexual preferences. David careens from the candy store, where, discovered "pimping" for Leo, he flees in shame. He then breaks into the *cheder*, where he tells Reb Pankower an hysterical, mangled version of his mother's shameful sexual history with the Polish "orghaneest." David then flies home, where the rosary—another bribe from Leo, offered so that David will "lay chickee"[65] (play watchman) for Leo during his sexual play with Esther—spills out of his pocket. This revelation becomes a sign, for David's paranoid father, confirming his fear that David is "no son of mine." His father's subsequent wrath compels David to run for his life. Finally, David sprints back to the street ("Arms up and gasping like a runner to the tape"), where he inserts a "milk-dipper" into the space between train tracks, in a search for redemption: "*Now! Now I gotta. In the crack, / remember. In the crack be born.*"[66]

Swirling around David during his street ordeal—he is briefly shocked unconscious by the electric currents conducted, through the milk ladle, from the rail to his foot—is a "stunning variety of street patois," in Thomas Ferraro's nice phrasing, an "orgy of multivocality."[67] In striking counterpoint to the richly aural-social world of the multicultural chorus, David's interior psychic journey is rendered poetically, in high modernist style. Throughout this famous section, Roth brilliantly blends fragments of dialogue, drawn from an array of immigrant tongues, incorporating a host of ethnic voices speaking in sexual overtones flecked with profane religious allusion. Half conscious, in a surreal, betwixt-and-between dreamlike state, David's mind recalls images condensed from his previous city experiences—in *cheder*, at the dock, in the cellar, in the words of the Bible, in Passover songs, coal, and so on—as he undergoes what most readers of *Call It Sleep* understand as an apocalyptic rebirth, "*in the clutch of a fatal glory.*"[68]

In the process, Roth implicitly offers the redemptive possibilities of what might be called "city light." "'Christchin light—it's way bigger . . . den Jew light,"[69] Leo brags to a curious David. But in the gritty urban landscape limned in *Call It Sleep*, only secular city light—the empowering light that flares between the tracks, together with the multicultural voices that mobilize a community into concerned collective action—can translate its deserving son, a city *boychick*, from a state of anxiety to a condition of ease. Earlier, Reb Pankower had ridiculed David about witnessing God's light in the cracks. But in Roth's critical vision, the rabbi—and, by extension his orthodox mode of belief—proves utterly impotent in the New World. Reb Pankower's thundering jeremiad about "Yiddish youth! Turd-worth"—"this sidewalk and gutter generation," this "corrupt generation," "a snide generation"—bespeaks his own hardness of heart (akin to Albert's) and his inability to appreciate the New World *as* a land unclean.[70] Reb Yidl (his name connotes "little man," in Roth's wicked satire) can only smell American *traife* in his "pious" nostrils; by contrast, Roth imagines David's profane territory as a site of spiritual *re*generation: the secular city, in effect, contains the potential for *kadosh*. Reb Pankower remains fixed in his ways of being. He cannot—or will not—adjust to the fluidity, the *mixing* that is the mark of New World negotiation.

By the end of *Call It Sleep*, however, Albert appears to have made some crucial adjustments to his sense of family history, especially to his identity as father. In the wake of David's injury, Albert speaks in dialect for the first time in the novel. Significantly, it is David who overhears his father's shakened response to (the son's) New World authority. It is significant, too, that David hears the response from the restorative space of motherlove:

In the kitchen, he could hear the policeman interrogating his father, and his father answering in a dazed, unsteady voice. That sense of triumph that David had felt on first being brought in, welled up within him again as he listened to him falter and knew him shaken.

"Yes, Yes," he was saying. "My sawn. Mine. Yes. Awld eight. Eight en'—en' vun mawnt'. He vas bawn in—"[71]

At the end of *Call It Sleep*, David sees his father *reduced* from his awesome status as tyrant, poised with a whip in his hand, speaking in the terrifying accents of threat and rebuke,[72] to a helpless immigrant, struggling in his hesitant, accented English, like a self-conscious greenhorn. David's first triumph thus occurs at the level of language. His other, perhaps greater, victory, of course, takes place at the level of genealogy, for Albert now acknowledges David's correct age, and therefore his own identity—legally and emotionally—as David's father.

Ultimately, of course, David remains his mother's child. Forever in character, Genya provides David with the sustenance he craves: " 'Perhaps you'll be hungry in a little while,' his mother said persuasively. 'After you've rested a bit and we've put the medicine on your foot. And then some milk and a boiled egg. You'd like that?' . . . And then you'll go to sleep and forget it all. . . . Sleepy beloved?' "[73]

"In food there should be some trust," laments Reb Pankower, bewailing the fate of *kashrut* in America.[74] In the Schearl household at least, foodways possess a therapeutic, perhaps even holy office. In the end, David embraces a trust beyond even his faith in Genya's saintly kitchen; however hesitantly, his trust extends to his father, for whom he now feels "A vague, remote pity," a new empathy that "stirred within his breast."[75] At the end of *Call It Sleep*, Roth returns David to the center of the family, in apparent control of his New World destiny. No longer haunted by archaic fears—he has overcome the wrath of his father and banished the terror of the dark—David can now, presumably, sleep in peace, and dream of his mother's soothing, restoring *milchig* meals.

After the publication of *Call It Sleep* in 1934 Henry Roth, as noted above, remained virtually silent as a writer, his literary "blockage" the stuff of legend. The novel's subsequent "recovery," in 1964, is now considered a famous moment of American literary history. Ignored for almost thirty years, a younger generation of Jewish American literary critics and intellectuals helped restore *Call It Sleep*. Immigrant sons in their own right, breaking away from shtetl-like neighborhoods in Brooklyn and the Bronx, these critics—especially Irving Howe and Alfred Kazin—discovered in re-

reading *Call It Sleep* a book that evoked their own New York tenement stories in profound, indeed shattering ways. The most significant of these reassessments was Irving Howe's review of *Call It Sleep* on the front page of the New York *Times Book Review* on October 25, 1964.

Tellingly, Howe's review appeared at the same time as his *Commentary* article on the new hit Broadway musical, *Fiddler on the Roof* (November 1964). Looking back, it seems evident that Howe's celebration of Roth's immigrant narrative was, in part, shaped by his horrified response to the middle-brow show. For Howe, re-reading *Call It Sleep* thirty years later proved an exhilarating experience: "one has lived through a completeness of rendered life," he proclaimed, "and all one need do is silently to acknowledge its truth." Above all, Howe praised Roth for "ris[ing] above" the tired tones of "nostalgia," "parochialism," and sentiment that tended to characterize the "usual ghetto novel."[76]

By contrast, Howe hated *Fiddler;* in reality, Howe hated the *audience* that flocked to hear Zero Mostel's "gargling cantillation[s]" as Sholem Aleichem's Tevye. "It seems an equivalent in sound," he ungenerously observed, "to our deepest fantasies gratified." The source of Howe's substantial wrath involved what he called, again ungenerously, the "unearned nostalgia" of the emerging suburban Jewish middle class. "American Jews suffer these days from a feeling of guilt because they have lost touch with the past from which they derive. . . . As their own sense of Jewishness increasingly becomes fragile, more and more they feel—I would say, absurdly—grateful for any public recognition of Jewishness." The nostalgia on display in *Fiddler* embarrassed Howe, for it sweetened—with a fake saccharine aftertaste—the harshness of Eastern European ghetto life. Speaking of the staged Anatevka, Howe quipped that it was "the cutest *shtetl* we've never had." Howe felt that the nostalgia resulted in a fatal "surrender of dignity" in the representation of Jewish life. Thus in its capitulation to sentiment and stereotype, its serving up of fantasy and nostalgia, *Fiddler on the Roof* and its implied audience broke Irving Howe's heart.[77]

Forty years ago, Jewish critics celebrated Henry Roth for resisting sentiment and avoiding nostalgia; for them *Call It Sleep* chronicled (more or less) their own narrative of cultural deliverance, out of the old neighborhood and into the realm of art: "of art sustaining itself in a fallen world," in Alfred Kazin's deep appreciation of Roth's achievement. In this respect, Roth's David stands as a figure of the artist in—and of—the city. "Roth presents the city," Kazin continues, "not in an external documentary but as formed, instant by instant, out of David's perceptions." Writing against the aesthetic demands of "proletarian" theory in his own time, Roth "see[s] character as more important than environment."[78] For Howe and Kazin, David figures as the deeply Jewish, yet radically free artist-in-the making which, looking back, they themselves dreamed of becoming, also starting out in the thirties.

The publication of the volumes gathered as *Mercy of a Rude Stream* has not altered the achievement of *Call It Sleep*. In Mary Gordon's honest appraisal, "Nothing is lost from it, or added to it, by reading its sequels."[79] Still, it remains difficult to forge an imaginative–creative alliance between David Schearl and Ira Stigman. In the end, each figure achieves a kind of peace with the constraining world that has shaped him: David, content with his mother's milk and boiled egg; Ira, in willful flight from his mother's appeal via Jewish foodways. Roth, however, seems never to have made peace with *his* past. Howe was grateful for Roth's refusal of nostalgia in writing an astonishing book like *Call It Sleep* at the age of twenty-eight, less than ten years out of Jewish-Irish Harlem. What Howe could not have known was that sixty years later the memory of the Lower East Side continued to haunt Henry Roth. The past—in the form of familial shame and hazy nostalgia—proved immobilizing.

5

TO MAKE "A JEW"

Projecting Antisemitism in Post-War America

To see your own face look to what you say of the Jews.[1]
—Cynthia Ozick

In this moment her eyes had made a Jew of him.[2]
—*Focus*

For the anti-Semite, the Jew is a living Rorschach inkblot . . . the anti-Semite sees whatever he needs to see in the Jew.[3]
—*Anti-Semitism and Emotional Disorder*

In the wake of World War II and the horrors revealed by the Holocaust, Americans were confronted by the dark legacy of European antisemitism. For young writers like Saul Bellow and Alfred Kazin, the palpable shock of Nazi genocide was revealed in the darkness of the movie theaters, in footage of the liberation of concentration camps, and in the sickening images of bodies piled in mass graves. Commenting later on the impact of watching these terrifying newsreels, Bellow recalled the "deeply troubling sense of disgrace and human demotion" in witnessing these images; he was appalled and sickened that "the Jews had lost the respect of the rest of humankind."[4] Working in the shipfitting department of the Brooklyn Navy Yard during the war (deferred from the draft because of an injury), a young Arthur Miller pondered the fate of antisemitism in America after the war. "It is no longer possible to decide," Miller wrote in the Afterward to a later edition of his 1945 novel, *Focus,* "whether it was my own Hitler-begotten sensitivity or the anti-Semitism itself that so often made me wonder whether, when peace came, we were to be launched into a raw politics of race and religion, and not in the South, but in New York."[5]

To judge from the evidence of post-war American literary and popular culture, the matter of antisemitism in America, with its complex social and psychological manifestations, and the larger question of the fate—resilience—of American ideals in light of the sordid revelations of the Holocaust, consumed writers, filmmakers, and dramatists alike. In works as various as Hollywood's two film portraits in 1947 of antisemitism, *Crossfire* and *Gentleman's Agreement,* Arthur Laurents's stage play *Home of the Brave* (1945), Saul Bellow's *The Victim* (1947), and Miller's *Focus* (1945), his first and only published novel, the meaning of Jewish identity in relation to various forms of antisemitism—genteel in *Gentleman's Agreement,* brazen in *Home of the Brave,* murderous in *Crossfire,* psychologically complex and ambiguous in *The Victim* and *Focus*—became perhaps *the* overarching subject of post-war cultural expression.

In America of the 1940s, the "scientific" study of antisemitism preoccupied psychologists and sociologists, as evidenced in the collection *Jews in a Gentile World* (1942), subtitled "The Problem of Anti-Semitism," and *Anti-Semitism and Emotional Disorder* (1950), based on a series of essays published in the late 1940s by its authors, Nathan W. Ackerman and Marie Jahoda (sponsored by the American Jewish Committee under the "Studies in Prejudice" series, which produced the famous post-war study, *The Authoritarian Personality* [1950]). Its deepest readings, however, are to be found in *Focus* and *The Victim,* post-war novels that explore in profound ways the social-psychological dynamics of antisemitism as an obscene system of belief afflicting American society in general (*Focus*) and subverting the possibilities of intimacy across the ethnic divide (*The Victim*). Setting these texts in dialogue reveals how the "great hatred," to recall the title of Maurice Samuel's 1940 study of antisemitism, enabled authors as different as Miller and Bellow to dramatize the modern condition of "alienation"—the label often ascribed to that moment of post-war American writing marking the emergence of the so-called Jewish American novel. In retrospect, Miller's *Focus* may be said to have inaugurated the

Arthur Miller in his Brooklyn study with copy of *Focus,* circa 1945.
Photograph courtesy Culver Pictures.

thematic strain of American literature concerned with the figure of the Jew
as the *face* of modernity itself.[6] Anticipating Sartre's famous *Réflexions sur
la question juive* (1946), published in the United States as *Anti-Semite
and Jew* in 1948, *Focus* explores the intrinsic and extrinsic figurations of
the Jew projected by the gentile imagination. With Sartre, Miller's novel
images "the Jew" as the terrifying reflection in the eyes of the gentiles—the
uncanny sign of alienation, the specter mirroring the condition of modernity itself.

Looking back, Miller recalled "the sense of emergency that surrounded
the writing of" *Focus.*[7] Sixty years later, readers may wonder at the situation
of crisis that stirred the young playwright, who was not yet thirty, to
compose it. The straightforward plot of the fable-like *Focus* concerns
the psychic journey of Lawrence Newman (does Miller consciously echo

Henry James?), a self-consciously mannered, middle-level office worker whose job is to screen applicants for a restricted company. He prides himself on being able to tell—to "make," or identify, as in street language—a "Jew" when he sees (or smells, or suspects) one. When he fails to flag an applicant who, after she is hired, turns out to be a Jew, thus unsettling the placid gentile tones of the office (" 'Miss Kapp is obviously not our type of person, Newman,' " remarks Newman's supervisor; " 'I mean she's obvious. Her name must be Kapinsky or something.' "), Newman is ordered to get fitted for a pair of glasses.[8] Yet it turns out that wearing glasses *makes* Newman look "Jewish" in the eyes of the world ("a little Hebey," according to his antisemitic next-door neighbor), even in the eyes of his invalid mother. *Focus* is thus a moral–political fable enabling Miller to explore the transformations in consciousness of an antisemite who begins, acutely, to feel persecuted by a world that now "takes" him for a "Jew," indeed that "makes" a "Jew" of him, despite himself.[9]

At a crucial point in his journey, from generalized resentment to emergent empathy, Newman begins to identify with the preyed-upon neighborhood newspaper vendor Mr. Finkelstein, who challenges Newman's own slowly destabilized, abstracting antisemitism by forcing Newman to look at him (Finkelstein) and thus at himself (Newman) face to face. In the end, Newman joins Finkelstein in defending his life and property against local "Christian Front" hooligans (Miller's version of the quasi-Nazi collective who follow the antisemitic rantings of an unnamed Father Coughlin-like figure, a "priest from Boston"). Questioned in a police station after fighting off the neighborhood antisemites with a baseball bat, battered and psychically altered by the "cleansing fury" of his actions, Newman has the following exchange with a policeman, to whom he has reported the assault:

> "How many of you people live there? . . ."
> "There are just the Finkelsteins on the corner . . .
> "Just them and yourself?" the policeman interrupted.
> "Yes. Just them and myself," Mr. Newman said.[10]

This is *Focus*'s concluding dramatic dialogue: Newman's "confession" that he, too, lives among "you people," a testament to Newman's striking personal growth, from his previous garden variety, genteel antisemitic stereotyping to an awakened psychic space of self-identification as a "Jew."

As it turns out, Saul Bellow did not admire *Focus* when it was published in late 1945. Writing in the *New Republic*, the thirty-year-old novelist, in the midst of composing his own meditation on antisemitism, which he published less than two years later as *The Victim*, felt that in Newman Miller had created a character not fully adequate to the situation. "He is not conscious enough," Bellow observed of Newman. "If only he had more substance to begin with." Bellow continued: "He finds himself in Mr. Finkelstein's predicament. He tries to escape it, but fails; the gift of glasses is not to be refused; and eventually he accepts his identification as a Jew as a course of wisdom and justice and attains to the dignity of a brother's keeper. . . . [I]t would be splendid to believe it. But the whole thing is thrust on him. He is too docile."[11]

For Bellow, Newman's psychological passage from antisemite to honorary "Jew" (think of the conclusion to Bernard Malamud's novel *The Assistant* [1957] in this respect, where Frank Alpine undergoes a ritual circumcision, the physical and symbolic expression of his awakened "Jewish" empathy), remains too pat, uncomplicated. Whatever form of "dignity" he may "attain"—and "dignity" is, perhaps, the key word in *The Victim*'s vision of what it takes to be human—feels unearned. Why doesn't Newman (in Bellow's cynical speculation) simply "carry his baptismal certificate around to the neighbors as proof that he was not a Jew"?[12] Bellow's question, designed to expose the thinness of Miller's characterization, radically misses the point about Newman's reversal (so to speak) of gentile fortune. What Miller understood sixty years ago—in an insight that carried, as Matthew Jacobson has argued,[13] a substantial charge of social criticism—is that there can be no *material* defense against the perverse "logic" of antisemitism, no *rational* proof of Newman's hereditary "gentile" identity, since the act of being "taken" as a "Jew" exposes the "raving" unconscious of the antisemite himself.[14]

Listen to Lawrence Newman, in one of his early reflections, bordering on epiphany, on the meaning of his "new," glasses-transforming "Jewish face":

> For he knew that in the old days in the glass cubicle [where, in an uncanny New World version of *judenrein*, Newman labors, separating Jew from gentile] no proof, no documents, no words could have changed the shape of a face he himself suspected.
>
> A face . . . The monstrous mockery of the thing started tears to his eyes. He got up and started walking again as though to find ahead of him in the dark the clue to his confusion. Was it possible, he wondered, that Mr. Stevens looked at me and thought me untrustworthy, or grasping, or loud because of my face? . . . Because I am not untrustworthy and I am a quiet person . . . There must be something he could do that would henceforth indicate to an employer that he was what he was, a man of great fidelity and good manners. . . .

> His face. Beside a lamppost on a corner he came to a halt. *He* was
> not this face. Nobody had a right to dismiss him like that because of his
> face. Nobody! He was *him,* a human being with a certain definite history
> and he was not this face which looked like it had grown out of another
> alien and dirty history.[15]

In this complex interior monologue, we overhear Newman's psychic
confusion and despair as he begins his bewildering rite of passage. Entering the territory of "alienation," Newman tries to fathom, to rationalize
how he could be seen ("taken") for what he believes he "knows" he is not.
Tellingly, his only recourse is denial of the imagined (hallucinated?) accusations of "bad manners," or of being "loud" and "grasping." He has no
identity, we might say, except through negation of stereotypes. Unconscious (for now) of the operation of antisemitism as ideology, Newman
nevertheless begins to feel the existential–political process that would
empty him of individual history and replace it with one that defines him,
both in his own eyes and in the eyes of the world, as "alien and dirty." (In
this respect his tears betray the dislodging of emotion—another gesture
toward empathy, self-empathy.) Newman thus begins his eventual transforming encounter with the haunting face of the "Jew": the uncanny
image he sees in the mirror is that of the "Jew" and the "antisemite." Both,
ironically, are his.

At the beginning of *Focus,* Miller emphasizes Newman's strict personal
habits. Newman strives to be neat, to appear unruffled in public. Indeed,
"When he awakened [in the morning] there would hardly be a crease in the
bedding and his reddish hair, trained flat from the part on the left side,
would really not need combing." Taking the train downtown from Brooklyn, "He wore a starched collar and a meticulously-tied cravat. . . . His
fingernails were roundly pared and shone baby pink. There was hardly a
crease in his soul." Newman's obsessions at the level of the body, however,
bespeak a soul struggling for *self*-mastery; his neat, "creaseless" habits
betray a latent fascist mentality: "Walking *neatly* now, watching along the
already baking sidewalk, he tried to think of his block and the houses all
identical standing there like pickets on a fence. The memory of their
sameness soothed his yearning for order."[16]

The political–psychic drama of *Focus* follows Newman, the crypto-
fascist antisemite, in his overturning passage from order to chaos, figured
in his ultimate identification with the "dirty history" of the Jews. In the
process, he relinquishes (in Miller's understanding of historical stereotypes) an ingrained "gentile" fear of intimacy and "Jewish odors" ("He did
not want to touch the odor" emanating from "the old cooking" in Mrs.

surely beside him, for consciously he did not think of himself that way. It was only that he saw the man in possession of a secret that left him controlled and fortified, while he himself was circling in confusion in search of a formula through which he could again find his dignity.[22]

In Sartrean terms (that is, Sartre's particular way of understanding Jewish identity in *Anti-Semite and Jew*), we might say that at this moment Mr. Finkelstein represents the "authentic" Jew, linked by bonds of history and memory to his people. In this respect, the Old World parable of the shtetl-bound Itzik, which Finkelstein recalls at his father's grave, seems important as a cautionary tale on how to become the duped middleman for the gentiles. The parable fills Finkelstein with indignation; he vows never to be an "Itzik," playing the fool for the master. (Realizing how his accommodating, self-interested behavior leads to the death of his family and community, Itzik goes mad.) In a subsequent impassioned face to face encounter, Finkelstein challenges Newman ("'You look at me and you don't see me. You see something else.'") to feel his (i.e., Finkelstein's) passion, to acknowledge his existence. The result is transforming: "Where once [Newman] had seen a rather comical, ugly, and obsequious face, now he found a man, a man throbbing with anger. And somehow his anger made him comprehensible to Newman. His clear anger, his relentless and controlled fury opened a wide channel into Newman's being. . . . he had no complaint against Finkelstein in particular and he could not face the man like this."[23]

The voicing of Finkelstein's righteous anger, we might say, *creases* Newman's very being. Anger clarifies; it confers humanity. To recall another Bellovian theme, this emotional exchange with Finkelstein (now no longer "the Jew") begins to open a channel to Newman's soul, replacing antisemitic abstractions with the flesh and blood and pain and despair of Jewish history (memory?) itself. That is why Newman can't "face" Finkelstein; for an antisemite, such a face-to-face encounter is apocalyptic, a threat to his very being. As a result, Newman himself undergoes an astonishing consciousness-*razing* transformation, an ordeal by identification that literally overwhelms his previous self, displacing the "Northern man that he *was*"[24] with the soul of a "new-man," an agent able to act in the world with a measure of dignity.

To achieve such a condition, however, Newman must first begin to "make" himself a "Jew"—or, at least, sense how the "gentile" imagines Jews feel under the palpable weight of his judging gaze. In his present liminal condition, caught between his once secure non-Jewish self and a new-man waiting to be born, Newman becomes displaced in the city, which "kept carving a new shape against his soul . . . it scoured silently against the sides of his mind."[25] (In this striking image, Miller suggests that the crust of Newman's closed world is being softened, penetrated by figures arriving, implicitly, from the East. It also recalls Henry James's anxious sense of witnessing, just forty years earlier, the Old World's unsavory invasion at Ellis Island.) His certainties gone, his confidence assaulted, Newman feels "off balance":

> He could no longer simply enter a restaurant and innocently sit down to a meal. Certain tall and broad types of fair-haired men, with whom he fancied his appearance most in contrast, threw him off balance. When they happened to be seated nearby he found himself speaking quite softly, always wary of any loudness in his tone. . . . When he spoke he kept his hands under the table, although he had always needed gestures. In the glances of people, in the fleet warpings of their eyes, he sought to learn where he stood. . . . The things he had done all his life as a gentile, the most innocent habits of his person, had been turned into the tokens of an alien and evil personality.[26]

In this astonishing reflection, we witness the newly self-conscious New man experience—perhaps at the level of paranoia—what might be called the David Levinsky syndrome: the ghetto Jew's restaurant anxiety, the self-monitoring—really, repressing— of voice and gesture signifying the shame and self-hatred that comes with the territory of alienation. And like his American namesake, James' Christophers Newman, at sea in the Old World, Lawrence Newman also finds himself "off balance," seeking "to learn where he stood" in the eyes of a world he takes as authorizing, legitimizing his own, no longer stable, identity.

On one level, Miller places Newman in such destabilizing situations in order to explode the foundations of antisemitic thinking itself: If a gentile like Newman can be compelled to act (and feel) like a ghetto Jew, then the attendant stereotypes can, perhaps, be drained of local, self-arraigning power; thus demystified, this debilitating habit of mind can be exposed as a debased psychological–political structure of feeling, overcome by seeing through its external and internal impositions. By contrast, David Levinsky cannot, alas, see through his own shame and self-hatred. Yezierska's daughters of loneliness continuously struggle to overcome the syndrome. Henry Roth's Ira Stigman flees an imagined parvenu world by heading downtown.

At the same time, Newman's self-hatred seems like a necessary stage in a process leading to its ultimate shedding. He must "make" a "Jew" of himself; he must "take" himself for a "Jew" on the road to dignity. In this questions concerning human responsibility, guilt, revenge, the meaning of dignity, and the possibility of empathy in a jittery post-war world of recrimination and pain. *The Victim* thus participates in and is deeply shaped by the key themes that occupied both Jewish American expression and post-war American culture in the late 1940s.

The Victim was Bellow's second novel. When it appeared in late 1947, it was heralded by important critics like Diana Trilling, Leslie Fiedler, and Elizabeth Hardwick as a brilliant work of fiction. Its reception elevated the thirty-two year-old Bellow into the ranks of major American novelists. He has the "chance," observed Hardwick, "to become the redeeming novelist of his period."[37]

Reading *The Victim* almost sixty years later, the interpretive challenge remains gauging the levels of complexity in Bellow's portrait of Asa Leventhal, the city Jew, alone in New York during a few sultry weeks in August (the novel famously opens, "On some summer nights New York is as hot as Bangkok")[38] and Kirby Allbee, a down-on-his luck, antisemitic WASP, who suddenly surfaces with a long-harbored grievance against Leventhal, whom he associates with the beginning of his fall into destitution. At first Leventhal is baffled by Allbee's accusation (" 'You ruined me.' ");[39] he feels innocent of the charge, and resists any claim of responsibility for Allbee's personal situation. The core drama of *The Victim* involves Allbee's literal stalking—haunting—of Leventhal, his obsession with the Jew as the symbol of all his woe. As Hardwick recognized long ago, "More than anything else [Allbee] seems to want Leventhal to recognize the possibility of his guilt."[40]

What is the source of Allbee's grievance? The short answer concerns a fairly convoluted story (Fiedler speaks of *The Victim*'s "slow, gray, low-keyed exposition")[41] involving Leventhal's search, after the war, for a new job in publishing. Although Leventhal knew Allbee socially (and then only indirectly), Allbee agrees to recommend Leventhal for a position to his employer, Rudiger, the editor of *Dill's*, where Albee himself works. During the subsequent interview, Leventhal engages in a heated argument with Rudiger; as a direct result—at least in Allbee's reading of the episode—Allbee is fired by Rudiger. In his own mind, Allbee links Leventhal's outburst at Rudiger with his own loss of a job, thus marking the onset of his financial and personal ruin. Allbee has now materialized, after years of decline and personal tragedy (his wife died a few years before in a car accident) to remind Leventhal of his forgotten but still outstanding moral and monetary debts. But more than anything else, Allbee seeks retribution and confession from Leventhal *as a Jew*.

The deeper meanings contained in the Leventhal–Allbee "story," however, are located in the rich if (at times) abstract narrative that shapes *The Victim*'s dense plot: the psychologically charged exchanges between Allbee and Leventhal played out as a version of Bellow's own Sartre-like drama of "antisemite and Jew." As the novel unfolds, Allbee surfaces from nowhere, a return of the repressed figure from Leventhal's unconscious. As a native New Yorker, Allbee is obsessed with the "swarming" (to recall Henry James own unsettling encounter with the Lower East Side) presence of upstart Jews in *his* city. The object of his passion (desire?) is Leventhal, the second-generation son of an immigrant father sensitive, we soon discover, about the subject of Jews—specifically, their manners and civility—in a gentile world.

The origins of the complicated Allbee–Leventhal "relationship," the source of their eventual debate, begins with a troubling episode: a social gathering during which a Jew named Harkavy behaves in ways that shamed Leventhal and "delighted" Allbee.[42] *The Victim*'s deep analysis—in effect, its genealogy of antisemite and Jew—requires a close reading of this moment of ethnic-social drama, for the scene contains the foundations of the novel's profound evocation of Jews ill at ease—haunted—in the New World, struggling to locate a zone of stability under the condition of psychic exile, alienated even in the familiar territory of post-war New York City.

The incident in question takes place at a party, where a group of mixed company (Jews and gentiles), including Leventhal's boss (at the time) Williston, Allbee and his wife, and Leventhal's roommate Dan Harkavy gather together and witness Harkavy's comic "performances." Harkavy, we're told, loves an audience. In Bellow's description: "He liked to talk and at these parties he was easily kindled, for some reason. Any trifle made him enthusiastic, and when he spoke his hands flew up and his brows slanted up, sharpening the line of his nose." His subject—really his shtick—amounts to a comic routine "giving imitations of auctioneers, in reality [in Leventhal's assumption] burlesquing his father." Crucially, during these antic performances Leventhal watches *Allbee* watching Harkavy, for Leventhal is obsessed with Allbee's reactions. During these routines, "Allbee studied him, grinning and curious; Harkavy appeared to delight him."[43]

For his part, Leventhal is "annoyed" at Harkavy's spectacle, above all at his friend's utter lack of self-consciousness at playing the type of the comic Jew before Allbee's "grinning and curious" gaze. For some reason, Leventhal is shamed by Harkavy's unconscious gesticulations; during these routines, "for all his traits," Leventhal muses, "the Jewish especially, became accentuated"—a brilliant description, pointing toward Harkavy's "Jewish" gestures and suggesting his theatrical inflections [is

Harkavy imitating Milton Berle? Eddie Cantor? Or perhaps Bellow's own dear friend and legendary mimic, Isaac Rosenfeld?], including the un-welcome accents (in Leventhal's ears at least) that sound from his "Jewish voice." (Harkavy's routine also *accent*uates his "Jewish" nose.) Leventhal "watched" this spectacle, we're told, "unsmiling and even forbidding," thus offering another great touch by Bellow: chagrined by Harvaky, Lev-enthal privately seeks to banish these "Jewish" gestures so relished by Allbee. If the aim of shame is invisibility, then Leventhal wishes Harkavy would disappear.[44]

Leventhal's private ordeal of witnessing *a shanda for the goyim* ("shame before the gentiles") isn't over, however. At one of these parties, while in a drunken state, Allbee asks Harkavy to stop his singing (in this instance) of "spirituals and old ballads," protesting that " 'It isn't right for you to sing them. You have to be born to them. It's no use trying to sing them.' " He further presses Harkavy, charging that he is not "bred" to sing this music; instead, he requests, " 'Then sing any Jewish song. Something you really got feeling for. Sing us the one about the mother.' "[45] Enjoying the collec-tive wince in the wake of his wicked antisemitic "advice" (at least that's how the aghast audience appears to take Allbee's impertinence), he sur-veys the shocked assembly of friends; then, "deeply pleased; he smiled at Harkavy . . . and he even had a glance for Leventhal, too."[46]

Bellow focuses so intensely on this early, determining episode in *The Victim* because it highlights the main characters' respective habits of imag-ination. Years later, ruined and degenerate, Allbee continues to be literally consumed by the matter of "breeding." He announces his once-proud lineage as a descendant of Governor Winthrop, now usurped by the chil-dren of immigrants. The irony continues to astonish him: "His voice vibrated fiercely; there was a repressed laugh in it." A dethroned New York aristocrat (think of Tom Buchanan knocked off his polo pony by Mr. Finkelstein), Allbee feels utterly *displaced* in his city where the cafeterias now serve only "Jewish" food; where people with names like "Lipshitz" publish books on Emerson and Thoreau (is Bellow gently satirizing his friend Alfred Kazin, author of *On Native Grounds* [1942]?); where "the children of Caliban were running everything." Above all, Allbee is ob-sessed with the (bodily) figure of Leventhal as "Jew." He is fascinated, for example, by Leventhal's "Jewish" hair ("It's like an animal's hair," he ex-claims in wonder): " 'Your hair amazes me. Whenever I see you, I have to study it. . . . Is it hard to comb?' " and assumes, on the evidence of a photograph, that Leventhal's absent wife must have descended from an-cestors in Eastern Europe.[47]

Thus Allbee constructs Leventhal as a textbook "Jew" who has usurped Allbee's position in the city. He can't "see" Leventhal, face to face, for a history of stereotyping and a personal rage at feeling unhoused, adrift on the streets of his old home, mediate the encounter. A paranoid consumed by "descent" identity, a social scientist manqué driven by a morbid fascination with the new Jewish New York, Allbee seeks to examine Leventhal (as he had earlier studied Harkavy) as "Jewish" specimen; he desires to know, up close, the source of his personal pain, embodied in the figure of Leventhal.

The unwelcome encounter with Allbee forces Leventhal to re-examine his own life. Allbee's sudden appearance disrupts Leventhal's usually "impassive" composure—the habitual demeanor of his public, "indifferent" face[48]—adding yet another complication to his summer of crisis (in a subplot, Leventhal's brother's son is very sick on Staten Island, compelling the uncle to assume the role of surrogate father while the brother is in Texas, searching for work and a new home). Indeed, Allbee's invasion (at least that's how it feels to Leventhal, even if out of a growing concern he invites Allbee into his apartment) challenges Leventhal's deepest assumptions; his sudden return dislodges long-buried anxieties about Leventhal's identity as son, as brother, as husband and (above all) as "Jew." "Eventually he had to have a reckoning with himself,"[49] Leventhal admits. It's a crucial moment of honest (if rare) introspection, among the earliest articulations of the now familiar Bellovian invitation to self-analysis. During the course of *The Victim*, Leventhal begins to recognize Allbee's claim upon him, which means that Leventhal begins to learn (to recall Newman's dilemma in *Focus*) the meaning of "dignity," what *in-deed* is truly "dignified."

In this respect, a key sequence in *The Victim* involves Leventhal's re-interpretation of the "primal scene" that haunts Allbee: the fateful encounter with Rudiger at *Dill's*, which, Allbee feels, cost him his job. As it turns out, for all his confidence about the meaning of his behavior with Rudiger, upon deeper reflection, prodded by his ex-boss Williston, Leventhal begins to feel unsure of his true motivations. Could Allbee be right? Did he intend for Allbee to lose his job, in revenge (unconscious or not) for the antisemitic behavior (however benign) toward Harkavy? For Leventhal, the condition of his very soul seems at stake.

These questions literally haunt Leventhal as he revisits the argument with Rudiger. To distill this key episode, on Allbee's recommendation, Leventhal, in search of a better position, is granted an interview with Rudiger, but their exchange immediately turns sour, descending into a shouting match. Rudiger insults Leventhal's sense of his abilities as a writer; in reply, Leventhal insults Rudiger by stating how much he feels *he* could improve *Dill's* magazine, but since the business of newspapers amounts to a "guild," " 'Any outsider hasn't got a chance.' "[50] Let me quote at length from Bellow's narration of this incident, related (of course) from Leventhal's perspective:

> The air between them must have shaken, it was so charged with insult and rage. Under no circumstances could he [Leventhal] imagine doing now what he had done then. But he had determined not to let his nose be pulled. That was what he told himself. "He thinks everybody who comes to him will let his nose be pulled." Too many people looking for work were ready to allow anything. . . .
>
> "Get out!" Rudiger cried. His face was aflame. He rose with a thrust of his stocky arm while Leventhal, evincing neither anger nor satisfaction, although he felt both, smoothed the groove of his green velours hat, and said, "I guess you can't take it when people stand up to you, Mr. Rudiger."
>
> "Out, out, out!" Rudiger repeated, pushing over his desk with both arms. "Out, you case, you nut, you belong in the asylum! Out! You ought to be committed!"
>
> And Leventhal, sauntering toward the door, turned and retorted, made a remark about two-bit big shots and empty wagons. . . . He did remember, and very clearly, too, that he was elated. He congratulated himself. Rudiger had not pulled his nose.[51]

Looking back, struggling to remember what in fact he had said to set off Rudiger (Allbee accuses him of swearing), Leventhal feels mortified. During this heated exchange, Leventhal remains utterly in character, always projecting an "impassive" mask of composure, an air of "indifference" before the eyes of the world. "Angry and tense" during the interview, Leventhal "managed to present a surface of dry, uncaring calm."[52] Beneath Leventhal's façade of indifference, however, raw emotion rages, uncontained affect reigns (rains?), linked, at some level, with his self-consciousness as "outsider"—to the closed newspaper guild, perhaps to the world in general. Without directly acknowledging his situation, Leventhal nonetheless *feels* his outsider status as a Jew.

"He had determined not to let his nose be pulled." Significantly, Leventhal voices this private injunction three times in recalling the Rudiger incident. Clearly, the shame of having one's nose pulled is associated with his threatened, self-conscious Jewish identity shaped, ultimately, by a history of stereotyping. Indeed, Leventhal's sense of Jewish identity seems formed in visceral reaction to the limited models of selfhood available in his horizon of experience (i.e., Harkavy, his absent brother, his immigrant father). In his row with Rudiger, Leventhal refuses to play the part of the passive, insinuating Jew of the gentile stereotype, a figure hovering near the surface of his imagination. (Are long Jewish noses naturally more accessible to gentile pulling? Do Jews push their big noses forward so that they may be pulled?) "Too many people looking for work were ready to allow anything,"[53] he tells himself; the act of letting one's nose be pulled issues in degradation, in the loss of self-worth, indeed, of self image.

Leventhal's psychic defense against playing—being *taken for*—the Jew of his own worried self-reflection finds curious expression in his studied *act* of composure (Bellow speaks of Leventhal's "appearance of composure"), which masks his growing rage during the interview, as well as the "elation" he experiences after his feigned display of control incites (excites?) *Rudiger* into making a scene. Rudiger, that is, *acts out* the rage that Leventhal tries to keep under wraps. In a complex scene of "projection," it may be that Rudiger's loss of composure is the source—and aim—of Leventhal's elation—indeed, the measure of his victory in a losing cause. Savoring his revenge, expressive of Leventhal's private Jewish "delight," he performs what is clearly an exaggerated exit, "sauntering toward the door," "smooth[ing]" the groove of his green velours hat"—a show (shtick?) emphasizing his own false "indifference."[54] His behavior can thus be read as a way of getting even with Rudiger, the arrogant reminder (and symbol) of Leventhal's own outsider status.[55]

At the same time, perhaps unconsciously, Leventhal's actions appear as an act of revenge against Allbee. Although he can't *as yet* admit the possibility, Leventhal's behavior, nevertheless, might be construed as a belated response to being uncomfortably fixed (during the Harkavy incident), if only for a second, by Allbee's antisemitic gaze. Watching Allbee watching Harkavy's "Jewish" performance, we recall, made Leventhal cringe, for Harkavy's gesticulations bring to light the repressed Jewish self that Leventhal seeks to keep buried: the *accent*uated Jew of his deeply embedded shame and self-hatred. Thus the antisemitic Allbee doesn't *make* Harkavy a "Jew" (although he takes him for one); Allbee remains a passive, if "delighted," witness to Harkavy's Jewish shtick. And Harkavy doesn't in theory make a "Jew" of himself, since he appears at ease in his performing (Jewish) self. In the end, it is *Leventhal* who makes a "Jew" of Harkavy. To recall the core rhetoric of *Focus*, Leventhal takes Harkavy for a "Jew"; in the process, he projects his own shame-ridden anxiety as a Jew onto Harkavy. Thus the figure of Harkavy, under repression, haunts Leventhal as much as it does Allbee.

He wondered why it was that lately he was more susceptible than he had ever been before to certain kinds of feeling. With everyone except Mary [his absent wife] he was inclined to be short and neutral, outwardly a little like his father [this recognition seems important], and this short-ness of his was, when you came right down to it, merely neglectfulness. When you didn't want to take trouble with people, you found the means to turn them aside. . . . You couldn't find a place in your feelings for everything.[62]

It takes a disorienting conversation with his gentile ex-boss Williston for Leventhal to begin to gain an altered perspective on the past. After Allbee surfaces in his life, Leventhal rushes to Williston, seeking con-firmation of his own reading of the Rudiger incident. Despite Leventhal's "pushy" demand to meet, his face-to-face encounter with the always-composed Williston proves unnerving; "he began to feel unsure of his ground. . . . He suddenly felt weak and confused; his face was wet. He changed the position of his feet uneasily on the soft circle of carpet."[63] Here is a portion of their exchange:

WILLISTON: "You were wrong."
LEVENTHAL: "Maybe . . . My nerves were shot. And I never was any good at rubbing people the right way. I don't know how to please them."
WILLISTON: "You're not long on tact, that's perfectly true."
LEVENTHAL: "I never intended to hurt Allbee. That's my word of honor."
WILLISTON: "I believe you." . . .
LEVENTHAL: "I don't see what he's after. I can't find out what he wants."
WILLISTON: "You ought to . . . You certainly ought."[64]

In the wake of this demystifying moment, Leventhal's strategies of indifference and impassivity begin to lose their defensive power; softened under the pressure of self-analysis, he begins to feel the palpable truth of Allbee's claims. In the process, Leventhal emerges as a recognizable Bello-vian hero, a self overwhelmed, consumed by a need to understand what primal forces drive the human heart. After the unnerving conversation with Williston, Leventhal "felt that he had not said everything he had come to say. The really important things, the deepest issues, had not been touched."[65] Lying in bed, Leventhal revisits in his mind the scene with Rudiger and winces in recollection: "He stifled his emotion altogether and all expression, merely moving his lids downward. He did not try to spare himself; he recalled them all, from his attack on Williston tonight to the original scene in Rudiger's office. When he came to this, he turned on his back and crossed his bare arms over his eyes."[66] Leventhal's telling ges-ture—he covers his eyes in defense against shame—opens him to the truth of his intentions, which include, he now admits, the possibility of revenge. He has begun to "see," indeed perhaps begun to recognize what Allbee is "after."

Thus the source of Leventhal's convicting shame—his revelation—is the memory of the "scene" at Rudiger's. For all his appearance of composure, to his discomfort Leventhal now sees that he had, literally, lost it, while "losing his head at *Dill's*." As he recounts, Rudiger "made me believe what I was afraid of"; under his judging gaze, Rudiger made him feel unworthy and rejected. His deepest self thus insulted, Leventhal became "his own worst enemy."[67]

Having reached this insight—that his defensive pride (an instinctual backlash that surfaces in the wake of self-hatred) determined his behavior at *Dill's*—Leventhal no longer can claim antisemitism in defense of his actions or summon the history of Jewish stereotyping in anticipation of an imagined (gentile) reading of his intentions: "'If you believe I did it on purpose, to get even,'" Leventhal heatedly says to Williston, strenuously defending himself against the (presumed) "gentile" charge of "plotting" to have Allbee fired, "'then it's not only because I'm terrible personally but because I'm a Jew.'" But a clear-eyed, rational Williston refuses to accept Leventhal's "logic": "'You were fighting everybody, those days,'" he reminds Leventhal; "'You were worst with Rudiger, but I heard of others.'" "'The Jewish part of it,'" he points out to Leventhal, in the role of sober analyst, "'is your own invention.'"[68]

Stripped of all his defenses, Leventhal is left alone with Allbee; the result is a gradual but steady recognition of the legitimacy of Allbee's claims, not simply with respect to the incident at *Dill's* but, more importantly, in relation to Allbee's struggle to recover his own dignity after a long ordeal of degradation. At the same time, Allbee undergoes his own personal reckoning, a rite of passage that involves moving beyond his own dehumanizing abstractions born of antisemitism to see Leventhal face to face. If in the beginning each figure becomes the other's stereotype,[69] as in an ancient script, in the end Leventhal and Allbee each achieves a kind of dignity, perhaps even a mutual empathy. They achieve the dignity of the "exactly human"—not more or less—in the famous words of old Schlossberg. The signs of dignity, we might say, are inscribed in gestures of recognition and forgiveness: Leventhal and Allbee each begins to soften his respective grievances with the world, adjusting expectations, refusing to displace or project personal disappointments onto the "other."

Significantly, Leventhal moves from impassivity to empathy as he begins to *feel* Allbee's presence in his life. It represents a momentous transition. Exchanging instinctual feelings of "harassment" for a kind of heart, in direct response to Allbee.[76] At the same time, Leventhal does not separate himself from the scene of farce; he, too, is implicated in the comedy, as witness and participant—another sign of Leventhal's emergent empathy. Finally, to complete the stunning set of reversals, Leventhal watches Allbee's losing effort in shame management, unconscious that the comic situation recalls his own not so funny scene with Rudiger, where he, too, lost his head, and could dare not say what he truly felt.

Thus by the end of *The Victim*—I refer now to the Epilogue—the initially fixed positions of the "antisemite" and the "Jew" have become blurred; the unhealthy zones of stereotyping and mutual enmity have been breached, giving way to empathy and perhaps, at some level, identification. Each has helped engineer the other's transformation. Leventhal enables Allbee to move beyond despair and recrimination by slowly making room for Allbee, first in his home and (at some level) in his heart. Based on the evidence, Allbee, it appears, has worked through his suicidal impulses, arriving at a healthier, better "adjusted" relation to the larger world. This is in radical contrast to our last image of Allbee (before the Epilogue), crouching at Leventhal's open oven door, inhaling gas fumes, seeking only his own death, not intending, he claims, Leventhal's. (" 'Me, myself!' Allbee whispered despairingly.") Not surprisingly, after this ordeal, Leventhal's self reverts to *its* familiar territory of defense: "He looked impassive, under the cloud of his hair."[77]

In the remarkable final pages of *The Victim,* at Leventhal's and Allbee's chance encounter a few years later in the lobby of a Broadway theater, we observes each character's "progress." Leventhal, Bellow remarks, has stopped lashing out against the world. "Something recalcitrant seemed to have left him"; "he was not exactly affable, but his obstinately unrevealing expression had softened." Looking "years younger," his wife pregnant, Leventhal is about to fulfill a generative office we caught only a glimpse of during his fatherly gestures with his nephew Philly. (A subplot in *The Victim* concerns Asa's tender parental relationship with his sick nephew, who sadly passes away at the end of the novel.) What has softened (of course, only to a degree) in Leventhal is his heart; he is now more inclined to empathy, rather than bristling against the insults of the world.[78]

Tellingly, however, Bellow expresses *The Victim*'s deepest wisdom through the example of Allbee who, unlike the still baffled Leventhal, has apparently acquired a self-preserving, ironic sense of humor. Indeed, Allbee seems to have taken to heart the key insight that, earlier, Leventhal had noted of Allbee, without really recognizing the import of his observation (even in the Epilogue Leventhal continues to be either deaf or unresponsive to comic nuance): "By clowning," Leventhal says of Allbee, reflecting

on the incident in the bedroom, "he could pass off his own feelings."[79]
Burlesque as emotional release; clowning as way to salve the pain of in-
curred or imagined insult; *accent*uated routines as a mode of defense;
comedy as revenge. Of course these are among the familiar strategies of
Jewish humor. Indeed, by the end of *The Victim*, Allbee has become
something of a (Jewish?) comedian.

Meeting Leventhal and his expectant wife, Allbee cracks ("smil[ing]
broadly, displaying his teeth"), " 'Congratulations. I see you're following
orders. "Increase and multiply." ' " Still (alas) in character, Leventhal can
only respond "with a dull, short nod"; he misses, that is, Allbee's genial
tone, above all the levels of irony embedded in Allbee's line.[80] In light of
their shared history, Allbee's joking (to my Jewish ears at least) sounds
like the self-mocking humor of an *ex*-antisemite who, nevertheless, *acts*
the role of the wise-ass antisemite for someone who shares, or can remember, their previous intimacy. The joke banks on intimacy; only Leventhal
knows—or ought to remember—how unironic Allbee used to be, when he
was obsessed with Leventhal's "animal"-like, "Jewish" hair, or protested
Harkavy's singing. " 'Increase and multiply' " amounts to Allbee's shtick,
his way of "signaling" (a key word in sociological–anthropological studies
of ethnic humor) that he is a changed man. " 'You haven't changed much,' "
Allbee remarks, again, with an ironic tone. " 'I wasn't the one who was
going to change much,' " Leventhal dryly admits, in reply. At last Leventhal
voices a truth about himself.[81]

In yet another striking example of self-transformation through humor, voiced perhaps in this instance, from within a less self-conscious
comedic space, Allbee utters a startlingly ironic line. We overhear Allbee,
arriving late to the theater, arguing with a cabbie about overcharging
(" 'He took us the long way around' "), exclaiming, " 'Does he think I don't
know the city? I'm no greenhorn here.' "[82] In light of his earlier obsessive
exchange with Leventhal on the matter of "breeding," recalling the unsettling scene of immigrant Jews overtaking his New York, Allbee's statement
registers, on many levels, with even more stunning irony. As voiced by
someone like Allbee, " 'I'm no greenhorn' " could mean any one (or more)
of the following:

"I'm not a 'Jew,' " either an innocent immigrant (recall that *greenhorn*
is a key word in Cahan and Yezierska) or a "Jew" in general.

"I'm not a 'greenhorn' Jew, but rather a Jew who knows the city."

"I've lived in New York all my life, so I know when I've been taken for
a ride."

"Don't make a [greenhorn] Jew of me."

Whichever meanings one might choose, the point is that, finally, Allbee appears at ease in "Jewish" New York; he can now appropriate—crucially, without rancor or despair—the latent resonances of "greenhorn" for his own purposes, ironically or not. In this respect, Allbee's gesture seems related to Newman's at the end of *Focus,* though obviously from a very different perspective. For Allbee now seems able to identify as a "Jew"—not, of course, as a Jew fresh off the boat or a Jew as a matter of "descent," but rather as a *symbolic* "Jew" in—and of—the city: argumentative, wise-ass, ironic, refusing to be "taken."

And, finally, Allbee appears to be reconciled with a universe that tends to ignore him. " 'I've made my peace with things as they are,' " he confesses to Leventhal; " 'I'm not the type that runs things. I could never be. I realized that long ago. I'm the type that comes to terms with whoever runs things. What do I care? The world wasn't made exactly for me. What am I going to do about it?' "[83] Arriving at this hard-won reality principle (recall the Freudian vogue among the New York intellectuals in the forties and fifties), a worldview at odds with the paranoid isolationist maxims of Leventhal's immigrant father, living on "the old system," Bellow's phrase (and title of a great 1967 story) connoting Old World styles of belief and behavior, Allbee's personal insight sounds with the authority of a lifetime of pain, loss, and humiliation. " 'When you turn against yourself,' " he continues, voicing perhaps the deepest insight any character is allowed in *The Victim,* " 'nobody else means anything to you either.' " Significantly, Allbee utters these heartfelt words in a "bitterly shame-faced and self-mocking" mood; "he took Leventhal's hand and pressed it."[84]

Thus in *The Victim,* the self may be healed through a psychic journey from self-hatred to empathy, a condition of selfhood that, in the end, Allbee appears to have achieved more than his "victim." Allbee, that is, seems to have worked through his grievances, to have adjusted his expectations: adjustment through self-mockery. Chafing under the system, Leventhal, by contrast, continues to worry about "who runs things." In light of Talcott Parsons's famous observations in "The Sociology of Modern Anti-Semitism," does Leventhal remain an "emotional victim"? True, his previous "impassive," "recalcitrant" self has been softened, but it remains unclear whether his heart now inhabits a zone of enlarged feeling. After all, "Leventhal pulls his hand away" from Allbee at the very end.[85] Reversing (unconsciously?) the office of the "Jew" in *Focus,* Bellow's Allbee serves as the agent of Leventhal's choosing, or effort to choose, "dignity."

In *Focus,* the antisemite gazes into the Jew's face in order to be spiritually cleansed; in *The Victim,* the Jew must learn how to read the antisemite in order to read himself. In each drama, a heart is stirred to empathy, piercing layers of stereotype, breaking through the crust of animosity.

Despite his critical dismissal, Bellow, like Miller, participated in the post-war examination of Jewish–gentile relations. Would the possibilities of such mutual recognition lead to personal and social renovation, if not redemption? The answer to these ultimate questions remains open, unresolved. But for both Miller and Bellow, the "situation" of the Jew was crucial for resolving the political and psychological dilemmas of post-war America. Whatever the future might bring, the "Jew" would figure in the outcome.

6

MEMORY AND REPRESSION

Goldberg Variations

The assimilation of a people always begins with the women.[1]
—Joseph Roth, *The Wandering Jews*

It is difficult, I suppose, to imagine in our age of proliferating cable TV stations a time when people gathered around a lone radio set and listened attentively to the continuing saga of a Jewish American family trying to "rise" in the world, despite the desperate social and economic conditions of the 1930s. In November 1931, two years into the Depression and exactly two years after the radio show created by Gertrude Berg (1899–1966) as *The Rise of the Goldbergs* premiered on NBC, a crowd of people in a Chicago neighborhood huddled around a radio between 6:45 and 7:00 P.M., causing the businessman whose radio drew the audience to lament, " 'Oi, I won't make a sale for 15 minutes!' " If we can believe this anecdote, reported in the Milwaukee *Journal* as "The Goldbergs Go Over in the Ghetto,"[2] it seems as if years before the Tuesday night ritual of watching the zany figure of Milton Berle in drag compelled urban shopkeepers to close their stores, *The Goldbergs* on radio had the same mesmerizing effect. In fact, the show's popularity was truly enormous, second only nationally to *Amos 'n Andy*, a series that *The Goldbergs* followed in most radio markets in the early thirties; they even shared the same Chicago announcer, Bill Hay. It may also be impossible to recover radio's power, at least in its early days, to generate a cohesive, indeed comforting, aural space for segments of the population; the "new media" of radio, especially "the absurd soap opera," as historian Warren Susman explains, "provid[ed] a huge public with a body of symbols and myths" whose continuing narrative it could, at some level, bond with, enabling the listener to forge an imagined community—or idealized family, in the case of *The Goldbergs*—in the face of apparent despair. "The 1930s was *the* decade of participation and belonging," Susman argues; and in this respect radio functioned as a source and, indeed, as an agent, of national identity.[3]

Just before the onset of the Depression, having returned to her native New York from a sojourn in New Orleans, where her English-born husband Lewis Berg had worked as a chemist-engineer in sugar manufacturing, Gertrude Berg peddled her idea for a radio show about an immigrant family in the process of "Americanization." Interestingly, Berg initially had called the first "Molly Goldberg" *Maltke*, and the family *Talnitzky*, but she altered the names, explaining in her autobiography *Molly and Me* (1961) that "Talnitzky was no longer suitable. It was too much, it was trying too hard, and I couldn't take my character seriously. I changed the name to Goldberg because it sounded right."[4] Although the reasoning may remain obscure, what does seem apparent is that Berg adjusted the name of the more heavily "ethnic" *Maltke Talnitzky* to reflect her own sense of what felt more appropriate, perhaps even more palatable, as she began to shape her particular vision of Jewish American family life sounding along the airwaves, in the ears of the host culture.

How can we begin to locate Berg's imagined radio family: her husband "Jake," her children "Samily" and "Rosily," and "Uncle David"— all modeled on members of Berg's own family? What are the ideological and cultural contexts of *The Goldbergs*? And why, for fifteen minutes each day, *was* the "nation's ear . . . attuned to the conversation of the best-known family in America," as the fan magazine *Radioland* announced in 1934?[5] The answers may be found by sampling a portion of Berg's apparently huge radio audience. During the month of May 1932, for example, the show's initial sponsor, Pepsodent toothpaste, reported to Berg that *The Goldbergs* received 3,302 letters, of which 2,838 were complimentary, while only 11 voiced objections.[6] We also can measure Berg's popularity by betrayal in terms of foodways and civility: " 'The old Jewish eating is poison to her,' " he yells, " 'she must have *trefe* ham—only forbidden food . . . She makes herself so refined, she can't stand it when we use the knife or fork in the wrong way.' "[11]

It was this kind of raw, Yiddish-inflected encounter between perceived greenhorn parents and shame-riven children that generated the deepest sources of humor in the early twentieth-century Jewish American imagination. The humor took many forms and exhibited various modes, from the acting out of "greenhorn" predicaments on the Yiddish stage, to Abraham Cahan's "ghetto" stories about the comedy of acculturation in the late nineteenth century, to the popular genre of "Cohen on the Telephone" monologues of the early twentieth century. The latter presented heavy dialect performances on record (a few were filmed as well) drawing on the long tradition of ethnic stereotypes from vaudeville routines to create comedy based on "mis-hearing/mid-readings" of exchanges between a "Jew comic" and his American interlocutor.[12] Dialect humor flowered in the teens and twenties, with such emerging vaudeville stars as Monroe Silver (who recorded a number of "Cohen on the Telephone" albums), Fannie Brice (who recorded "Mrs. Cohen at the Beach" in 1927), and Sophie Tucker (who included in her repertoire bawdy Yiddish ballads along with her signature "coon" songs) forging successful careers out of Yiddish-flecked routines. The richest example of dialect humor, however, may be the now obscure sketches of Milt Gross, who achieved a measure of popularity with his collections *Nize Baby* (1926) and *Dunt Esk!!* (1927). Along with Yezierska, Gross is an important figure in locating Berg, for it was his particular style of dialect humor that she admitted later to be consciously working against. Starting out in 1930, she explained that her own portrait of Jews issued from a reaction to "Jewish types portrayed on the stage," a tradition of Jewish popular culture which, she confessed, "was very revolting to me."[13]

What must have disgusted Berg about the Gross material (by the 1950s one could speak, derogatively, of a "Milt Gross" style of dialect humor) was how the mangled Yiddish-English voicings along with his strange drawings—Gross was also a fairly primitive cartoonist—rendered immigrant family life as unsavory, an endless screaming match between lazy, streetwise children and shrill, quick-to-holler-and-hit immigrant parents. Berg also must not have appreciated, in light of her grandfather's unalloyed patriotism, Gross's wicked parodic send-ups of various American tales and legends: "Cuttsheep from Miles Stendish"; "Sturry from Hurratio Halger"; "Sturry from Reep Wen Weenkle"; "Give a Look is in

De Raven" ("Wance oppon a meednight drirry / While I rad a Tebloid chirry— / 'Pitches Hinnan gatting litty— / Odder peectures on Page Furr"; / Gredually came a whecking, / Tutt I: 'Feitlebaum is smecking / Goot for notting Isidore!['] / Smecks heem where de pents is lecking / In de rirr from Isidore. / Wheech hez hepped huft befurr!!").[14]

In retrospect, Gross may have offended some of his (Jewish) readers' assimilationist tendencies; perhaps they were embarrassed by how awkward and "uncivilized" Jews were made to sound in his unbuttoned parodies. Perhaps, too, they heard (at some level) tones of a darker world beneath the raw generational exchanges, often leading to physical violence and filial flight, in brutal sketches filled with the mocking humor subversive to both the authority of the family and to the dominant culture in general. Above all, troubled readers in the late twenties—perhaps like Berg herself—may have sensed the anarchic potential of Yiddish dialect humor that in Gross's art explodes American mythologies through the overturning linguistic power of parody. Ultimately, that is, Gross's richly comic but harsh immigrant landscape is the lowbrow version of Henry Roth's utterly unsentimental, harrowing canvas of immigrant coming-of-age, *Call It Sleep,* where Yiddish is rendered as a lyrical English and English is represented in severely fractured, disjointed, often incomprehensible street Yinglish.

By contrast, Gertrude Berg's career in radio and television amounts to a gigantic effort to soften the jagged edges of historical alienation through the supremely maternal figure of Molly Goldberg and her special accommodating vision—the dream of a loving family, of interdenominational brotherhood, of the political ideals associated with the American founders (on the set of the television show, ovals of Washington and Lincoln grace the wall of the Goldberg family's Bronx apartment). Above all, Berg's inviting representation of Jewish American life ("Molly" famously invites us into her home each day with a warm "Yoo hoo"), in contrast to the dangerous world rendered in *Call It Sleep,* is that of a family unconflicted, untainted by new world irony and despair: the bitter tones that nourish the parodic sensibility.

Berg's "Molly" is thus no Hannah Breineh, to recall the Old World mother from Yezierska's "The Fat of the Land," suffering the despair wrought by generational shame or cultural liminality; nor is she a "red hot mama," like Sophie Tucker who, along with her cohort of early vaudeville entertainers, drew on her ethnic identity to construct a distinctive, often unbuttoned comedy of satire and sexual innuendo.[15] Despite—or, perhaps, because—of its unabashed sentiment, its wholesale embrace of na-

Publicity still for the radio *Goldbergs,* circa 1931. Photograph by
Ray Lee Jackson, NBC Studios. Used by permission of the Estate of
Gertrude Berg.

tional ideals, *The Rise of the Goldbergs,* as the series was initially called,
offered an inspiring testament to the wonder-working powers of the
American dream, a daily chapter in the saga of hope and perseverance that
struck a profound answering chord in the hearts and minds of what soon
became her millions of listeners during the Great Depression.

We can, perhaps, begin to explain Berg's, and her show's, astonishing
popularity by listening to a sampling of responses drawn from her radio
audience, in some cases sent directly to Berg in New York, or forwarded to
her from the show's first sponsor, the Pepsodent Company in Chicago.
From a woman in Seattle, Wash., Feb. 1933:

> My dear Molly: I am not in the habit of writing letters to the Radio Stars,
> but Molly Dear you are the Star of Stars. To my way of thinking you are

the most wonderful person in the Radio today. The Goldberg's to our family is something real and true and beautiful. You play your part to perfection [from the beginning there was a blurring of Berg as Molly in the imagination of her auditors] and I am sure you must be very good and gracious in your own life to reflect such beauty in character on the air. You are divine, and we love you so.

From a man in Pierre, South Dakota, Dec., 1932:

Dear Friends: All year my family and I have selfishly been waiting for your evening knock at 6:45 C.S.T. and living with your bit of Jewish life with you. Many times I have meant to write and tell you how we have grown to love you all—Molly and Jake and "Samilly" . . . we see[!] you every night and God forbid that anyone should induce you to appear in pictures to spoil the illusion . . . It's folks like you—and I believe that you're really truly Jewish, that make us believe in the radio! Stay with you? Of course, we will!

From a woman in Oklahoma City, Jan., 1933:

There is not a single thing about the "Goldbergs" I can find to criticize, for they present life as it should be. The fact that they are Jews does not at all detract from our enjoyment, but rather adds to it. We like the democratic and friendly feeling they have for Jew, Gentile and Catholic. . . . "Molly" is a beautiful character, an example for all wives and mothers, and her philosophy is practical for our every day living. . . . We like their patriotism, their constructive, charitable acts, their sympathy for friends in pleasure or trouble. In fact, we cannot imagine any portrayal of family life more perfect.

From a woman in Maine, Dec. 1932:

My mother and I live here alone together. She is 84, still mentally alert, and there's nothing on the radio for her like "The Goldbergs." We never miss the 7:45 appointment unless we are compelled to and then regrets are always expressed. We call it "visiting with the Goldbergs." We have no "better people" within the range of our acquaintance . . . I continue to marvel at the uniform excellence of the sketches. You seem to draw from a very deep well . . . I heard of a household in a nearby city where no telephone calls are answered between 7.45 and 8 P.M. because The Goldbergs are on the air. . . . Thank you very much, dear lady, for the clean, wholesome, helpful [like Pepsodent!] entertainment that you send nightly to this household . . . Truly, The Goldbergs "shine like a good deed in a naughty world." "May they live long and prosper."

Gertrude Berg surrounded by high culture in her Upper West Side apartment in the late 1930s. Photograph courtesy Culver Pictures.

From an anonymous writer to Pepsodent ca. 1931:

For many months all of my relatives and friends have all listened in to your program and consider it the best that the ether waves transmit. . . . We certainly admire the ideals this family stand for, and the way they reach the inner and higher feelings of us all. . . . The Goldbergs are to the mind what Pepsodent is to the mouth—they both leave a clean, whole-some feeling not to [sic] soon to be forgotten.

From a women in Detroit, 1934:

Allow me to ask whether in Jewish families nothing ever goes wrong. . . . Is it always "Papa darling" and "Mama darling"? . . . no wrangling, no quibbling?[16]

Read collectively, these letters convey a rare immediate sense of just how powerful—indeed, just how compelling—Berg's construction of the Jewish American family as *American* family proved to be. *The Goldbergs* appears to have truly inspired its listeners, and in the process seems to have filled an emotional void—the show literally became a surrogate family, enveloping households across the country in the thirties with the familiar sounds of middle-class experience, with the comforting messages of middle-class ideals. If in some sense that cultural moment can be understood as a time when people sought, in the face of an uncertain future, an explanatory, soothing narrative, or myth to embrace—think, in this respect, of the enormous appeal of various visionary movements, religious and political, in the decade, and, in counterpoint, think as well of that desire's dark apocalyptic underside, engineered by the Hollywood culture industry, in Nathanael West's doomsday text *Day of the Locust* (1939)—then *The Goldbergs* performed its office as an agent of cohesion—a utopian dream vision providing a redemptive light illuminating how "life should be." The figure of "Molly," we might say, inspired faith—and faithful listeners—during an interval of economic doubt and historical uncertainty.

About the overwhelmingly positive reaction to her characters, Berg was genuinely surprised; potential network executives had originally voiced severe doubts that a radio show about a Jewish family would find a national audience. Although Berg consciously labored to modify the extremely distasteful dialect tones of Gross's *Nize Baby,* what is remarkable about the early *Goldbergs* scripts is just *how* heavily "ethnic" in voice they, in fact, were. Listen, for example, to a portion from one of Berg's first dialogues:

> JAKE: Molly, your soup is feet for a kink.
> MOLLY: You mean a president. Ve're in Amerike, not in Europe.
> JAKE: Oy, Molly, Molly, soon ve'll be eating from gold plates.
> MOLLY: Jake, d'you tink it'll taste better?
> JAKE: Soch a question?[17]

This exchange, which Berg performed for Edward R. Murrow on *Person to Person* in 1954 and repeated in *Molly and Me,* already marks the imaginations of Berg's central characters: Jake (played originally on radio by James G. Waters, the star of *Abie's Irish Rose* on Broadway) always seeking a fuller material existence; and Molly, always tempering his impulsive, excessive desires with a down-to-earth reality check designed to remind him, and her listeners, about the spiritual costs of acquisition.

Cover of *The Rise of the Goldbergs* (1931), short stories based on the first year of *The Goldbergs* radio show. Collection of Donald Weber.

presenting—Jewish life to America in ways that made audience members feel better about their own uprooted condition, perhaps making them feel more at ease in their new world Zion. Ethnic memory in *The Goldbergs* is thus cohesive, a bonding ritual designed to defend against (imagined) host culture threat (or ignorance), as well as a source of collective nostalgia. Indeed, as if to compensate for her own "lack of Jewish training" in her private life, Berg redressed the religious balance in art by incorporating religiously "authentic" shows, rendering Jewish rituals and liturgy in the warmest, most affecting light.

Scanning her massive scrapbook of clippings from the fall of 1933 and the spring of 1934, one senses how important these Yom Kippur and (later) Passover shows were to Berg; *every* notice of the upcoming broadcast appears to have been saved, some taking up only a single line or two from the obscurest of newspapers. "Goldbergs Present Special Yom Kippur Program Tonight," with Cantor David Putterman and the Mechlenberg Boys Choir, announced the Youngstown *Vindicator;* it will be "one of the season's most unusual broadcasts," proclaimed the New York *News.* The sheaf of clippings also conveys a palpable sense of how geographically various a market *The Goldbergs* reached.[23]

The hallmark of these religious shows, even with the constraints of the fifteen-minute format, was Berg's desire for "authenticity." Following the first year of broadcasts, whose plots follow the family's rise from the Lower East Side to the Bronx by relating a variety of incidents and occasions in their daily (secular) and religious life—from Molly's secret saving of pennies in a cookie jar, which "saves the day" for Jake's frustrated business ventures, to "Sammy's Bar Mizvah [*sic*],"[24] Berg sought to inject as much Jewish tradition and culture as could be accommodated by the serial format. Thus, in 1932 she sought the advice of a well-known rabbi about the details of a Jewish marriage ceremony, which she subsequently incorporated on the air.[25] And in June 1933, she transformed *The Goldbergs* into a vehicle of middlebrow culture with a performance of "Sulameth," described by the Chicago *News* as "a popular Jewish opera of sixty years ago"—"Gertrude Berg introduces another Jewish novelty" is how the article begins.[26]

Two months earlier, on April 10 and 11, Berg had introduced the "novelty" of Passover to the national airwaves. Preparing for the Seder itself, Molly envisions "vone great big table. . . . Dat's how it should be, mein kind. . . . everybody at vone table." Concerned with "authenticity," Berg broadcast various Passover songs and rituals through the children, who ask each other about the symbolic meaning and use of the ritual foods and traditions; there is even a recitation of the Four Questions in Hebrew (followed by their English translation), and a collective rendering of "Dayenu" and other festive songs. Molly is moved by the chanting of "Adder-hu" ("Yes, darlink," she tells Rosily, "it's de song of freedom"); and David reacts to the sounds of "Hud Gadyo" with unalloyed nostalgia: "Oh, . . . De foist time I sang dat I vas tree years old."[27]

How did Berg's audience respond to such seemingly sentimental confessions? One Jewish listener remarked that he was "sure you proved to many a Jew how impressive the rituals of his religion are," while another was made to feel self-conscious about the public display of religious practice that the correspondent felt ought to be kept "for temple service only." In general, though, the Jewish American reception of *The Goldbergs*, especially from various official organizations—guardians and spokesmen for the Jewish middle-class—remained enthusiastic throughout the life of the radio series. To be sure, over the years letters would surface from more observant, more ritually precise listeners: "My dear Mrs. Berg: Shame on you for letting Molly Goldberg pare potatoes on Shabbos," reprimands a woman from Philadelphia in 1934; why did the family attend a "church affair on Friday nite?" asks another listener in December 1933; Molly chants the wrong Kiddush, according to a woman from Brooklyn, writing in May 1934. One 1934 listener, signed "A 'Goldberg' Enthusiast" from New York, even takes issue with Molly's dialect, which displays the "authentic speech defects of the middle class Jewish woman"; since Mrs. Goldberg is so "progressive a person, quick to learn and adapt herself," how can she "show so little improvement in her own grammatical expressions after months—no, years of broadcasting! . . . Please, sirs [the writer lodged these complaints directly to the radio station] may we ask for just a little better English from the noble lady!"[28]

The request for "better English," of course, misses the point—and source—of Berg's invention of "Molly's" signature verbal style, a rhetorical *performance* that endeared her to millions. Indeed, *The Goldbergs* almost immediately became something of a cultural commodity, especially the figure of "Molly," the archetypal Jewish matriarch that Berg inhabited for over thirty years. As early as 1932, there seems to have been a discussion about marketing a "Goldbergs'" puzzle; by 1934, Berg herself began a syndicated column in the Jewish press under the title, "Mamatalks," which served out morsels of homey philosophy—written not in "Molly's" dialect, but rather in Berg's own cultured, well-mannered English; and in 1944, Proctor and Gamble sought to put out a "good-will booklet" on the history of *The Goldbergs* show to coincide with a comic strip based on the series that was about to appear in the *New York Post*. Writing her sponsors about the idea for a comic strip, Berg assured Proctor and Gamble that she "would have the final say on what was done" and "would naturally see that characters represented would be in every way lovable and lifelike and would permit no caricatures."[29] Later on, after *The Goldbergs* was off television, Berg lent her character to *The Molly Goldberg Cookbook* (1955), which listed recipes based on the individual tastes of her TV family, like "Bagels Jake," and even personally marketed her own line of housedresses

Gertrude Berg, surrounded by years of *Goldbergs* scripts, makes the transition to television, *Life*, April 25, 1949. Courtesy of George Karger/Time Life Pictures/Getty Images.

designed for the "full-figured" woman, making highly advertised appearances at department stores in the Midwest and Northeast. Indeed, except for a brief interval in the mid-1930s, when Berg wrote and starred in a radio series based on her adolescence in the Catskills (titled "House of Glass"), *The Goldbergs* was never off the air; between 1929 and 1962, Berg remained a major presence in show business, starring in a short-lived Broadway play called *Me and Molly (1948)* (discussed briefly in the Epilogue), a feature film based on the series titled *Molly* (1951) (originally, Paramount's production materials called the film *The Goldbergs*), and then, in the late fifties, after the TV *Goldbergs* had become *Molly* in 1955, appearing in assorted TV dramas (among them "Paris and Mrs. Perlman" (*Alcoa Hour*, aired April 29, 1956) and "Mind Over Mama" (*Elgin Hour*, aired May 31, 1955, directed by Sidney Lumet), another Broadway play (*A Majority of One*, with Sir Cedric Hardwicke), and finally, her last, barely remembered TV show, called *Mrs. G Goes to College* (1961–62), again co-starring with Hardwicke.

Like a number of radio shows from the 1930s and 1940s, *The Goldbergs* joined the migration to television during the medium's first years (a host of vaudeville and comedy actors and popular singers switched over to television—Jack Benny, Eddie Cantor, Milton Berle are just a few examples). Berg barely changed the tone and subject matter in the early episodes, although the family "returns," so to speak, to Tremont Avenue in the Bronx from "Lastonbury," the small town in Connecticut where they had moved in the late thirties, and about which Berg had constructed a series of fantastic-sounding plots—including the family's encounter with encrusted New England prejudice from the town's older inhabitants, one of whom is descended from the original founders of Brook Farm (!).[30]

Perhaps the key aspect of the TV *Goldbergs* is revealed in the way Berg maintains Molly's office as an agent of reconciliation and reunion. In a remarkable *Commentary* interview in 1956, at a time when *The Goldbergs* had virtually run its course, and after the family had moved, one more time, from the Bronx to a town called "Haverville" (the "village of the haves," in David Marc's nice formulation),[31] Berg enumerated those sensitive areas she deemed inappropriate for treatment on *The Goldbergs*. Her list provides a revealing litany of taboo subjects:

> You see, darling [she tells the interviewer, who had noticed that in person Berg's speech "was careful and quite free of the accent that marks 'Molly Goldberg' "], I don't bring up anything that will bother people. That's very important. Unions, politics, fund-raising, Zionism, socialism, inter-group relations, I don't stress them. . . . after all, aren't such things secondary to daily family living? The Goldbergs are not defensive about their Jewishness, or especially aware of it.

"I keep things average," Berg continued in the same interview, adding, "I don't want to lose friends."[32] Or, of course, make trouble. The actor Philip Loeb, who played "Poppa Jake" on the radio and television *Goldbergs,* made trouble for Berg (despite her public pronouncements to the contrary) when his name appeared in *Red Channels,* the television industry's catalogue of actors and writers suspected for their left-wing sympathies and/or affiliations. In 1951, Loeb symbolized in his political behavior—which included support for the integration of baseball, among other subversive causes—all that Berg's worried, self-conscious version of Jewish life in America sought to repress. Loeb's listing, that is, brought to light an alternate, dissenting relationship to the host culture that Berg's middle-class sensibility could not tolerate.[33] Nor could Berg tolerate on the more visible television screen any overt, Yiddish-inspired inflections. Talking to the same interviewer, Berg explained that "as for Jewishness, you'll notice there's no dialect, just intonation and word order."[34] Earlier, as we have seen (heard?), *The Goldbergs* was marked by a rich dialect style—even the radio shows during the mid-forties contain what I hear as *very* strong Yiddish inflections, including occasional Yiddish words. But by the early fifties, a local debate over the embarrassing aural presence and awkward subject matter expressed in the routines of the dialect comedian broke out in pages of *Commentary*. The popular middle-brow raconteur Sam Levenson argued in earnest that "the dialect comic should vanish," citing as a moral counter the example of "Molly Goldberg, who speaks with an accent yet teaches love, kindness, honesty, respect for culture and decency on a high level, as does Mama in Scandinavian dialect."[35] (Levenson refers to the other famous 1950s "ethnic" television show starring Peggy Wood as the matriarch of an immigrant family in turn-of-the-century San Francisco.] In retrospect, the stir over dialect now seems to be about shame and visibility, about the anxious, if familiar, Jewish middle-class's worry about exposure, and about sounding "too Jewish" in the ears of the host culture.

By the late forties and early fifties, then, Berg was—by national consensus—*the* symbol of the emerging Jewish middle class, the most visible link between America and the affective life of her implied audience. "You symbolize for them the lives that they have lived," a letter from the director of a Jewish old age home declared in 1942.[36] But not, we should note, *all* Jewish lives, above all those narratives of working-class resentment and resistance, which were under repression in Berg's circumscribed version of Jewish American experience. Thus, even in the potentially dangerous subject area of landlord–tenant relations—the latent theme of a 1949 TV episode called "The Rent Strike"—the exposure of authentic social and class inequities, the arranging and implementing of a rent strike is contained through Molly's self-styled office as *fixerke*[37] that, so to speak, saves the day. Jake, played by Philip Loeb before the television blacklist, is outraged by another rent increase, and adamantly refuses to accept the landlord's demand. Loeb is so animated, so fiery in this role, that his agitated presence virtually overwhelms Berg's performance as calming mediator.

The crisis dramatized in "The Rent Strike" is resolved in the end, however, not by tough landlord–tenant negotiation, but rather through Molly's distinctive mode of reconciliation: her domestic art of cooking. Seeking to save the day, she bakes a cake especially for the landlord, since it happens to be his birthday. Uncle David—continued from the radio series, he is now living with the family and is the show's most "ethnic" character—squeezes lemons for lemonade as an offering to the landlord's wife, in order to soften her, and thus her husband, on the issue of the rent increase. In the end, the gift of food, and Molly's generous heart, overcome the potential of a Bronx tenement rift; "A landlord is also a person," she announces, as the episode closes with harmony and reconciliation.[38]

It may be that Berg's evasion of taboo political themes (in the case of "The Rent Strike," issues of power and property), together with her conscious avoidance of subjects keyed, at least in some segments of American imagination, as overtly "Jewish" ("unions," agitating for social justice, etc.) contributed to the enormous popularity of *The Goldbergs* on television. Swerving further from Jewish memory, even the show's representation of religious ritual became attenuated in the early fifties. Berg continued to create shows with overt religious content. For example, the script of the "Yom Kippur" show on television was virtually identical to an earlier radio program, but on TV it focused more on the unbreachable bond between father and son than on the spirit, much less than on the liturgy, of the sacred holiday itself. Unlike the earlier radio segments, the TV *Goldbergs* declined to represent the language and rituals of Jewish religious observance. Even the plot of the Passover show for television avoids addressing the meaning of the holiday; instead, its plot concerns the mildly funny situation of how many portions of gefilte fish Molly needs for a continually mounting number of guests she hears will attend the Seder. (By the early fifties, Berg's notes on these particular scripts indicate that other, non-religious shows, were replacing those with religious themes.)[39] Thus it may be that the implied TV audience for *The Goldbergs*—specifically, its Jewish American viewers—needed to repress the social-religious-political history embedded in Berg's litany of prohibited themes. It needed, at least in the early fifties, the figure of Molly Goldberg to help ease their self-conscious transition into the middle class.

In this respect, what marks the television incarnation of *The Goldbergs* is the show's anticipation—indeed, expression—of what, in 1956, the sociologist Herbert Gans labeled "symbolic Judaism," a term he later enlarged into "symbolic ethnicity"—a religious-cultural outlook linked in the fifties to the phenomenon of middle-class arrival:

As a result of the pressures, the training, and the rewards offered by American society at large, traditional Judaism has ceased to be a living culture for the second-generation Jew. Parts of it, however, have remained active in the form of habits or emotions; these are now providing the impetus for a new "symbolic Judaism" still in the process of development.[40]

In light of Gans's observations, *The Goldbergs* proved to be the perfect televisual medium "mirroring" this new class because it avoided the messier history of immigrant experience: the agitation for social change, the ordeal of Americanization. Of course, to speak of television's "mirroring" dimension simplifies the complex dynamic of legitimation and resistance—"how popular culture," in T. J. Jackson Lears's academic phrasing, "can simultaneously subvert and reproduce hegemony."[41] The themes and issues represented—or *not* represented—on *The Goldbergs* actively shaped, and were shaped by, the real aspirations of at least some portion of its implied audience: a new ethnic middle class looking to the dominant culture as an authorizing, legitimating sphere.

Gertrude Berg joined in the distinctively 1950s work of cultural legitimation through the performance of ethnic memory. But more than the voice of the network boardroom, it was voice of Molly Goldberg that sanctioned the new consumer culture. Listen, for example, to Berg's TV pitch for Sanka Coffee, a monologue that prefaced *The Goldbergs* broadcast on April 24, 1950:

> I'm just going over the recipe I used today. I made a cake—wait, you'll see it. I hope I didn't put in too much flour—it will be heavy. A recipe means ingredients . . . the right ingredients never fail to bring the right result, whether it's a cake or a house or a disposition . . . I mean it. If for instant, you are a person that should not drink coffee with caffein [*sic*] in it you do so regardless you know what happens . . . disturbed sleep—irritability—and do I have to tell you what irritability can do to the complexion of your family life? Don't ask. . . . I am already a Sanka drinker since time immemorial and I have never stopped thanking my friends that recommended Sanka to me. I am not asking you to thank me. I am only asking you to switch. That'll be my thank you . . . from you to me.

The language of Berg's commercial for Sanka reveals in suggestive ways the corporate appropriation of immigrant residues; the tones and rhythms of immigrant life, although in noticeably diluted form, are summoned to spur and sanction the purchase of commodities in response to Molly's authorizing voice. The ritualized invocation of "Don't ask," in this commercial context, resonates with terrific irony. In Gross's 1927 *Dunt Esk!!* this famous immigrant phrase bespeaks a weary but knowing exasperation with the comedy of ghetto life; by 1950, the expression has become a cute rhetorical utterance designed to win consumer confidence.[42] Even Molly's mild malaprop "for instant" highlights the attenuation of the once-lively language of the dialect artists (unless, of course, Berg intended this as a pun on a type of coffee).

The advertising format of Molly's opening monologue was eventually dropped from *The Goldbergs;* in the show's last incarnation, *Molly,* the opening shots, before the actual plot commences, depict the white-breaded landscape of suburbia—cars cruising slowly down Main Street, a picture of a water tower, manicured lawns. Yet in these post-Loeb *Goldbergs* episodes, Berg offers her viewers a Molly less sure of her mediating, negotiating abilities; a Molly whose identity is often challenged by the less ethnic, new suburban, commercial world of the fifties. Her efforts at personal and familial incorporation remain in uneasy dialogue with the lure of the compelling monetary rewards of that "New World." This cultural tension is richly conveyed in two key "Haverville" episodes, each broadcast in the fall of 1955, titled "Social Butterfly" and "Molly's Fish."

In their originally aired sequence, "Social Butterfly" followed "Moving Day," an episode about the family's transition from city to suburb. In "Moving Day," Molly sells off all the "Old World" Bronx furniture, even Rosalie's piano, to buy new furnishings for Haverville. In the end, only ovals of Washington and Lincoln remain in the empty foyer, serving as symbols of immigrant residue—the family's adoration of host culture, American icons—that survive, indeed oversee, the Goldberg family's Bronx evacuation.

"Social Butterfly" opens with Molly anxiously preparing to "receive," as she terms it, the stream of neighbors who, according to the authority of the etiquette manuals she has consulted, will be calling on this particular night—it is, after all, the end of their first week as emigrants to Haverville. "That's the regular procedure when new people move into the neighborhood," she explains to her family. Jake (now played by Robert H. Harris) assures Molly that their community will take her "to their hearts like Tremont Avenue." In her "hostess gown," Molly worries about Uncle David's (played by Eli Mintz) exposed suspenders and reminds her son, "Sammy, darling, did you put on your college pin?" To Molly's extreme dismay, no one appears that night, except the town fire chief selling raffles (he enlists Jake and David to join the town's volunteer fire department). Eventually Molly gives up any hope of "receiving," and this opening scene ends

The living room set of the Goldbergs' apartment in the Bronx,
presided over by George Washington, circa 1950. Photograph used
by permission of the Estate of Gertrude Berg.

with the surprise arrival of a huge "good luck" horseshoe wreath, sent by
the old Bronx crowd, a token of her past life—a symbol that leaves Molly
with the ache of bittersweet memory for the world she has left behind.
"Not everyone reads etiquette books," Jake gently advises, as the Goldbergs
all retire, each chanting the refrain, "Don't be lonesome, Molly."[43]

Determined to make new friends, Molly sets out the next morning to
survey the neighborly landscape. Three sharp, unsettling rebuffs ensue.
Watching portly Mrs. Carey cleaning her first-floor window (the intimate
scene of window-to-window exchange between neighbors has disappeared
in the suburbs, replaced by yard-to-yard dialogue), Molly immediately
brings up the impertinent (as it turns out) subject of food and dieting.
Molly's opening conversational gambit, "We like to eat, evidently" is met
with a pointed, huffy reply by Mrs. Carey ("I never discuss my eating

habits!"), which compels Mrs. Carey to leave. Next, Molly offers a little boy dressed in a Davy Crockett coonskin cap a chocolate cookie ("I'm the cookie lady," she announces). Next, she encounters Mrs. Peterson (the Goldbergs are evidently the only Jews in Haverville) hanging out her laundry and suggests that Mrs. Peterson visit Jake's new store (Jake has moved up from tailor to manufacturer) to buy a dress wholesale for her daughter's upcoming wedding. "I thought there was a law against wholesale selling to retail customers?" Mrs. Peterson questions in reply, and in extremely sharp language rebuffs Molly's offer. It turns out that her husband sells dresses retail in town; Molly's offer appears, therefore, "not very ethical." Finally, if matters could get any worse, the little boy's mother shows up (played by Florida Friebus, who later was Dobie Gillis's mom) to scold Molly for giving her son chocolate cookies; *of course* he's allergic to chocolate—she expects him to have a toxic reaction any minute.[44]

Thus the plot of "Social Butterfly" involves three social snubs, three blows to Molly's self-esteem, and three severe challenges to her identity. In reaction, Molly becomes forlorn, listless; she loses her appetite and even her desire to cook. During this time of trial (Berg portrays Molly as depressed; she is having an adjustment reaction to suburban life), she refuses to relinquish the token of her previous happier life, the Tremont Avenue good luck wreath. "When are you going to throw out that remembrance of your past?" an annoyed—and hungry—Jake asks. "Never, never," is Molly's mournful reply. In the meantime, the family arranges for a surprise visit by Mrs. Herman, Molly's closest Bronx neighbor, who forsakes her grandson's birthday party out of concern for her old friend.

In the meantime, too, Molly somehow jolts herself from lethargy and takes action, in the kitchen. In a rapid sequence of shots we see Molly at her work preparing . . . something, in a flurry of kneading, cutting, and tasting. As the episode approaches closure, Mrs. Herman arrives ("You of *all* people lonesome, Mrs. Goldberg!" she exclaims in disbelief). At the same moment, however, Mrs. Carey rings, to return a pot. Trying to pronounce the words correctly, she confesses that never in her life has she tasted such delicious food ("Mrs. Goldberg, you *genius*, you," is how she puts her rapt enthusiasm for Molly's culinary art; in another episode Uncle David praises Molly by remarking, "If your noodle soup could be put into a frame, Molly, you'd be hanging in a museum.") Struggling to pronounce the exotic words, Molly helps Mrs. Carey by naming the wonderful foods she has bestowed upon her new neighbor: *tsimmis,* gefilte fish, strudel.

In the next instant, other neighbors arrive at the family's door, welcoming Molly (this turns out to be the night prophesied by the manuals—

the marking of Molly's arrival in Haverville). Mrs. Peterson thanks her for buying a new dress from her husband's store (Molly just happens to be wearing it; "I'm all early American," she proclaims—a wonderfully ironic statement, suggestive of the immigrant desire, voiced with a mild Yiddish-English inversion, to appropriate the genealogical authority of the American founders); Davy Crockett's mother materializes to inform Molly that her son is not allergic to the cookies (so can she have Mrs. Goldberg's delicious recipe, please?). "Social Butterfly" concludes with Molly "receiving" invitations to speak before the local Garden Club, the Gourmet Club (would Molly give a talk on *tsimmis*?). Seeing her old friend surrounded by animated neighbors, Mrs. Herman decides to return to the city, promising Molly, "I'll tell the Bronx how busy you are!"[45]

What remains striking about "Social Butterfly" is how Berg imagines ethnic food as an agent of social incorporation; how, that is, the offering of (say) gefilte fish enacts a ritual of integration, a ritual of conformity, above all one of reassurance. "Traditional foods and ways of eating," remarks an anthropologist of ethnic foodways, "form a link with the past and help ease the shock of entering a new culture."[46] Yezierska's daughters of loneliness, we recall, are revolted by the gastronomic symbols of their ethnic affiliation; the aroma of herring generates the nausea of memory in the rising generation: they literally cannot tolerate, cannot swallow the world they seek liberation from. Molly, by contrast, resolves the problem of host culture acceptance (it does not matter whether Mrs. Carey is herself Irish American; she represents the new suburban turf that Molly's ex-Bronx self seeks to conquer) through what might be called the boundary-crossing power of gefilte fish. The gift of food (recall "The Rent Strike") is Molly's mode of conflict resolution, and indeed is her only mode of negotiating "otherness" in the new suburban fifties. In another context, or era, gefilte fish might have figured as a boundary-making symbol ("a marker of ethnic identity");[47] but in the television world of Haverville, whose opening filmed sequences have, ironically, the texture and look of the Waspy, "ethnically neutral" shows *Molly* will soon be displaced by, Berg presented a safe story of acceptance and toleration for the new Jewish middle class, thus consolidating a linear process of "symbolic ethnicity" already underway, if not virtually completed by the mid-fifties. In the end, a TV situation that might have exposed barriers between people or explored the dangerous territory of Americanization[48]—the strains of acculturation in the new suburban fifties—becomes instead a comical case study of social harmony and leveling through foodways, a mode of symbolic ethnicity— the gift of gefilte fish.[49] Few extant episodes of *The Goldbergs* hover around such taboo subjects as "Social Butterfly." One other example of Berg's imagination of the "mild" tensions between America and ethnic family life may be found in *The Goldbergs* show called "Molly's Fish," a wonderful episode that reveals how popular ethnic TV, perhaps still saturated with an immigrant-sedimented sensibility, could offer a potential critique of the dominant—or soon to be dominant—commodity culture of the fifties.

The plot of "Molly's Fish" turns on the desire, on the part of a national supermarket chain ("Peter Piper Supermarkets"), to mass produce and market Molly's unique and delicious "fish balls," as her gefilte fish are called throughout the episode. Indeed, it took two screenings of "Molly's Fish" for me to realize that *not once* is the term gefilte ever mentioned; it is as if the word itself is unutterable, taboo—as is, by the way, the required "matzoh meal" in the fish's preparation (instead it is called "cracker meal"). Were these terms "too Jewish" for Berg to name on television in the fifties? "This fish is commercial!" the store's traveling representative declares; "I can do something with your fish, Mrs. Goldberg." This enterprising dream runs into problems, however, when the scene of production shifts from Molly's kitchen to Chicago, where in the huge, antiseptic cooking area (it is "hospital clean," Molly remarks), overseen by Molly's *goyische* alter ego (the chief food inspector and her legion of turbanned, nurse-like assistants), Molly is invited to prepare "her" fish—"like Mama used to make," in the words of the supermarket chain's agent.[50]

The great comedy—and substantial critique—of "Molly's Fish" issues from the bafflement of those in the corporate, high-tech, mass production mentality world before the figure of Molly and her ethnic culinary art. Of course, no specific recipe exists to guide in the preparation. We observe Molly turning a huge food grater, surrounded by a group of the cooking aids, who are armed with clipboards and are attentively counting every turn of the grater, trying to demystify the secret of her fabulous fish balls. Sadly, however, because Molly is alienated from her own kitchen, the result is, in the words of one of the corporate designated food tasters, "Not your fish, Mrs. Goldberg."[51]

Perplexed by her failure to duplicate "her" fish in the assembly-line world of Chicago and big business, Molly calls Mrs. Herman back in the Bronx, for the exact amounts for the ingredients. "Who measures?" is her reply. "I cook blind," Molly explains to a boardroom filled with extremely genteel-looking, disappointed executives. But the real explanation for the dilemma involves the limiting, mechanistic, and quantifying mentality of the commercial world itself, which literally drains the ethnic flavor out of Molly's sacred fish, subverting, in the process, her domestic sphere.

Yet in the original ending to the script for "Molly's Fish," Berg has Molly return to Haverville dejected, her final conversation with Peter

Piper an apology for her poor performance: "From trying you can't build an industry. A fish that's good today and bad tomorrow is not a business. A flash in the pan. That's what I am." But in a flash of cooking revelation (or is it the return to the family that jogs her culinary memory?), Molly is able to make "her" fish once more. Her immediate impulse is to call Chicago ("Jake! David! I did it! I did it! I'm not a flash in the pan. I did it again. It's my fish.") Uncle David, however, has stopped by Peter Piper on the way home and has returned with a new item, a jar of "Fanny's Fish Balls." "They got somebody else?" Molly wonders; "They couldn't wait." Of course the commercialized fish proves inedible, and Jake is given the last, comforting word: "Molly, who needs them? Oscar in the Waldorf is also not commercial. He's exclusive like you, Molly." In the original conclusion to "Molly's Fish," then, Molly remains, at the very end, still lured by the promise, and by the monetary potential, of commodification.[52]

The revised aired TV version of "Molly's Fish" concludes, however, with an adjusted recognition on Molly's part: "A mother is not a corporation," she acknowledges. In the end, this insight helps her recover, to her family's delight, the art of making "her fish." Instead of running to the phone to call Chicago, Molly writes down the recipe for herself. "And what's your decision?" Jake asks, "Are you going back to Chicago?" (there is now no competing line of "Fanny's Fish Balls" to deter Molly from marketing herself); Molly's reply is an adamant "No. The big world is too wide for me, Jake. I found out a mother cooks best where she is needed the most." In the end, some areas of the self cannot be commodified; in this respect, ethnic memory—symbolized here by the culinary art of making gefilte fish—may at times be able to expose the contradictions of market capitalism (the arguments of some theorists of popular television) as it resists incorporation. From this perspective, "Molly's Fish" might be said to challenge the strategies of emergent commodity culture that, through the agency of network television, appropriated ethnic memory for the legitimization process itself. "A mother is not a corporation" is thus uttered from within the resisting space opened by the exposure of the commercial imagination's limitations; in turn, Molly's comic negotiations with the new technology of mass production become, at some level, the viewer's as well. At the historical-economic moment when TV validated, as it showcased, the new ideology of commodity, a show like "Molly's Fish," despite Berg's own participation in the rituals of legitimization, challenged the authority of commodity through the empowering memories of ethnic foodways.[53]

Still, in the end Berg envisioned her alter ego as a figure of cultural reconciliation and accommodation, overseeing those rituals of reassurance characteristic of situation comedies of the 1950s. "Popular culture," observes Todd Gitlin, "absorbs oppositional ideology, adapts it . . . domesticates it; at the same time, popular culture is a realm for the expression of forms of resistance and oppositional ideology."[54] Given this perspective, television—especially early ethnic television—can delineate both dynamics at work: critique and adaptation, as "Molly's Fish" and "Social Butterfly" amply reveal.

Gertrude Berg returned to network television one last time, in a short-lived series called *Mrs. G Goes to College* (1961–62), a show she did not herself write or produce, but (based on the evidence of the heavy revisions of her personal shooting scripts) a series whose content she had a substantial hand in determining. The premise of *Mrs. G* involves "Sarah Green" returning to college after a life as mother and wife (in the opening episode, made over forty years ago, a young Marion Ross escorts her "mother," Mrs. G, to the steps of the campus.)[55]

No longer surrounded by her television family, in *Mrs. G* Berg becomes the surrogate mother to an entire college dorm and assorted faculty. In the course of twenty-six half-hour episodes, Berg plays matchmaker, dabbles in contemporary child psychology ("The Baby Affair"), becomes a teacher to local merchants and working people, is humiliated in a speech class by a cocky, young debater ("How Now Brown Cow"), takes on The Kingston Trio (Mrs. G at first calls them "a waste of time," in "Mrs. G. versus the Kingston Trio"), and in one especially poignant episode, in light of "Mrs. G's" self evident, "intertextual" relation to "Molly Goldberg," she searches in vain for someone to share her Sunday dinner with— a feast of lamb and mint jelly, which she eventually serves to the local firemen who save her kitchen while she is out searching for guests (this show, called "Lonely Sunday," contrasts in remarkably ironic ways with our television memory of "Molly": *Sunday* dinner? *Lamb* and *mint jelly?*) In one revealing episode of *Mrs. G,* titled "Dad's Day," we return to the resonant theme of ethnic self-consciousness and generational shame, core emotions in ethnic expression in general. How Berg/"Mrs. G" addresses this subject, how the show tries to resolve the filial chasm, highlights those structures of feeling that lead to the heart of Berg's television imagination, and perhaps to the mental world of her audience as well.[56]

It's Father's Day at the college, and Mrs. G's dorm is hosting a reception for the students and their fathers. One student, Quentin Richards, when asked by Mrs. G whether his father is coming for the weekend, is vague: "He's sort of a business man," he answers, meaning that his father is too busy to attend. Quentin is depicted alone, isolated, as the festive preparations proceed. Concerned that Quentin's father should join in the special day (recall Molly's vision of "all vun table" from the thirties Passover show), Mrs. G calls and invites him herself. It turns out that Quentin Richards's father's name is, in reality, "Mr. Rickadmyack." Naturally, his son is quite vexed that Mrs. G has made his father materialize:

> RICKADMYACK: Hello, Quentie. [Quentin's smile vanishes. He seems disturbed]
> QUENTIN: Pop
> MRS. G: You see, Quentin. He wasn't so busy. Sometimes if you don't ask you don't know. So I asked. . . .
> QUENTIN: Uh . . . Swell, Mrs. G. Uh . . . Dad . . . I want to show you around . . . uh . . . my car's right outside. . . .
> MRS. G: Is something wrong, Quentin?
> QUENTIN: No, no . . . you just shouldn't have asked him here.
> MRS. G: He seems happy to be here.
> QUENTIN: Don't you see? . . . He just doesn't belong here that's all. [slightly angry] Why can't you stay out of things that don't concern you.[57]

The drama of "Dad's Day" involves Mrs. G's unsought discovery of Quentin's filial shame along with the classic sitcom question of whether Quentin, who wishes his father would disappear, will introduce him to his girlfriend Felicia's father, who (in Quentin's eyes) "looks like Mr. Wall Street." Before that scene takes place, however, Mrs. G and Quentin argue heatedly, but not according to the original script's intended dialogue; rather, the key exchange in this particular episode of *Mrs. G* that was filmed and broadcast nationally in early February 1962 was shaped by Berg's desire to impart a profound moral lesson that she felt "Quentin"—and perhaps a cohort of embarrassed American sons with him—needed to learn:

> Quentin, [Berg amended in her own hand to her copy of the script], If I thought you were ashamed of your father (let me talk) I never would have called him to come here—I feel very sorry for you Quentin and mostly I'm sorry for your father, so sorry that I could cry—One look at your father and I can see his life wasn't easy—I'm sure he had to push his way through the slings and arrows of life and in the end—what—a son that is ashamed of him—only—did he commit a crime[?] his pronunciation embarrasses you—his English is not grammatical—just a minute Quentin, I'm not finished yet . . . his bad English is making a very good life for you Quentin—don't forget that.[58]

With these heartfelt words, Berg performed what we now recognize as her self-proclaimed office as authority on immigrant generations and as (literal) embodiment of wisdom and experience, addressing the core affects shaping Jewish American expression. For over thirty years as "Molly," Berg had avoided "sensitive," taboo subjects; in 1962, in an uncharacteristic burst of emotion, Berg as "Mrs. G" drew on historical memory to heal the filial breach separating fathers and sons, to soothe the pain, to lift the shame under repression in immigrant family history.

Still, by the end of the episode much remains shrouded in mystery. Audiences in 1962 never watched the apparent scene of reconciliation between Quentin and his father.[59] By some unrevealed process, off camera, father and son bond together and return to the dorm arm and arm, displaying their newly awakened affection. Quentin now introduces the once banished fathers—the anxious moment he sought to avoid—and discovers that his girlfriend's father, "Mr. Stone," is really "Mr. Stalakowalski" (the construction of ethnic names here seems a bit overdetermined), who speaks with a heavy—it turns out to be Polish—accent as well. So the fathers meet, speak in Polish (tellingly, not in Yiddish), and remain at ease with their unburdened ethnicity. Their children exchange banalities (Quentin: the name "never bothered you at all, huh? / Felicia: Only the spelling"), but remain utterly silent about the truth of *their* shared but repressed shame. Everyone joins in a good episode-closing laugh, whose last lines are voiced by Mrs. G—again, *inserted* as a revision to the original script, in Berg's own hand: "America I love you. If I didn't hear an accent every day I'd think I was in a foreign country."[60]

We are not, at least not in 1962, allowed to overhear on television the intimate words or witness the lifting of the mask of shame separating Quentin from his father; nor are we allowed to know more of Berg's own character's "ethnic" origins (What *was* "Green" changed from?). Such intimacy would have been uncivil, perhaps taboo, given the historical moment in American culture, before the "ethnic revival" of the mid-1970s. (Ironically, Berg's celebration of ethnicity also looks forward to that revival a decade later.) By what liberating agency could the repression of dangerous subjects be lifted? Eventually, the emergence of stand-up comedy would generate a dislodging humor of subversive wit and social criticism *unavailable* in the ethnic family sitcom. *The Goldbergs*, we need to remember, faded from television at the threshold of Lenny Bruce, Shelly Berman, the Two Thousand Year-old Man, Mickey Katz, the young Jackie Mason, and the young Philip Roth. What was taboo, unutterable on *The Goldbergs* was grist for the stand-up comic. The show's often genial view of ethnic experience, its breezy assumption that the new Jewish middle class could be "tolerated" through a gift of gefilte fish, was overturned by the relentless, antic anarchic style of stand-up. By the early sixties, if not sooner, the night club stage, not the television screen, became the site for contested readings of the culture, the creative space where the emancipatory potential of popular culture could be enacted for—and by—an audience resisting, intolerant of, not only the official culture, but the saccharine middle-class vision of America symbolized by *The Goldbergs*.

In an interview in 1988, Philip Roth speaks of the now notorious response to his early stories (especially "Defender of the Faith" and "Eli, the Fanatic," which appeared almost fifty years ago), and how "the Jewish generation that didn't go for me is by now less influential, and the rest are no longer ashamed, if they ever were, of how Jews behave in my fiction. Because it *was* shame—theirs—that had a lot to do with that conflict." Roth's tough, absolutely correct observation highlights the nervous, self-conscious Jewish American world of the 1950s, a landscape of popular culture where the figure of Gertrude Berg as "Molly" and the Goldbergs's family had, for a time, a remarkably influential place. It may be, as television critics argue, that the sitcom is essentially a domesticating, reassuring medium, a cultural form that is careful not to cross boundaries or make trouble. It took another mode of popular culture for people to find an expressive outlet for nostalgia, for loss, for rage, and perhaps even for mourning. *The Goldbergs*, both on radio and on television, responded to its audience's particular historical needs, but a later generation would eventually find a more helpful and enabling outlet in the Yiddish-soaked patter of the lonely stand-up comic, a figure with whom they could join in the therapeutic process, in Roth's brilliant phrase, of "joking away its shame."[61]

7

THE "JEWISH OPERA"

Saul Bellow and Other Jewish Sons

The next conduct will have to come from the heart, from attachment to life despite the worst it has shown us, and it has shown us just about everything.[1]

—Saul Bellow, "The Trip to Galena"

I have known Bellow for more than half a century . . . and feel I understand the springs of his talent—which have to do with his innate sense of the primitive sources of life.[2]

—Alfred Kazin

From civility I now have some pain in my belly,' " laments Moses Herzog, trying on pants.[3] Saul Bellow's comic intellectual-schlemiel-hero, the voluble talker from the prize-winning novel *Herzog* (1964), voices perhaps *the* cosmic complaint that, for over fifty years, has occupied Bellow's various literary alter egos. What does it mean for Herzog to speak of a "pain from civility"? Why should "civility" induce such discomfort in everyday life? For Bellow, at least, the answers are complex, for the costs of "achieving" civilized behavior—as expressed by manners, "higher" education, belief systems (as proposed by theoreticians of various orientations, spiritual and political), and tempered, psychological "adjustment" to the overwhelming "distractedness" (another of Bellow's key words) of our world—are measured in repression and denial. Civility masks and obscures what Bellow often terms our individual "souls," or "essence"—"the characteristic signature of a person." Civility inhibits and thwarts our necessary quest for "unearth[ing] buried essences" that the clutter and growth of the modern world shroud, often in the name of material and technological progress.[4] Above all, civility pains because as we embrace—or conform to—its exacting demands, or strive to attain its surface appearance, we unwittingly labor against what, at the very end of *Seize the Day* (1956), Bellow famously calls "the consummation of [our] heart's ultimate need":[5] the need to connect, at the level of raw, unmediated *feelings*, with the deeper currents of our being, the enabling consciousness of our "essence" as feeling human beings who are linked to others through bonds of human solidarity and identification.

What does all this talk of "essences" and "distraction," of civility and manners have to do with the narrative of that sad sack Tommy Wilhelm, his stern, aloof father, and the bizarre philosopher-speculator Dr. Tamkin? The novel itself—by critical consensus Bellow's most brilliantly crafted, and in many ways his most representative work[6]—invites this kind of speculation. For *Seize the Day* dramatizes contrasting styles of behavior, moral and economic, as it explores the charged psychological relationship between fathers and sons. In fact, one of the pressing issues *between* Dr. Adler and Tommy involves the matter of civility, of proper personal deportment.

Dr. Adler, a "master of social behavior" in Bellow's description, is repelled by the son's often manic gesturings, Tommy's inability to control himself: "Dr. Adler felt that his son was indulging himself too much in his emotions." [7] Tommy's "problem," according to his socially self-conscious father, in other words, is that he "feels" too much; for Bellow, by contrast, Tommy's ability to feel is the prerequisite for personal freedom, the basis of his "bid for liberty"[8] —not just from his unfeeling father, but from a constraining (Protestant) business ethnic that measures the self only by the outward signs of material success: money and style. In this respect, *Seize the Day* locates itself as a work of substantial social criticism (ca. 1956) in commodity-obsessed America, limned by the teeming world of Broadway, along Manhattan's Upper West Side. As the novel follows Tommy's ordeal of material defeat and fatherly rejection, Bellow wishes us to understand that, at a deeper level of consciousness, Tommy is redeemed through his release of "uncivilized" emotion: Tommy's heartfelt tears at the end signal his moral victory over the rigid structures of affective restraint. His rush of feelings enables him to open a channel to the soul, the necessary passage to "overflowing comprehension"[9]—the moral activity that, in Bellow's imagination, makes us human.

In light of what might be called the sphere of manners, emotions, and civility in *Seize the Day*, I want to provide a fuller context for understanding the core themes explored in Bellow's great short novel. Why, I want to ask, does Dr. Adler feel so disgusted by Tommy's bad manners? What is the deeper genealogy of this particular father-son divide itself? Why does Bellow elevate emotion to a kind of cultural-expressive ideal? The answer to these (and other) questions requires placing *Seize the Day* within the social-psychological core of affects associated with immigrant Jewish American experience, as outlined in previous chapters.

Seize the Day makes passing reference to aspects of Jewish American life;[10] at one point, Tommy reflects that his father considers him the "wrong kind of Jew";[11] Mr. Rappaport alludes to the Day of Atonement while waiting with Tommy for the results of the fluctuating commodities market; and Dr. Tamkin in his zany *luftmensch* office looms as a familiar figure out of Yiddish folklore.[12] The novel's further relation to Jewish American culture may be distilled, first, from Bellow's own scattered but revealing pronouncements (along with one key story, "The Old System" [1967]) about his own relation to the immigrant Jewish experience, and second, by the cultural anxieties about civility and manners that in many ways shaped the immigrants' experience itself. From this perspective, *Seize the Day* emerges as a reverse immigrant novel, where the canonical narrative of striving, new world sons, embarrassed by the "barbaric" ways of their "greenhorn," old world fathers is inverted: in *Seize the Day*, old Dr. Adler represents new world (economic) arrival and its intrafamilial costs, while in his clownish behavior Tommy reverts back to what Bellow calls the "old system" of Jewish (sometimes styled "Russian" or "East European") affections, "a real, genuine old Jewish type" that, as a character in *Herzog* observes, "digs the emotions."[13]

The vexed encounter between the "old Jewish type" and an imagined genteel America proved both exhilarating and bewildering, especially for the new world voyagers. By the early twentieth century, cities—especially New York—were overflowing with immigrants, mainly from Eastern Europe and the Russian Pale of Settlement. Bellow's own family arrived in

Montreal during this huge wave of migration (he was born in Canada in 1915) and eventually settled in Chicago. From the beginning, the shock of immigrant arrival stunned and vexed guardians of the dominant culture. Debate swirled among defenders and detractors of these "new" Americans. As we have seen, Henry James worried at the turn of the century about the indelible impact the coarse tones of urban voices would have on the future of American speech. E. A. Ross, in his nativist attack *The Old World in the New* (1914), wrote specifically of "the Jewish invader": "What is disliked in the Jews," Ross admitted, without apology, "is not their religion but certain ways and manners." As a result of a "tribal spirit intensified by social isolation" in Europe, "they use their Old-World *shove* and wile and lie in a society like ours. . . . they rapidly *push up* into a position of prosperous parasitism, leaving scorn and curses in their wake" (emphasis added).[14]

Examples of nativist–antisemitic rant similar to Ross's—claiming that the Jews shoved and pushed their way into a once closed and orderly America—were pervasive during the early years of the twentieth century. Nightmares that social and economic and sexual boundaries would be blurred and transgressed, fears of the American "stock" tainted by foreign blood, and above all concern over the impact of perceived (or imagined) immigrant incivility rupturing through the polite surface of what sociologist John Murray Cuddihy terms "the Protestant etiquette"—all these cultural anxieties surfaced in the wake of early twentieth-century shocks to the national body politic.[15] With respect to Saul Bellow—and with him, the generation of immigrant sons, many of whom became important public intellectuals and academics—his experience, and thus memory, of nativist scorn proved crucial in shaping his literary imagination. As noted in the introduction, the sociological term for this creative, if stressful, encounter between the immigrant psyche and the "host" culture is Americanization, the complex dynamic of personal and collective negotiation—rejection, appropriation, refashioning—that accompanies the cultural rituals of new world adjustment. It is the attendant strain and—especially in Bellow—the comedy of Americanization that forms the core subject of much Jewish American creative expression. Set within and against this familiar canvas of immigrant fathers and intellectual sons, of provincial neighborhoods and the wider world, of "civilized" New World language and uncivil "Jewish" manners and emotion, *Seize the Day* now appears to be a book that effectively plays with, and indeed overturns, the traditions of immigrant narrative that Bellow inherited.

In numerous interviews, essays, and some of his fiction (notably in marginality and detachment. Above all, Howe confesses, "*He has lost the sense of continuity which was such sustenance to his forefathers*" (emphasis in the original).[30] The primal scene depicting this filial rupture usually occurs in public, in the "Americanizing" spheres of the classroom and the street. As Howe relates these primordial traumas, it is the public display of the private, familiar, *heimisch,* heartfelt Yiddish—or a heavily Yiddish-inflected accent—that signals the son's abject alienation from the world of the Bronx fathers. In one traumatic scene (tellingly, Howe shifts into the first person to relate these still raw experiences), the young Irving Howe utters the Yiddish word for "fork"—*goopel*—in an imagined alert response to his kindergarten teacher's query to name that utensil (it was, after all, the first day of class, and Irving sought to impress his teacher with his knowledge of the world). His classmates laugh at his lapse (Yiddish-speaking children, they all know the difference between "fork" and "goopel"). Riven with shame, Howe vows never to speak Yiddish again.[31]

A more momentous occasion of rupture occurs when Irving cringes at being summoned home for dinner by his old world shopkeeper father. Listen to the lost, young Jewish intellectual recount the trauma:

> When I was a few years older, about eight or nine, my parents had a grocery store in an "Americanized" Jewish neighborhood, the West Bronx. I used to play in an abandoned lot about a block away from the store, and when I'd neglect to come home at supper time, my father would come to call for me. He would shout my name from afar, giving it a Yiddish twist: "Oivee!" I would always feel a sense of shame at hearing my name so mutilated in the presence of amused onlookers, and though I would come home—supper was always supper!—I would always run ahead of my father as if to emphasize the existence of a certain distance between us.[32]

This "primal" scene of shame and alienation leads to the heart of the generational abyss that forms the affective core of Jewish American (and perhaps all ethnic/immigrant) fiction, at least in the early twentieth century. Howe's father "squawks" (to recall Bellow's startling term characterizing the abrasive immigrant tone) the name of the son before the "amused" eyes of the more "Americanized"—that is, *civilized*—world of the West Bronx. The son would like to disappear ("The aim of shame," to recall psychoanalyst Léon Wurmser once again, "is invisibility"),[33] but all he can do is "run ahead," making a helpless gesture toward separation, conscious of the filial divide, a chasm marked by the barbaric "gabblings" of "East" (as opposed to "West"?) Bronx voice and inflection. Of course only in retrospect does the son recognize the deeper meanings of filial distancing; only later can he name it as a symbolic precursor to the collective "angst" of his generation—"a feeling," Howe relates, "that can be described as one of total loneliness, of complete rootlessness."[34]

As we have observed, scenes of filial shame pervade Jewish American expression in the first half of the twentieth century. It was a characteristic feature in early cinema, in Edward Sloman's *His People,* in Anzia Yezierska's stories of immigrant life, and in Henry Roth's *Call It Sleep,* where the terrifying chasm separating fathers and sons shapes the entire novel. Like Roth, the evocative power of immigrant speech and the redemptive potential of the city turned out to be one of Bellow's major subjects. Perhaps the most poignant evocation of these core themes in Jewish American literature is Isaac Rosenfeld's *Passage from Home* (1946), a neglected but richly suggestive work that also helps clarify some of the thematic and interpretive issues related to *Seize the Day.* Rosenfeld was among Bellow's most cherished friends growing up in Chicago, and in some respects he was a version of Tommy Wilhelm, had Tommy studied philosophy instead of trying his luck in Hollywood. (Rosenfeld died still a young man of thirty-eight in the year that *Seize the Day* was published.) In a personal reflection Bellow remarks that Rosenfeld "was a marvelous clown" who "preferred to have things about him in a mess"[35]—as a personal protest against the conventions of middle-class cleanliness.

Without offering an extended analysis of *Passage from Home,* let me mention that the novel concerns the journey of a fastidious and sensitive young man, Bernard, into a new zone of sensibility that is at odds with the traditional Jewish worlds of his father and grandfather. My interest in the figure of Bernard concerns his attitude toward his "fathers," and the way he fashions himself against their ways of being. Above all, I am curious about how and why—Bernard is repulsed by the manners (table and personal) of his immigrant grandfather. In a crucial passage Bernard observes how, while in the public street, the patriarch devours his food: "I felt rather disgusted as I saw him tear out a deep, doughy chunk [of "bread smeared with chicken fat"], avoiding the crust, chewing with his mouth open and rolling the bread over his gums. He smeared his fingers on his beard, and wiped his hands on his jacket before drawing out a crusty handkerchief with which he dabbed at his lips."[36] Like an anthropologist observing the table manners of a primitive tribe (but without the "objectivity"—he's too close to the subject), Bernard, as (grand)son, cannot tolerate the "barbarous" eating styles of the father(s), despite the pull, the "ecstatic" potential of orthodoxy represented by the spiritual fire of the pious older generation. He can't tolerate this display of raw desire because he himself, as son, has become (or yearns to be) "civilized," identified with

Dr. Adler remains adamantly blocked, either to the display of feeling or to the recollection of family history. Wilhelm is blocked as well, his roiling emotions pent up, seeking release ("He hadn't been able to get rid of his energy").[48] In its movement and structure, *Seize the Day* works toward the release of all that Tommy has repressed, which include fragments of poetry once deeply felt, the true meaning of his relationship with his father, and above all his need to connect, to be moved by, and to move, other people. "Dad," Tommy thinks to himself, in a crucial moment of recognition, "I couldn't affect one way or another."[49] It's a brilliant flash of insight, revealing, however briefly, his father's *affect*-less style and his own efforts (born of love) to adjust Dr. Adler's habitual aloofness.

The problem is that, for the father, Tommy *embodies* all that Dr. Adler seeks to repress, to deny in himself. When he observes, clinician that he always is, his son's manic behavior, he is disgusted, repelled by Tommy's bad manners. The residue of grime that Tommy's dirty fingers leave on the white eggshell at breakfast confirms Dr. Adler in his rejection. He cannot tolerate—neither stomach nor swallow—how Tommy lives (in sublime filth, using the red plastic seals of cigarette packs as makeshift dental floss, randomly tossing garbage into the back seat of his car); he cannot understand Tommy's chronic fidgeting ("Why the devil can't he stand still when we're talking? He's either hoisting his pants up and down by the pockets or jittering his feet. A regular mountain of tics he's getting to be," Dr. Adler thinks to himself, observing Tommy's "antics"); most tellingly, Dr. Adler cannot bear Tommy's embarrassing habit of gesticulating.[50]

In perhaps the key scene between father and son, Tommy starts to strangle himself, in order to dramatize for his aloof, *affect*-less father his current feelings of helplessness and despair (really, to demonstrate what his wife, who refuses to grant him a divorce, is doing to him):

> Wilhelm took hold of his broad throat with brown-stained fingers and bitten nails and began to choke himself.
> "What are you doing?" cried the old man.
> "I'm showing you what she does to me."
> "Stop that—stop it!" the old man said and tapped the table commandingly.

During the same exchange, dumbfounded by his father's incapacity to listen to his plight, Tommy "struggle[s] for breath and frown[s] in his father's face":

> "I don't understand your problems," said the old man. "I never had any of them."

By now Wilhelm had host his head and he *waved his hands* and said over and over, "Oh, Dad, don't give me that stuff, don't give me that. Please don't give me that sort of thing."

"It's true," said the father. "I come from a different world. Your mother and I led an entirely different life."

"Oh, how can you compare Mother," Wilhelm said. "Mother was a help to you. Did she harm you, ever?"

"*There's no need to carry on like an opera,*" Wilky . . . this is only your side of things."[51]

Tommy, we might say, speaks from the heart in this exchange. His histrionic behavior is expressive of the old system, the old Jewish mode of "operatic" feeling.[52] In demanding that the son tone down his "silly" behavior, to act with restraint, the father betrays his own assimilative anxieties, exposing the roots of his disgust toward his "uncivilized" son.

The commandment against public display is laced with ironies, in light of the exchange at breakfast with Mr. Perls. Discussing family history, Dr. Adler asserts that *he* represents "tradition": "I uphold tradition," he explains to those who ask, in the context of Tommy's change of name from Adler to Wilhelm; "He's for the new."[53] But at the level of affective style and the religion of the heart, it is just the opposite. Tommy Wilhelm represents the grand traditions of the Jewish opera *against* which his father labors to repress. Indeed, he calls his son by the archaic "Wilky" in order to "tone down" Tommy's operatic gestures, which shame the father into memory. Why else does Dr. Adler resist discussing family history (especially his married life)? Because Tommy conjures, by his extravagant behavior, the living presence of his mother: "From his mother he had gotten sensitive feelings, a soft heart, a brooding nature, a tendency to be confused under pressure."[54] In short, Tommy's maternal inheritance dislodges the repressed, emotional world of the past, both his own family's and the larger Jewish past of immigrant experience—the buried realm of the primordial. In this respect, Tommy's "truest" name may indeed be "Velvel," his deeper identity signaled by the *mamaloshen* (mother-tongue) Yiddish, uttered by the grandfather(s).

Thus Tommy still remembers, as Bellow sketches his hero's spiritual biography, how his mother "tried to stop me, and we carried on and yelled and pleaded" (an intimation of Adler family opera?) when he decided to start out in the thirties by making a new beginning in Hollywood. For all the wonderfully comic dimension of the scenes with the "talent" scout Maurice Venice, we should note that he at least senses *some* enabling potential about Wilhelm, a possibility of self that Bellow, I believe, wants us to recognize as well: "Let yourself go. . . . Don't be afraid to make faces and be emotional. Shoot the works. . . . You don't behave the same way as the average." The advice touches the pent-up, throttled source of Tommy's deepest desires: "to be freed from the anxious and narrow life of the average."[55] Acting thus becomes an outlet for his substantial reservoirs of affect, letting go—the "gesture" (Bellow's key word; gestures/gesturing lead us to the soul) of becoming "Tommy Wilhelm"—as the heart's ultimate need, in contrast to his father's labor of self-mastery, his effort at social control. Venice's injunctions thus implicitly oppose the worried commandments of the father; and Tommy, in search of personal validation unavailable at home, grasps at the talent scout's ego-nourishing promise, however insubstantial, of Hollywood.

Through his inheritance of his mother's emotionally receptive line, Tommy embodies the "old system" of immigrant Jewish opera; and this genealogy of the heart gives him access to realms of feeling, or the *potential* of feeling proscribed by the implicitly WASP-identified world of reserved Dr. Adler. Tommy's "channels" of emotion are blocked, in part by the father's authority, in part by the overbearing urban scene of New York City in the 1950s, in part by the cult of success against which Tommy's behavior looms as an implicit critique.[56] In subtle ways, then, Tommy's "pathology" (if we can term his behavior pathological) comments on the "Americanizing" process itself; Dr. Adler, and rapacious Mr. Rappaport are its materialist, money-craving symbols.

Can we say, with some recent psychoanalytic theorists, that Tommy's symptoms reveal "the parents' repressed doubts about their own ideals and ambitions"?[57] Does Tommy's unconscious quest for affective bonding with all of humanity—the axial lines of democratic solidarity tugging at him in the subway—expose the fathers' guilty embrace of the American mania for success? (In other moments of insight, Tommy sees through the materialist cult, recognizing the deformations wrought by the money culture.) At some level, Tommy's "symptoms" provide an indirect critique, both of the "heartless" commodity-obsessed 1950s and of Americanization itself, a culturally attenuating process that absorbs all vibrant traces of ethnic/immigrant residues in the ordeal of achieving WASP "civility and manners." The cautionary tale of such a denaturing procedure is, of course, Dr. Adler himself, whom Bellow tellingly describes as "a rather bland old man." Dr. Adler is continuously characterized in the verbal exchanges with Tommy as not "a father"—the implication being that "America" has drained him of any and all paternal attributes: "The fathers were no fathers."[58]

On the matter of psychoanalysis itself, and of Freudian modes of therapy in general, Bellow has been outspoken, for the most part critical.[59] In this respect, the character of Dr. Tamkin represents Bellow's wicked satire on the obsession with therapeutic styles (emerging as very popular, especially among angst-ridden [Jewish] intellectuals in the 1950s). Most critics tend to view Tamkin as a figure out of Yiddish folklore, a flighty character whose office is "in his socks" (the reference is to Bernard Malamud's great story, "The Magic Barrel"); but whatever he is, he succeeds as a self-styled therapist of the sick 1950s Jewish soul, offering succor to Tommy, in desperate need of attention and affection ("This was what he craved, that someone should care about him, wish him well. Kindness, mercy, he wanted.").[60]

Tamkin may not provide Jewish mercy *(rachmones)*, but he does help Tommy in his journey toward the soul by distracting him from the troubling business with his father and by relieving the constant pressure building inside Tommy through the therapy of laughter. Above all, Tamkin's words—and the quack therapist is one of Bellow's great talkers—"caught Wilhelm's heart"; his words tug at Tommy where it counts, enabling him to reconnect, notably, with fragments of poems that continue to resonate in his heart. Through Tamkin's therapeutic office Tommy begins to comprehend what Bellow calls "the peculiar burden"[61] of his existence, to carry a heavy load of feeling (Tamkin?), for himself—Tommy learns to take pity on himself rather than wallow in self-hatred (the self-castigating, father-imposed "Wilky" aspect of the self)—and for mankind in general.

This redemptive realm of the soul always remains active for Bellow, but it tends to be obscured by the overgrown thickets of civility, by the modern cult of emotional aloofness (recall Dr. Braun's late-day meditations). "There were depths in Wilhelm," "some remote element in his thoughts," Bellow informs us, in what is perhaps the most important passage in *Seize the Day,* where he receives the intimation "that the business of life, the real business—to carry his peculiar burden, to feel shame and impotence, to taste these quelled tears—the only important business, the highest business was being done." Dr. Tamkin points Tommy toward this realm of consciousness by helping banish the figure of the father: "The sight of Dr. Tamkin brought his quarrel with his father to a close. He found himself flowing into another channel." Tamkin, who speaks "a kind of truth," opens a necessary channel to the soul; in the case of Tommy Wilhelm, the channel opens out into general, Whitmanesque "involuntary feelings" for the crowds of Manhattan.[62] On this, his "day of reckoning" (or is it his true Day of Atonement?), Tommy allows the cumulative emotional blockage to break through, to let go; his blockage flows into breakthrough as he mourns for himself, crying "with all his heart."[63]

Much has been written about the closing epiphany of *Seize the Day,*
with some critics arguing for its brilliant aptness (in light of the metaphoric resonances in the pattern of water imagery, the movement toward
catharsis, etc.) while others finding Tommy's effusive release ambiguous,
and thus the novel's final imaging of Tommy problematic. Rather than
enter that debate, let me suggest that the famous scene of mourning and
release resembles, in light of the genealogy of manners and emotions I
have outlined, an uncanny scene of Jewish "opera." For it turns out that
unhinged, unalloyed (Jewish) feeling provides, in Bellow's metaphysics, a
pure channel leading to the soul.

Beyond the forces of repression symbolized by the dominant culture,
no longer heeding the father's self-conscious injunction against emotion
(Dr. Adler speaks on behalf of that culture), Tommy allows his feelings to
flow, uncontained:

> Standing a little apart, Wilhelm began to cry. He cried at first softly and
> from sentiment, but soon from deeper feeling. He sobbed loudly and his
> face grew distorted and hot, and the tears stung his skin. . . . Soon he was
> past words, past reason, coherence. He could not stop. The source of all
> tears had suddenly sprung open within him, black, deep, and hot, and
> they were pouring out and convulsed his body, bending his stubborn
> head, bowing his shoulders, twisting his face, crippling the very hands
> with which he held the handkerchief.[64]

To my own (Jewish) ears, I hear operatic notes sounding, indeed swelling
through this description. Tommy sobs "loudly," his face registers the physical and spiritual extremes of released emotion: "grew distorted," his "con-
vulsed" body, his "crippled" hands no longer under rational control. One
can perhaps hear as well old Dr. Adler rebuking the son to tone down his
behavior—"There's no need [Wilky] to carry on like an opera." Bellow,
however, welcomes Tommy's convulsions, a type of those "European Ju-
daic, operatic *fist-clenchings.* Tears," to recall the perspective of Tommy's
fictional cousin, Isaac Braun.[65]

In an even more compelling vision, Bellow would claim that Tommy's
tears—his cosmic confusion—like Herzog's, are "barbarous." Writing twenty
years ago in "The Civilized Barbarian Reader," Bellow spoke of Herzog's
need to "return . . . to some primal point of balance," a zone of elemental
connectedness sought after the failure of all systems of belief, of education,
of civilization to help him cope with the confusions of the modern world.
"Herzog's confusion is barbarous," Bellow explained. "Well, what else can
it be?" "In the greatest confusion," Bellow continues, in something of a
moral-aesthetic manifesto,

there is still an open channel to the soul. It may be difficult to find because by midlife is it overgrown, and some of the wildest thickets that surround it grow out of what we call our education. But the channel is always there, and it is our business to keep it open, to have access to the deepest part of ourselves—to that part of us which is conscious of a higher consciousness, by means of which we make final judgments, and put everything together.[66]

At the end of *Seize the Day,* Tommy Wilhelm gains long-deferred access to the deepest registers of the self. His "barbarous confusion" in the noisy Babel of the choking, smoke-filled city proves ultimately to be a means of spiritual redemption, for his (unconscious?) habit of emotion helps him break through the empty, impotent (recall the last image of the father, limp in the lower depths of the Gloriana hotel steam baths) civility that his *new world* father employs in defense against dangerous emotion itself. Tommy and his nervous antics may resemble those of a textbook neurotic; he may be the pathetic schlemiel we would all prefer not to recognize in the mirror. But in the end, Tommy's operatic mode exposes the blandness, the dis-ease of pork-pale civility; his neuroses critique indeed challenge the cult of 1950s success.

In the end, Tommy's "barbarous confusion," a symptomatic response to the American world at mid-century, links him implicitly to the immigrant past of the emotional Jewish fathers (and mothers), his "gesture"/ gesticulations expressive of a necessary process of becoming. "Having love," Irving Howe observed years after his youthful confession of alienation, of Sholem Aleichem's Old World shtetl, "they had no need for politeness."[67] Love versus politeness; enabling emotions versus artificial manners; redemptive barbarism versus repressive civility. In *Seize the Day,* Tommy recuperates the old (world) system of the heart. In the process he recovers, in Bellow's ultimate vision of personal success, indeed of personal redemption, a "primal point of balance."[68]

state, up front, that I share Howe's irritation with the often breezy senti-mentalizing of Jewish American experience. With its hazy, disabling mem-ory, nostalgia can dangerously obscure the hurts of history, salving the pain of immigrant life, tempering its rawness, softening the rough edges of acculturation.[5]

In the same essay-reflection, wickedly titled "Immigrant Chic," Howe continued his relentless "turn to ethnicity"-bashing with the following cri de coeur, a lament that voices an implicit challenge to students of Jewish American popular culture, hopelessly nostalgic for their parents' nostalgia:

> For I don't want the immigrant-Jewish milieu—it's my life you under-stand—to become "material" for the chic museum displays and cozy Yinglish musicals. I don't want the world of my youth to be worked over (I almost said pawed) by sweet-tempered but ignorant filmmakers. I don't want the lost hopes and surviving pains, the memories that still chafe, to become occasions, or pretexts, for philistine observances among affluent Jews.[6]

One understands Howe's dismay at the burgeoning scene of (re)-turns to ethnicity ten years after *World of Our Fathers* (a bestseller, that, ironically, bestowed on Howe wealth and fame and countless invitations to address the philistines). Yet I also detect the middle-class, generational bias at the heart of the matter. Where were the "cozy Yinglish musicals" of 1986? Howe, I believe, is stewing about the past rather than the present here, perhaps conjuring the Broadway season of 1951, when two Yinglish musi-cal reviews, *Bagels and Yox* and Mickey Katz's *Borscht Capades*, opened within a week of each other in September. Or perhaps Howe is still think-ing (really wincing) about the remarkable success—twenty-two years earlier—of *Fiddler on the Roof*, a show he detested.

In a now famous *Commentary* review of *Fiddler*, discussed briefly in Chapter 4 above, Howe spoke in bitter, unforgiving tones of "a tasteless jumble of styles: some in good, others in bad, and therefore the whole in no taste. The 'book' provided by Joseph Stein is closer in tone and quality to Harry Golden (sometimes Gertrude Berg) than to Sholem Aleichem, and the production, despite its expensiveness of surface, reflects the spiri-tual anemia of Broadway and of the middle-class Jewish world which by now seems firmly linked to Broadway."[7]

Fiddler proved a demeaning spectacle to the Yiddishist Howe (in his early forties) in the fall of 1964; according to Howe, the musical was expressive of a deep-seated "guilt" on the part of its affluent *alrightnik* audience:

guilt because they have lost touch with the past from which they derive . . . and . . . compound[ed] . . . by indulging themselves in an
unearned nostalgia. The less, for example, they know about East European Jewish life or even the immigrant experience in America, the more
inclined they seem to celebrate it. As their own sense of Jewishness
increasingly becomes fragile, more and more they feel—I would say,
absurdly—grateful for any public recognition of Jewishness. A politician
drops a Yiddish phrase, and they roar with delight. A TV comic slips in a
Yiddish vulgarism, and they regard this as a communal triumph.

Above all, the saccharine sentimentality of *Fiddler on the Roof* signaled,
in the key phrase from Howe's attack, "a surrender of dignity." Watching
the brilliant Zero Mostel's "gargling cantillation[s]"—"an equivalent in
sound," Howe brutally asserted, "to our deepest fantasies gratified"—
Howe witnessed the ultimate degradation of Jewish experience: he read,
sadly, the fate of *his* world of (Yiddish) fathers in the schmaltzy middlebrow construction of the shtetl on Broadway.[8]

Now I don't propose either to defend the (a)historical imagination of
Fiddler on the Roof or mindlessly appropriate the pleasures of "unearned
nostalgia"; nor do I wish to pile on by joining the culture-bashing of the
implied middlebrow audience of *Fiddler,* and by further implication,
Gertrude Berg, Mickey Katz and Milton Berle (Howe associates Berg directly with the middle class, and is perhaps thinking of Berle among the
group of vulgar comics). After all, Howe is talking about *my* family in
1964, and (at some level) about me a generation later. I want, instead, to
speculate about the complex cultural transactions between these figures
and their various audiences. Why was *The Goldbergs* continually popular
on radio and television from 1929 to 1955? The show was so popular, in
fact, that Berg wrote and starred in *Me and Molly* for the 1948 Broadway
season. Indeed, after its strong Broadway run, *The Goldbergs* moved the
next year to television, with virtually the same core cast. Why *did* Berle
capture the (Jewish) imagination in the Bronx, and elsewhere? Why did
the neighbors, as my Aunts Annie, Bebe, and Tiny vividly recall, bring
down folding chairs to the Webers' apartment to watch Uncle Miltie after
my father—big spender that he was—bought the very first TV to 3031
Holland Avenue in the late forties? Why were Mickey Katz's parodies of
"Home on the Range," ("Haim afn Range"), or "The Ballad of Davy
Crockett" ("Duvid Crockett"), or "The Cry of the Wild Goose" ("Geshray
of devilde Kotchke"), filled with Yiddish and Yinglish send-ups, among
the bestselling records of the early fifties? And why am *I,* a sometime

scholar of early American literature and culture, so interested in these figures, so moved by these matters?

Before turning to the examples of Berg, Berle, and Katz, let me return, briefly, to my own story. I would describe myself as, for the most part, utterly representative of my generation of baby boomers who came of age in the provincial middle-class Jewish world of New York City in the fifties and sixties. Invoking the figure of Doctorow's radical son, Daniel, as a model of the self, I want to emphasize how a number of key histories that mark Jewish American life *flow* and indeed continue to pulsate through me. I suppose I would claim, perhaps even take a certain pride in, what I would call a series of hybrid, disjunctive selves: although I identify with the Bronx as the "old neighborhood," I grew up in the northernmost reaches of Manhattan, among the working-class Irish of Inwood. My mother—a true Yiddishist in her own right, in contrast to my father—was born in Cleveland, where Mickey Katz was raised (in the 1920s, his sister Jeanne was my mother's counselor at Camp Alliance,[9] one among many striking coincidences of this narrative). My world is thus split—regionally and culturally and psychologically—between brash Bronx Jews and quieter *greeners* from Cleveland who arrived in New York City during World War II (my mother settled into the small apartment at 165 Seaman Avenue with my grandmother in the mid-forties, summoned by her brother who had already established his career as a famous flutist in New York).

More tellingly, I was lucky enough to leave Inwood during the enervating city summers for the safe, shtetl-like existence of Cortlandt Colony in Mohegan Lake, a summer bungalow community with a left-leaning atmosphere, a *heimisch* world where Yiddish filled the air at night, and where some families sent their kids to Camp Kinderland, the legendary summer camp for Red Diaper babies. In 1963, two years before I myself saw Tevye on Broadway (with Luther Adler and not, alas, Zero Mostel as the star), I spent a month at Kinderland. The night before I left, I went to hear the Weavers in their extraordinary reunion concert at Mohegan Colony (the concert, I eventually learned, was their first since they had been blacklisted in the fifties.). At Kinderland, I participated in the Labor Olympics (the ILGWU was my team; I recall vividly writing our own union fight songs), signed time capsules ("No More Hiroshimas"—a mantra I later recognized in a photo of a poster on the wall of the SDS office in New York), and listened attentively to evening bunk discussions ("Should Red China be admitted into the UN?").[10] At twelve, all I wanted was to play baseball (and *be* Mickey Mantle), but in retrospect I realize how formative my summer at Kinderland, filled with Yiddishkayt and politics (as Sidney Lumet's film adaptation of Doctorow's *Book of Daniel* warmly portrays), proved for my adult cultural and political identity. As for Cortlandt Colony, only much later did I realize how profoundly it, too, shaped my cultural outlook. (I was startled to discover, many years later, that our weird "Mrs. Landau," a tiny old lady with a long grey pony tail who didn't own a car and thus hiked, with her towering hiking stick, into town for supplies, was the widow of the famous Yiddish poet Zisha Landau.)

Of course my parents had *no* idea about the urgent political atmosphere of Kinderland or the traditions of secular Jewish radicalism that inspired its daily activities (in the summer of 1963, college-age counselors would share their experience of the Freedom Rides); my father, let me emphasize, was no Irving Howe—or Jules Dassin or Herbert Gutman, two of the many distinguished Kinderland alumni. After working at the Daitch dairy, he went into the hotel business, first in Brooklyn (running a sad roominghouse called Nostrand Studios—an exhausting commute from Upper Manhattan) and then, by the early fifties, as a hotel manager in midtown Manhattan, in a ramshackle transient hotel in perhaps the fanciest area of the city, around the corner from Delmonico's. I don't know if he really liked his life running the Hotel Nassau on East 59th street; I can say, however, that he loved Perry Como's crooning, Milton Berle's zany cross-dressing, Buddy Hackett's "blue" comic style, and Rickie Layne and his Yiddish-speaking dummy Velvel's routine—this last performer presenting another obscure vaudeville act that we would watch together when they appeared, with some regularity, on the *Ed Sullivan Show* through the early sixties. (It turns out that "Rickie Layne and Velvel" was a regular act in the Yiddish reviews in 1951, another nice coincidence to this personal case study.)[11] And I can also say that my father was a brilliant comedian manqué, legendary for his "Bar Mitzvah Boy Speech" ("Today I am a fountain pen") and other routines. "Fun wouldn't begin until the Weber boys came in," my Aunt Tiny tells me, about my father and his brother, my zany Uncle Benny; together they were "loud and wild and crazy"—I have the testament of old movies to prove this. Silent movies from Cortlandt Colony show them, along with my athletic Uncle Leo, dolled up as bathing beauties (with suits lent by their kid sister, my spirited, Sinatra-crazy Aunt Bebe), rouged up, with large grapefruits stuffed in their bodices. Laughing and crying at their hysterical voguing (à la Milton Berle),[12] I now recognize in their unbuttoned, antic displays the weekend release from the weekly grind in the city (both my uncles were cabbies), the safely exhibited surge of comic energy, vulgar I suppose from a certain (intellectual) perspective, but for me it was the indelible image of the Bronx fathers who loved Berle, Sid Caesar, and the (slightly younger) generation of boy–man schlemiel Jewish comics from the 1950s, with whom they identified.[13]

Hyman Weber and author in the "foyer" of Apartment 2C, 165 Seaman Avenue, circa 1957. Note the Davy Crockett patch on the author's right thigh.

Thus my world at home was solidly middle class and utterly provincial; at the same time, I entered another existence during the long summers filled with the enveloping atmosphere (and aromas) of Yiddishkayt and the still felt legacies of the Peekskill riots, the blacklist, and so on. In addition, I absorbed my father's taste ("tasteless," in Howe's estimate) in popular culture, especially for a style of (Jewish) comedy played for audiences Howe ridiculed as empty of real (intellectual) culture, afflicted with guilt over a vanishing Yiddish world. This was "a new Yinglish popular culture," according to the young sociologist Herbert Gans, writing in 1953.[14] Researching this world, trying to write about it fifty years later, I feel, palpably, the various currents of post-war Jewish American history coursing through me. And I want to understand: Why do I vividly remember watching Rickie Layne and Velvel with my father on Sunday nights (I can still hear him laughing)? Why do I suddenly recall meeting Berle himself, with my father, at a Sunday doubleheader at Yankee Stadium, during Ted Williams's last year? (I still have Berle's autograph on a Yankee scorecard). What is the meaning of a Jewish son's nostalgia for his father's nostalgia?

As a partial answer to these large questions (which are both personal and cultural), let me turn, once again, to the career of Gertrude Berg. By the early fifties, Berg had come to represent *the* image of the Jewish matriarch in American culture. So fused, so blurred in the popular imagination was Berg and her alter ego Molly Goldberg that fans would address letters to her as Molly (she would even sign autographs as "Molly Goldberg"). In this respect, Berg as Molly performed, we might say, cultural work for her audience (both Jewish American and gentile), easing them through various cultural transitions, from the Depression through the 1950s. Brooks Atkinson, in his *New York Times* review of the modest Broadway play *Me and Molly*—written by Berg and co-starring her radio and later television husband "Jake" Philip Loeb—recognized in 1948 the distinctive quality, indeed the cultural office, performed by Berg's vision of (Jewish) American life: "Even those who tossed it away as trash were compelled to respect some quality in it. For basically it is authentic, not only of the Goldbergs in the Bronx, but of middle-class people all over America who are trying to bring up their children well and live respectable lives. 'Me and Molly' strikes an American average. . . . The real quality of 'Me and Molly' lies in its recognition of familiar things."[15]

Authentic, average, familiar: these terms resonate as the key, if now (for us) contested words in Atkinson's appreciation; for despite its ethnic particularity—depicting the moral and economic crisis afflicting a Jewish family in 1919, striving for middle-class respectability in a new apartment uptown, in the Bronx—*Me and Molly* is, more or less, a bland narrative of Americanization, with the matriarch heroine saving the day, and thus solving the chronic problem of her bitter husband's longing to run his own dress business, by anticipating the emergent need for ready-to-wear dresses sized proportionately, so that all women can find an appropriate dress according to her body shape, and so on. Looking forward, Molly longer defined the lives of most American Jews."[21] In this respect, Berg richly exemplifies Wenger's claim: as Molly, Berg became in effect a symbol of intimacy for her assimilating (Jewish) audiences; and as an (ethnic) artist searching for new material, even if she refrained—in striking contrast to the early radio scripts of *The Goldbergs*—from incorporating heavy Yinglish dialect on both Broadway and television,[22] she immersed herself in the "authentic," "vibrant" scene of the vanishing, (perhaps already vanished) world that had been the Lower East Side.

Yet from another perspective, Berg remained quite removed from an alternate style of popular Jewish American female entertainers. Molly was no "bawd" comedienne, no high voltage "red-hot mamma" in the mode, say, of Sophie Tucker or Fannie Brice, or their later "unkosher" incarnations (most famously the vulgar Belle Barth) who played the nightclub circuits of New York and Miami Beach.[23] In contrast to Berg, I want to explore a very different form of "intimacy" in Jewish American popular culture, a mode of (linguistic) intimacy represented by the phenomenon of Milton Berle—"Uncle Miltie"—and his relatively brief but by all accounts commanding influence on television in the early fifties.

Both *The Goldbergs* and *Texaco Star Theater* had large audiences in the Bronx and elsewhere; indeed, as the Berg Papers reveal and extant videos in the television archives testify, Berg in character as Molly was a frequent guest on the *Texaco Star Theater* (there was even talk of making *The Goldbergs* a regular segment of the Berle show, when in 1953 the initial variety–vaudeville style changed to a scripted, plot-centered format under the direction of Goodman Ace).[24] Berle mentions Berg in his autobiography; and a few years ago Berle (who passed away at age ninety-three in 2002) was reported to be working on a Broadway show titled *Milton and Me*—of course a direct allusion to both Berg's 1948 play and her own autobiography, *Molly and Me*.[25]

Thus Gertrude Berg and Milton Berle tend to be linked in early television history, as they are fused in my own imagination as entertainers whom my Northeast Bronx and Inwood families watched religiously. The "intimacy" I feel when watching Berle—and with him, the brilliant Sid Caesar—is captured by Theodore Reik in his study of Jewish Wit (1962): "It is difficult," Reik observed, "to characterize the special kind of intimacy in Jewish wit. It is even more difficult to define its nuances and shades. That familiarity reaches from an almost naive kind of intimacy to impudence, to a demonstrative sidling up to the other person."[26] Throughout his long career, Berle has often been reviled for his "impudence," what the critic of early twentieth-century American popular culture Gilbert Seldes (who, we should recall, was enamored with the "galvanic" figure of Al

Jolson thirty years earlier) termed in 1956 Berle's "cocky assurance," his "rude honesty." "Berle's vulgarity flowed like the Mississippi," Seldes remarked of Berle's vaudeville's routines, "muddy but powerful, and he spent his strength in knocking out the audience."[27]

So why, from the beginning, despite the vulgar style, did audiences take to Berle? What was the appeal of his legendary "impudence"? On a purely demographic level, the huge popularity of the *Texaco Star Theater* issued from the concentration of television sets in urban areas. Television historian Arthur Wertheim reminds us that at the height of Berle's popularity (1949–52), around five million people tuned into "Uncle Miltie" each week, the majority of whom lived in New York City. Wertheim estimates that 35 percent of Berle's viewers came from New York, whose residents accounted for almost 42 percent of the nation's TV sets. In addition, Wertheim reminds us that of the 108 operating stations in 1952, 63 were in metropolitan regions, and of the total number of stations, 64 were already NBC affiliates (Berle's home network). Thus, in retrospect, "Mr. Television" had something of a captive audience, until the networks expanded west, coaxial cables were laid, and his particular brand of brash, vaudeville-indebted, "New York" style of comedy did not play well beyond the urban centers along the East Coast.[28]

Still, Berle's now legendary television antics elicited loud shrieks from the live audience, as the video archive of the Museum of Television and Radio reveals. Dressed in a sailor suit for the last episode of the 1949 season (6/14/49—a month earlier Berle's face appeared on the covers of both *Time* and *Newsweek*), he cries out, "I'm *schvitzing* in here!" to the loud response of knowing audience laughter. In the same show, appearing as a Spanish contessa, Berle adjusts his wig with the Jewish insider line, "My *sheytal* is falling," in a Spanish accent. Again, I hear the audience roar in intimate recognition of the Yiddish word for "wig."[29]

"We just knew that [Berle] was one of us," my Aunt Tiny tells me. I am sure that her memories of watching Berle on Holland Avenue match those of the vast majority of his (Jewish) viewers in the early fifties. Of course, the invocation of Yiddish was nothing new in American popular culture, as the careers of Eddie Cantor (notably in *Paleface*) and the Marx Brothers ("Did someone call me *schnorrer*?") attest. I just know that my family up in the Bronx *howled* at Berle, too, enjoying the pleasures of intimacy at the public display of such "insider"/"sidling" language—"a sly insertion of Jewishness in his skits"[30]—feeling at home with Berle's *heimisch* if brash, impudent vaudeville-trained Borscht Belt *tummler* style, on the still very new democratic medium of television. Berle's particular comic style touched spaces of repressed Jewish memory in his audience; indeed, the

Milton Berle as "Carmen Miranda" on the cover of *Newsweek*,
May 16, 1949. © 1949 Newsweek, Inc. All rights reserved.
Photograph by Ed Wergeles. Used by permission.

knowing, insider laughter is itself the expressive sign of release, through recognition.[31]

The Milton Berle phenomenon was not a universal success at the time, however. We can detect the terms of contemporary dissent in the brutal description of Philip Hamburger, reviewing a now famous shtick between Berle and the emerging superstar comedy team of Martin and Lewis in *The New Yorker,* in the fall of 1949, which marked the beginning of Berle's first full season on television:

After a brief and glowing introduction by Mr. Berle, two comedians, the Messrs. Dean Martin and Jerry Lewis, came on. It is just possible that they represent a trend in television, so they are worth consideration. . . . For the most part, their humor consisted of behaving like delinquent children: poking their fingers in each other's eyes, putting their hands in each other's mouths, and in the classic tradition, insulting each other. . . . Mr. Berle joined them, and by his presence made them look like genuine comics. Berle was at his best—or worst—with Martin and Lewis. He demonstrated a few sorry tricks that may conceivably be the real reason for his television success. No. 1, he puts *his* hand in somebody's mouth. No. 2, he crooks his elbow and simultaneously bends his fingers in a clawlike gesture that gives him the air of a singularly distressed primate. No. 3, he twists his mouth and reveals his teeth in an exertion that, at least to me, signifies nothing.[32]

Berle's manic television antics, we might say, left a bad taste in Hamburger's "civilized" mouth. Is it possible to imagine (or defend?) Berle's regressive behavior before the eyes of the American world as similar to the loosening of restraint, of civility, depicted in the famous satiric imaging of "uptown" versus "downtown" Jewish audiences in the Yiddish newspaper *The Big Stick*? Note, for example, the various scenes of eating, where in one image a woman appears to be inserting her hand in the mouth of another woman. In another, a man is taking off his socks—clearly he feels "at home," downtown, among his people.[33] At some affective level, Berle's television persona elicited equivalent liberated reactions: the laughter of identification, of homey Yinglish tones and gestures, of Yiddish as insider tongue displayed—perhaps with brazen, unself-conscious abandon—before the ignorant gaze of the goyim. In Berg, of course, the *opposite* cultural dynamic takes place: from local ethnic intimacies to national cultural consensus. "Jewish humor in mid-twentieth-century America," writes Albert Goldman, "was not gentle, ironic, Sholom Aleichem folksiness. . . . It was the plaint of a people who were highly successful in countless ways, yet who still felt inferior, tainted, outcast." If Goldman's characterization is right—and I believe that his description of mid-century Jewish American humor as "potent, explosive," releasing a "cathartic laughter" captures perfectly the moment of Berle and the more talented Sid Caesar as it looks forward to the anarchic "Yidditude" of Lenny Bruce—then we can begin to understand Irving Howe's dismay at the vulgarization of Yiddish in the rising generation of TV comics, for they represented something quite different from the "folksy" (if nevertheless still biting) traditions of satire and self-mockery he associated with the world of Sholom Aleichem.[34]

In this respect, the figure of Berle anticipates Philip Roth's candid

Cartoons of (top) a Jewish American audience behaving sedately at the "uptown" theatre and (bottom) the same audience "unbuttoned" at the "downtown" Yiddish theatre. From *Der groyser kibitzer* 1, no.1, January 22, 1909.

explanation (from his 1990 novel *Deception*) of why "he" feels himself at home, among the "tough" Jews of New York: "Jews with force, I'm talking about. Jews with appetite. Jews without shame. Complaining Jews who get under your skin. Brash Jews who eat with their elbows on the table. Unaccommodating Jews, full of anger, insult, argument, impudence."[35] Perhaps I mis-remember, perhaps I am a victim of (unearned?) nostalgia, or perhaps I romanticize, but the brash Bronx Jews I love watched Uncle Miltie *act out* their own deepest, perhaps even taboo desires, and in the process, they felt more at home, if not in the already *heimisch* Bronx, then at least in the (as yet) unknown neighborhoods beyond Pelham Parkway, in the wilderness of America.

By contrast, in both life and art, Gertrude Berg shied away from such discomforting (Jewish) styles and stereotypes. In the *Commentary* profile from 1956, cited above, Berg enumerated those subjects she deemed inappropriate ("I don't bring them up") for representation on the television *Goldbergs*, a revealing litany of prohibited themes, including "unions, politics . . . socialism."[36] Her list of taboos reads like the daily activities at Camp Kinderland: time capsules that look forward to the political millennium of nuclear disarmament; labor olympics vs. bourgeois color war; obligatory bunk raps on the political issues of the day engineered by true believing counselors, who often came from the "Amalgamated" co-ops in the still Jewish working-class Bronx.

So despite a tendency to link them together, the contrasting images of Gertrude Berg and Milton Berle open out into strikingly different realms of Jewish American popular culture. In each case, however, the artist achieves a kind of intimacy with the audience—Berg through the celebration of America, Berle through the exhibition of impudence, with a Bronx-inflected brashness summoned to negotiate feelings of marginality, despite the proffered riches of America. Each figure, however, speaks *to* the Americanizing world of the early 1950s from different cultural spaces, in different linguistic modes and registers.

The example of Mickey Katz and his Yinglish parodies offers us an even richer case study in appropriation and resistance, as well as the opportunity to examine the ways that audiences in the 1950s related to an attenuated world/word of Yiddish that, by the second and third generation in America, was indeed entering the zone of nostalgia—"a quick and superficial nostalgia," in Gans's contemporaneous critique of the Katz phenomenon.[37] In our time, however, the music of Mickey Katz has undergone something of a revival, mainly through the surge of interest in klezmer music, along with the faith-keeping covers of his instrumentals and parodies by the jazz clarinetist Don Byron. "The parody numbers are a healthy take on the 1950s," Byron observed in 1990, as he prepared to showcase Katz's art, "a real way to deal with pluralism. . . . They're tasteless enough to be funny, and tasteful enough to be cool." The Yinglish world conjured by Mickey Katz tells us much about Jewish American culture in the 1950s, as well as about our own various turns to ethnicity and the growing appeal of "Yiddi-tude" among the post-Tevye "Klezmania" generation.[38]

After starting out in the thirties in Cleveland, where he played in local bands, Katz's career included a stint with the Spike Jones orchestra—famous for its parodic sendups of popular tunes and novelty songs—and as the bandleader for Betty Hutton. After leaving Spike Jones in 1947, Katz went out on his own, recording the first of his numerous parodies of Hit Parade songs. As he tells it in his autobiography, *Papa, Play for Me,* these novelty records sold wildly: "In three days the stores [in Times Square] sold out the original ten thousand records [of "Haim afen Range"] and took orders for twenty-five thousand more!" The parody of "Davy Crock-ett" a few years later sold two hundred thousand copies and (as Katz recalls) hit number two on the charts, "all over the country."[39] Based on this success, Katz created a Yiddish-English revue in Los Angeles in 1948 called *Borscht Capades,* and brought it to New York in the fall of 1951. Through his heyday in the fifties and into the mid-sixties, Katz performed with his "Kosher Jammers," mainly in New York, Los Angeles, and Miami Beach, recording numerous albums, including dialect stories based on popular fables and American literary and folk legends (including, for example, "Moby Glick").

Can we recover the appeal of Katz's Yinglish parodies? "The way Katz did 'Davy Crockett' in Yiddish, your side split,'" recalls an older woman, speaking with the authority of someone who saw Katz perform in Florida, in 1957.[40] The Broadway critics in September 1951, however, weren't as taken with the arrival of either *Bagels and Yox* or *Borscht Capades.* "It may be that all the Yiddish jibes are devastatingly funny," wrote Brooks Atkin-son (who had loved Gertrude Berg's "Molly" three years earlier), "but this department cannot vouch for that, and even suspects that in *Bagels and Yox* all Yiddish words are regarded as funny, whatever they mean." An even tougher critique ran in *Cue:* "for anybody who can catch occasional home-folk phrases, an uneasy feeling that religious sentiment and street-corner smut make a pretty poor mix. You can't combine the Kaddish with "Come on-a My House" [another of Katz's best-selling parodies] and get what even Broadway thinks is art."[41]

What the official critics-outsiders missed in 1951, William and Sarah Schack understood in profound ways. Writing in *Commentary* about this

Salamis and clarinets hang together. Mickey Katz as musical deli
man. Album cover for *Mish Mosh* (Capitol Records, 1957). Used by
permission.

moment of "Yinglish"—a term they appear to have coined—they recognized in the Katz revue and its large audiences the expression of a now
familiar, but then emergent, "hybrid life," "the mixed world of halvah and
Hershey almond bar" that had come to characterize Jewish American
experience by mid-century. More importantly, the Schacks recognized
that this large segment of "culturally hybrid variety of American Jew . . .
responds to the hybridization of language that developed in the Yiddish
popular theater."[42] In this respect, the art of Mickey Katz draws on, as it

reinvents, the traditions of dialect humor and parody that nourished the Jewish American popular imagination, a comedic angle of vision that flourished in the early 1950s on television (in the example of Sid Caesar, among others) and in Katz's recordings.

Earlier, I briefly outlined the traditions of Jewish dialect humor that help locate the parodic Yinglish world of Mickey Katz, a line that would include the early twentieth-century recordings of "Cohen on the Telephone," the rude mid-twenties collections of dialect sketches by Milt Gross, which for some (like the young Gertrude Berg) represented Jewish life in shameful, embarrassing ways.[43] After Katz, we would need to highlight the early parodies of Mel Brooks and Carl Reiner (doesn't the heavy Yiddish accent of the Two-Thousand Year Old Man authorize the wicked satire?), Lenny Bruce, the Allan Sherman craze in the early sixties, and, of course, the entire corpus of Woody Allen. With *Borscht Capades* and *Bagels and Yox* there was a brief stir, in the pages of *Commentary,* over the incivilities—and dangers—of dialect humor, with the middle-brow raconteur Sam Levenson arguing that "The Dialect Comedian Should Vanish," because (in Levenson's argument) the outside world is laughing at us ("It is my belief that any Jew who, in humor or otherwise, strengthens the misconceptions and the prejudices against his own people is neither a good Jew nor a responsible human being.").[44]

What Levenson's proscriptions failed to realize, or perhaps admit, are the unmasking, demystifying powers of dialect humor; its ability to see through pretension; its rich potential (often through the art of the pun) to expose, to reduce the mighty and awesome through the leveling playfulness of the earthy (sometimes scatological) "other" tongue. Of course I am describing here the familiar linguistic-political-social registers often attributed to Yiddish as a "minority" language—its ability to overturn, via tones of (self-) mocking irony, the powers of the dominant (and dominating) host culture. And I am also describing the cultural office of parody, the literary-musical mode of Katz's Yinglish hits.

What was so "side-splitting" about Katz's parody of Davy Crockett? The song itself, as every child of the fifties (living in the Bronx or Inwood and elsewhere) can remember, tells of the heroic-mythic exploits of Davy Crockett, "king of the wild frontier" (in the famous Bill Hayes lyric of 1955). What is remarkable listening to the original tune now is how the figure of Davy Crockett emerges as a symbol of the American Way—going off to Congress, "fixing up the government's laws," "patch[ing] up the crack in the Liberty Bell," and above all "serving his country well." In the last stanza the song takes on a wider perspective, celebrating Davy's America:

His land is biggest, and his land is best
From grassy plains to the mountain crest
He's ahead of us all, meeting the test
And following his legend right into the West

In wise-ass response, Katz's parody transforms the American hero into "Duvid Crockett," "King of Delancey Street," where we learn of *his* childhood exploits—"He flicked him a chicken when he was only t'ree"—and his schlemiel-like journey West. Unlike the mythical frontiersman, however, *our* Duvid treks to Las Vegas, where he gambles his money away: "Up came two sixes in drerd di geldt" (lost his money; idiom: "into the ground"). In the end, Duvid "farlorn di heysn un he went on nakhet" (he lost his pants and went on naked). So much for Duvid Crockett, who's "back on Delancey Street."[45]

What marks Katz's achievement in parody, and what (obviously) can't be demonstrated on the page, are the Yinglish intonations and rhythms registered by his high pitched voice and the musical intervention of a klezmer-inspired interlude in every song ("his in-your-*punim* parodic subversion," in Katz scholar Josh Kun's memorable characterization), a style that, in effect, counters the smooth pop tune orchestrations of the fifties with the sound of Jewish difference (according to Kun, a key aspect of Katz's aural stance as "anti-crooner.")[46] In the end, Katz's idiomatic Yiddish phrasings explode, deflating the authorizing American voice of Bill Hayes, and the frontier legend of whom he sings. Duvid Crockett of Delancey street loses his pants, and goes *home,* not to the territory of American myth, but to the familiar Lower East Side, where he still belongs.[47]

Katz's sendup of Tennessee Ernie Ford's 1955 hit "Sixteen Tons" ("a kosher deli work song," in Kun's view)[48] is filled with even more piercing Yinglish ironies. Listen to the opening stanza:

Oh, I vent to woyk in a delicatessen
Far draysik toler [for $30] and plenty to fresn [gorge]
The balebast [head cook] promised me a real gedila [glory/honor]
Instead of gedila I catched me a kila [hernia]

As the parody unfolds, Katz threads Jewish foodways (characteristic of his Yinglish parodies as well as most forms of symbolic ethnicity) with a darker, edgier, if still comic vision:

Sixteen tons all kinds smooked fishes
Latkes, blintzes, un heyse [hot] knishes
O Lordy nem es shnell [take me quickly] to the promised land

A fayer afn bus zol er vein farbrent [a fire on the boss may he get burned up!]
You load sixteen tons of lekakh [cake] un tagl
Herring mislines [fish intestines] stuffed heldzl and beygl
Genig tsu shlepn [enough to shlep] just like a ferd [horse]
Hert zikh tsu tsu mir mentshn [listen to me people]
Es teyg in dred [it's good for nothing!][49]

If for Tennessee Ernie Ford "fightin' and trouble are my middle name," then for Mickey Katz's deli man, chained to the counter, life offers hernias instead of honor ("kilas" instead of "gedila"—"Don't catch yourself a 'kila,' " my mother always warned, when I attempted to lift a heavy object). Life "es teyg in dred!" the song announces, concluding with a familiar Yiddish twist in the form of an idiomatic curse that, I imagine, filled his listeners with the knowing laughter of (insider) recognition.

Most of Katz's parodies are not as "serious" as "Sixteen Tons." The majority of his recordings have a "zest and zaniness," almost a manic exuberance inscribed in their imaginative punning style.[50] In the brilliant parody of "C'est si Bon"—perhaps already parodied in Eartha Kitt's 1953 rendition—Katz presents "a ridiculous pastiche of trite French and irrelevant Yiddish," as in "Madame Piaf Gut Yontef," "kishke voulez-vouz," "cherchez la tschotske," or "Cadillac de Ville oys geshpilt" (trans: "Cadillac de Ville, no way").[51] This sort of wordplay has its own traditions of bilingual punning (including in James Joyce, as the Schacks understood about Katz and Yinglish in general in 1951); combined with his comic, davening-inflected "anti-crooner" voice, we can hear in Mickey Katz overtones of what Robert Alter richly describes as the qualities and characteristics of "the Jewish voice":

> a certain caustically ironic tonality; a fondness for exuberant shuttling among disparate layers of diction in a language; a predisposition to turn written language into quasi-oral performance, art into shtick. . . . Behind these speech habits stands the oral culture of Yiddish, with its delight in verbal performance and the resourceful awareness in its speakers of the disparate constituents of the language.[52]

I realize, of course, that the corpus of Mickey Katz's Hit Parade shtiklach may not fit perfectly into Alter's academic definition. But surely at some level Katz's Yinglish art participates in the traditions and styles that Alter associates with a "Jewish" voice. And that voice issued from the hybrid, betwixt-and-between liminal spaces of fifties Yiddish popular culture to Americanizing Jewish audiences, speaking to them on (Yinglish) wavelengths to which they were still ethnically and linguistically attuned. Rather than offering his audiences "a quick and superficial nostalgia," rather than "selling nostalgia,"[53] as Gans worried about in 1953, Mickey Katz's Yinglish art provided a space of subculture identification, perhaps even a mode of parodic defense or (at least) temporary resistance against the forces of acculturation. Katz's parodies signify the voice of resistance against the (Jewish American) compulsion to forget as they (nevertheless) *ease* the audience's transition into the consensual American 1950s. The "nostalgia" of Jewish foodways that fills his hilarious parodies, the exuberant klezmer-inspired rhythms that make the instrumentals more than just "novelty songs" (as Don Byron recognizes) are expressive of the generational needs—and desires—of an audience worried about the inexorable loss of cultural identity.[54] In this respect, Katz's musically hybrid style, his anticrooner "Jewish voice," affected audiences in the early fifties, applying the salve of nostalgia while softening the hurts—or the exclusions—of (American) history. Above all, Katz's irreverent parodies made us—perhaps still make us—laugh the therapeutic(?) laughter of insider pleasure.

"To enter into parody," observes Judith Butler, "is to enter into a relationship of both desire and ambivalence."[55] There is no parody, we might say, without a certain intimacy. The Yinglish universe of Mickey Katz's parodic imagination offers me, third-generation son that I am, the "primitive pleasures of recognition";[56] entering into Jewish American parody is, I suppose, my way of returning (to recall the immigration historian Marcus Hansen's theory of "third-generation return"), of getting back to the Bronx, to the world of my father.[57] "Parody," Butler continues, "requires a certain ability to identify, approximate, and draw near."[58] Thus taking Jewish American popular culture seriously enables me to create a space (intellectually and psychologically) where I can perform—act out—those complexities of desire (identification) and of ambivalence (resistance) that mark filiality itself.

Is the nostalgia of Jewish sons—or nostalgia itself—always disabling? immobilizing? Why can't the son's nostalgia for the father's nostalgia generate an altered relationship with the past, with memory—personal and collective—itself, enabling the construction of counter-memories and histories that highlight how Yinglish voices in the fifties bespeak intimacies now forgotten, solidarities long sundered. I'd prefer, in the end, not to think of my analysis of the worlds of Gertrude Berg, Milton Berle, and Mickey Katz as an academic's expression of mourning, but rather as an act of empathic, imaginative recuperation, a way of re-viewing, of *feeling* the worlds of my father (and mother, aunts, and uncles): to draw near their old (Bronx, and Cleveland) worlds, in order to negotiate better the complex and (at times) bewildering Jewish American dilemmas of my own.

NOTES

INTRODUCTION

1. Abraham Cahan, *The Rise of David Levinsky* [1917] (New York: Harper and Row, 1960), p. 61.

2. "America-in-the-large-sense," writes Marcus Klein, "had demanded Americanization, no matter that the term was so ambiguous or that America also established formidable barriers to assimilation. The essential business of the immigrants, on their side, had been to try to become Americans, no matter what the recalcitrance or frustrations." Marcus Klein, *Foreigners: The Making of American Literature, 1900–1940* (Chicago: University of Chicago Press, 1981), p. 36. "Between 1870 and 1915," observed Irving Howe in the mid-1960s, just beginning his research for *World of Our Fathers* (1976), "the population of New York City increased from one and a half to five million. In 1880 there were some 80,000 Jews living in the city; by 1910, a million and a quarter. . . . Has there ever, one wonders, been a migration of comparable speed and density in recent Western history?" "The Lower East Side: Symbol and Fact," in *The Lower East Side: Portal to American Life (1870–1924)*, ed. Allon Schoener (New York: The Jewish Museum, 1966), p. 11. On the social history of Jewish migration to America see Ronald Sanders, *The Downtown Jews: Portraits of an Immigrant Generation* (New York: Harper and Row, 1969) and Gerald Sorin, *A Time for Building: The Third Migration, 1880–1920* (Baltimore: Johns Hopkins University Press, 1992). About the label "green," Abraham Cahan's Gitl, the initially bewildered Old World wife in his great short novel *Yekl* (1896), sees through its debilitating linguistic power: "What an ugly word to apply to people! She had never been green at home, and here she had suddenly become so. What do they mean by it, anyhow? Verily, one might turn green and yellow and gray while young in such a dreadful place." Abraham Cahan, *Yekl*, in *The Imported Bridegroom and other Stories* (New York: Penguin Books, 1996), p. 207.

3. By *affect*, I mean how the self expresses and discharges emotions, often at the level of the body, in psychodynamic reaction to strain, whether as a result of physical, social, or spiritual transition, or any situation that induces a complex emotional response. "*Affect* is a feeling tone," according to psychiatric textbooks, "that accompanies an idea. Affect and emotion are used interchangeably and include such feelings as rage, grief, and joy. Affect determines the general attitude, whether of rejection, acceptance, flight, fight, or indifference. Thus, the affects provide the motivational drive or psychodynamic component in relation to every life situation and play a determining role in the thoughts and actions of a person in health and disease." *Comprehensive Textbook of Psychiatry/IV*, ed. Harold I. Kaplan and Benjamin J. Sadock (Baltimore: Williams and Wilkins, 1985), p. 575.

4. Quoted in Isaac B. Berkson, *Theories of Americanization: A Critical Study* [1920] (New York: Arno Press, 1969), p. 59. "Broadly speaking," Berkson continued, "we mean by it an appreciation of the institutions of this country, absolute forgetfulness of all obligations or connections with other countries because of descent of birth."

5. E. A. Ross, *The Old World in the New: The Significance of Past and Present Immigration to the American People* (New York: The Century Co., 1914), p. 164.

6. Mary Antin, *They Who Knock at Our Gates: A Complete Gospel of Immigration* (Boston: Houghton Mifflin, 1914), p. 98.

7. Anzia Yezierska, "Mostly About Myself," in *Children of Loneliness: Stories of Immigrant Life in America* (New York: Funk and Wagnalls, 1923), p. 27. On the ways "ethnic" writers like Antin and Yezierska seized early American history to authorize their own position as New World citizens see Werner Sollors, *Beyond Ethnicity: Consent and Descent in American Culture* (New York: Oxford University Press, 1986).

8. Horace Kallen, "Americanization," in *Culture and Democracy in the United States* (New York: Boni and Liveright, 1924), p. 161.

9. Abraham Cahan, "Forward Editorial, 1916," quoted in Sanders, *The Downtown Jews,* pp. 429–30. For more about Cahan's relation to history and politics while writing *The Rise of David Levinsky* see Sanders, *The Downtown Jews,* chapter 18, "The Exile Is an American at Last," pp. 415–36.

10. Svetlana Boym, *The Future of Nostalgia* (New York: Basic Books, 2001), p. xvi.

11. Jonathan Freedman, *The Temple of Culture: Assimilation and Anti-Semitism in Literary Anglo-America* (New York: Oxford University Press, 2000), p. 12. For Freedman, these "affective complexities," resulting from the "process" of Jewish intellectuals' "assimilation by culture," are "the admixture of reverence and rage, accommodation and aggression" (p. 12).

12. Henry James, *The American Scene* [1907], ed. Leon Edel (Bloomington: Indiana University Press, 1968), p. 84; p. 139. On the question of James's relation to "the oncoming citizen" (p. 127), see the nuanced readings by Ross Posnock, *The Trial of Curiosity: Henry James, William James, and the Challenge of Modernity* (New York: Oxford University Press, 1991) and Alan Trachtenberg, "Conceivable Aliens," *Yale Review* 82 (1994): 42–64. For Trachtenberg, James's complex response to "the drama of immigration" enabled him, at some level, to identify with the "alien" in his "unfixed, provisional, and improvisational 'American' identity" (p. 62). Thus despite his "garden-variety" antisemitism, James nonetheless sensed the emerging "Jewish" aspect (my reading, since Trachtenberg's key words also tend to be ascribed to Jews under the pressure of modernity) of the "new" New York City, its "Accent of the Future" (*American Scene,* p. 139). "The Jew," shrewdly observes Jonathan Freedman, "became the vehicle through which James staged an encounter with his deepest anxieties about himself, his art, and the relation of both to his culture." See Jonathan Freedman, "Henry James and the Discourses of Antisemitism," in *Between "Race" and Culture: Representations of "the Jew" in English and American Literature,* ed. Bryan Cheyette (Stanford, Calif.: Stanford University Press, 1996), p. 62. I borrow the phrase "garden variety" from Freedman, p. 62.

13. John F. Kasson, *Rudeness and Civility: Manners in Nineteenth-Century Urban America* (New York: Hill and Wang, 1990), p. 43. For the story of etiquette manuals into the twentieth century see Cas Wouters, "Etiquette Books and Emotion Management in the Twentieth Century: American Habitus in International Comparison," in *An Emotional History of the United States,* ed. Peter N. Stearns and Jan Lewis (New York: New York University Press, 1998), pp. 283–304. The classic work on this subject remains Arthur Schlesinger, *Learning How to Behave: A Historical Study of American Etiquette Books* (New York: Macmillan, 1946).

14. Karen Halttunen, *Confidence Men and Painted Women: A Study of Middle-Class Culture in America, 1830–1870* (New Haven, Conn.: Yale University Press, 1982), p. 96.

15. Ross, *The Old World in the New,* Preface, n.p.

16. Bauman, Zygmunt, *Modernity and Ambivalence,* (Ithaca, N.Y.: Cornell University Press, 1991), p. 135.

17. Norbert Elias, *Power and Civility* (New York: Pantheon Books, 1982), p. 312. In addition to a number of essay reviews by important historians upon the English publication of Elias's work (especially Keith Thomas, "The Rise of the Fork," *New York*

Review of Books (March 9, 1978): 28–31), see the following recent work by and about Elias for the biographical and cultural contexts of his achievement: Norbert Elias, *Reflections on a Life* (Cambridge: Polity Press, 1994); Steven Russell, *Jewish Identity and the Civilizing Process* (New York: St. Martin's Press, 1996); Robert van Kreiken, *Norbert Elias* (London: Routledge, 1998).

18. Elias, *Power and Civility,* p. 313. The matter of "poise"—of imitating (imagined) high-toned, upper-class manners and civility—leads to the source of comedy and parody in much immigrant popular culture and beyond.

19. Bauman, *Modernity and Ambivalence,* p. 130. Under the rubric of "Jewish Shame," Hasia Diner writes, "In a profound way, modern Jewish history *is* a history of the emotions. They provide *the* central tension in the Jewish confrontation with modernity, regardless of where it played itself out" (emphasis in the original). Hasia Diner, "Ethnicity and Emotions in America: Dimensions of the Unexplored," in *An Emotional History of the United States,* p. 205. These behaviors might include "gesticulating" hands ("talmudic gesticulations," in David Levinsky's phrase) or the use of "*mauschlen,*" a mode of "Jewish" speech mixing German with Yiddish rhythm and intonation that marks the Jew. "Mauschlen" and other shame-producing "Jewish" behaviors are richly theorized by Sander L. Gilman in *Jewish Self-Hatred: Anti-Semitism and the Hidden Language of the Jews* (Baltimore: Johns Hopkins University Press, 1986). Shulamit Volkov describes *mauschlen* as having "the remnants of talmudic colloquialism, and a dose of Galician wit." See Volkov, "The Dynamics of Dissimilation: *Ostjuden* and German Jews," in Jehuda Reinharz and Walter Schatzberg, eds., *The Jewish Response to German Culture* (Hanover, N.H.: University Press of New England, 1985), pp. 203–204. Volkov explains, following Elias's model of decoding "the civilization game," the shame-producing impact of East European migrants to German cities. "*Ostjuden* began to be conceived as a major source of embarrassment, haunting the better-situated, better-acculturated, better-assimilated Jews" (p. 210).

20. Silvan Tomkins, *Affect, Imagery, Consciousness: The Negative Affects,* vol. 2 [1963], quoted in *Shame and Its Sisters: A Silvan Tomkins Reader,* ed. Eve Kosofsky Sedgwick and Adam Frank (Durham, N.C.: Duke University Press, 1995), p. 133. The literature on shame is vast. I have benefited most from Léon Wurmser, *The Mask of Shame* (Baltimore: Johns Hopkins University Press, 1981). I borrow the phrase "abyss of unlovability" from Wurmser, p. 92.

21. On Howe's irritation with the nostalgia culture that coincided with the ethnic revival of the late 1970s see "Immigrant Chic," *New York* 19 (May 12, 1986), p. 76. In *The Anatomy Lesson* (1983), Philip Roth plays with Howe's vexations (getting even with Howe for an earlier, scathing attack) in the character of "Milton Appel," who makes a career taking on what Roth's narrator, Nathan Zuckerman, calls "the distortions of the Jewish nostalgists" and their "cheap middlebrow crap." Philip Roth, *Zuckerman Bound: A Trilogy and Epilogue* (New York: Farrar, Straus and Giroux, 1985), pp. 480, 484.

22. Bauman, *Modernity and Ambivalence,* 154.

23. In this respect I begin to understand the personal implications of the following dictum, offered by Pierre Nora:

> To understand the force and appeal of this sense of obligation ["the constraint of memory"], perhaps we should think of Jewish memory, which has recently been revived among many nonpracticing Jews. In this tradition, which has no other history than its own memory, to be Jewish is to remember that one is such; but once this incontestable memory has been interiorized, it eventually demands full recognition. What is being remembered? In a sense, it is memory itself. The psychologization of memory has thus given every individual the sense that his or her salvation ultimately depends on the repayment of an impossible debt.

33. Cahan, *Rise of David Levinsky,* p. 396.

34. Cahan, *Rise of David Levinsky,* p. 167.

35. Cahan, *Rise of David Levinsky,* pp. 397, 398.

36. Cahan, *Rise of David Levinsky,* p. 495. As mentioned in the Introduction, Mary Antin's *They Who Knock at Our Gates: A Complete Gospel of Immigration* voices the *unironic* version of the immigrants as latter-day Pilgrims: "The ghost of the Mayflower pilots every immigrant ship, and Ellis Island is another name for Plymouth Rock." Antin, *They Who Knock at Our Gates* (Boston: Houghton Mifflin, 1914), p. 98. On the matter of the country's "ingestion" of the alien, Antin offered the following solution: "The remedy for the moral indigestion which unchecked immigration is said to induce is enlarging the organs of digestion." *They Who Knock,* p. 122. By contrast, for Henry James Ellis Island was a haunted place, difficult to fathom: a chilling scene of apocalyptic knowledge from where he experienced the irreversible American future, not—as in Antin—the completion of his country's sacred Protestant past.

37. Cahan, *Rise of David Levinsky,* pp. 259, 259–60.

38. Cahan, *Rise of David Levinsky,* pp. 259–60.

39. Cahan, *Rise of David Levinsky,* p. 260. In *Rudeness and Civility: Manners in Nineteenth-Century Urban America* (New York: Hill and Wang, 1990), John F. Kasson mentions that in his research into etiquette manuals "none of the books in my sample or in the bibliographies I uncovered addressed recent immigrants" (p. 54). There were, in fact, "manuals" for immigrants. See Esther Romeyn, "Eros and Americanization: David Levinsky and the Etiquette of Race," in *Key Texts in American Jewish Culture,* ed. Jack Kugelmass (New Brunswick, N.J.: Rutgers University Press, 2003), pp. 25–45. See especially p. 29, discussing "*Etikete,* a Yiddish etiquette book published in 1908." In Romeyn's shrewd reading, Cahan's novel "reads as a classic *Bildungsroman*—in this case a cross between an etiquette book and Dale Carnegie's *How to Win Friends and Influence People* (p. 31). For more on Yiddish etiquette manuals see p. 42 (note 21). As *Levinsky* also reveals, manners could be mediated during social interaction rituals or—even more dramatically, for the immigrant experience, through popular culture, especially the early cinema.

40. Cahan, *Rise of David Levinsky,* p. 380.

41. Cahan, *Rise of David Levinsky,* p. 515. In rich and poignant contrast, James visited—really, revisited—the Waldorf Astoria (part of the "hotel spirit" celebrated in *The American Scene*) in 1907, and like Levinsky, was taken with a virtual trance of soothing nostalgia. The Waldorf scene "was a social order in positively stable equilibrium . . . a world whose relation to its form and medium was practically imperturbable . . . a gorgeous golden blur, a paradise peopled with unmistakable American shapes." *American Scene,* p. 105. One can only imagine how perturbed James might have been observing poor Gitelson dining in *his* Waldorf. Significantly, in this instance Levinsky shares James's patrician tastes and anxieties.

42. Alter Brody, "Yiddish: Our Literary Dominion," *The Nation* 124 (April 20, 1927): 435.

43. Cahan, *Rise of David Levinsky,* p. 530. In this respect, Stephen Whitfield captures a key aspect of *Levinsky:* "Much of the evocative power of *The Rise of David Levinsky* emanates from its self-exposure of homelessness, which a new American could not palliate despite the giddy sensations of prosperity and freedom." Stephen J. Whitfield, *In Search of American Jewish Culture* (Hanover, N.H.: University Press of New England, 1999), p. 48. In this respect, too, Priscilla Wald nicely articulates a major theme of early Jewish American literature: "Nostalgia finds expression in the work of East European Jews often indirectly, emerging as an isolated memory. . . . It could lead variously to the reclaiming of traditions long abandoned and other times to the alienation attendant upon the failure to do so. A sense of loss, an experience typically

described in the language of melancholy, infuses the experience of assimilation." Priscilla Wald, "Of Crucibles and Grandfathers: The East European Immigrants," in *The Cambridge Companion to Jewish American Literature*, ed. Michael P. Kramer and Hana Wirth-Nesher (Cambridge: Cambridge University Press, 2003), p. 53.

2. GASTRONOMIC NOSTALGIA

1. Anzia Yezierska, "You Can't Be an Immigrant Twice," *Children of Loneliness* (New York: Funk and Wagnalls 1923), p. 265.

2. Margaret Visser, *The Rituals of Dinner: The Origins, Evolution, Eccentricities, and Meaning of Table Manners* (New York: Penguin, 1991), xiii.

3. Isaac Rosenfeld, "The Fall of David Levinsky" [1952], in *Preserving the Hunger: An Isaac Rosenfeld Reader*, ed. Mark Shechner (Detroit: Wayne State University Press, 1988), pp. 153, 155.

4. Over the past few years there has been something of a Yezierska revival, both in scholarship and in the republication of her works. The richest study of Yezierska's imagination is found in Magdalena J. Zaborowska, *How We Found America: Reading Gender through East European Immigrant Narratives* (Chapel Hill: University of North Carolina Press, 1995), chapter four. For recent editions of Yezierska, each with impressive introductions, see Anzia Yezierska, *Salome of the Tenements* [1923] (Urbana and Chicago: University of Illinois Press, 1995) [introduction by Gay Wilentz] and Anzia Yezierska, *Arrogant Beggar* [1927] (Durham, N.C.: Duke University Press, 1996) [introduction by Katherine Stubbs].

5. Louise Levitas Henriksen, "Afterword about Anzia Yezierska," in *The Open Cage: An Anzia Yezierska Collection*, ed. Alice Kessler-Harris (New York: Persea Books, 1979), p. 254.

6. Mary V. Dearborn, *Love in the Promised Land: The Story of Anzia Yezierska and John Dewey* (New York: The Free Press, 1988), p. 130. Dearborn's account of the Yezierska-Dewey romance and its larger cultural implications remains the best portrait of their complicated relationship.

7. Anzia Yezierska, *Hungry Hearts* [orig. 1920] (New York: Persea Books, 1985), p. 173.

8. Yezierska, "Wings," in *Hungry Hearts*, p. 5.

9. Anzia Yezierska, "Children of Loneliness," in *The Open Cage*, p. 161.

10. Yezierska, "Wings," p. 3.

11. Anzia Yezierska, *Arrogant Beggar* (New York: Doubleday, Page & Co., 1927), p. 152.

12. Yezierska, "Wings," p. 3.

13. Yezierska, "Wings," pp. 17, 20, 17.

14. Yezierska, "Wings," pp. 21, 30, 34. Note Shenah's rough grammar, the rhetorical sign of her greenhorn status. For a reading of "Wings" see Zaborowska, *How We Found America*, p. 134.

15. Anzia Yezierska, "Hunger," in *Children of Loneliness*, pp. 56–57.

16. Yezierska, "Hunger," pp. 58, 64.

17. Alice Kessler-Harris speaks of "the dangerous territory of Americanization" in her Introduction to Anzia Yezierska's *Bread Givers* (New York: Persea Press, 1975), p. xiii.

18. Yezierska, "Hunger," p. 64.

19. Anzia Yezierska, "To the Stars," in *Children of Loneliness*, pp. 75, 74, 86. See Zaborowska, *How We Found America*, pp. 135–37 for a smart reading of this story.

20. Yezierska, "To the Stars," pp. 96, 97.

21. Anzia Yezierska, "My Own People," in *Hungry Hearts*, p. 242. According to

Yezierska's daughter, "My Own People" was also the title of a novel that Yezierska was hoping to write. See Louise Levitas Henriksen, *Anzia Yezierska: A Writer's Life* (New Brunswick: Rutgers University Press, 1988), pp. 132–33.

22. On the film version of *Hungry Hearts* see Dearborn, *Love in the Promised Land*, 144–46; Kevin Brownlow, *Behind the Mask of Innocence* (New York: Knopf, 1990), pp. 392–404; and Delia Caparoso Konzett, "From Hollywood to Hester Street: Ghetto Film, Melodrama, and the Image of the Assimilated Jew in *Hungry Hearts*," *Journal of Film and Video* 50 (1998–99): 18–33.

23. Anzia Yezierska, *Salome of the Tenements* (New York: Grosset and Dunlap, 1922), p. 121. For recent helpful discussions of *Salome* see Gay Wilentz's Introduction to *Salome of the Tenements* pp. ix–xxvi; Zaborowska, *How We Found America*, pp. 139–47; Christopher N. Okonkwo, "Of Repression, Assertion, and the Speakerly Dress: Anzia Yezierska's *Salome of the Tenements*," *MELUS* 25 (2000): 129–45; and Priscilla Wald, "Of Crucibles and Grandfathers: The East European Immigrants," in *The Cambridge Companion to Jewish American Literature*, ed. Michael P. Kramer and Hana Wirth-Nesher (Cambridge: Cambridge University Press, 2003), pp. 64–66. Werner Sollors calls *Salome* "this weak and odd novel" in his review of the reprint edition, *Journal of American Ethnic History* 17 (1998): 98. A. O. Scott recognizes the novel's suitability for the silent movies, its "outsized, almost parodic theatricality," in his review of the 1995 reprint in "When We Read Red," *The Nation* 263 (Sept. 23, 1996): 31.

24. Yezierska, *Salome of the Tenements*, pp. 7, 9, 11.

25. Yezierska, *Salome of the Tenements*, pp. 59, 10, 65.

26. Yezierska, *Salome of the Tenements*, p. 65.

27. Yezierska, *Salome of the Tenements*, p. 135.

28. Yezierska, *Salome of the Tenements*, p. 64.

29. Yezierska, *Salome of the Tenements*, pp. 137, 134.

30. Yezierska, *Salome of the Tenements*, p. 177.

31. Yezierska, *Salome of the Tenements*, pp. 64–65, 177. The Manning-Sonya relationship recalls another James novel, *Portrait of a Lady* (1881): in her Emersonian yearning Sonya partly resembles Isabel Archer's highest desires, while Manning, in his appeal to tradition, resembles Gilbert Osmond's soul-killing office.

32. Yezierska, *Salome of the Tenements*, p. 180.

33. Yezierska, *Salome of the Tenements*, pp. 181, 236.

34. Yezierska, *Salome of the Tenements*, p. 198. For an analysis of the "aim" of shame and other brilliant insights into this key affect see Léon Wurmser, *The Mask of Shame* (Baltimore: Johns Hopkins University Press, 1981), p. 84.

35. Yezierska, *Salome of the Tenements*, pp. 205, 207.

36. Yezierska, *Salome of the Tenements*, p. 232.

37. Yezierska, *Salome of the Tenements*, pp. 278, 279.

38. Yezierska, *The Open Cage*, pp. 211, 209.

39. Yezierska, *The Open Cage*, pp. 218, 219.

40. Anzia Yezierska, *Bread Givers* (New York: Persea Books, 1975), pp. 10, 138, 4.

41. Yezierska, *Bread Givers*, p. 212.

42. Yezierska, *Bread Givers*, p. 237.

43. Henriksen, *Anzia Yezierska*, pp. 219, 220.

44. Yezierska, *Bread Givers*, p. 278–79, 286. My reading draws on Laura Wexler, "Looking at Yezierska," in *Women of the Word: Jewish Women and Jewish Writing* ed. Judith R. Paskin (Detroit: Wayne State University Press, 1994), 153–81.

45. Yezierska, *Bread Givers*, pp. 296–97.

46. Anzia Yezierska, *Arrogant Beggar* (Garden City, N.Y.: Doubleday, 1927), pp. 1, 6. For a very smart reading of *Arrogant Beggar,* drawing out its political and cultural

contexts see Katherine Stubbs, "Introduction," *Arrogant Beggar* (Durham: Duke University Press, 1996), vii–xxxiv.

47. Yezierska, *Arrogant Beggar*, pp. 94, 95.

48. Yezierska, *Arrogant Beggar*, p. 70.

49. Yezierska, *Arrogant Beggar*, pp. 71, 152–53.

50. Yezierska, *Arrogant Beggar*, pp. 164, 165.

51. Yezierska, *Arrogant Beggar*, pp. 178, 179.

52. Yezierska, *Arrogant Beggar*, p. 252.

53. Yezierska, *Arrogant Beggar*, p. 264. In this respect Yezierska's lost immigrants are textbook examples of the portraits in exile limned by Leon Grinberg and Rebeca Grinberg in their powerful study *Psychoanalytic Perspectives on Migration and Exile* (New Haven, Conn.: Yale University Press, 1989). The reference to Winnicott's idea of "transitional space" and its relation to migration and adjustment is on p. 14.

54. Dearborn, *Love in the Promised Land*, p. 158. For the most recent authoritative assessment of Yezierska's career, listen to Ruth Wisse: "Once her autobiographical heroines move out of their neighborhoods and into their new tailored suits, the author loses the Yiddish pungency that was her trademark." *The Modern Jewish Canon: A Journey through Language and Culture* (New York: Free Press, 2000), p. 273.

55. See in this respect, Henriksen, *Anzia Yezierska*, passim.

56. Anzia Yezierska, *All I Could Never Be* (New York: Brewer, Warren, and Putnam, 1932), p. 14.

57. Yezierska, *All I Could Never Be*, pp. 19, 23, 24.

58. Yezierska, *All I Could Never Be*, pp. 28, 40, 66. In contrast to the aroma of certain ghetto types—and the commercial air of Christopher Newman—Scott gives off an intoxicating aura of New World metaphysics.

59. Yezierska, *All I Could Never Be*, pp. 33, 107. Elsewhere Fanya speaks of Scott/Dewey's "rigid Puritan pose" (p. 68).

60. Yezierska, *All I Could Never Be*, pp. 55, 56. At this point, Yezierska links Fanya with another immigrant daughter of the Puritans, Mary Antin, who also understood the immigrant journey as a fulfillment of the famous "errand" into the wilderness. In this respect, we should note that it is the obligation of the Dewey figure to help relocate the "past-less" immigrant within the sacred design of American prophetic history. On the immigrant appropriation of early American history see Mary Antin, *They Who Knock at Our Gates* (Boston: Houghton Mifflin, 1914), p. 98: "The ghost of the Mayflower pilots every immigrant ship, and Ellis Island is another name for Plymouth Rock." On Antin's typological imagination see Werner Sollors, *Beyond Ethnicity: Consent and Descent in American Culture* (New York: Oxford University Press, 1986).

61. See Dearborn, *Love in the Promised Land*, 128.

62. Yezierska, *All I Could Never Be*, p. 194.

63. Yezierska, *All I Could Never Be*, pp. 200, 202.

64. Yezierska, *All I Could Never Be*, pp. 215, 218.

65. Yezierska, *All I Could Never Be*, p. 253. "This novel ends the cycle of my experiences as an immigrant," Henriksen quotes her mother, writing to her publisher, William Lyon Phelps, in light of the failure of *All I Could Never Be*. See Henriksen, *Anzia Yezierska*, pp. 241–44 on the difficulties Yezierska had in composing and publishing this last novel.

66. Rosenfeld, "The Fall of David Levinsky," p. 156.

67. Alter Brody, "Yiddish: Our Literary Dominion," *The Nation* (20 April 1927): 435.

68. Letter to the "Bintel Brief" ("Bundle of Letters") section of the *Jewish Daily Forward*, dated 1908, in *A Bintel Brief: Sixty Years of Letters from the Lower East Side to the Jewish Daily Forward*, ed. Isaac Metzker (New York: Ballantine Books, 1971), p. 76.

3. THE CLAIMS OF DESCENT

1. Joseph Roth, *The Wandering Jews* (New York: W. W. Norton, 2001), pp. 84–5.

2. Henry James, *The American Scene* (1907), ed. Leon Edel (Bloomington: Indiana University Press, 1968), pp. 139, 138.

3. See in this respect Hasia Diner, *Lower East Side Memories: A Jewish Place in America* (Princeton, N.J.: Princeton University Press, 2000) and the essays gathered in *Remembering the Lower East Side,* ed. Hasia Diner, Jeffrey Shandler, and Beth S. Wenger (Bloomington: Indiana University Press, 2000).

4. Irving Howe, "The Lower East Side: Symbol and Fact," in *The Lower East Side: Portal to American Life (1870–1924),* ed. Allon Schoener (New York: The Jewish Museum), 1966), p. 11.

5. Irving Howe, *World of Our Fathers* (New York: Harcourt, Brace, Jovanovich, 1976), p. 558.

6. Alfred Kazin, "The Jew as Modern American Writer," in *Jewish-American Literature,* ed. Abraham Chapman (New York: New American Library, 1974), pp. 588–89.

7. Gilbert Seldes, "The Daemonic in the American Theatre," in *The Seven Lively Arts* (New York: Harper and Brothers, 1924), pp. 191–200.

8. Seldes, "The Daemonic in the American Theatre," p. 200.

9. For a map locating the scores of nickelodeon theaters dotting the Lower East Side ca. 1910 see the reproduction in *Entertaining America: Jews, Movies, and Broadcasting,* ed. J. Hoberman and Jeffrey Shandler (Princeton, N.J.: Princeton University Press, 2003), p. 25.

10. Patricia Erens, *The Jew In American Cinema* (Bloomington: Indiana University Press, 1984), p. 57.

11. Edward Sloman, quoted in Kevin Brownlow, *Behind the Mask of Innocence* (New York: Knopf, 1990), p. 409. On the phenomenon of Jewish sons fighting under Irish names, in *The Old World in the New* E. A. Ross relates the following anecdote: "The second generation [of "denizens of the Ghetto"], to be sure, overtop their parents and are going in for athletics. Hebrews under Irish names abound in the prize-ring, and not long ago a sporting editor printed the item, 'Jack Sullivan received a letter in Yiddish yesterday from his sister.'" E. A. Ross, *The Old World in the New* (New York: Century, 1914), p. 290.

12. *His People,* dir. Edward Sloman (Universal, 1925), National Center for Jewish Film, Brandeis University.

13. Michael Rogin, *Blackface, White Noise: Jewish Immigrants in the Hollywood Melting Pot* (Berkeley: University of California Press, 1996), p. 54. In light of the response his work has stimulated, Rogin's provocative argument concerning the Jews' problematic appropriation of blackface (via the tradition of minstrelsy) on their journey to "whiteness" deserves a clarifying essay itself. For dissenting views see Neal Gabler, "Making Faces," *The Forward* (May 24, 1996): 1, 10 [also see Rogin's response, "Seeing the Faces of Hollywood Jews," *Forward* (July, 5, 1996): 6]; Hasia Diner, "Trading Faces," *Common Quest* 2 (Summer 1997): 40–44; Paul Buhle and Edward Portnoy, "Al Jolson in Black and White," *Tikkun* 11 (Nov./Dec. 1996): 67–70); Michael Alexander, *Jazz Age Jews* (Princeton, N.J.: Princeton University Press, 2001), pp. 171–72; Joel Rosenberg, "Rogin's Noise: The Alleged Historical Crimes of *The Jazz Singer,*" *Prooftexts* 22 (Winter/Spring 2002): 221–39; Joel Rosenberg, "What You Ain't Heard Yet: The Languages of *The Jazz Singer,*" *Prooftexts* 22 (Winter/Spring 2002): especially 12–14.

14. Joel Rosenberg, "What You Ain't Heard Yet," p. 27.

15. For an illuminating timeline charting the various incarnations of *The Jazz Singer* see J. Hoberman, "*The Jazz Singer:* A Chronology," *Entertaining America,*

pp. 84–92. Perhaps the key issue in the debate over Jolson and the many other "ethnic" performers in early twentieth-century popular culture who donned blackface is the extent such palpably racist performances proved socio-politically enabling in the way Rogin claims: "Blackface is the instrument that transfers identities from immigrant Jew to American" (*Blackface, White Noise*, p. 95). Missing from Rogin's account of what might be termed "transferring to whiteness" is a more complicated sense of the inherent ambiguities and ambivalences in the psychological and political passage itself. Daniel Itzkovitz, for example, highlights "the unsettled place of *Jewishness* in early-twentieth century American culture" (emphasis in original). Indeed, Jews *troubled* white America's notion of citizenship and identity, especially in the zone of popular culture. See Daniel Itzkovitz, "Passing Like Me," *South Atlantic Quarterly* 98 (Winter/Spring 1999): 36. See also Daniel Itzkovitz, "Secret Temples," in *Jews and Other Differences: The New Jewish Cultural Studies*, ed. Jonathan Boyarin and Daniel Boyarin (Minneapolis: University of Minnesota Press, 1997), pp. 176–202 (see especially p. 198n on Rogin). On the more complicating dimension of blackface and Jewish identity also see Marshall Berman, "Love and Theft: From Jack Robin to Bob Dylan," *Dissent* 49 (Summer 2002): 67–73. "For Jewish kids who did not want to become comfortable 'allrightniks,' blackface enabled them to feel firmly, even righteously American without having to feel white" (p. 70). Ultimately, for Berman, "When Jolson paints himself black, he performs multicultural America's first sacrament: he constitutes himself as both the mixer and the mix" (p. 73).

16. Anzia Yezierska, *All I Could Never Be* (New York: Brewer, Warren, and Putnam, 1932), p. 171.

17. In *Bread Givers*, Sara briefly encounters a version of this "Broadway type" in the figure of the charismatic, restless Max Goldstein, who admits that he can't "sit still and be quiet five minutes. I've got to be on the go. Excitement is like eating to me." Sarah eventually rejects his entreaties, stating, "'I'm no excitement eater like you.'" Anzia Yezierska, *Bread Givers* (New York: Persea Books, 1975), p. 196.

18. Seldes, "The Daemonic in American Theatre," pp. 196, 193, 200.

19. Samson Raphaelson, "The Day of Atonement," in Robert L. Carringer, ed., *The Jazz Singer* (Madison: University of Wisconsin Press, 1979), p. 147; Raphaelson, quoted in Carringer, "Introduction: History of a Popular Culture Classic," p. 11. On the matter of "cantoring" in immigrant popular culture see Jeffrey Melnick, *A Right to Sing the Blues: African Americans, Jews, and American Popular Song* (Cambridge, Mass.: Harvard University Press, 1999), pp. 168–77.

20. Raphaelson, "The Day of Atonement," pp. 160, 160–61, 165.

21. Raphaelson, "The Day of Atonement," pp. 164, 147. Interestingly, "The Day of Atonement" embeds (as it reverses) a Yezierska-like subplot: Jack falls in love with an upscale "daughter of a Boston lawyer," his eyes seeking out her "simple, unruffled Anglo-Saxon quality of temperament." Yet such an embrace proves fatal for his "daemonic" stage presence. Her "unruffled" quality "served to beat him down into a soothing numbness which was bad for the audiences." "Day of Atonement," p. 154. In this scenario Jack looms as one of Yezierska's unbridled "hungry hearts."

22. In another incarnation, Jack might have been a stand-up comic drawing on the restlessness and cynicism of ghetto life, hurling vulgar insults at both the world that shaped and constrained him *and* the authorizing Anglo-Saxon culture he emulates and resists at the same time—recall Joe's "salacious banter" in *Levinsky*, or the career of the late Milton Berle—see the Epilogue, below.

23. Raphaelson, "The Day of Atonement," p. 155.

24. Samson Raphaelson, *The Jazz Singer* (New York: Brentano, 1925), pp. 38–39, 49, 48. For a very smart reading of the theatrical version of *The Jazz Singer* see Andrea Most, *Making Americans: Jews and the Broadway Musical* (Cambridge, Mass.: Harvard University Press, 2003), pp. 33–39. With Most I agree that the "Jack Robins" in both

play and movie are "figured as identities of *descent*, not *consent*" (p. 39). On the question of the play's contemporary meanings see Melnick, *A Right to Sing the Blues*, 104–108. "The play version of *The Jazz Singer*," Melnick writes, "afforded Jewish audiences the opportunity to visit a social space which was not blatantly marked as Jewish but which nonetheless provided entertainment with special in-group meanings" (p. 105).

25. Raphaelson, *The Jazz Singer*, pp. 58, 57, 107, 50, 50.

26. Raphaelson, *The Jazz Singer*, pp. 144, 143, 148, 150. Emphasis in the original.

27. Raphaelson, *The Jazz Singer*, pp. 150, 151. Emphasis in the original. "The play ends ambiguously," observes Andrea Most, "as the producer and costar of Jack's show overhear his chanting in the synagogue and express great admiration for his talent and hope that he will return to the stage." Most, *Making Americans*, p. 33.

28. Jessel's relation to the play is itself fascinating. During *The Jazz Singer*'s thirty-eight week run in New York, it seems that Jessel was converted to a more committed Judaism. "I had found faith," he said in 1926, "and I turned about face and became a new George Jessel. . . . [I] became in reality the man I am portraying on stage." George Jessel, quoted in Carringer, "Introduction," p. 14.

29. Neal Gabler, *An Empire of Their Own: How the Jews Invented Hollywood* (New York: Doubleday, 1988), p. 141.

30. Quoted in Gabler, *An Empire of Their Own*, p. 141. Note, in this respect, the connection to Yezierska, especially to the figure of Sara in *Bread Givers* who claims "America" as the authority for her dissent from orthodox ways.

31. *The Jazz Singer*, dir. Alan Crosland (Warner Bros. 1927).

32. Carringer, ed., *The Jazz Singer*, p. 70.

33. Herbert G. Goldman, *Jolson: The Legend Comes to Life* (New York: Oxford University Press, 1988), p. 5.

34. J. Hoberman, *Vulgar Modernism: Writing on Movies and other Media* (Philadelphia: Temple University Press, 1991), p. 65.

35. Carringer, ed., *The Jazz Singer*, p. 71. "The whole scene," observes J. Hoberman, "is redolent of his liberation from tribal taboo. Jack wolfs down an unkosher breakfast with ragtime ebullience . . . and then launches into 'Toot, Toot, Tootsie' with lascivious assurance." Such extreme emotions bespeak "Jack/Jolson's" affective transition. Hoberman, "My Songs Mean as Much to My Audience as Yours Do to Your Congregation," [review of Rogin, *Blackface, White Noise*], *London Review of Books* 18 (July 18, 1996): 22. Hoberman's review is by far the most reasoned response to Rogin. His conclusion: "*The Jazz Singer* [is] a movie about the psychic costs of becoming American" (p. 23).

36. Seldes, "The Daemonic in American Theatre," pp. 192, 196. Seldes continues: "On the great nights when everything is right, Jolson is driven by a power beyond himself" (p. 196). With only film, newsreel and recordings left in the Jolson archive, it may well be impossible to recover Jolson's apparently profound stage presence, his authentic charisma as a performer.

37. Seldes, "The Daemonic in the American Theatre," pp. 193, 192. The ad-lib quotation is from the filmed (not scripted) version of *The Jazz Singer*.

38. In another context, Michael Rogin speaks of *The Jazz Singer* as a "liminal movie." *Blackface, White Noise*, p. 116.

39. Gabler, *Empire of Their Own*, p. 145. For a deep reading of the emotionally rich "encounter" between Jack and Cantor Rosenblatt, emphasizing the "contagion of mourning" inscribed in the scene, see Rosenberg, "What You Ain't Heard Yet," pp. 22–29

40. Hoberman, *Vulgar Modernism*, p. 67.

41. For the story of Jolson's depressing private life see Goldman, *Jolson*, passim.

42. For information on *It Is to Laugh* see its folder in the Performing Arts Library, Lincoln Center Library. "The Gold in Fish" was reprinted in Hurst's story collection

Song of Life (New York: Knopf, 1927). A number of Hurst stories and novels were adapted for the screen, including, most famously, "Humoresque" (1919) and *Imitation of Life* (1933) [each was subsequently remade]. For more on Hurst's fiction onto film see Abe C. Ravitz, *Imitations of Life: Fannie Hurst's Gaslight Sonatas* (Carbondale: Southern Illinois Press, 1997).

43. *The Younger Generation,* dir. Frank Capra (Columbia, 1929).

44. Hurst, "The Gold in Fish," p. 102. Birdie has an errand before she arrives with her mother uptown: "We could take the Bronx express up, but the local is better because I want to stop at Lipschutz's Fish Market and get a miltz so you can *gedaemfte* [to stew, as in pot roast] it for supper, ma." Hurst's description of Ma Goldfish's reaction is priceless: "The atavistic look of a woman backed by whole centuries of women who have known how to tear the entrails from fish." Indeed, Ma is "Going home." (p. 102).

45. Gabler, *An Empire of Their Own,* p. 167.

46. For a shrewd reading of *The Younger Generation* see Raymond Carney, *American Vision: The Films of Frank Capra* (Cambridge: Cambridge University Press, 1986), pp. 53–55.

47. J. Hoberman, *Bridge of Light: Yiddish Film between Two Worlds* (New York: Schocken, 1991), p. 262.

48. *The Cantor's Son,* dir. Sidney Goldin (Eron Pictures, 1937). For more about the response to *The Jazz Singer* see Eric A. Goldman, "*The Jazz Singer* and Its Reaction in the Yiddish Cinema," in *When Joseph Met Molly: A Reader on Yiddish Film,* ed. Sylvia Paskin (Nottingham: Five Leaves Publications, 1999), pp. 39–48.

49. For a brilliant discussion of the meaning of nostalgia in early immigrant cinema see Jeffrey Shandler, "*Ost und West,* Old World and New: Nostalgia and Anti-nostalgia on the Silver Screen," in *Going Home,* ed. Jack Kugelmass (Evanston, Ill.: Northwestern University Press, 1993), pp. 153–88.

50. Hoberman, *Bridge of Light,* p. 165.

51. Asch, Sholom, *Uncle Moses,* 1918 (New York: G. P. Putnam's Sons, 1938), pp. 40, 41, 21. David G. Roskies notes the connections between Levinsky and Moses in "Yiddish on Screen," *Commentary* 93 (April 1992): 47–50 (especially p. 49). For Roskies's fuller reading of *Uncle Moses* see "Coney Island, USA: America in the Yiddish Literary Imagination," in *The Cambridge Companion to Jewish American Literature,* ed. Michael P. Kramer and Hana Wirth-Nesher (Cambridge: Cambridge University Press, 2003), pp. 75–78.

52. Compare Hoberman's view of nostalgia in *Uncle Moses,* in *Bridge of Light,* p. 163. Ultimately, Hoberman observes, "*Uncle Moses* coincided with a new literary awareness, as first-generation Jewish-American writers addressed the pathos of immigration and the circumstances of their childhoods" (p. 166). In this respect, the film looks forward to Henry Roth's *Call It Sleep,* discussed in the next chapter.

53. Asch, *Uncle Moses,* p. 176.

4. HAUNTED IN THE NEW WORLD

1. Henry Roth, *Call It Sleep* [1934] (New York: Avon, 1964), p. 375.

2. Henry Roth, letter to Byron Franzen (4 Nov. 1968), in Henry Roth, *Shifting Landscape* (Philadelphia: Jewish Publication Society, 1987), p. 47.

3. Mary Gordon, "Confession, Terminable and Interminable," review of Henry Roth, *A Diving Rock on the Hudson, The New York Times Book Review* (Feb. 26, 1995): 5.

4. James Wood, "Portrait: Roth of God," *The Guardian* (Feb. 18, 1994): 20.

5. Marshall Berman, "The Bonds of Love" (review of Henry Roth, *From Bondage*), *The Nation* 263 (Sept. 23, 1996): 26.

6. Henry Roth, *Requiem for Harlem,* vol. IV of *Mercy of a Rude Stream* (New York: St. Martin's 1998), p. 64.

7. Henry Roth, *A Diving Rock on the Hudson,* vol. II of *Mercy of a Rude Stream* (New York: St. Martin's, 1995), p. 399.

8. Numerous profiles of Henry Roth living in relative obscurity in New Mexico remark on this particular image. See, for example, Hana Wirth-Nesher: "Towering over his desk in his living room in Albuquerque, New Mexico, is a many times enlarged photograph of New York's Lower East Side at the turn of the century." Hana Wirth-Nesher, "Introduction," *New Essays on Call It Sleep,* ed. Hana Wirth-Nesher (New York: Cambridge University Press, 1996), pp. 1–2.

9. Henry Roth, *A Star Shines over Mt. Morris Park,* vol. I of *Mercy of a Rude Stream* (New York: St. Martin's, 1994), pp. 18–19.

10. Roth, *A Star Shines over Mt. Morris Park,* pp. 17, 16.

11. Henry Roth, "On Being Blocked & Other Literary Matters," *Commentary* 64 (Aug. 1977): 32–33.

12. Roth, *A Star Shines Over Mt. Morris Park,* p. 160.

13. Roth, *A Diving Rock on the Hudson,* pp. 379, 382.

14. Roth, *A Diving Rock on the Hudson,* pp. 190, 210.

15. Roth, *A Diving Rock on the Hudson,* p. 225.

16. Roth, *A Diving Rock on the Hudson,* p. 412.

17. Roth, *A Diving Rock on the Hudson,* pp. 10, 55.

18. Allegra Goodman, "About Time" (review of Henry Roth, *Requiem for Harlem*), *The New York Times Book Review* (April 1, 1998): 16.

19. Gordon, "Confession, Terminable and Interminable," p. 5.

20. Roth, *Requiem for Harlem,* p. 172.

21. Roth, *A Diving Rock on the Hudson,* p. 410.

22. Roth, *Requiem for Harlem,* p. 266.

23. Roth, *A Diving Rock on the Hudson,* p. 340.

24. Roth, *Requiem for Harlem,* p. 271.

25. Roth, *Requiem for Harlem,* p. 272.

26. Roth, *Call It Sleep,* p. 11.

27. Roth, *Call It Sleep,* p. 15.

28. Roth, *Call It Sleep,* p. 393.

29. Ruth R. Wisse, *The Modern Jewish Canon: A Journey through Language and Culture* (New York: The Free Press, 2000), p. 278.

30. Roth, *Call It Sleep,* pp. 22, 35, 23. For a brilliant reading of *Call It Sleep* (a reading to which I am much indebted), see Werner Sollors, " 'A World Somewhere, Somewhere Else': Language, Nostalgic Mournfulness, and Urban Immigrant Family Romance in *Call It Sleep,*" in *New Essays on Call It Sleep,* pp. 127–82.

31. Roth, *Call It Sleep,* p. 38.

32. Roth, *Call It Sleep,* p. 40.

33. Roth, *Call It Sleep,* pp. 43–44. I have distilled the Luter-Genya dialogue from Roth's narrative, eliminating his intra-dialogue commentary.

34. Roth, *Call It Sleep,* pp. 45–46. " 'Let's go to bed then,' " the mother replies to the son's tacit agreement; " 'it grows late.' " Given the charged oedipal atmosphere of *Call It Sleep,* Genya's seeming matter of fact statement sounds like a long dreamed-of invitation.

35. Roth, *Call It Sleep,* p. 95.

36. Roth, *Call It Sleep,* pp. 95, 92.

37. Listen, in this respect, to Alfred Kazin's memories of foodways in Williamsburg, and the anxious imprecations that attended this now virtually canonic territory of immigrant experience. Of course the mothers' greenhorn anxiety now sounds comical in Kazin's sophisticated ears:

As I went down Belmont Avenue, the copper-shining herrings in the tall black barrels made me think of the veneration of food in Brownsville families. I can still see the kids pinned down to the tenement stoops, their feet helplessly kicking at the pots and pans lined up before them, their mouths pressed open with a spoon while the great meals are rammed down their throats. "*Eat! Eat! May you be destroyed if you don't eat! What sin have I committed that God should punish me with you! Eat! What will become of you if you don't eat! Imp of darkness, may you sink ten fathoms into the earth if you don't eat! Eat!*"

Alfred Kazin, *A Walker in the City* (New York: Harcourt, Brace, 1951), p. 32. Genya may not sound like Kazin's crazed Williamsburg mothers (Yezierska's Hanna Breinah would seem a better example), but she does hover around David, pressing him with soothing meals, designed to allay his fears. See especially the conclusion to *Call It Sleep*, discussed below.

38. Roth, *Call It Sleep*, pp. 332, 209.

39. Roth, *Call It Sleep*, pp. 65, 71.

40. Roth, *Call It Sleep*, pp. 228, 230.

41. Cf. *Call It Sleep*, p. 231: "But your mouth don't get dirty. I don't feel no dirt. (He rolled his tongue about). Maybe inside. Way, way in, where you can't taste it. What did Isaiah say that made his mouth dirty? Real dirty, so he'd know it was?"

42. Roth, *Call It Sleep*, p. 227.

43. Roth, *Call It Sleep*, p. 227.

44. Roth, *Call It Sleep*, p. 246.

45. Roth, *Call It Sleep*, pp. 247, 248.

46. Roth, *Call It Sleep*, p. 248.

47. See Sollors, " 'A World Somewhere, Somewhere Else,' " p. 142, on the matter of David and nostalgia: "The mother's warm and living body, the goal of David's oedipal yearnings, is also the physical space designating his origins, a space all the more important to David since he does not directly know his geographic place of birth."

48. Roth, *Call It Sleep*, p. 67. Genya relates her grandmother's story to David, pp. 65–68.

49. Roth, *Call It Sleep*, p. 68.

50. Roth, *Call It Sleep*, p. 71. Roth renders Genya's complexity by juxtaposing the awesome Sabbath light ("The hushed hour, the hour of tawny beatitude") with Genya's recognition of New World (proto-feminist?) Sabbath burdens:

His [David's] eyes roamed the kitchen: the confusion of Friday afternoons. Pots on the stove, parings in the sink, flour smeared on the rolling pin, the board. The air was warm, twined with many odors. His mother rose, washed the beets, drained them, set them aside.

"There," she said. "I can begin cleaning again."

David, of course, can't fathom his mother's wicked deflating irony. His senses envelop her in the realm of the sacred.

51. Roth, *A Diving Rock on the Hudson*, p. 6.

52. Roth, *Call It Sleep*, p. 252.

53. Roth, *Call It Sleep*, p. 253.

54. Roth, *Call It Sleep*, p. 253.

55. Roth, *Call It Sleep*, p. 257.

56. Roth, *Call It Sleep*, p. 257.

57. Roth, *Call It Sleep*, p. 261.

58. Roth, *Call It Sleep*, p. 226.

59. Roth, *Call It Sleep*, pp. 146, 153. In answer to Genya's question about whether she would ever return to her village in Austria, Aunt Bertha replies with a tour-de-force comedic riff—in the spirit of Jolson and, later, Mel Brooks, on the advantages of the New World: " 'But there's life here, isn't there? There's a stir here always. Listen! The street! The cars! High laughter! Ha, good! Veljish [Bertha's Old-World shtetl] was still as a fart in company. Who could endure it? Trees! Fields! Again trees! Who can talk to trees! Here at least I can find other pastimes than sliding down the gable on a roof!' "

60. Roth, *Call It Sleep*, pp. 305, 319, 303.

61. Roth, *Call It Sleep*, p. 320.

62. Roth, *Call It Sleep*, p. 322.

63. "Leo gives the illusion of having transcended his boyhood, mastered the neighborhood," observes Thomas J. Ferraro, in his very smart reading of *Call It Sleep*. See *Ethnic Passages: Literary Immigrants in Twentieth-Century America* (Chicago: University of Chicago Press, 1993), p. 109.

64. Roth, *Call It Sleep*, p. 326.

65. Roth, *Call It Sleep*, p. 345.

66. Roth, *Call It Sleep*, pp. 403, 411.

67. Ferraro, *Ethnic Passages*, pp. 113, 116.

68. Roth, *Call It Sleep*, p. 419. For a stunning reading of this famous "high modernist" section of *Call It Sleep* see Sollors, " 'A World Somewhere, Somewhere Else.' "

69. Roth, *Call It Sleep*, p. 322.

70. Roth, *Call It Sleep*, pp. 374, 375.

71. Roth, *Call It Sleep*, p. 437.

72. In an important essay Robert Alter speaks of "the famous Yiddish gift for invective," translated by Roth into the mouths of various characters, especially David's "menacing father," whose cursings sound to Alter's ears sounds like Melville's Ahab. See Robert Alter, "Awakenings," *The New Republic* 198 (Jan. 25, 1988): 36–37.

73. Roth, *Call It Sleep*, p. 441.

74. Roth, *Call It Sleep*, p. 375. For the rich social history of foodways in immigrant America see Hasia R. Diner, *Hungering for America: Italian, Irish, and Jewish Foodways in the Age of Migration* (Cambridge, Mass.: Harvard University Press, 2001).

75. Roth, *Call It Sleep*, p. 440.

76. Irving Howe, "Life Never Let Up," *The New York Times Book Review* (Oct. 25, 1964): 60.

77. Irving Howe, "Tevye on Broadway," *Commentary* 38 (Nov. 1964): 73; 75; 74. I return to Howe's critique of middle-class Jewish nostalgia in the epilogue. In retrospect, it seems clear that Howe's celebration of Roth was, in part, inspired by his loathing of *Fiddler*. In the Fall of 1964 Howe, not yet the guardian of Yiddish culture in America, thus had a complicated encounter with radically opposed modes of Jewish American expression. For additional discussions of Howe's response to *Fiddler* see Edward Alexander, *Irving Howe: Socialist, Critic, Jew* (Bloomington: Indiana University Press, 1998), pp. 173–74 (in the context of Howe's later attack on Philip Roth), and Stephen J. Whitfield, "Fiddling with Sholem Aleichem: A History of *Fiddler on the Roof*," in *Key Texts in American Jewish Culture*, ed. Jack Kugelmass (New Brunswick, N.J.: Rutgers University Press, 2003), pp. 105–106. For a very helpful essay explaining the response to Howe's *World of Our Fathers* in terms of Howe's relation to Yiddishkayt in general see Hasia Diner, "Embracing *World of Our Fathers*: The Context of Reception," in *Key Texts*, 210–22.

78. Alfred Kazin, "The Art of *Call It Sleep*," *New York Review* (Oct. 10, 1991): 15; 16.

79. Gordon, "Confession, Terminable and Interminable," p. 6.

5. TO MAKE "A JEW"

1. Cynthia Ozick, participant in "Is There a Cure for Anti-Semitism?" *Partisan Review* 61 (1994): 388.

2. Arthur Miller, *Focus* (New York: Reynal and Hitchcock, 1945), p. 33.

3. Nathan W. Ackerman and Marie Jahoda, *Anti-Semitism and Emotional Disorder: A Psychoanalytic Interpretation* (New York: Harper, 1950), p. 58.

4. James Atlas, *Bellow: A Biography* (New York: Knopf, 2000), p. 126.

5. Arthur Miller, "The Face in the Mirror: Anti-Semitism Then and Now," "Afterword" to *Focus* [1945] (London: Methuen, 2002), p. 213. Looking back in 2003 about his encounter with antisemitism and the origins of *Focus* Miller further reflected: "The anti-Semitism I ran into all over the place was fierce. And yet there was no sign of any recognition of it or acknowledgement of it in the public domain, not in novels, not in plays. . . . I felt it had to be unearthed. It had to be brought to light." Quoted in Hilary Leila Krieger, "Withstanding the Crucible," *The Jerusalem Post* (June 19, 2003) [Internet edition].

6. Malcolm Bradbury asserts that *Focus* "has some claim to being the first postwar Jewish-American novel, appearing at a time when that distinctive genre underwent a powerful, internationally influential revival." "Arthur Miller's Fiction," in *The Cambridge Companion to Arthur Miller* ed. Christopher Bigsby (Cambridge: Cambridge University Press, 1997), p. 215. Michael Walzer speaks of "The Jew in Europe" as "the exposed face of modern life" in the Preface to Jean-Paul Sartre's *Anti-Semite and Jew* (New York: Schocken Books, 1997 [orig. 1948]), p. xviii. "The post-war writers," observes Morris Dickstein, "moved away from social problems toward metaphysical concerns about identity, morality, and man's place in the larger scheme of the universe." Both *Focus* and *The Victim* amply illustrate his point. Morris Dickstein, *Leopards in the Temple: The Transformation of American Fiction, 1945–1970* (Cambridge, Mass.: Harvard University Press, 2002), p. 63.

7. Miller, "The Face in the Mirror," p. 214. Miller's original title for *Focus* was "Some Shall Not Sleep." This and other interesting factoids about Miller's first novel are reported by Martin Gottfried in *Arthur Miller: His Life and Work* (Cambridge, Mass.: Da Capo Press, 2003), pp. 88–90 (reference to original title on p. 88).

8. Miller, *Focus*, p. 17 ("a little Hebey," p. 175)

9. In this respect *Focus* uncannily anticipates the core rhetorical/philosophical discourse of Sartre's *Anti-Semite and Jew*. "Miller had completed *Focus* before *Réflexions* were [sic] published, and it is not clear how familiar he was with any writings on Sartre available by then. However, whether owing to Sartre's direct influence or in response to the broader intellectual climate, many of his works show clear analogies with existentialism." Ladislaus Löb, "'Insanity in the Darkness': Anti-Semitic Stereotypes and Jewish Identity in Max Frisch's *Andorra* and Arthur Miller's *Focus*," *Modern Language Review* 92 (1997), p. 547.

10. Miller, *Focus*, pp. 155, 217.

11. Saul Bellow, "Brothers' Keepers" [review of Arthur Miller, *Focus*], *The New Republic* 114 (Jan. 7, 1946): 30.

12. Bellow, "Brothers' Keepers," p. 30.

13. For a smart reading of *Focus*, which connects the novel to Laura Z. Hobson's *Gentleman's Agreement* (1947), see Matthew Jacobson, *Whiteness of a Different Color: European Immigrants and the Alchemy of Race* (Cambridge, Mass.: Harvard University Press, 1998), pp. 187–99.

14. "It is not a natural and clean anger," Maurice Samuel observes of antisemitism in *The Great Hatred;* "it is rage, plus disgust at the sight of something both dangerous and repulsive. It is the difference between being fighting mad and raving mad." *The Great Hatred* (New York: A. A. Knopf, 1940), p. 143.

15. Miller, *Focus*, pp. 66–67. Newman's agony over the loss of social identity at the level of his "face" looks forward to Miller's later cautionary 1952 fable *The Crucible*, where John Proctor, falsely accused of witchcraft, agonizes over losing his "name"—and thus his "history"—if he accepts the judges' *devil's* bargain to save his life. Mr. Finkelstein also voices a Proctor-like accusation against the antisemites of the Christian Front. " 'I will not move,' " he tells Newman, who has asked him to consider leaving the neighborhood. " 'I like it here. I like the air. . . . I don't know how to fight them but I will fight them. . . . They are a gang of devils and they want this country.' " *Focus*, pp. 182–83. Thus antisemitism in the 1940s looks forward to blacklisting in the 50s. Each ideology of negation *possesses* a totalitarian face. Miller, it should be remembered, refused to answer the summons to appear before HUAC.

16. Miller, *Focus*, pp. 3, 58, 13 (emphasis added).

17. Miller, *Focus*, p. 6. On the utopian aspect to the ending of *Focus* see Jacobson, *Whiteness of a Different Color*, p. 198.

18. Miller, *Focus*, pp. 32, 35, 34.

19. Miller, *Focus*, pp. 34, 32–34. In Jacobson's view, Miller provides "a stunning treatment of the complex process of projection" in the figure of Lawrence Newman (p. 192). In the 1940s "projection" was taken to be *the* psychological defense mechanism of antisemites.

20. Miller, *Focus*, p. 134. Anticipating one of key issues of *The Victim*, Miller has Newman ask himself, "What was dignified, what in God's name was dignified!" p. 137. "Finkelstein's secret," observes Löb, "is his unwavering confidence in his Jewish identity. Newman eventually finds his dignity by identifying himself with the Jews." Löb, " 'Insanity in the Darkness,' " p. 550.

21. Miller, *Focus*, pp. 135, 166.

22. Miller, *Focus*, p. 165.

23. Miller, *Focus*, pp. 168, 169. In this respect, Finkelstein offers Newman a (psychoanalytic) mirror reflecting the gentile's deepest anxieties. "What do you see that makes you so angry?" (p. 166) Finkelstein asks? The query exposes the complex dynamic of antisemitic projection limned in *Focus*.

24. Miller, *Focus*, p. 186 (emphasis added).

25. Miller, *Focus*, p. 184.

26. Miller, *Focus*, pp. 185–86.

27. Miller, *Focus*, p. 117. Further ironies abound, especially in relation to the film version of *Gentleman's Agreement*. Passing as a Jew, Gregory Peck as "Phil Green" confronts the manager at the restricted Flume Inn on the matter of admitting Jews. In the tense exchange, Peck—who has made a "Jew" of himself—seeks to expose the hotel's genteel antisemitism, but his moral outrage remains helpless before the steely gaze of the Inn's manager who, made uneasy by Peck's increasingly belligerent tone, quickly banishes the "loud" "Jew" from the lobby. During this scene of palpable shame Peck begins to "feel" his self-declared "Jewish" identity in new ways. For a fuller reading of *Gentleman's Agreement* along with *Crossfire*, the other famous 1947 film on antisemitism, see Donald Weber, "The Limits of Empathy: Hollywood's Imaging of Jews ca. 1947," in Jack Kugelmass, ed., *Key Texts in American Jewish Culture* (New Brunswick, N.J.: Rutgers University Press, 2003), pp. 91–104.

28. Miller, *Focus*, pp. 209, 210.

29. Miller, *Focus*, p. 212.

30. Miller, *Focus*, p. 217.

31. Miller, *Focus*, p. 211.

32. Miller, "The Face in the Mirror," p. 213.

33. Miller, *Focus*, p. 217.

34. Jacobson, *Whiteness of a Different Color*, p. 198.

35. Walzer, "Preface" to Sartre, *Anti-Semite and Jew*, pp. xx–xxi.

36. Leslie A. Fiedler, "Saul Bellow," in *Saul Bellow and the Critics,* ed. Irving Malin (New York: New York University Press, 1967), p. 6. Fiedler also reviewed *The Victim* in the *Kenyon Review* 10 (1948): 526–27.

37. Elizabeth Hardwick, rev. of *The Victim, Partisan Review* 15 (1948): 114. Other significant reviews include Diana Trilling in *The Nation* 166 (Jan. 3, 1948): 24–25, and Martin Greenberg, "Modern Man as Jew," *Commentary* 5 (1948): 86–87.

38. Saul Bellow, *The Victim* (New York: Vanguard Press, 1947), p. 3.

39. Bellow, *The Victim,* p. 77.

40. Hardwick, review of *The Victim,* p. 116. Morris Dickstein helpfully locates Bellow's second novel in terms of "forties concerns" (racism and antisemitism); it is, Dickstein observes, "almost a parody of the literature of social protest." *Leopards in the Temple,* p. 61.

41. Fiedler, "Saul Bellow," p. 6.

42. Bellow, *The Victim,* p. 39.

43. Bellow, *The Victim,* p. 39.

44. Bellow, *The Victim,* p. 39. For the complicated cultural genealogy of Harkavy's "Jewish" antics see Sander Gilman's chapters on "the Jewish voice" and "the Jewish nose" in *The Jew's Body* (New York: Routledge, 1991), pp. 10–37, 169–93.

45. Is Allbee thinking of the popular classic "My Yiddishe Mama"? Written by Jack Yellen, it was a huge hit for Sophie Tucker in the mid-thirties, and for the Barry Sisters in the forties. Thanks to Mount Holyoke master librarian Bryan Goodwin for this factoid.

46. Bellow, *The Victim,* pp. 40, 41.

47. Bellow, *The Victim,* pp. 144, 144–45, 224. In an early exchange Allbee notes with interest the picture of Leventhal's wife and seeks to divine her "descent" identity:

> Allbee: She's positively Asiatic.
> Leventhal: She comes from Baltimore.
> A: First generation?
> L: Her mother is native-born, too. Further back than that I don't know.
> [Here Leventhal sounds like Sara confessing her lack of genealogical memory to Hugo in *Bread Givers.*]
> A: I'm willing to bet they came from Eastern Europe, originally.
>
> It's apparent enough; it doesn't need any investigating. Russian, Poland . . . I can see at a glance. (p. 72)

Recent scholarship on *The Victim* highlights the racialized dimension of the Allbee-Leventhal relationship. See, for example, Philip McGowan, "The Writing of Blackness in Saul Bellow's *The Victim,*" *Saul Bellow Journal* 16 17 (2000 2001). 74–103.

48. Bellow, *The Victim,* pp. 7, 13. Elsewhere Bellow notes Leventhal's "unimpassioned face" (p. 98).

49. Bellow, *The Victim,* p. 241. In this respect Leventhal's looming personal crisis looks forward to that of Tommy Wilhelm. See chapter 7 below.

50. Bellow, *The Victim,* p. 44.

51. Bellow, *The Victim,* pp. 45–46.

52. Bellow, *The Victim,* p. 44.

53. Bellow, *The Victim,* p. 45.

54. Bellow, *The Victim,* p. 45.

55. "Composure, if it is a quality," observes Adam Phillips, "is the least innocent of virtues." "Provoked by an excess of excitement, composure becomes a way of accommodating such experience, a belated refusal; it becomes, in fact, a superstition of confidence in the integrity of the self." Asa's mask of composure exemplifies Phillips's stunning observation about the raging underbelly of composure, acted out at the end

Cohen: "Hullo! Are you dere? Yes—are you de benk? Yes, I want to see the manager, please. I say I vant to SEE de manager, please. Vot do you say? This is not a telescope, it is a telephone? Say, you tink you're very clever ain't it? Vell, du mehr favor. Just hang a small of crepe on your nose, your brains are dead."

Transcribed by Michael G. Corenthal in *Cohen on the Telephone: A History of Jewish Recorded Humor and Popular Music, 1892–1942* (Milwaukee: Yesterday's Memories, 1984), p. 53

13. Quoted in Joan Jaffe, "This is Molly Goldberg Speaking of the Rise of the Goldbergs," Correspondence Scrapbook I, 1931–32, Berg Papers.

14. Milt Gross, *Dunt Esk!!* (New York: George H. Doran, 1927), pp. 9, 206, 219, 229. Milt Gross was a cartoonist for the *Sunday World* when he began a humor column called "Down the Dumbwaiter" in 1924. To judge from reviews of his books, his ethnic sketches had a substantial following in the late 20s. See, for example, Robert Littell, "Nize Baby," *New Republic* 47 (June 9, 1926): 93–94. "The Jewish East Side speaks through Milt Gross," according to Ernest Sutherland Bates, in "American Folklore," *Saturday Review of Literature* 2 (July 10, 1926): 914. Paul Buhle briefly discusses the figure of Milt Gross in relation to a tradition of other Jewish comic strip artists in *From the Lower East Side to Hollywood: Jews in American Popular Culture* (London: Verso, 2004), pp. 97–98.

15. On Tucker and Jolson's contemporary, Fannie Brice see June Sochen, "From Sophie Tucker to Barbra Streisand: Jewish Women Entertainers as Reformers," in *Talking Back: Images of Jewish Women in American Popular Culture* ed. Joyce Antler (Hanover, N.H.: University Press of New England, 1998), pp. 68–84.

16. All letters are from the Correspondence Scrapbooks, Berg Papers.

17. Berg, *Molly and Me*, p. 179.

18. Radio and TV Scripts, 1930, Berg Papers.

19. Correspondence Scrapbook, 1935, Berg Papers. In this instance the show in question is *House of Glass*, a radio serial that Berg wrote briefly between long runs of *The Goldbergs. House of Glass* concerned family life revolving around a modest resort hotel in the Catskills modeled on a similar hotel operated by Berg's own father.

20. Correspondence Scrapbook, 1935, Berg Papers.

21. Correspondence Scrapbook, 1943, Berg Papers.

22. Correspondence Scrapbook, 1949, Berg Papers.

23. Correspondence Scrapbooks, 1934–35, Berg Papers.

24. These 1929–30 radio serial plots were eventually transformed by Berg into a collection of short stories, printed with slightly less Yiddish inflection, and published by NBC as *The Rise of the Goldbergs* (New York: Barse & Co., 1931) with a preface by Eddie Cantor.

25. "I am glad to help in any little way that I can," wrote Rabbi David de Sola Pool of the Spanish and Portuguese Synagogue in New York, after providing a detailed synopsis of a Jewish marriage ceremony, "because I believe that you are doing more for better understanding and good will of an interdenominational and interracial character than all the organized movements." Rabbi David de Sola Pool to Gertrude Berg, June 8, 1932, Berg Papers.

26. Scrapbook, 1933, Berg Papers.

27. Radio and TV Scripts, 1933 (Episode 593, "The 'Seder' at the Neighborhood Club House"), Berg Papers.

28. Correspondence Scrapbooks 1933 and 1934, Berg Papers.

29. Correspondence Scrapbook, 1944, Berg Papers. For examples of *The Goldbergs* puzzle and comic strip, see the illustrations in *Entertaining America,* 124. The comic strip did indeed begin in the *Post,* in June 1944, revisiting the plot of "Mama

Saves the Day." The panels often conclude with a box titled "Mama Says," with a fitting moral tag. For more on this aspect of Berg's career see Antler, " 'Yesterday's Woman.' "

30. In the words of Berg's own plot outline-narrative, the Goldbergs save the town by injecting a spirit of commercial enterprise (through Jake's dress business) and the "new [i.e., ethnic] families" embrace of "My America"—which becomes the title of Molly's "new Pilgrim's progress," a gathering of her own thoughts and insights, written in "Molly's style . . . the right style," which is published to great success. Throughout these late thirties and early forties soaps, as Berg herself explains, Molly continues in character, "constantly bringing . . . people together, forcing them to realize what their role in life must be. In a sense she transfigures and saves each character." Gertrude Berg, Plot Outline, ca. early 1940s, Berg Papers.

31. David Marc, *Comic Visions: Television Comedy and American Culture* (Boston: Unwin Hyman, 1989), p. 51. For another perspective on the transitions/transformations of early ethnic television with specific reference to *The Goldbergs* see Brook, "The Americanization of Molly: How Mid-Fifties TV Homogenized *The Goldbergs*."

32. Morris Freedman, "The Real Molly Goldberg: Balesbostah of the Air Waves," *Commentary* 21 (April 1956): 359–60.

33. A brief account of the Loeb affair: In the summer of 1950 Loeb was listed in *Red Channels*, the blacklist bible of the television networks and sponsors. After much debate with CBS and General Foods, Loeb was fired by Berg (although Berg tried to keep him on the show) in January 1952. *The Goldbergs* eventually returned to TV that spring with three new sponsors (paying for three fifteen-minute segments a week) on NBC. Bitter, exhausted, burdened with tremendous personal debts, and hounded by the IRS, Loeb committed suicide in September 1955. Interestingly, Berg kept a separate scrapbook on the Loeb affair, gathering the flurry of newspaper accounts of Loeb's detractors (by influential columnists like Ed Sullivan and Victor Reisel) and defenders (like the New York-based Actor's Equity and revered columnist Murray Kempton. Responding to the obituary notice for William S. Paley, the founder of CBS and supporter of the blacklist, in a letter to the *New York Times* Berg's daughter, Harriet Berg Schwartz, defended her mother's behavior during this sorry episode of television history: Mentioning Loeb, she remarks, "My mother would not go along with this injustice." "In the McCarthy Era, TV Networks Cowered," *New York Times* (Nov. 11, 1990): E16. On the Loeb affair and TV blacklisting in general, see Merle Miller, *The Judges and the Judged* (New York: Doubleday, 1952); and Stefan Kanfer, *A Journal of the Plague Years* (New York: Atheneum, 1973). For contemporary journalism on Loeb, see "Loeb and Red Channels," *New Republic*, vol. 126 (Jan. 1, 1952): 8; and "Red Channels Rides Again," *New Republic*, vol. 126 (Feb. 18, 1952): 22. For an evaluation of his life, see the moving column by Murray Kempton, "The Victim," *New York Post* (Sept. 13, 1955). See also Lipsitz, "The Meaning of Memory," pp. 62–63. The Philip Loeb Papers at the New York Public Library hold precious little information about the Loeb case. There are, however, letters of encouragement from such figures as Harold Clurman and Elia Kazan, and copies of letters protesting Loeb's firing from outraged fans of *The Goldbergs*. Loeb, who had been living at Zero Mostel's apartment on West Eighty-Sixth Street, tragically gave up the fight for his political and professional integrity and committed suicide. Mostel eventually honored the memory of his friend's tragic life by playing a version of Loeb ("Hecky Green") in *The Front* (Columbia, 1976), Martin Ritt's attack on the sordid era of blacklisting in early television.

34. Freedman, "The Real Molly Goldberg."

35. Sam Levenson, "The Dialect Comedian Should Vanish," *Commentary* 14 (Aug. 1952): 169.

36. Correspondence Scrapbook 6, 1939–42, Berg Papers.

37. I borrow this Yiddish term from Charles Angoff, " 'The Goldbergs,' " *The Reconstructionist* (Dec. 24, 1954): 20. In another essay on *The Goldbergs,* Angoff observed, "I have found the simpler the people, the less complicated, the more they are likely to enjoy 'The Goldbergs,' and that the *ersatz* intellectuals, especially the females, tend to look down upon it." Angoff, " 'The Goldbergs' and Jewish Humor," *Congress Weekly: A Review of Jewish Interests* 18 (March 5, 1951): 12. Both articles are in the Berg Papers.

38. Copies of various episodes of the television *Goldbergs* may be screened at the Museum of Television and Radio (in New York and Los Angeles), the National Jewish Archive of Broadcasting, the Jewish Museum in New York, and the UCLA Radio and Television Archive. UCLA has by far the largest collection of *Goldbergs* episodes, although drawn for the most part from the later seasons, after the family moved from Tremont Avenue in the Bronx to the suburbs of Haverville.

39. "Passover Program" (April 18, 1949), Scripts, Berg Papers. By contrast, a Passover show broadcast on radio (April 3, 1939) includes Passover liturgy sung in Hebrew and the sound of a rock smashing through the Goldbergs's window (Berg's allusion to Kristallnacht?). "Passover Program" (April 3, 1939), R86:0791, Museum of Television and Radio.

40. Herbert J. Gans, "American Jewry: Present and Future," *Commentary* 21 (May 1956): 425. Over twenty years later, Gans revised "symbolic Judaism" into the overarching term, "symbolic ethnicity," to describe the transformation of traditional religious observance into modes of sentiment, including nostalgia, foodways, the "old neighborhood," and so on. See Herbert J. Gans, "Symbolic Ethnicity: The Future of Ethnic Groups and Culture in America" [1979], in *Theories of Ethnicity: A Classical Reader,* ed. Werner Sollors (New York: New York University Press, 1996), pp. 425–52.

41. T. J. Jackson Lears, "Making Fun of Popular Culture," *American Historical Review* 97 (1992): 1417–26.

42. Radio and TV Scripts, 1950, Berg Papers. The Sanka ad is in Berg's own hand.

43. "Moving Day" (Sept. 22, 1955), videotape 2591T, UCLA Film and Television Archive. For some shrewd insights into the contradictions of the Goldbergs in the suburbs see Brook, "The Americanization of Molly."

44. "Moving Day," UCLA Film and Television Archive.

45. "Social Butterfly," UCLA Film and Television Archive. Earlier, on the radio in the thirties, Molly conquered genteel/gentile Lastonbury, Connecticut with a volume of her observations called "My America."

46. Susan Kalcik, "Ethnic Foodways in America: Symbol and the Performance of Identity," in *Ethnic and Regional Foodways in the United States: The Performance of Group Identity,* ed. L. K. Brown and K. Mussell (Knoxville: University of Tennessee Press, 1984), p. 37. For the larger social history of ethnic foodways among immigrant groups see Hasia R. Diner, *Hungering for America: Italian, Irish and Jewish Foodways in the Age of Migration* (Cambridge, Mass.: Harvard University Press, 2001).

47. Kalcik, p. 38.

48. I borrow this phrase from Alice Kessler-Harris, Introduction to Anzia Yezierska, *Bread Givers* (New York: Persea, 1975), xiii.

49. Interestingly, a late episode titled "The Hansens' Rise in the World," virtually repeats this theme. Mama senses that she is accepted into the snooty "Bayside Ladies Culture and Conversation Club" because, she comes to realize, "they like my recipes." "The Hansens' Rise in the World," *Mama,* videotape T86 1128, Museum of Television and Radio.

50. "Molly's Fish" (Jan. 5, 1956), VA2004, UCLA Film and Television Archive.

51. In ironic contrast, in *Molly and Me* Berg describes her grandmother's magical fish-making, a symphony of culinary labor that recalls the utopian aspect of Dinah's

kitchen in *Uncle Tom's Cabin:* "Grandma," Berg recalls, "was busy filleting pounds of carp, pike, whitefish. . . . These were the ingredients of gefillte fish that were chopped by hand in a wooden bowl that made a sound like music." *Molly and Me,* p. 39.

52. "Molly's Fish," UCLA Film and Television Archive.

53. "Molly's Fish," Script, Radio and TV Manuscripts, 1955, Berg Papers. "Ethnic and local loyalties," observes Donna Gabaccia, "repeatedly generate critiques of mass consumer culture, even while the marketplace remains the arena for expressing ethnic and local identities." "Molly's Fish" anticipates this keen insight. See Donna R. Gabaccia, *We Are What We Eat: Ethnic Food and the Making of Americans* (Cambridge, Mass.: Harvard University Press, 1998), p. 230.

54. Todd Gitlin, "Prime Time Ideology: The Hegemonic Process in Television Entertainment," in *Television: The Critical View,* 3rd ed., ed. Horace Newcomb (New York: Oxford University Press, 1982), p. 452 and passim.

55. All twenty-six episodes of *Mrs. G Goes to College* (later called *The Gertrude Berg Show*) are available on film from Four Star Productions, based in Los Angeles. I was able to screen the various episodes discussed below at the UCLA Television archive facilities. In an amazing factoid, Marion Ross eventually played a mother of the 1950s (in *Happy Days*) and then a grandmother of the same era (in *Brooklyn Bridge*). Did she base her more recent TV incarnation of an Old World Brooklyn grandmother on Gertrude Berg? For a brief analysis of *Brooklyn Bridge* and contemporary nostalgia see Donald Weber, "Accents of the Future: Jewish American Popular Culture," in *The Cambridge Companion to Jewish American Literature,* ed. Michael P. Kramer and Hana Wirth-Nesher (Cambridge: Cambridge University Press, 2003), pp. 144–45.

56. Remember, as David Marc explains, the early 1960s was a cultural threshold in television history, a moment when ethnicity was virtually erased—symbolized by the fascinating story of *The Dick Van Dyke Show,* whose creator, Carl Reiner, was either deemed, or deemed himself, "too Jewish" to play the lead in a series à clef about his own life as a television writer living in New Rochelle. See Marc, *Comic Visions,* pp. 97–99. Also on this subject see Jeffrey Shandler, "At Home on the Small Screen: Television's New York Jews," in *Entertaining America,* pp. 244–56 (esp. pp. 246–47 on Reiner). Note, in this respect, the continuing "emptying out" (*oisgrinung?*) aspect of Berg's self-naming over time, from "Talnitzky" in the first imagined *Goldbergs* incarnation in 1929, to *The Goldbergs,* to *Molly* (on television, during the Haverville episodes in 1955), to, by 1961, the "Mrs. G."

57. "Dad's Day," *Mrs. G Goes to College* (1962), manuscript shooting script, in Berg Papers. This episode is listed as #4650 in the Four Star synopses list.

58. "Dad's Day," Television Scripts 1962 (including Berg's manuscript revisions), Berg Papers.

59. Nor did the audience overhear the following exchange between Mrs. G and Mr. Rickadmyack, for the scene was never included in the final cut:

> Mr. R: I'm Quentin Richards['s] father.
> Mrs. G: Oh . . . I'm so happy you could. I didn't recognize the name. I . . .
> Mr. R: The boy changed his name to Richards. He thought it would be more up to date . . . more American.
> Mrs. G (smiles): We weren't always the Greens either [this line is crossed out by Berg]
> Mr. R: (he smiles at this . . . seems a little more at ease)

"Dad's Day," Shooting Script, p. 25.

60. "Dad's Day," Shooting Script, p. 32, Berg Papers.

61. Asher Z. Milbauer and Donald G. Watson, "An Interview with Philip Roth," in *Conversations with Philip Roth,* ed. George J. Searles (Jackson: University of Mississippi Press, 1992), pp. 245, 244. For a stinging critique of *The Goldbergs* as an "unfunny early

ethnic sitcom that reveals the inherent limitations of the genre see Judith Shulevitz, "'The Cosby Show,' Starring . . . Heavily Accented Jews?" *New York Times* (July 20, 2003): 24, 34 ["Arts and Leisure" section].

7. THE "JEWISH OPERA"

1. Saul Bellow, "The Trip to Galena," *Partisan Review* 17 (1950): 789.

2. Alfred Kazin, *A Lifetime Burning in Every Moment: From the Journals of Alfred Kazin* (New York: HarperCollins, 1996), p. 327.

3. Saul Bellow, *Herzog* (New York: The Viking Press, 1964), p. 20.

4. These key phrases are taken from Saul Bellow, "The Distracted Public" (1990), in Bellow, *It All Adds Up: From the Dim Past to the Uncertain Future* (New York: Penguin Books, 1994), p. 168.

5. Saul Bellow, *Seize the Day* (New York: Penguin Books, 1956, 1974), p. 118.

6. Most recently, Sanford Pinsker describes *Seize the Day* as "arguably Bellow's tightest, most perfectly executed fiction." "Saul Bellow: 'What, in all of this, speaks for man?'" *Georgia Review* 49 (1995): 90–91.

7. Bellow, *Seize the Day*, pp. 28, 47.

8. Bellow, *Seize the Day*, p. 25.

9. Bellow, "The Distracted Public," p. 168.

10. For the deeper historical resonances of *Seize the Day* see Michael P. Kramer, "The Vanishing Jew: On Teaching Bellow's *Seize the Day* as Ethnic Fiction," in *New Essays on Seize the Day*, ed. Michael P. Kramer (Cambridge: Cambridge University Press, 1998), pp. 1–24.

11. Bellow, *Seize the Day*, p. 86.

12. On the subject of Bellow's relation to the traditions of Yiddish literature see Ruth R. Wisse, *The Schlemiel as Modern Hero* (Chicago: University of Chicago Press, 1971), chapter 6. For Bellow's relation to Jewish writing in general see his famous Introduction to his edition of *Great Jewish Short Stories* (New York: Dell, 1963), pp. 9–16.

13. Bellow, *Herzog*, p. 84.

14. Edward A. Ross, *The Old World in the New: The Significance of Past and Present Immigration to the American People* (New York: The Century Co., 1914), pp. 164, 154.

15. Cf. John Murray Cuddihy, *The Ordeal of Civility: Freud, Marx, Levi-Strauss, and the Jewish Struggle with Modernity* (New York: Basic Books, 1974), p. 4. Cuddihy briefly treats Bellow in terms of the Jewish encounter with modernity on pp. 217–21.

16. Bellow, *It All Adds Up*, p. 74.

17. Bellow, *It All Adds Up*, pp. 145, 152.

18. Bellow, *It All Adds Up*, p. 234.

19. "Free to Feel: Conversation with Saul Bellow" (1979), in *Conversations with Saul Bellow*, ed. Gloria L. Cronin and Ben Siegel (Jackson: University Press of Mississippi, 1994), p. 163.

20. Pinsker, "Saul Bellow," p. 93; Daniel Fuchs, *Saul Bellow: Vision and Revision* (Durham, N.C.: Duke University Press, 1984), p. 298. One of the strongest readings of "The Old System" is Gregory Johnson, "Jewish Assimilation and Codes of Manners in Saul Bellow's 'The Old System,'" *Studies in Jewish American Literature* 9 (1990): 48–60. Most recently, Morris Dickstein explains that "'The Old System' sets the pattern for Bellow's later work": "the figure of the aged intellectual who has seen everything." Morris Dickstein, *Leopards in the Temple: The Transformation of American Fiction, 1945–1970* (Cambridge, Mass.: Harvard University Press, 2002), p. 176.

21. Saul Bellow, "The Old System" (1967), in *Mosby's Memoirs and Other Stories* (New York: Fawcett World Library, 1969), p. 58. Interestingly, "The Old System" appeared in *Playboy* in 1967.

22. Bellow, "The Old System," pp. 61, 73–74, 61.

23. Bellow, "The Old System," p. 70.

24. Fuchs, *Saul Bellow,* p. 298.

25. Bellow, "The Old System," p. 69.

26. Bellow, "The Old System," pp. 71, 82, 83.

27. On this rich subject see Jonathan Freedman's "Henry James among the Jews," in his superb *The Temple of Culture: Assimilation and Anti-Semitism in Literary Anglo-America* (New York: Oxford University Press, 2000), pp. 155–209.

28. Alfred Kazin, *Bright Book of Life: American Novelists and Storytellers from Hemingway to Mailer* (New York: Dell Publishing Co., 1973), p. 134; Alfred Kazin, "The World of Saul Bellow" (1959), in Kazin, *Contemporaries* (Boston: Little, Brown, 1962), p. 219.

29. In fact, as Howe recounts it in his intellectual autobiography *A Margin of Hope,* his shock of recognition upon reading—and subsequently reviewing—Rosenfeld's novel led him to write, almost immediately, his own interpretation of the tortured passage out, from the Bronx to the wider world. See Irving Howe, *A Margin of Hope* (New York: Harcourt Brace Jovanovich, 1982), pp. 112–14. Interestingly, Howe remembers the original title as the "alienated" rather than "lost" Jewish intellectual (p. 114).

30. Irving Howe, "The Lost Young Intellectual," *Commentary* 2 (Oct. 1946): 361, 362. For a helpful discussion of Howe's youthful essay, along with shrewd analyses of Rosenfeld, Bellow and the general intellectual-political-psychological milieu of the "New York Intellectuals" see Mark Shechner *After the Revolution: Studies in the Contemporary Jewish-American Imagination* (Bloomington: Indiana University Press, 1987), esp. pp. 16–17, 201–202. "The piece is a nearly perfect example of Howe's ambivalence about his immigrant origins and reveals his continuing struggle with the question of Jewish identity," succinctly observes Gerald Sorin. See *Irving Howe: A Life of Passionate Dissent* (New York: New York University Press, 2002), p. 62.

31. Informing his parents of his decision, Howe recalls that "It was a shock to them, the first in a series of conflicts between immigrant and America." Howe, "The Lost Young Intellectual," p. 364. Of course, Howe's abstracting of this family crisis sounds like the plot of a Yezierska story, with Howe figured among the Americanizing generation's "children of loneliness."

32. Howe, "The Lost Young Intellectual," p. 364. Almost forty years later, in his intellectual autobiography *A Margin of Hope,* Howe revisits this traumatic scene in this way: "As a boy, when I played in the streets too long, my father would come from his grocery store, wearing a white apron, to find me. He would shout 'Oivic,' and his pronunciation of my unloved name, together with his apron, so embarrassed me that I would run home ahead of him, as if to keep a distance. Half a century later, I still feel the shame." Howe, *A Margin of Hope,* p. 114.

33. Léon Wurmser, *The Mask of Shame* (Baltimore: The Johns Hopkins University Press, 1981), p. 84. "Shame anxiety," Wurmser observes, "is accompanied by a profound estrangement from world and self, present and past" (p. 53).

34. Howe, "The Lost Young Intellectual," p. 366. Issues of class may also have played a part in Howe's youthful chagrin. By the late twenties the West Bronx symbolized upward mobility, the emerging middle class's escape from the Lower East Side.

35. Bellow, "Isaac Rosenfeld" (1956), in *It All Adds Up,* p. 265. The best introduction to Rosenfeld's career and importance is by Shechner, *After the Revolution,* pp. 102–20.

36. Isaac Rosenfeld, *Passage from Home* [1946] (Cleveland: World Publishing, 1961), p. 86. On the figure of Rosenfeld see Mark Shechner, ed., *Preserving the Hunger: An Isaac Rosenfeld Reader* (Detroit: Wayne State University Press, 1988); and James

p. 215. Howe's title suggests that he eventually discovered the answer to his youthful angst and alienation in the implicitly collective world of Yiddishkayt.

68. Bellow, "The Civilized Barbarian Reader," p. 38.

EPILOGUE

1. Michael M. J. Fischer, "Ethnicity and the Post-Modern arts of Memory," in *Writing Culture: The Poetics and Politics of Ethnography*, ed. James Clifford and George E. Marcus (Berkeley: University of California Press, 1986), p. 231.

2. Leon Wieseltier, "Yidfellas," *The New Republic* 218 (May 25, 1998): 42. Wieseltier is reviewing Rich Cohen, *Tough Jews* (1998). The other recent book with the same title is Paul Breines, *Tough Jews: Political Fantasies and the Moral Dilemma of American Jewry* (New York: Basic Books, 1990).

3. Examples of this mode of scholarship include the essays collected in *People of the Book: Thirty Scholars Reflect on Their Jewish Identity*, ed. Jeffrey Rubin-Dorsky and Shelley Fisher Fishkin (Madison: University of Wisconsin Press, 1996) and *Jews and Other Differences: The New Jewish Cultural Studies*, ed. Jonathan Boyarin and Daniel Boyarin (Minneapolis: University of Minnesota Press, 1997). This academic genre is not limited of course to Jewish scholars. See Marianna Torgovnick, *Crossing Ocean Parkway: Readings by an Italian American Daughter* (Chicago: University of Chicago Press, 1994).

4. Irving Howe, "Immigrant Chic," *New York* 19 (May 12, 1986): 76. The most recent studies of Howe are by Edward Alexander, *Irving Howe: Socialist, Critic, Jew* (Bloomington: Indiana University Press, 1998) and Gerald Sorin, *Irving Howe: A Life of Passionate Dissent* (New York: New York University Press, 2002). Alexander discusses Howe's responses to the "turn to ethnicity" and *World of Our Fathers* on pp. 177–89. Howe anticipates Wieseltier's remark about nostalgia, quoted above. Howe's observation also looks forward to Martin Peretz's own meditation on similar themes: "Identity, History, Nostalgia," *The New Republic* 200 (Feb. 6, 1989): 43: "What is generally left of the immigrant cultures in the lives of their heirs is sparse. It's largely nostalgia for twice-removed memories, a few foul words, and a residual culinary preference." I offer this Epilogue as a case study in "twice-removed nostalgia," but—I hope—shorn of the pejorative tones imputed by these critics.

5. Howe's toughest critique of the ethnic revival remains "The Limits of Ethnicity," *The New Republic* 176 (June 25, 1977): 17–19. I draw on some of his language in this paragraph: "Some of us remember with discomfort our days in high school when well intentioned but willful teachers tried to smooth the Jewish creases out of our speech and psyches" (p. 19).

6. Howe, "Immigrant Chic," p. 76.

7. Irving Howe, "Tevye on Broadway," *Commentary* 38 (Nov. 1964): 73. Alexander discusses this review in relation to the famous literary-cultural battle between Howe and Philip Roth. See *Irving Howe*, pp. 173–74. For meanings of *Fiddler* around the world see Stephen J. Whitfield, "Fiddling with Sholem Aleichem: A History of *Fiddler on the Roof*," in Jack Kugelmass, ed., *Key Texts in American Jewish Culture* (New Brunswick, N.J.: Rutgers University Press, 2003), pp. 105–25.

8. Howe, "Tevye on Broadway," pp. 75, 73. For a brilliant discussion of the mid-1960s cultural moment of *Fiddler* on Broadway for Jewish American life see Steven J. Zipperstein, *Imagining Russian Jewry: Memory, History, Identity* (Seattle: University of Washington Press, 1999). Building on Howe, see Ruth Franklin's smart reading of the contemporary resonances of the 2004 revival of *Fiddler*. Franklin, "Shtetl Shtick," *New York Times* (Feb. 29, 2004): 4; 5 [Sunday Arts and Leisure Section].

9. Katz speaks briefly of his sisters' relation to Cleveland-area camps for under-

privileged children in his autobiography, *Papa, Play for Me* (New York: Simon and Schuster, 1977), pp. 42–43.

10. On the social history of "red diaper baby" camps see Paul C. Mishler, *Raising Reds: The Young Pioneers, Radical Summer Camps, and Communist Party Political Culture in the United States* (New York: Columbia University Press, 1999). See also the exhibition catalogue *A Worthy Use of Summer: Jewish Summer Camping in America* (Philadelphia: National Museum of American Jewish History, 1993), which includes an essay by I. Sheldon Posen on the variety of songs—parodies, "political and social causes," "antifascist/civil rights/nuclear peace/anti-Vietnam War," among them—taught in these camps. See Posen, "*Lomir Zingn, Hava Nashira* (Let Us Sing): An Introduction to Jewish Camp Song," pp. 29–36 (the essay includes many Kinderland voices). Eugene Goodheart's personal essay in *Culturefront* on "Jews in America" confirms my own memory—around twenty years later—of the ritual-pageantry atmosphere of Camp Kinderland: "Summer camp was just another opportunity to further our political and Jewish education. The only difference between our lives in the city and our lives in camp was the pastoral setting. It was a time of pageants about Jewish history and working-class struggle in which campers and counselors marched and sang in the presence of visiting parents and dignitaries of the sponsoring organization." Learning of an elderly counselor's life among the Indians, Goodheart recalls, "We were the Jewish-Indians of Camp Kinderland, multicultural before the word ever existed." Eugene Goodheart, " 'I Am a Jew,' " *Culturefront* 5 (Winter 1997): 62, 63.

11. Sadly, the archive of the Museum of Television and Radio in New York has no extant tapes of the Sullivan Show with Rickie Layne and Velvel. From what I can glean from reviews of the earlier Yinglish reviews, Layne spoke in English while "Velvel" answered in Yiddish—a routine expressive of the linguistically schizoid world of the audience. By the early 60s, "Velvel" no doubt spoke (talked back) in Yiddish-inflected tones. My affection for "Velvel" is also connected to Bellow's great short novel, *Seize the Day*, where Tommy Wilhelm's deepest name, the name conferred upon him by his grandfather is "Velvel."

12. Manly to the core, my father and uncles were, like Berle, not afraid to cross-dress.

13. I borrow "boy man schlemiel" from Albert Goldman's key 1967 essay "Boy-Man Schlemiel: The Jewish Element in American Humor," in Goldman, *Freakshow* (New York: Atheneum, 1971), pp. 169–86. An early profile of Milton Berle, on the threshold of his television success, speaks of how "at forty, Berle, the adult, is still much the carefree boy that he has to be virtually held down while a barber cuts his hair." Robert Sylvester, "The Strange Career of Milton Berle," *Saturday Evening Post* 221 (March 19, 1949): 38.

14. Herbert J. Gans, "The 'Yinglish' Music of Mickey Katz," *American Quarterly* 5 (1953): 214.

15. Brooks Atkinson, review of *Me and Molly* (*New York Times* [March 7, 1948]), Clippings File, Billy Rose Collection, Performing Arts Library of Lincoln Center, New York.

16. Synopsis of Gertrude Berg, *Me and Molly*, in Harry Horner Collection [#7179], Research Department, Performing Arts Library of Lincoln Center, NY. *Me and Molly* contains even more touching coincidences for me: the two young neighbors in the play are named "Hymie" and "Benny" (my father's and uncle's names respectively); as gifts for his Bar Mitzvah (where the play also ends), "Samily" (the Goldbergs' son) receives no less than twenty fountain pens—Berg's gentle comedy, I suppose, but for me a nice confirmation of the truths which authorize my father's "Today I Am a Fountain Pen" routine.

The reviewer for the *Daily Worker* (March 1, 1948) was less infatuated with *Me and Molly;* Lee Newton observed that "Miss Berg is no Odets, and the rich dramatic potentialities of the material are ignored in favor of an emphasis on the surface characteristics of Jewish families like the Goldbergs in that period and locale. . . . the basic social realities—anti-Semitism, sweat-shop conditions, etc. . . . are ignored, or, if mentioned, are treated in soap opera style." Billy Rose Theatre Collection, Performing Arts Library of Lincoln Center, New York. Rather than associating Berg negatively with Odets, I would suggest that Arthur Miller (especially the Miller of *Death of a Salesman* [1949]) is the better comparison. Miller shifts the focus from "Molly" to the bitter and disillusioned yet still dreaming of success "Willy Loman," obviously a more complex figure than "Jake."

17. For more information on Gertrude Berg see chapter 6, above. The piece about Berg and the Lower East Side is from *PM Magazine* (Dec. 1, 1940): 57, in Gertrude Berg Clippings File, Performing Arts Library of Lincoln Center, New York.

18. June Sochen, "From Sophie Tucker to Barbra Streisand: Jewish Women Entertainers as Reformers," in *Talking Back,* in Joyce Antler, ed., *Talking Back: Images of Jewish Women in American Popular Culture* (Hanover, N.H.: University Press of New England, 1998), p. 81.

19. Mel Heimer, "Here's the Secret of 'Molly Goldberg's' TV Success—'Pushcarts' Keep Her on Park Avenue," *Pictorial Review* (Sept. 13, 1953), Scrapbook 1953, Berg Papers, Syracuse University Library. To speak up in her defense, we should note that Berg was a truly *beloved* actress in her own time. Subsequent dramatic performances on television and the stage received glowing reviews by such important voices as Gilbert Seldes and Kenneth Tynan. See their respective reviews of "Paris and Mrs. Perlman" [Gilbert Seldes, "The Great Gertrude," *Saturday Review* 39 (June 2, 1956): 26] and *A Majority of One* [Kenneth Tynan, "The Matriarchal Principle," *New Yorker* 35 (Feb. 28, 1959): 62–63].

20. Beth S. Wenger, "Memory as Identity: The Invention of the Lower East Side," *American Jewish History* 85 (1997): 10.

21. Wenger, "Memory as Identity," pp. 13, 14.

22. On the various adjustments in the use of dialect on *The Goldbergs* see chapter 6.

23. On this tradition of Jewish American (female) entertainers see the various essays by Sarah Blacher Cohen, including "The Unkosher Comediennes: From Sophie Tucker to Joan Rivers," in Cohen, ed., *Jewish Wry: Essays on Jewish Humor* (Bloomington: Indiana University Press, 1987), pp. 105–24 and "From Critic to Playwright: Fleshing Out Jewish Women in Contemporary Drama," in *Talking Back,* pp. 191–203. See also Sochen, "From Sophie Tucker to Barbra Streisand," in *Talking Back,* pp. 68–84.

24. On the idea of making *The Goldbergs* a regular segment of the *Texaco Star Theater* see Lynn Spigel, *Make Room for TV: Television and the Family Ideal in Postwar America* (Chicago: University of Chicago Press, 1992), p. 149. On Berle's general television career see the catalogue for the Museum of Broadcasting's (now the Museum of Television and Radio) retrospective, *Milton Berle: Mr. Television* (New York: Museum of Broadcasting, 1985). The catalogue contains an interview, along with a detailed chronology of Berle's various shows (both comedy and drama) from 1948 to 1984.

25. For Berle on Berg and the Loeb affair see Milton Berle, *Milton Berle: An Autobiography* (New York: Delacorte Press, 1974), pp. 293–94. For Berle's idea for a musical based on his career see Marvine Howe, "Chronicle," *New York Times* (July 28, 1992): B6.

26. Theodore Reik, *Jewish Wit* (New York: Gamut Press, 1962), p. 198.

27. Gilbert Seldes, "The Good-Bad Berle," in Seldes, *The Public Arts* (New York: Simon and Schuster, 1956), p. 144. Cf. Reik on "Jewish impudence": "impudence is not as harmless, stupid and sly as that of the peasant, but rather sophisticated and perceptive. It keenly observes and discerns human nature. It is also not poker-faced

and controlled, but accompanied with vivid facial expressions and dramatic gestures." *Jewish Wit*, p. 200. While working in radio, Sylvester reports, Berle "adamantly refused to change his timing and curb his explosiveness to meet microphone auditory demands. He also insisted on being his own brash, overpowering self, regardless of what the script required in character or story line." "The Strange Career of Milton Berle," p. 153. Such overpowering impudence is abundantly clear in Berle's opening monologues and sketch work on the *Texaco Star Theater*.

Writing fifty years later, Frank Rich captures the essence of Milton Berle: "Berle was to television what an electric cord is to a socket, sheer energy the moment someone plugged him in." See Rich's assessment of Berle's career in "TV Guy," *The New York Times Magazine* (Dec. 29, 2002): 22, 24 (quotation, p. 24).

28. I distill this demographic information from Arthur Frank Wertheim, "The Rise and Fall of Milton Berle," in *American History American Television*, ed. John E. O'Connor (New York: Frederick Ungar, 1983), pp. 55–78 (esp. p. 69), and Wertheim, "The Milton Berle Craze," in *Milton Berle: Mr. Television*, pp. 18–25.

29. *Texaco Star Theater* (June 14, 1949), Museum of Television and Radio. In general, Berle's skits are not as inflected with Yiddishisms as, say, Sid Caesar's various sketch parodies on *Your Show of Shows*; still, the *Texaco Star Theater* for Oct. 25, 1949 has Bert Gordon play "Professor Mischa Gos," as an Indian called "Princess Latke." On Sept. 18, 1951, Berle introduced in the audience the minor racketeer Harry Gross—dark and heavy set, he appears to me, uncannily, a dead ringer for my father.

30. Albert Goldman, "Laughtermakers," in *Jewish Wry*, p. 84. Goldman makes this observation in reference to Caesar, but the same could be said about Berle.

31. I refer to the famous essay by E. Lifschutz, "Merrymakers and Jesters among Jews (Materials for a Lexicon)," *YIVO Annual of Jewish Social Science* 7 (1952): 43–83. "A wedding," Lifschutz remarks, was "a kind of carnival and festive holiday" (p. 43). In this respect, we might think of the ritual of Tuesday nights in the early 1950s as a kind of urban-Jewish carnival, with Milton Berle presiding over the festivities. In a wonderful essay, Jeffrey Rubin-Dorksy revisits his own memory of watching, with his extended family, Berle perform in the Catskills and describes the deeper meanings of his enormous popularity in resonant terms: "But I believe that for men like my father and my uncles—and for the countless Jewish fathers and uncles of their generation—Berle provided something more than 'recognition.' . . . Uncle Miltie created the space—sanctioned and safe—for liberation, provided the secret pleasure of 'acting out' in front of the gentiles without any consequences." Jeffrey Rubin-Dorsky, "The Catskills Reinvented (and Redeemed): Woody Allen's *Broadway Danny Rose*," *The Kenyon Review* 25, nos. 3/4 (2003): 264–81 (quotation, p. 274).

32. Philip Hamburger, "The World of Milton Berle," *The New Yorker* 25 (Oct. 29, 1949): 91. "When the history of the early days of television is eventually written," Hamburger predicted, "several chapters will no doubt be devoted to the strange art of Milton Berle. In my book they will be dark and bloodcurdling pages" (p. 91).

33. This rich illustration may be found in Nahma Sandrow, *Vagabond Stars: A World History of Yiddish Theater* (New York, Seth Press, 1977), p. 93.

34. Goldman, "Laughtermakers," pp. 83, 84. Interestingly, in 1951, the young Irving Howe speculated on the style of Jewish humor in the *American Mercury* magazine, inaugurating a theme that would surface again in the *Fiddler* review: "Though there was a Yiddish cultural movement of some proportions in America during the early part of the century, it has recently been restricted to an increasingly narrow circle. What has percolated into American life is a sad substitute—the dialect joke, often vicious and always cheap; [and] the Broadway clowns [Berle?] who can only vulgarize Jewish humor." Again, I think that Howe had a limited sense of the range, variety, and offices of Jewish wit. Howe's essay is reprinted in *Jewish Wry*, pp. 16–24 (quotation, p. 24).

35. Philip Roth, *Deception* (New York: Simon and Schuster, 1990), p. 204.

36. Morris Freedman, "The Real Molly Goldberg," *Commentary* 21 (April 1956): 59, 60.

37. Gans, "The 'Yinglish' Music of Mickey Katz," p. 216.

38. Peter Watrous, "Remember Mickey Katz? No? Well, Just Listen to This," *New York Times* (Jan. 19, 1990): C24. "To me," Byron writes in the notes to *Don Byron Plays the Music of Mickey Katz* (Electra-Nonesuch, 1993), "Mickey Katz is one of the most important artists America has produced." On the current vibrant klezmer scene see James Loeffler, "Klezmania," *The New Republic* 218 (April 6, 1998): 42.

39. Katz, *Papa, Play for Me*, pp. 123, 131.

40. Quoted in Stephen Sherrill, "Don Byron," *New York Times Sunday Magazine* (Jan. 16, 1994): 18.

41. Atkinson, review of *Borscht Capades*, quoted in William and Sarah Schack, "And Now—Yinglish on Broadway," *Commentary* 12 (Dec. 1951): 588; anonymous review of *Borscht Capades* in *Cue* 20 (Sept. 29, 1951): 17, Billy Rose Collection, Performing Arts Library of Lincoln Center, New York. For another harsh review see Wolcott Gibbs, "Off Like a Tortoise," *New Yorker* 27 (Sept. 29, 1951): 58.

42. Schack and Schack, "And Now—Yinglish on Broadway," pp. 588, 587.

43. That list would also include the more benign, folksy sketches of Bronx life gathered in Arthur Kober's now obscure *Thunder Over the Bronx* (1935).

44. Sam Levenson, "The Dialect Comedian Should Vanish," *Commentary* 14 (Aug. 1952): 168. Implicit in Levenson's hierarchies is the "safe" dialect voiced by ethnic mothers; Berg, we recall, did not wish to "make trouble" on television. Dialect humor, in this respect, always has the potential for troublemaking. An even wider context for this debate would include the more complicated story of *Amos 'n Andy*, and that show's transition from radio to television. We can follow that story in Melvin Patrick Ely, *The Adventures of Amos 'n Andy: A Social History of an American Phenomenon* (New York: Free Press, 1991).

45. Transcribed, with the help of Henny Lewin of the National Yiddish Book Center, from *Mickey Katz and His Orchestra* (Capital T 298, 1951, 1961).

46. Josh Kun, "The Yiddish Are Coming: Mickey Katz, Antic-Semitism, and the Sound of Jewish Difference," *American Jewish History* 87 (2001): 351. With Kun, I agree that figures like Katz (and with him, Menasha Skulnick, who also appeared on the radio and television, *Goldbergs'*, are "undertheorized" in current Jewish cultural studies.

47. In "Duvid Crockett," Katz also sends up "Western" styles of singing, at least to my ears, especially in his "country" rendering of "He sat in the sun *un gerocket un gebocket*." For the richest of Katz's parodies of "American" folksiness see "Haim afen Range."

48. Kun, "The Yiddish Are Coming," p. 351.

49. Mickey Katz, "Sixteen Tons," *Mickey Katz "Mish Mosh"* (Capital T 799, 1957).

50. I borrow this phrase from Robert Alter, "The Jewish Voice," *Commentary* 100 (Oct. 1995): 45.

51. Mickey Katz, "C'est si Bon," *Mickey Katz and His Orchestra*. On the resonances of "kishke" in the early 1950s, the Schacks write: "What a word—*kishkeh!* The very sound of it fills your belly with lead [among the tonic phrases, always in Yiddish, in many Katz parodies: cf. "Sixteen Tons": "To eat a piece kishke you must have *koyach* (strength) / Just like a *shteyn* (rock) it lays in your *boyakh* (stomach)]. But you still love it, or think you do, or would like to, but anyway, with the gusto that actor puts into the word, you can't help laughing." "And Now—Yinglish on Broadway," p. 588. The quotation about Katz's French-Yiddish punning is taken from Ira Steingroot, "Lauding Bryon," *Tikkun* 9 (March 1994): 78.

52. Alter, "The Jewish Voice," p. 43. See also Sander L. Gilman, "The Jewish Voice:

Chicken Soup or the Penalties of Sounding Too Jewish," in Gilman, *The Jew's Body* (New York: Routledge, 1991), pp. 10–37.

53. Gans, "The 'Yinglish' Music of Mickey Katz," p. 216.

54. In this respect, we might note that unlike Katz, Anzia Yezierska was never able to transform her obsession with gastronomic nostalgia into a potentially enabling mode like parody. What burdened her notably *un*ironic children of loneliness was parodic grist for later figures like Mel Brooks and Woody Allen. Can we say that the onset of Jewish parody is generationally determined? That parody *needs* a distancing generation (i.e., the 1950s) to gestate into brilliant (and at times subversive) comedic art?

55. Judith Butler, "Merely Cultural," *New Left Review* no. 227 (Jan./Feb. 1998): 35. On the subject of parody (which is quite vast), see Linda Hutcheon, *A Theory of Parody* (1985) and the entire issue of *Quarterly Review of Film & Video* 12 (1990).

56. Schack and Schack, "And Now—Yinglish on Broadway," p. 589.

57. In the more conventional meaning of the word, both Gertrude Berg and the Yinglish review have had their "returns" over the years. Berg, of course, after *Molly* (as *The Goldbergs* was renamed) aired for the last time in 1955, returned to Broadway in *A Majority of One* (1959) and *Dear Me, the Sky Is Falling* (1963), as well as to television in a variety of roles, discussed briefly in chapter 6. In 1973, Kaye Ballard opened on Broadway in *Molly,* a musical version of *The Goldbergs,* with Eli Mintz, the original Uncle David in *Me and Molly* and on television, in the same role of twenty-five years earlier. See Robert Wahls, "The Return of 'Molly,'" *New York Daily News* (Oct. 7, 1973), Billy Rose Theater Collection, Performing Arts Library of Lincoln Center, New York. As for the fate of *Bagels and Yox,* it too was revived in the New York area, opening in Brooklyn's Brandt's Theater in Coney Island on Christmas Day 1965 ("Close to 8000 people saw 'Bagels and Yox' over the weekend," reports the New York *World Telegram & Sun,* Dec. 27, 1965, Billy Rose Theater Collection, Performing Arts Library of Lincoln Center, New York); it was also revived at the Westbury Theater in October 1995. See *Newsday* (Oct. 19, 1995): B9. Billy Rose Theater Collection, Performing Arts Library of Lincoln Center, New York.

58. Butler, "Merely Cultural," p. 34.

BOOKS

Ackerman, Nathan, and Marie Jahoda. *Anti-Semitism and Emotional Disorder: A Psychoanalytic Interpretation.* New York: Harper, 1950.

Alexander, Edward. *Irving Howe: Socialist, Critic, Jew.* Bloomington: Indiana University Press, 1998.

Alexander, Michael. *Jazz Age Jews.* Princeton, N.J.: Princeton University Press, 2001.

Antin, Mary. *They Who Knock at Our Gates: A Complete Gospel of Immigration.* Boston: Houghton Mifflin, 1914.

Antler, Joyce, ed. *Talking Back: Images of Jewish Women in American Popular Culture.* Hanover, N.H.: University Press of New England, 1998.

Arendt, Hannah. *The Jew as Pariah: Jewish Identity and Politics in the Modern Age.* New York: Grove Press, 1978.

Asch, Sholem. *Uncle Moses* [1918]. New York: G. P. Putnam's Sons, 1938.

Atlas, James. *Bellow: A Biography.* New York: Knopf, 2000.

Banta, Martha, ed. *New Essays on the American.* New York: Cambridge University Press, 1987.

Baskin, Judith R., ed. *Women of the Word: Jewish Women and Jewish Writing.* Detroit: Wayne State University Press, 1994.

Bauman, Zygmunt. *Modernity and Ambivalence.* Ithaca, N.Y.: Cornell University Press, 1991.

Bellow, Saul. *Herzog.* New York: Viking Press, 1964.

———. *It All Adds Up: From the Dim Past to the Uncertain Future.* New York: Viking Press, 1994.

———. *The Last Analysis: A Play.* New York: Viking Press, 1965.

———. *Mosby's Memoirs and Other Stories.* New York: Fawcett World Library, 1969.

———. *Seize the Day.* New York: Penguin Books, 1956.

———. *The Victim.* New York: Vanguard Press, 1947.

———, ed. *Great Jewish Short Stories.* New York: Dell, 1963.

Berg, Gertrude. *Molly and Me: The Memoirs of Gertrude Berg.* New York: McGraw Hill, 1961.

———. *The Rise of the Goldbergs.* New York: Barse & Co., 1931.

Berkson, Isaac. *Theories of Americanization: A Critical Study* [1920]. New York: Arno Press, 1969.

Berle, Milton. *Milton Berle: An Autobiography.* New York: Delacorte Press, 1974.

Bigsby, Christopher, ed. *The Cambridge Companion to Arthur Miller.* New York: Cambridge University Press, 1997.

Boyarin, Jonathan, and Daniel Boyarin, eds. *Jews and Other Differences: The New Jewish Cultural Studies.* Minneapolis: University of Minnesota Press, 1997.

Boym, Svetlana. *The Future of Nostalgia.* New York: Basic Books, 2001.

Breines, Paul. *Tough Jews: Political Fantasies and the Moral Dilemma of American Jewry.* New York: Basic Books, 1990.

Brown, L. K., and K. Mussell, eds. *Ethnic and Regional Foodways in the United States: The Performance of Group Identity.* Knoxville: University of Tennessee Press, 1984.

Brownlow, Kevin. *Behind the Mask of Innocence.* New York: Knopf, 1990.

Buhle, Paul. *From the Lower East Side to Hollywood: Jews in American Popular Culture.* New York: Verso, 2004.

Cahan, Abraham. *The Imported Bridegroom and other Stories.* New York: Penguin Books, 1996.

———. *The Rise of David Levinsky* [1917]. New York: Harper and Row, 1960.

Carney, Raymond. *American Vision: The Films of Frank Capra.* New York: Cambridge University Press, 1986.

Carringer, Robert L., ed. *The Jazz Singer.* Madison: University of Wisconsin Press, 1979.

Chapman, Abraham, ed. *Jewish-American Literature.* New York: New American Library, 1974.

Cheyette, Bryan, ed. *Between "Race" and Culture: Representations of "the Jew" in English and American Literature.* Stanford, Calif.: Stanford University Press, 1996.

Clayton, John Jacob. *Saul Bellow: In Defense of Man.* Bloomington: Indiana University Press, 1968.

Clifford, James, and George E. Marcus, eds. *Writing Culture: The Poetics and Politics of Ethnography.* Berkeley: University of California Press, 1986.

Cohen, Sarah Blacher, ed. *Jewish Wry: Essays on Jewish Humor.* Bloomington: Indiana University Press, 1987.

Corenthal, Michael G., ed. *Cohen on the Telephone: A History of Jewish Recorded Humor and Popular Music, 1892–1942.* Milwaukee: Yesterday's Memories, 1984.

Cronin, Gloria L., and Ben Siegel, eds. *Conversations with Saul Bellow.* Jackson: University of Mississippi Press, 1994.

Cuddihy, John Murray. *The Ordeal of Civility: Freud, Marx, Levi-Strauss, and the Jewish Struggle with Modernity.* New York: Basic Books, 1974.

Dearborn, Mary V. *Love in the Promised Land: The Story of Anzia Yezierska and John Dewey.* New York: The Free Press, 1988.

Dickstein, Morris. *Leopards in the Temple. The Transformation of American Fiction, 1945–1970.* Cambridge, Mass.: Harvard University Press, 2002.

Diner, Hasia R. *Hungering for America: Italian, Irish and Jewish Foodways in the Age of Migration.* Cambridge, Mass.: Harvard University Press, 2001.

———. *Lower East Side Memories: A Jewish Place in America.* Princeton, N.J.: Princeton University Press, 2000.

———, Jeffrey Shandler, and Beth S. Wenger, eds. *Remembering the Lower East Side: American Jewish Reflections.* Bloomington: Indiana University Press, 2000.

Elias, Norbert. *Power and Civility. The Civilizing Process,* vol. II. New York: Pantheon Books, 1982.

———. *Reflections on a Life.* Cambridge: Polity Press, 1994.

Ely, Melvin Patrick. *The Adventures of Amos 'n Andy: A Social History of an American Phenomenon.* New York: Free Press, 1991.

Erens, Patricia. *The Jew in American Cinema.* Bloomington: Indiana University Press, 1984.

Ewen, Elizabeth. *Immigrant Women in the Land of Dollars: Life and Culture on the Lower East Side, 1890–1925.* New York: Monthly Review Press, 1985.

Ferraro, Thomas. *Ethnic Passages: Literary Immigrants in Twentieth-Century America.* Chicago: University of Chicago Press, 1993.

Freedman, Jonathan. *The Temple of Culture: Assimilation and Anti-Semitism in Literary Anglo-America.* New York: Oxford University Press, 2000.

———, ed. *The Cambridge Companion to Henry James.* Cambridge: Cambridge University Press, 1998.

Fuchs, Daniel. *Saul Bellow: Vision and Revision.* Durham, N.C.: Duke University Press, 1984.

Gabaccia, Donna R. *We Are What We Eat: Ethnic Food and the Making of Americans.* Cambridge, Mass.: Harvard University Press, 1998.

Gabler, Neal. *An Empire of Their Own: How the Jews Invented Hollywood.* New York: Doubleday, 1988.

Gilman, Sander L. *Jewish Self-Hatred: Anti-Semitism and the Hidden Language of the Jews.* Baltimore: Johns Hopkins University Press, 1986.

———. *The Jew's Body.* New York: Routledge, 1991.

Goldman, Albert. *Freakshow.* New York: Atheneum, 1971.

Goldman, Herbert G. *Jolson: The Legend Comes to Life.* New York: Oxford University Press, 1988.

Gottfried, Martin. *Arthur Miller: His Life and Work.* Cambridge, Mass.: Da Capo Press, 2003.

Graeber, Isacque, and Steuart Henderson Britt, eds. *Jews in a Gentile World.* New York: Macmillan, 1942.

Grinberg, Leon, and Rebeca Grinberg. *Psychoanalytic Perspectives on Migration and Exile.* New Haven, Conn.: Yale University Press, 1989.

Gross, Milt. *Dunt Esk!!* New York: George H. Doran, 1927.

Halttunen, Karen. *Confidence Men and Painted Women: A Study of Middle-Class Culture in America, 1830–1870.* New Haven, Conn.: Yale University Press, 1982.

Henriksen, Louise Levitas. *Anzia Yezierska: A Writer's Life.* New Brunswick, N.J.: Rutgers University Press, 1988.

Hoberman, J. *Bridge of Light: Yiddish Film between Two Worlds.* New York: Schocken Books, 1991.

———. *Vulgar Modernism: Writing on Movies and other Media.* Philadelphia: Temple University Press, 1991.

———, and Jeffrey Shandler, eds. *Entertaining America: Jews, Movies, and Broadcasting.* Princeton, N.J.: Princeton University Press, 2003.

Hobson, Laura Z. *Gentleman's Agreement.* New York: Simon and Schuster, 1947.

Howe, Irving. *A Margin of Hope: An Intellectual Autobiography.* New York: Harcourt Brace Jovanovich, 1982.

———. *A World More Attractive: A View of Modern Literature and Politics.* New York: Horizon Press, 1963.

———. *World of Our Fathers.* New York: Harcourt Brace Jovanovich, 1976.

———, ed. *Classics of Modern Fiction.* New York: Harcourt Brace, 1968.

Hurst, Fannie. *Song of Life.* New York: Knopf, 1927.

Hutcheon, Linda. *A Theory of Parody: The Teachings of Twentieth-Century Art Forms.* New York: Methuen, 1985.

Jacobson, Matthew. *Whiteness of a Different Color: European Immigrants and the Alchemy of Race.* Cambridge, Mass.: Harvard University Press, 1998.

James, Henry. *The American.* Edited by James W. Tuttleton. New York: W.W. Norton, 1978.

———. *The American.* Edited by William Spengemann. New York: Penguin, 1980.

———. *The American Scene* [1907]. Edited by Leon Edel. Bloomington: Indiana University Press, 1968.

———. *Hawthorne* [1879]. Ithaca: Cornell University Press, 1966.

———. *The Question of Our Speech [and] The Lessons of Balzac: Two Lectures.* Boston: Houghton, Mifflin and Co., 1905.

Kallen, Horace. *Culture and Democracy in the United States.* New York: Boni and Liveright, 1924.

Kanfer, Stefan. *A Journal of the Plague Years.* New York: Atheneum, 1973.

Kaplan, Harold, and Benjamin Sadock, eds. *Comprehensive Textbook of Psychiatry/IV.* Baltimore: Williams and Wilkins, 1985.

Kasson, John. *Rudeness and Civility: Manners in Nineteenth-Century Urban America.* New York: Hill And Wang, 1990.

Katz, Mickey. *Papa, Play for Me.* New York: Simon and Schuster, 1977.

Kazin, Alfred. *Bright Book of Life: American Novelists and Storytellers from Hemingway to Mailer.* New York: Dell, 1973.

———. *Contemporaries.* Boston: Little, Brown, 1962.

———. *A Lifetime Burning in Every Moment: From the Journals of Alfred Kazin.* New York: HarperCollins, 1996.

———. *A Walker in the City.* New York: Harcourt, Brace, 1951.

Kessler-Harris, Alice, ed. *The Open Cage: An Anzia Yezierska Collection.* New York: Persea Books, 1979.

Klein, Marcus. *Foreigners: The Making of American Literature, 1900–1940.* Chicago: University of Chicago Press, 1981.

Kramer, Michael P., ed. *New Essays on Seize the Day.* Cambridge: Cambridge University Press, 1998.

Kramer, Michael P., and Hana Wirth-Nesher, eds. *The Cambridge Companion to Jewish American Literature.* Cambridge: Cambridge University Press, 2003.

Kugelmass, Jack, ed. *Going Home.* Evanston, Illinois: Northwestern University Press, 1993.

———. *Key Texts in American Jewish Culture.* New Brunswick, N.J.: Rutgers University Press, 2003.

Levi-Strauss, Claude. *Tristes Tropiques* [1955]. New York: Atheneum, 1974.

Lewin, Kurt. *Resolving Social Conflicts: Selected Papers on Group Dynamics [1935– 1946].* New York: Harper and Brothers, 1948.

Lipsitz, George. *Time Passages: Collective Memory and American Popular Culture.* Minneapolis: University of Minnesota Press, 1990.

Malin, Irving, ed. *Psychoanalysis and American Fiction.* New York: E. P. Dutton, 1965.

———. *Saul Bellow and the Critics.* New York: New York University Press, 1967.

Marc, David. *Comic Visions: Television Comedy and American Culture.* Boston. Unwin Hyman, 1989.

Melnick, Jeffrey. *A Right to Sing the Blues: African Americans, Jews, and American Popular Song.* Cambridge, Mass.: Harvard University Press, 1999.

Metzker, Isaac, ed. *A Bintel Brief: Sixty Years of Letters from the Lower East Side to the Jewish Daily Forward.* New York: Ballantine Books, 1971.

Miller, Arthur. *Focus.* New York: Reynal and Hitchcock, 1945.

———. *Focus.* London: Methuen, 2002.

Miller, Merle. *The Judges and the Judged.* New York: Doubleday, 1952.

Milton Berle: Mr. Television. New York: Museum of Broadcasting, 1985.

Mishler, Paul C. *Raising Reds: The Young Pioneers, Radical Summer Camps, and Communist Party Political Culture in the United States.* New York: Columbia University Press, 1999.

Most, Andrea. *Making Americans: Jews and the Broadway Musical.* Cambridge, Mass.: Harvard University Press, 2003.

Newcomb, Horace, ed., *Television: The Critical View,* 3rd ed. New York: Oxford University Press, 1982.

O'Connor, John E., ed. *American History American Television.* New York: Frederick Unger, 1983.

Ozick, Cynthia. *Fame and Folly.* New York: Alfred A. Knopf, 1996.

Phillips, Adam. *On Flirtation.* Cambridge, Mass.: Harvard University Press, 1994.

———. *On Kissing, Tickling, and Being Bored: Psychoanalytic Essays in the Unexamined Life.* Cambridge, Mass.: Harvard University Press, 1993.

Poirier, Richard. *The Comic Sense of Henry James.* New York: Oxford University Press, 1967.

Posnock, Ross. *The Trial of Curiosity: Henry James, William James, and the Challenge of Modernity.* New York: Oxford University Press, 1991.

Raphaelson, Samson. *The Jazz Singer* [play]. New York: Brentano, 1925.

Ravitz, Abe C. *Imitations of Life: Fannie Hurst's Gaslight Sonatas.* Carbondale: Southern Illinois University Press, 1997.

Red Channels: The Report of Communist Influence in Radio and Television. New York: American Business Consultants, 1950.

Reik, Theodore. *Jewish Wit.* New York: Gamut Press, 1962.

Reinharz, Jehuda, and Walter Schatzberg, eds. *The Jewish Response to German Culture.* Hanover, N.H.: University Press of New England, 1985.

Rogin, Michael. *Blackface, White Noise: Jewish Immigrants in the Hollywood Melting Pot.* Berkeley: University of California Press, 1996.

Rosenfeld, Isaac. *Passage from Home.* Cleveland: World Publishing, 1961.

Ross, E. A. *The Old World in the New: The Significance of Past and Present Immigration to the American People.* New York: The Century Co., 1914.

Roth, Henry. *Call It Sleep* [1934]. New York: Avon Books, 1976.

———. *Mercy of a Rude Stream.* New York: St. Martin's Press, 1994-98. 4 vols. [*A Star Shines Over Mt. Morris Park; A Diving Rock on the Hudson; From Bondage; Requiem for Harlem*]

———. *Shifting Landscape.* Philadelphia: Jewish Publication Society, 1987.

Roth, Joseph. *The Wandering Jews.* New York: W.W. Norton, 2001.

Roth, Philip. *The Anatomy Lesson.* New York: Farrar, Strauss, and Giroux, 1983.

———. *Deception.* New York: Simon and Schuster, 1990.

———. *Zuckerman Bound: A Trilogy and Epilogue.* New York: Farrar, Straus and Giroux, 1985.

Rovit, Earl. *Saul Bellow.* Minneapolis: University of Minnesota Press, 1967.

———, ed. *Saul Bellow: A Collection of Critical Essays.* Englewood Cliffs, N.J.: Prentice-Hall, 1975.

Rubin-Dorsky, Jeffrey, and Shelley Fisher Fishkin, eds. *People of the Book: Thirty Scholars Reflect on Their Jewish Identity.* Madison: University of Wisconsin Press, 1996.

Russell, Steven. *Jewish Identity and the Civilizing Process.* New York: St. Martin's Press, 1996.

Samuel, Maurice. *The Great Hatred.* New York: A. A. Knopf, 1940.

Sanders, Ronald. *The Downtown Jews: Portraits of an Immigrant Generation.* New York: Harper and Row, 1969.

Sandrow, Nahma. *Vagabond Stars: A World History of Yiddish Theater.* New York: Seth Press, 1977.

Sartre, Jean-Paul. *Anti-Semite and Jew* [1948]. New York: Schocken Books, 1997.

Schlesinger, Arthur. *Learning How to Behave: A Historical Study of American Etiquette Books.* New York: Macmillan, 1946.

Schoener, Allon, ed. *The Lower East Side: Portal to American Life (1870–1924).* New York: The Jewish Museum, 1966.

Searles, George J., ed. *Conversations with Philip Roth.* Jackson: University of Mississippi Press, 1992.

Sedgwick, Eve Kosofsky, and Adam Frank, eds. *Shame and Its Sisters: A Silvan Tomkins Reader.* Durham, N.C.: Duke University Press, 1995.

Seldes, Gilbert. *The Public Arts.* New York: Simon and Schuster, 1956.

———. *The Seven Lively Arts.* New York: Harper & Brothers, 1924.

Shechner, Mark. *After the Revolution: Studies in the Contemporary Jewish-American Imagination.* Bloomington: Indiana University Press, 1987.

———. *Preserving the Hunger: An Isaac Rosenfeld Reader.* Detroit: Wayne State University Press, 1988.

Sollers, Werner. *Beyond Ethnicity: Consent and Descent in American Culture.* New York: Oxford University Press, 1986.

———, ed. *Theories of Ethnicity: A Classical Reader.* New York: New York University Press, 1996.

Sorin, Gerald. *Irving Howe: A Life of Passionate Dissent.* New York: New York University Press, 2002.

———. *A Time for Building: The Third Migration, 1880–1920.* Baltimore: Johns Hopkins University Press, 1992.

Spigel, Lynn. *Make Room for TV: Television and the Family Ideal in Postwar America.* Chicago: University of Chicago Press, 1992.

Stearns, Peter, and Jan Lewis, eds. *An Emotional History of the United States.* New York: New York University Press, 1998.

Stratton, John. *Coming Out Jewish: Constructing Ambivalent Identities.* London: Routledge, 2000.

Susman, Warren. *Culture as History.* New York: Pantheon, 1984.

Torgovnick, Marianna. *Crossing Ocean Parkway: Readings by an Italian American Daughter.* Chicago: University of Chicago Press, 1994.

Trachtenberg, Stanley, ed. *Critical Essays on Saul Bellow.* Boston: G. K. Hall, 1979.

van Kreiken, Robert. *Norbert Elias.* London: Routledge, 1998.

Visser, Margaret. *The Rituals of Dinner: The Origins, Evolution, Eccentricities, and Meaning of Table Manners.* New York: Penguin, 1991.

Whitfield, Stephen. *In Search of American Jewish Culture.* Hanover, N.H.: University of New England Press, 1999.

Wirth-Nesher, Hana, ed. *New Essays on Call It Sleep.* New York: Cambridge University Press, 1996.

Wisse, Ruth. *The Modern Jewish Canon: A Journey through Language and Culture.* New York: Free Press, 2000.

——. *The Schlemiel as Modern Hero.* Chicago: University of Chicago Press, 1971.

Wurmser, Léon. *The Mask of Shame.* Baltimore: Johns Hopkins University Press, 1981.

Yezierska, Anzia. *All I Could Never Be.* New York: Brewer, Warren, and Putnam, 1932.

——. *Arrogant Beggar.* New York: Doubleday Page & Co., 1927.

——. *Arrogant Beggar* [1927]. Durham, N.C.: Duke University Press, 1996.

——. *Bread Givers* [1925]. New York: Persea Books, 1975.

——. *Children of Loneliness: Stories of Immigrant Life in America.* New York: Funk and Wagnalls, 1923.

——. *Hungry Hearts* [1920]. New York: Persea Books, 1985.

. *Salome of the Tenements.* New York: Grosset and Dunlop, 1922.

——. *Salome of the Tenements* [1923]. Urbana and Chicago: University of Illinois Press, 1995.

Zaborowska, Magdalena. *How We Found America: Reading Gender through East European Immigrant Narratives.* Chapel Hill: University of North Carolina Press, 1995.

Zipperstein, Steven J. *Imagining Russian Jewry: Memory, History, Identity.* Seattle: University of Washington Press, 1999.

ARTICLES

Alter, Robert. "Awakenings." *The New Republic* 198 (January 25, 1988): 33–37.

——. "The Jewish Voice." *Commentary* 100 (October 1995): 39–45.

——. "Manners & the Jewish Intellectual." *Commentary* 60 (August 1975): 58–64.

Angoff, Charles. "The Goldbergs." *The Reconstructionist* (December 24, 1954): 19–22.

——. "'The Goldbergs' and Jewish Humor." *Congress Weekly: A Review of Jewish Interests* 18 (March 5, 1951): 12–13.

Atkinson, Brooks. "Review of *Me and Molly.*" *New York Times* (March 7, 1948).

Atlas, James. "Golden Boy." *The New York Review of Books* (June 29, 1989): 42–46.

Bates, Ernest Sutherland. "American Folklore." *Saturday Review of Literature* 2 (July 10, 1926): 914.

Bellow, Saul. "The Art of Fiction XXXVII Saul Bellow: An Interview." *Paris Review* 36 (1966).

——. "Brothers' Keepers." Review of Arthur Miller, *Focus. The New Republic* 114 (January 7, 1946): 29–30.

——. "The Civilized Barbarian Reader." *The New York Times Book Review* (March 8, 1987): 1, 38.

——. "The Trip to Galena." *Partisan Review* 17 (1950): 779–94.

Berman, Marshall. "The Bonds of Love." *The Nation* 263 (September 23, 1996): 25–30.

——. "Love and Theft: From Jack Robin to Bob Dylan." *Dissent* 49, no. 3 (Summer 2002): 67–73.

Bourne, Randolph. "Trans-National America." *Atlantic Monthly* 118 (1916): 86–97.

Boyarin, Daniel. "Épater L'Embourgeoisement: Freud, Gender, and the (De)Colonized Psyche." *Diacritics* 24 (Spring 1994): 17–41.

Boyers, Robert T. "Literature and Culture: An Interview with Saul Bellow." *Salmagundi* 30 (1975): 6-23.

Brody, Alter. "Yiddish: Our Literary Dominion." *The Nation* 124 (April 20, 1927): 435–36.

Brook, Vincent. "The Americanization of Molly: How Mid-Fifties TV Homogenized The Goldbergs (and Got 'Berg-larized in the Process)." *Cinema Journal* 38 (1999): 45–67.

Buhle, Paul, and Edward Portnoy. "Al Jolson in Black and White." *Tikkun* 11 (November/December 1996): 67–70.

Butler, Judith. "Merely Cultural." *New Left Review* no. 227 (January/February 1998): 33–44.

Diner, Hasia. "Trading Faces." *Common Quest* 2 (Summer 1997): 40–44.

Drucker, Sally Ann. "Yiddish, Yidgin, and Yezierska: Dialect in Jewish-American Writing." *Modern Jewish Studies* 6 (1987): 99–113.

Engel, David. "The 'Discrepancies' of the Modern: Towards a Revaluation of Abraham Cahan's *The Rise of David Levinsky.*" *Studies in Jewish American Literature* 2 (1982): 36–60.

Fiedler, Leslie A. "Review of Saul Bellow, *The Victim.*" *Kenyon Review* 10 (1948): 526–27.

Franklin, Ruth. "Shtetl Shtick." *The New York Times* (February 29, 2004): 4–5.

Freedman, Morris. "The Real Molly Goldberg: Balesbostah of the Air Waves." *Commentary* 21 (April 1956): 359–64.

Fuchs, Daniel. "Bellow and Freud." *Studies in the Literary Imagination* 17 (1984): 59–80.

Gabler, Neal. "Making Faces." *The Forward* (May 24, 1996): 1, 10.

Gans, Herbert J. "American Jewry: Present and Future." *Commentary* 21 (May 1956): 422–30.

——. "The 'Yinglish' Music of Mickey Katz." *American Quarterly* 5 (1953): 213–18.

Gibbs, Wolcott. "Off Like a Tortoise." Review of Borscht Capades. *The New Yorker* 27 (September 29, 1951): 58–60.

Gitlin, Todd. "Prime Time Ideology: The Hegemonic Process in Television Entertainment." In Horace Newcomb, ed., *Television: The Critical View*, 3rd ed. New York: Oxford University Press, 1982: 426-54.

Goldman, Eric A. "The Jazz Singer and Its Reaction in the Yiddish Cinema." In Sylvia Paskin, ed., *When Joseph Met Molly: A Reader on Yiddish Film*. Nottingham: Five Leaves Publications, 1999: 39-48.

Goldsmith, Meredith. "Dressing, Passing, and Americanizing: Anzia Yezierska's Sartorial Fictions." *Studies in Jewish American Literature* 16 (1997): 34–45.

Golub, Ellen. "Eat Your Heart Out: The Fiction of Anzia Yezierska." *Studies in American Jewish American Literature* 3 (1983): 51–61.

Goodheart, Eugene. " 'I Am a Jew.' " *Culturefront* 5, no. 3 (Winter 1997): 60–64, 73–74.

Goodman, Allegra. "About Time." Review of Henry Roth, *Requiem for Harlem. The New York Times Book Review* (April 1, 1998): 16.

Gordon, Mary. "Confession, Terminable and Interminable." Review of Henry Roth, *A Dividing Rock on the Hudson*. *The New York Times Book Review* (February 26, 1995): 5–6.

Greenberg, Martin. "Modern Man as Jew." *Commentary* 5 (1948): 86–87.

Hamburger, Philip. "The World of Milton Berle." *The New Yorker* 25 (October 29, 1949): 91–92.

Hardwick, Elizabeth. Review of Saul Bellow, *The Victim*. *Partisan Review* 15 (1948): 114–17.

Heimer, Mel. "Here's the Secret of 'Molly Goldberg's' TV Success—'Pushcarts' Keep Her on Park Avenue." *Pictorial Review* (September 13, 1953). Scrapbook 1953, Berg Papers, Syracuse University Library. 4p–5p.

Hoberman, J. "My Songs Mean As Much to My Audience As Yours Do to Your Congregation." (Review of Michael Rogin, *Blackface, White Noise*.) *London Review of Books* 18 (July 18, 1996): 22–23.

Howe, Irving. "Immigrant Chic." *New York* 19 (May 12, 1986): 76.

———. "Life Never Let Up." *The New York Times Book Review* (October 25, 1964): 1, 60.

———. "Limits of Ethnicity." *The New Republic* 176 (June 25, 1977): 17–19.

———. "The Lost Young Intellectual." *Commentary* 2 (October 1946): 361–67.

———. "Of Fathers and Sons." (Review of Isaac Rosenfeld, *Passage from Home*) *Commentary* 2 (August 1946): 190–92.

———. "Tevye on Broadway." *Commentary* 38 (November 1964): 73–75.

Howe, Marvine. "Chronicle." *The New York Times* (July 28, 1992): B6.

Itzkovitz, Daniel. "Passing Like Me." *South Atlantic Quarterly* 98 (Winter/Spring 1999): 35–57.

Johnson, Gregory. "Jewish Assimilation and Codes of Manners in Saul Bellow's 'The Old System.'" *Studies in Jewish American Literature* 9 (1990): 48–60.

Kazin, Alfred. "The Art of 'Call It Sleep.'" *New York Review of Books* 38, no. 16 (October 10, 1991): 15–18.

Kempton, Murray. "The Victim." *New York Post* (September 13, 1955). New York Public Library Clippings File.

Konzett, Delia Caparoso. "Administered Identities and Linguistic Assimilation: The Politics of Immigrant English in Anzia Yezierska's Hungry Hearts." *American Literature* 69 (1997): 595–619.

———. "From Hollywood to Hester Street: Ghetto Film, Melodrama, and the Image of the Assimilated Jew in Hungry Hearts." *Journal of Film and Video* 50 (1998–99): 18–33.

Krieger, Hilary Leila. "Withstanding the Crucible." *The Jerusalem Post* (June 19, 2003).

Kun, Josh. "The Yiddish Are Coming: Mickey Katz, Antic-Semitism, and the Sound of Jewish Difference." *American Jewish History* 87 (2001): 343–74.

Lears, T. J. Jackson. "Making Fun of Popular Culture." *American Historical Review* 97 (1992): 1417–26.

Levenson, Sam. "The Dialect Comedian Should Vanish." *Commentary* 14 (August 1952): 168–70.

Lifschutz, E. "Merrymakers and Jesters among Jews (Materials for a Lexicon)." *YIVO Annual of Jewish Social Science* 7 (1952): 43–83.

Littell, Robert. "Nize Baby." *New Republic* 47 (June 9, 1926): 93–94.

Löb, Ladislaus. "'Insanity in the Darkness': Anti-Semitic Stereotypes and Jewish Identity in Max Frisch's *Andorra* and Arthur Miller's *Focus*." *Modern Language Review* 92(1997): 545–58.

"Loeb and Red Channels." *New Republic* 26 (January 1, 1952): 8.

Loeffler, James. "Klezmania." *The New Republic* 218 (April 6, 1998): 42.

Maxwell, Perriton. "The Mother of the Goldbergs." *Radioland* II, no. 1 (March 1934): 40–41, 53, 70. Berg Papers.

McGowan, Philip. "The Writing of Blackness in Saul Bellow's *The Victim.*" *Saul Bellow Journal* 16–17 (2000+2001): 74–103.

Newton, Lee. Review of *Me and Molly. Daily Worker* (March 1, 1948). Clippings File, New York Public Library.

Nora, Pierre. "Between Memory and History: *Les Lieux de Memoire.*" *Representations* 26 (1989): 7–25.

Okonkwo, Christopher. "Of Repression, Assertion, and the Speakerly Dress: Anzia Yezierska's Salome of the Tenements." *MELUS* 25 (2000): 129–45.

Ozick, Cynthia [symposium participant]. "Is There a Cure for Anti-Semitism?" *Partisan Review* 61 (1994): 388.

Peretz, Martin. "Identity, History, Nostalgia." *The New Republic* 200 (February 6, 1989): 43.

Pinsker, Sanford. "Saul Bellow: 'What, in all of this, speaks for man?' " *Georgia Review* 49 (1995): 89–95.

Posen, I. Sheldon. "Lomir Zingn, Hava Nashira (Let Us Sing): An Introduction to Jewish Camp Song." In *A Worthy Use of Summer: Jewish Summer Camping in America* (exhibition catalog). Philadelphia: National Museum of American Jewish History, 1993.

"Red Channels Rides Again." *New Republic* 126 (February 18, 1952): 22.

"Review of Borscht Capades." *Cue* 20 (September 29, 1951): 17.

Rich, Frank. "TV Guy." *The New York Times Magazine* (December 29, 2002): 22, 24.

Rogin, Michael. " Seeing the Faces of Hollywood Jews." *The Forward* (July 5, 1996): 6.

Rosenberg, Joel. "Rogin's Noise: The Alleged Historical Crimes of *The Jazz Singer.*" *Prooftexts* 22 (Winter/Spring 2002): 221–39.

———. "What You Ain't Heard Yet: The Languages of *The Jazz Singer.*" *Prooftexts* 22 (Winter/Spring 2002): 11–54.

Rosenfeld, Isaac. "The Fall of David Levinsky." [1952] In Mark Shechner, ed., *Preserving the Hunger: An Isaac Rosenfeld Reader.* Detroit: Wayne State University Press, 1988: 152-59.

Roskies, David G. "Coney Island, USA: America in the Jewish Literary Imagination." In Michael P. Kramer and Hana Wirth-Nesher, eds., *The Cambridge Companion to Jewish American Literature.* New York: Cambridge University Press, 2003: 70-91.

———. "Yiddish on Screen." *Commentary* 93 (April 1992): 47–50.

Roth, Henry. "On Being Blocked & Other Literary Matters." *Commentary* 64 (August 1977): 27–38.

Rowe, John Carlos. "The Politics of the Uncanny: Newman's Fate in The American." *The Henry James Review* 8 (1987): 79–90.

Rubin-Dorsky, Jeffrey. "The Catskills Reinvented (and Redeemed): Woody Allen's *Broadway Danny Rose.*" *The Kenyon Review* 25, nos. 3/4 (2003): 264–81.

Schack, William, and Sarah Schack. "And Now—Yinglish on Broadway." *Commentary* 12 (December 1951): 586–89.

Schwartz, Harriet Berg. "In the McCarthy Era, TV Networks Cowered." *The New York Times* (November 11, 1990): E16.

Scott, A. O. "When We Read Red." *The Nation* 263 (September 23, 1996): 30–32.

Seldes, Gilbert. "The Great Gertrude." *Saturday Review* 39 (June 2, 1956): 26.

Shandler, Jeffrey. "*Ost und West,* Old World and New: Nostalgia and Antinostalgia on the Silver Screen." In Jack Kugelmass, ed., *Going Home. YIVO Annual,* vol. 21. Evanston, Ill.: Northwestern University Press, 1993: 153–88.

Sherrill, Stephen. "Don Byron." *The New York Times Sunday Magazine* (January 16, 1994): 18.

Shulevitz, Judith. " 'The Cosby Show,' Starring . . . Heavily Accented Jews?" *The New York Times* (July 20, 2003): 24, 34.

Siegel, Lee. "Ozick Seizes Bellow." *The Nation* 262 (February 26, 1996): 34–36.

Sollors, Werner. " 'A World Somewhere, Somewhere Else': Language, Nostalgic Mournfulness, and Urban Immigrant Family Romance in Call It Sleep." In Hana Wirth-Nesher, ed., *New Essays on Call It Sleep*. New York: Cambridge University Press, 1996: 127-82.

Sollers, Werner and Keith Thomas. "Review of Yezierska, Salome of the Tenements." *Journal of American Ethnic History* 17 (1998): 98.

Steingroot, Ira. "Lauding Byron." *Tikkun* 8 and 9 (March/April 1994): 76–78.

Sylvester, Robert. "The Strange Career of Milton Berle." *The Saturday Evening Post* 221 (March 19, 1949): 38–39, 150, 152–54.

Thomas, Keith. "The Rise of the Fork." *New York Review of Books* (March 8, 1978): 28-31.

Trachtenberg, Alan. "Conceivable Aliens." *Yale Review* 82 (1994): 42–64.

Trilling, Diana. "Fiction in Review." (Review of Saul Bellow, *The Victim.*) *The Nation* 166 (January 3, 1948): 24–25.

Tynan, Kenneth. "The Matriarchal Principle." *New Yorker* 35 (February 28, 1959): 62–63.

Wald, Priscilla. "Of Crucibles and Grandfathers: The East European Immigrants." In Michael P. Kramer and Hana Wirth-Nesher, eds., *The Cambridge Companion to Jewish American Literature*. New York: Cambridge University Press, 2003: 50-69.

Wahls, Robert. "The Return of 'Molly'." *New York Daily News* (October 7, 1973). Clippings File, New York Public Library.

Watrous, Peter. "Remember Mickey Katz? No? Well, Just Listen to This." *The New York Times* (January 19, 1990): C24.

Weber, Donald. "Accents of the Future: Jewish American Popular Culture." In Michael P. Kramer and Hana Wirth-Nesher, eds., *The Cambridge Companion to Jewish American Literature*. New York: Cambridge University Press, 2003: 129-48.

——. "The Limits of Empathy: Hollywood's Imaging of Jews circa 1947." In Jack Kugelmass, ed., *Key Texts in American Jewish Culture*. New Brunswick: Rutgers University Press, 2003: 91-104.

Wenger, Beth S. "Memory as Identity: The Invention of the Lower East Side." *American Jewish History* 85 (1997): 3–27.

Wexler, Laura. "Looking at Yezierska." In Judith R. Paskin ed., *Women of the Word: Jewish Women and Jewish Writing*. Detroit: Wayne State University Press, 1994:153-81.

Wieseltier, Leon. "Yidfellas." *The New Republic* 218 (May 25, 1998): 42.

Wood, James. "Portrait: Roth of God." *The Guardian* (February 18, 1994): 20.

INDEX

Donald Weber is Lucia, Ruth, and Elizabeth MacGregor Professor of English at Mount Holyoke College. His essays on Jewish American literature and popular culture have appeared in the *Forward* and other publications, and he is author of *Rhetoric and History in Revolutionary New England*.

DAVID ELLIOT COHEN

THE WRONG DOG

yellow pear 🍐 press

For Hank—

You were a great cat!

THE WRONG DOG

Dave Shields

Library of Congress Cataloging-in-Publication Data

Cohen, David Elliot, date.
The Wrong Dog: a tale of unconditional love /
David Elliot Cohen
p.   cm.
1. Dogs   2. Dogs—Travel Anecdotes
3. U.S Travel   4. Cohen, David Elliot, 1955— I. Title.
X000.000   2017
000.0'0—xx00   17-00000
                          CIP

ISBN 978-0-9970664-1-8

Manufactured in China.

Designed by David Elliot Cohen.
Type styling by Peter Truskier.
This book has been set in Adobe Garamond Pro and Avenir.

Published by Yellow Pear Press, LLC.
www.yellowpearpress.com

10 9 8 7 6 5 4 3 2 1

Distributed by Publishers Group West.

CONTENTS

1. A NEW PUPPY, PART 1

Atlanta, Georgia
November 2000

Way back in November 2000, my future wife Laureen sent her first husband, Guenter, to a well-regarded Labrador breeder with very straightforward instructions: please pick up the eight-week-old female pup that Laureen had selected after weeks of research and more than three months on a waiting list. But Guenter—who's a dashing celebrity chef from Germany's Black Forest and frankly a little bit wild   often flouted instructions. And when he arrived at the breeder's place of business, he was unimpressed with Laureen's selection and smitten instead by a little rough-and-tumble white male with honey-dipped ears and a proud bearing. So true to his Teutonic nature and without any further consultation with Laureen, Guenter swapped her sleepy female for a hyperkinetic, testosterone-infused ball of fur.

Meanwhile, back at the house, Guenter and Laureen's two young daughters—bashful, blonde four-year-old Angela and sweet freckled two-year-old Grace—couldn't wait to meet their new puppy. When they heard Guenter's fire-engine red Porsche roar up the long gravel driveway, they leapt up and down on the gray velvet sofa screaming, "He's here, Mommy! He's here!" And when Guenter strode through the front door bearing the stylish black tote he had acquired just for the occasion, the girls were practically bursting to meet the amiable ingénue whose baby picture they had passed one to the other for weeks. But what they got instead was a frenzied, out-of-control hellion—rolling, yipping, and slip-sliding his way across their slick oaken floor like a tiny Tasmanian devil.

Laureen, a seasoned trial lawyer who tends to maintain her cool even in vexing situations, said as calmly as possible, "Guenter, this is not the puppy we discussed."

"*Ja, ja,*" Guenter replied, "but let me explain…"

Laureen cut him off right there. "Guenter, there were only two females in the litter. Three other families wanted them. And I spent two months, Guenter, two months convincing the breeder to give one of those females to us. I let the breeder inspect our house, Guenter. He made me sit through an interview for Christ's sake."

"*Ja, ja,* I know all that," Guenter replied, still confident for some reason. "But believe me, Laureen, this is a very *gut* dog. He was the biggest puppy in the litter. He is strong and healthy. And he has… how do you say… a very *spirited* personality."

Any further objection on Laureen's part was preempted by the girls' ecstatic reaction to their new puppy's antics.

"I like *this* puppy," Angela declared. And on the spot she named him Simba after the hero of Disney's *The Lion King* movie. Well, she didn't precisely name the new puppy after the lion king. Angela, who even now deplores change of any stripe, actually named him after the family's recently deceased Samoyed, who tragically succumbed to liver cancer at the tender age of four. Samoyeds are big Siberian sled dogs with fluffy white manes. So Simba I actually did look like a lion—or perhaps more accurately an albino lion. Simba II didn't—at least not yet. But despite that quibble, Angela christened the new puppy in his predecessor's memory.

So at the beginning of this story, Simba II was the wrong dog with a secondhand name. Laureen had wanted a sweet, even-tempered female suitable for two little girls and a quiet suburban routine. Simba II, on the other hand, couldn't have been more macho or frenetic. He would have been far better suited to a farm or a cattle ranch or some other outdoorsy situation where his size, strength, and stamina would have made him the ideal companion. But as fate and Guenter would have it, Simba II began his life in a sleek modern house, all done up in black, white, and gray, in leafy Buckhead, Atlanta, with an ambitious hard-working lawyer mom, two pretty little girls, and a rakish Prada-clad chef.

In time Simba II would grow up to be a handsome, robust dog that at ninety muscular pounds was immense for his breed—a Labrador XL we'd call him. And as big as he was, he would have an even bigger head that lent him an air of masculine wisdom. That, combined with his proud carriage and noblesse oblige toward lesser members of his species, would mark Simba II as canine aristocracy—or at least that's how we'd see him. And well down the road Angela's spur-of-the-moment decision to name Simba II after an animal king would seem, if not terribly original, then certainly fitting.

Not for nothing would we someday bestow upon Simba II a string of nonsensical alliterative honorifics. For in our family's opinion, Simba II would indeed become Duke of the Dogs, Lord of the Labradors, and King of the Canines. And nearly fourteen years later, near the end of this story, my determined efforts to drive Simba from one end of the country to the other—so he could see Laureen and the girls one more time before he died—would seem less like an act of mercy and more like a matter of respect— and by that point, love.

2. COURTING THE DOG

San Francisco, California
October 2003

I met Laureen at a snazzy San Francisco watering hole called the Redwood Room three years after Simba joined her household but only hours after the Fulton County Court finalized her divorce from Guenter. A volatile brew of alcohol, late nights, and star-struck young women eventually propels nearly every celebrity chef toward the cheatin' side of town. And as Laureen always said, Guenter wasn't built for fidelity. So after eleven years of marriage and a remarkable fourteen-year run as an undefeated trial lawyer, forty-two-year-old Laureen found herself a single working mother of two small girls and one very large dog.

With fifty-something Guenter off playing house with a waitress-slash-ballerina less than half his age, Laureen resolved to spend more time at home with Angela and Grace. And since in-house lawyers keep far shorter, more regular hours than trial lawyers, she reluctantly quit the courtroom she loved and took a new position—as head lawyer of the technology division of a mammoth health-care conglomerate called the McKesson Corporation. McKesson's tech operations were based in Atlanta, where Laureen lived. But its parent company was headquartered in a thirty-seven-story office tower in downtown San Francisco, which was my hometown.

When McKesson's worldwide law department meeting wound to a close on October 23, 2003, four of Laureen's colleagues—three men and a woman—informed her in no uncertain terms that they were taking her out on the town. The purpose of the mission, the lawyers half-joked, was to celebrate Laureen's brand-new officially single status and to scout some fresh romantic prospects. So when the PowerPoints faded and the laptops snapped shut, the four pushy lawyers grabbed up Laureen and dragged her across San Francisco's Union Square to the Redwood Room in the hip Clift Hotel.

By coincidence, I was also at the Redwood Room that evening. At forty-eight, I was bravely enduring my own immensely crappy divorce. And I had three school-age children—sixteen-year-old Kara, fourteen-year-old Willie, and nine-year-old Lucas. So generally speaking, you wouldn't have found me whiling away a crisp autumn eve at some ritzy downtown nightspot. But that particular crisp autumn eve my New York editor was in town to help me celebrate my new book's debut on the *New York Times* bestseller list (after, it must be said, a prolonged bestseller drought).

When our self-congratulatory wine-soaked dinner wound to a close, I realized I needed some air. So I offered to walk the editor back to his hotel. He said he was staying at the Clift, which was only twelve blocks away, so off we went.

When we hit the Clift's lobby, the festive din emanating from the Redwood Room matched our high spirits, so we decided to drop in for a nightcap. As I pushed my way into the cavernous redwood-paneled bar packed with what must have been two hundred or more significantly younger revelers, I had no idea that I was about to become the target of a romantic manhunt mounted by a team of corporate lawyers. All I knew was that my bad back was kicking up. And I desperately wanted to plunk myself down in a chair somewhere so I could nurse my L4 vertebra and a Grey Goose martini. But it was a Friday night. The joint was jumpin'. And it looked like standing room only.

Within a matter of minutes, I lost sight of my tipsy publishing colleague, who had likely retreated to his room. So I bemoaned by plight instead to a well-tailored young woman who was loitering at the jammed art deco bar tapping her Jimmy Choos to the house music. Her name was Ami Patel. And she turned out to be one of the intrepid McKesson attorneys who were hard on the hunt for Laureen's new mate.

After a quick glance at my ring finger, the wily Ms. Patel posed a few deceptively casual questions about my age, occupation, and marital status. And then, sensing prey, she deftly steered me toward a burgundy velvet settee where Laureen—slim, blonde, and elegant—was already in the process of being wooed by another suitor, a gawky six-foot-five anesthesiologist who was up from LA for some sort of medical convention.

I subsequently learned that the McKesson lawyers had also recruited the towering anesthesiologist, whom they dubbed Bachelor Number One. Which of course made me Bachelor Number Two—doomed to languish in the bull pen until the starter lost his mojo.

But since I was still oblivious to any of this nonsense, I was just grateful for the seat and content to sip my ice-cold martini while smugly eavesdropping on the good doctor's tortured mating patter.

For better or worse, Laureen has always skewed toward impetuous creative types—like chefs and authors—so when the monotonous MD took a bathroom break, she finally turned her attention my way. I decided to open with a joke. So I asked her if the anesthesiologist was putting her to sleep. Admittedly weak, but Laureen was kind enough to chuckle. So we bantered back and forth for maybe twenty minutes. And during that brief interval, I'm reliably informed (by Laureen) that I blustered on shamelessly about my new bestseller and issued an impromptu invitation to its upcoming launch party at the New York Public Library—a brash solicitation she prudently declined. When our conversation ran its natural course and I realized, perhaps too late, that vodka poured on top of red wine might actually be rendering me less, rather than more, debonair, I bid Laureen adieu. We routinely exchanged business cards—hers very corporate, mine recently printed at Kinko's—and that, I figured, was that.

Laureen was a stunner—five foot nine, with an enormous smile and a quietly confident demeanor. But she lived clear on the other side of the country, in Georgia of all places, where she apparently had a proper corporate job, two pretty little girls, and a big crazy dog. I was bound to San Francisco, a city I loved, not by my work—I could do that anywhere—but by three school-age children and a sporadically belligerent ex-wife with whom I shared custody on a fifty-fifty basis. Laureen didn't seem like a casual relationship kind of gal. So what would be the point?

Anyway that was the logic of it. But as we all learn at some point in our lives, logic has its limits. And about two months after our fleeting barroom encounter, I received a "remember me?" email from Laureen. She wrote that she was returning to San Francisco for the company Christmas party. She also said I looked a bit like Ryan O'Neal. And she wondered whether I might like to have a drink with her.

Of course, I remembered her. And I sincerely hoped she meant the handsome *Love Story*-era Ryan O'Neal and not the puffy, old man-boob Ryan O'Neal who occasionally turned up in "Where Are They Now?" photos—although I knew the latter was probably closer to the mark. But, yes, either way, I did want to reconnect. So I threw all prudent geographical considerations to the wind and invited Laureen to meet me at the very same bench in the Redwood Room which seemed, to me at least, to be a vaguely romantic gesture.

On the appointed evening, I found myself getting all dressed up in a blue blazer, gray slacks and a powder blue shirt, all courtesy of the Brooks Brothers factory outlet in Petaluma. I arrived an hour early so I could secure the seats in question. And when Laureen wafted in wearing a starched white blouse with French cuffs and silver cufflinks, a charcoal pencil skirt, and some pretty pricey-looking riding boots, she was just as engaging and sophisticated as I remembered through my wine-and-vodka haze. Laureen flashed her megawatt smile. Sparks flew. And that very evening we initiated a long-distance romance that would culminate at the altar two years later—all thanks to four very pushy lawyers who tried to play Cupid and, oddly enough, succeeded.

During our two-year courtship, Laureen visited San Francisco every other month, and on alternating months, I traveled to Atlanta—usually for a weekend, but sometimes for as long as a week. At that point, Simba was three years old and at the peak of his impressive physical prowess. I wasn't around for his wayward puppy years, but by all accounts, Simba was a holy terror.

Laureen—Lolly to her family and childhood friends—grew up the youngest of ten children in a ridiculously small (given the number of occupants) red brick house in a pleasant residential section of Milwaukee called Whitefish Bay. There—as if ten children weren't enough—her staunchly Catholic parents bred Boston terriers and bichon frises to make a little scratch on the side. As a consequence, Laureen was intimately familiar with the care and training of puppies and had every reason to believe that she could tackle even a hard case like Simba. Early on, when Laureen still harbored that illusion, she signed Simba up for a standard six-week puppy-training course at her local pet store in Atlanta. The program's goals were modest. Puppies would learn the basic commands—sit, stay, lie down, and come. They would be taught to parade around on their leashes, and if all went well, to amicably commingle with other members of their species.

Simba refused to do any one of those things. During his very first training session, he leapt up on every other dog and human in the room. He ignored Laureen's commands. He repeatedly crashed through the low plastic fence that defined the training area. And he made it clear that he regarded his leash a grave personal insult. At the end of the first two-hour session, Simba was branded a delinquent and summarily expelled from the group.

"I think it would be better for the other dogs," said the young female trainer in khaki shorts and a polo shirt.

Laureen took a deep breath, looked the trainer straight in the eye, and employed her most persuasive trial-lawyer tone—which, believe me, is pretty persuasive.

"I understand this evening's session didn't go particularly well," Laureen said very calmly, like she was addressing a jury. "But if you would be kind enough to give us one more opportunity, I'm confident that we can do better next week. Can you give us that opportunity?"

"Yeah, I'd like to help you with that," the young trainer replied. "But you saw what happened here tonight. It was chaos. I've been teaching the puppy class for more than a year, and I've never seen anything like it. I'm pretty sure we won't be able to do anything with *that* dog." Then she pointed at little Simba in a very "*J'accuse!*" sort of way, and he gazed up at her and smiled.

"If I were you," she continued, "I would look into private lessons. Or better yet, give that dog back to whoever sold him to you." And with that, she turned on her heel and walked briskly toward the break room.

"It's my ex-husband's fault," Laureen cried out after her. "He brought home the wrong dog!"

But by then, of course, it was too late.

Laureen, who is accustomed to across-the-board success in all of her endeavors, was humiliated but undaunted. She swooped into her trademark research mode and quickly turned up a no-nonsense "canine behavior consultant" who lived in Brooklyn. Despite the ridiculous expense, Laureen flew the tough New Yorker down to Atlanta. And in less than two weeks, she transformed Simba from a feral little brute into something roughly approximating a family pet. I don't know exactly what the trainer did or how she did it. But it was such a traumatic experience for baby Simba that years later if Laureen barked orders at him in a Brooklyn accent ("Go-wahn, Simba, go-wahn,") he would immediately recall his boot-camp days, shudder, and meekly comply.

The first time I visited Laureen in Atlanta, I knew that if I truly wanted a future with her, I would have to win the hearts of both her daughters and her dog. Because, as anyone who's ever tried it will tell you, when you date a single mom, you pretty much date her entire family.

Grace, who was four at the time, was the easiest nut to crack. When her mother told her I was coming for a visit, Grace misheard my name and thought it was Chen—the same as an Asian girl at her nursery school. So, naturally, she expected me to be Chinese—a prospect that seemed to please her immensely. When she first clapped eyes on my plainly Caucasian features, she was visibly disappointed. But within a matter of days, I was able to win her over with a few of the classics—piggyback rides, the tickle monster, candy, and a stupid song I made up about frozen polar bear poop.

At six, Angela was so shy that she literally shook with fear whenever she was compelled to attend a classmate's birthday party. So it took us a bit longer to forge a connection. Fortunately, she didn't expect me to be Chinese. But when her father ran off with his lanky young paramour, Angela zeroed in on a very specific replacement—namely Atlanta Falcons starting quarterback Michael Vick. Angela, who was every inch a tomboy at the time, thought Vick might be better than her original German-born, soccer-raised father when it came to tossing a ball around the backyard—which was probably a fair assumption.

It took awhile for Angela to relinquish her NFL dreams, but I can throw a ball as well as the next native-born American. And four years later, when Michael Vick was sentenced to twenty-three months in Leavenworth for operating a vicious dog-fighting ring, I looked pretty good by comparison. Angela also thought for some reason that Dr. Martin Luther King was a leprechaun. But I decided not to disabuse her of that particular historical inaccuracy, at least for the time being.

Simba was a whole other story. In my admittedly limited experience, Labradors—even proud Labradors like Simba—can be seduced in four ways:

1. Feed them.
2. Throw them a ball.
3. Take them for walks.
4. Scratch their tummies.

Dispensing treats all day would have been the quickest, most efficacious way to go. Labs, after all, are all about the grub. But in the long run, it wouldn't have been the healthiest regime. This was subsequently proven by Angela and Grace's Brazilian au pair, Andrea. During her otherwise very pleasant year with us, Andrea tried to win Simba's heart and mind through his stomach. And by the time Laureen discovered her nefarious scheme, she'd managed to plump Simba up into a happy, lazy, 110-pound couch potato.

Laureen would have come down harder on Andrea, but honestly, she had already punished herself. Because as Andrea massively overfed the dog, she, like a surprisingly large number of foreign au pairs, became enamored with the caloric wonders of a chain restaurant called the Cheesecake Factory. And in a stroke of karmic justice, the Cheesecake Factory did to her exactly what she did to Simba, piling twenty-five pounds onto her previously slender frame. Happily, when Andrea finished her year in America and returned to her native land, both she and the dog resumed their original size and weight.

As for fetching a ball . . . well, Simba simply wouldn't do it. I could never quite wrap my mind around that cold, hard fact. In my mid-thirties and early forties, I had an affable yellow Lab named Ginger who devoted the best years of her life to incessantly dropping a neon green tennis ball at my feet. Whenever I relented and took her out to the backyard, she would retrieve the ball a hundred times in a row with no visible decrease in enthusiasm. I'm convinced that if I'd thrown the ball for three hours straight, Ginger—who wasn't exactly the Einstein of Labradors—would have cheerfully returned it over and over again until she dropped dead from exhaustion, an ecstatic smile plastered across her guileless face.

But whenever I took Simba outside, threw a tennis ball across the lawn, and bellowed, "Get it, Simba! Get it!"—even in a Brooklyn accent—he would just sit there and look at me in his bemused patrician way as if to say, "And what would be the point of *that*?"

And I would patiently explain to him that this is what Labradors are meant to do. "For more than two hundred years," I told him, "your ancestors have been bred as hunting dogs. That means when I shoot a duck, you joyously leap into the pond and bring it to me. Well, luckily for you, I don't hunt ducks, and we don't have a pond. But when I throw a tennis ball—which, in this case, is a proxy for the duck—you are compelled by two full centuries of breeding to fetch it. It's in your blood, Simba. In fact, the full name of your breed is Labrador *retriever*, not Labrador "Just-sit-there-and-look-at-me-when-I-throw-a-ball.""

But Simba, who was trained by a New York dog whisperer, not a Georgia duck hunter, had no interest whatsoever. And he was smart and proud enough to know that all of that running back and forth signified nothing and hardly befit his august stature.

So in terms of winning Simba over, that left affectionate scratching and long walks. The scratching was no problem. Simba was only too happy to roll right over and receive his due. He would lie on his back, curl up his front legs, and loll his head back with an appallingly goofy look on his enormous face. With his big brown eyes bulging and his long pink tongue hanging out from the side of his mouth, it was one of the few circumstances when he didn't look the least bit noble.

Walking Simba was a much bigger challenge. The tip-off came the first time I approached Laureen's front door in Atlanta. As I climbed the steps of the red brick townhouse where Laureen moved after her divorce, Simba barked with immense enthusiasm. Clearly, whatever qualities he lacked as a gun dog, he more than made up for them as a watchdog. From the first day Simba joined her household, Laureen no longer needed an alarm system or even a doorbell. Because whenever an unsuspecting citizen mounted her steps, pulled into her driveway, or even casually strolled past her house on a sultry Georgia eve, Simba would sound the alarm with gusto.

But to be clear, Simba was a watchdog, not a guard dog. He was still a Labrador after all. And Labradors, with few exceptions, are far more bark than bite. In fact, Simba often found himself fiercely woofing at his front end while cordially wagging in the rear. He seemed unbothered by the contradiction, and any intruder who ignored his ruckus would have had very little to fear.

So despite his big show of protective clamor as I mounted Laureen's steps, when I actually got inside, Simba didn't growl, jump up, or bare his fangs. Instead, he inexplicably turned tail and sprinted full speed down a long hallway toward the rear of the house. Then he rounded the kitchen island, zoomed back through the dining room and across the living room to his starting point. Adults and small children alike pressed their backs to the wall in alarm as ninety pounds of galloping Labrador barreled by.

"Is there something wrong with him?" I asked Laureen.

Laureen shrugged and said, "I don't know. Maybe. It's just what he does. He gets overexcited when new people come to the house. And I guess all that running around calms him down. But don't worry. Once he does a few laps, he'll be fine."

And that turned out to be true. After sprinting his indoor loop three times in succession, Simba was sufficiently composed to greet me, which he then did quite nicely.

So if that was how Simba said hello, what would he do when we sallied forth together into the great outdoors?

In the late eighteenth and early nineteenth centuries, when people still lit their homes with whale oil lamps, Nantucket Island, off the coast of Cape Cod, was the hub of America's energy industry. That's because stout Nantucket whalers were intrepid enough to set forth in twenty-foot open boats, harpoon giant sperm whales, and then hang on for dear life as the leviathans made a run for it. This was called a "Nantucket sleigh ride," and it was sort of what it was like to walk Simba. From the moment we stepped through the front door, Simba strained his leather leash to the breaking point. And I just held on as best I could.

The Nantucket whalers would have to keep their harpoon lines taut until the whale exhausted itself. But I only had to maintain my grip on Simba's leash until he stopped to poop—precisely three times per walk—or pee—every few hundred yards since Simba dispensed his urine judiciously in order to mark as much territory as possible.

As you might guess, Laureen was far more disciplined about all of this than I was. When Laureen walked Simba, she shortened his leash, yanked hard on his choke collar, and yelled, "Heel, Simba, heel!" every few steps until the dog more or less submitted to her will—usually less. My goal, however, was not to train Simba but to win his affection. So I left that particular aspect of Simba's pedagogy to Laureen, and I only reined in the galloping Labrador when we encountered other dogs—confrontations that occasionally turned contentious.

Despite his alpha disposition, or perhaps because of it, Simba almost never barked or growled at his fellow canines. But a surprisingly large number of dogs—almost always much smaller dogs—felt the compulsion to bark and growl at him. Simba generally brushed off these *poseurs* with haughty disdain. But every so often, he sensed a genuine threat. Then, as he silently assumed his defensive posture, his hackles rose and his big brown eyes went flat and steely cold.

The way I saw it, Simba was an old-fashioned "Greatest Generation" sort of dog. He practiced what my father, a former Eighty-second Airborne paratrooper, preached. Namely, that you should never start a fight, but you always finish it. In fact, the one time Simba was physically attacked—by a pair of ridiculous off-leash Pomeranians on a California nature trail—he acquitted himself with conspicuous valor, wounding one Pomeranian in the haunch but stopping well short of the canicide of which he was clearly capable.

Simba's inclination to use only the minimum necessary violence was confirmed years later when Laureen's best friend Tamera brought her handsome, six-month-old, cinnamon-colored vizsla over for a visit. Simba had recently returned from a walk and just wanted to lie down in peace. But young Mikos, full of beans, kept yapping in his face, trying to get Simba to play with him. After several minutes of that nonsense, Simba slowly rose to his feet and shook himself briefly. And then, with neither bark nor growl, he simply took Mikos's entire head into his enormous mouth.

Simba didn't chomp down on Mikos's skull or hurt him in any way. He just wanted to let the young whippersnapper know that he was the boss. And if pushed too far, the boss could literally bite his head off. This had the desired effect. Mikos skulked away whimpering with his tail between his legs and spent the next several hours tucked safely between his owner's knees. Simba, point made, resumed his siesta.

Anyway, whenever I traveled to Atlanta to visit Laureen and the girls, I tried to walk Simba as often as possible. Every evening after dinner, I scratched his belly. And during the course of the day, I dispensed treats sparingly. (Laureen might take issue with that.) In time, Simba accepted me as a member of his pack and eventually as his alpha. He stopped barking maniacally when I climbed Laureen's steps. And he no longer broke into his frenzied hundred-yard dash when I stepped inside. Despite all that—and despite the fact that Simba would eventually become my most constant companion for nearly a decade—he never, ever, even once, fetched a ball for me.

Two years into our long-distance romance, I bought an engagement ring and filled my bedroom with twenty candles of various heights. Then I waited forty minutes for Laureen to get off an evening conference call, dropped to one knee, and proposed marriage. Now we could no longer delay the inevitable. One of us would have to move.

Laureen had a perfectly good job in Atlanta. But after six years as a divisional general counsel she was pretty bored with the work. We figured her digital law experience might land her a more interesting, better-paying job in the Bay Area's booming tech sector. And more to the point, the terms of Laureen's divorce settlement granted her sole custody of Angela, Grace, and Simba. So Guenter the Chef couldn't prevent her from leaving Atlanta even if he wanted to—which, it turned out, he didn't.

There was no way my ex-wife would have had the same laissez-faire attitude. And I knew my California kids would never move to Atlanta. So given all that, Laureen agreed to relocate to San Francisco where we would merge our families.

At the time, I told Laureen how much I appreciated the fact that she was willing to leave a city she loved full of friends she adored to marry the likes of me. And to assuage my guilt, I handed her a chit she could redeem somewhere down the road.

"This time, you're coming to San Francisco to be with me," I told her, "and you know I'm grateful for that. But I know you, Laureen. You're smart and ambitious. And someday you're going to want to take a bigger, better job in some other city. So here's my promise. Once Lucas heads off to college, which is only six years from now, you can move anywhere you want. And I will follow without complaint."

"I appreciate that," said Laureen. "But for now, why don't we just focus on finding me a job in San Francisco and a house big enough for seven people. You know how deep rooted I am. I moved to Atlanta right after law school, and I stayed there for more than twenty years. I'd still be living there if you hadn't come along. So we'll probably end up living in San Francisco for the rest of our lives."

The moment Laureen said that, I had a strong premonition we'd be moving someday. But all I said was, "Well, that would be great, but remember: the offer stands."

Although I did chauffeur Laureen to a few random job interviews—like the general counsel position at brand new Virgin America Airlines—it turned out to be unnecessary. Because in a stroke of great timing, McKesson's own general counsel—the company's top lawyer and Laureen's boss's boss—suddenly decided to retire after more than two decades at the helm. And while Laureen no longer wanted to head up a divisional law department—the equivalent of middle management—McKesson's top legal job, based in San Francisco and far more prestigious—appealed to her striving nature.

Laureen and I had long discussions about whether she should pursue the position. The $300 billion drug distribution business has always been a boys' club—even more so than other industries. And in the storied 173-year history of the McKesson Corporation, no woman had ever been chief legal officer or chief anything officer for that matter. And even if you put gender aside, Laureen objectively lacked the deep securities experience normally required to be head lawyer of a large, publicly traded company.

There would also be some unpleasantness involved. To prevail, Laureen would have to leapfrog her own boss, McKesson's longtime deputy general counsel, who, with a certain degree of justification, considered the top job his hard-earned due. He would view any expression of interest on Laureen's part as rank insubordination. And whoever lost that battle would likely have to pack up their files and set sail for another company.

Despite all that—and despite the fact that McKesson mounted a formal nationwide search—Laureen threw her hat in the ring, arguing that what the company really needed was a rock-solid manager and battle-tested trial lawyer—for the times when McKesson, like all large corporations, faced existential legal conflict. As for securities law, Laureen assured her CEO that she could hire a specialist to handle that aspect of the job while she got up to speed.

Laureen must have been persuasive, because after a months-long vetting process, the company's dynamic young CEO—a fellow Midwesterner from Minnesota—decided to give her the shot. Suddenly Laureen was no longer a mid-level corporate lawyer. She was now executive vice president, general counsel, and corporate secretary of America's fourteenth largest corporation by sales. And she headed up an international law department that employed nearly 400 attorneys, paralegals, and assistants. McKesson wasn't a household name like General Electric or Wells Fargo, but it was a hundred-billion-dollar a year enterprise in a tightly regulated industry. So for a lawyer, this was the big time.

In May 2006, Laureen and I bought a house roomy enough for five kids and a dog. It was your typical Bay Area craftsman home with brown shingles and hunter-green trim set on a quiet wooded acre eight miles north of the Golden Gate Bridge in scenic Marin County. I prepared the house for our newly merged family while Laureen frantically flew back and forth across the country, trying to do her old job in Atlanta and her new job in San Francisco at the same time. In June, Laureen, Angela, Grace, and Simba bid Atlanta a teary farewell and joined Kara, Willie, Lucas, and me in our new home.

It was Simba's first, and as it turned out last, airplane ride. And he was not amused. Simba was ensconced as comfortably as possible with his chew toys and bed in what must have been the largest dog crate ever manufactured. And he was mildly sedated for the four-and-a-half-hour flight. Still, it seemed somehow disrespectful to incarcerate the King of the Canines in a big plastic box and shove him into the luggage compartment of an airplane.

When Simba was finally discharged into the baggage claim area of the San Jose airport[1] he was a bit groggy and suitably annoyed. And in his drug-addled state, he nipped Grace's finger when she tried to hug him around the neck. It was a minor injury to be sure. But to Grace, who used to ride around the house on Simba's back, it was an astonishing betrayal. We forgave Simba his bad temper and eventually convinced Grace to do the same. And we figured Simba would forgive us too when he saw his big, new yard, lushly inhabited by deer, raccoons, and wild turkeys that he could chase to his heart's content but never quite catch.

At this point, Kara was about to graduate from high school. Will was a high school junior; Lucas, a sixth-grader; Angela, a second-grader; and Grace, a kindergartener. Our blended family was blessed in many ways. Thanks to Laureen's fancy new job, we could actually afford the big house we just bought. My kids adored Laureen. Hers were willing to give me a chance. And most importantly, all five kids got along well with each other right from the get-go. In fact, they got along a little too well. The five of them promptly formed an ironclad alliance against their common enemy, Laureen and me. And when either of us tried to discipline one child, the other four would vigorously rally to the miscreant's defense with outspoken Angela invariably bearing their standard.

On August 19, 2006, Laureen and I were married at an old stone winery in nearby Napa Valley. The wedding got off to a rocky

---

[1] Laureen didn't fully understand Bay Area geography yet—specifically that Mineta San Jose Airport was an hour and a half from our house as opposed to SFO, which was only thirty minutes away.

start. During the previous year, my seventy-six-year-old mother, who lived in Pittsburgh, Pennsylvania, had become progressively less steady on her feet. In fairly quick progression, she had dislocated her shoulder in one fall and cracked a vertebra in another. But like her mother before her, she stubbornly refused to use either a wheelchair or a walker—only a cane. So as she shuffled up the uneven flagstone path that led from the parking lot to the outdoor wedding site, she tripped and fell flat on her face.

Although the spill was initially dramatic—my mother has never suffered quietly—two of Laureen's many brothers helped her to her feet and cleaned her wounds with a handful of wet paper towels they grabbed from the men's room. Then my sainted father, Norm, rushed over and attempted to calm her down. Twenty minutes later, she hobbled into the ceremony with only a few conspicuous scrapes on her nose and chin. And for the remainder of the happy day, she basked in the solicitous attention of the other wedding guests.

At roughly the same time, Angela—stunning in her black and white bridesmaid's dress—was struck with a serious bout of stage fright and flatly refused to participate in the ceremony. It took Laureen a full thirty minutes to convince Angela—who sat crying on the floor of a hotel closet—that it was her categorical duty to stand up with her younger sister and three new stepsiblings. Eventually she acquiesced. And although the ceremony was delayed, she performed flawlessly in the end.

While we certainly discussed it, we weren't quite crazy enough to march Simba down the aisle with the rest of the wedding party. Somehow that seemed to cross the fine line between dog lover and lunatic. But he did watch majestically from the sidelines, a white bow tied to his leather collar, as a grumpy rabbi and a charismatic defrocked Irish Catholic priest took turns pronouncing us man and wife. When the ceremony concluded with a smattering of applause from Laureen's side of the aisle and a few shouts of "*L'chaim*" from mine, Simba was officially my stepdog.

As you might imagine, five children and a very large dog make for a boisterous household. But it was a happy home, and Simba was no small part of that. I loved watching the kids come home from school each day, one after the other, and break into big smiles when they saw Simba faithfully waiting for them by the front door. Simba greeted each child as a long-lost pack member. But he was practically ecstatic when Laureen came home from work, usually around seven thirty. When Simba heard the garage door rumble open, he leapt up from his customary spot on the brown family-room rug and ran to the top of the stairs that led down to the garage. There he waited, tail madly flailing, until Laureen emerged from the basement. Then he gazed upon her with an unsullied love, buried his enormous head between her knees like a giant Labrador baby, and gratefully received her ministrations.

One secret of Laureen's success is that she has always dressed the part of the chic corporate executive. You'd be shocked at the difference this makes for women approaching the top rung of corporate America. (For men, it hardly matters.) But haute couture wasn't always easy with Simba around. On days when Laureen wore a black skirt or charcoal slacks, Simba would inevitably rub up against her mere seconds before she left for work, instantly blanketing her smart ensemble with hundreds of short, white dog hairs. In fact, all of our clothes and most of our furniture were perpetually upholstered in Labrador fur. And when Simba rode in the car with us, the air vents would kick up visible cyclones of dog hair that eventually settled like fresh snow on everyone in the vehicle.

But that was a small price to pay for Simba's companionship. Because in this much too serious world, dogs give us license to act foolishly. Since I have that propensity anyway, I took full advantage of the situation. But, believe me, I wasn't the only one who did that. Grace set up a Facebook page where she faithfully reported Simba's noteworthy activities to his twenty-four "friends." Every Halloween Lucas dressed him up in costumes that inevitably involved Ray-Bans and a fedora. And every few months or so, Angela painted his black toenails pink, blue, or both.

When Willie pissed off his younger siblings (which happened fairly regularly), they would often sneak into his room, swipe a pair of his boxer shorts, and let Simba wear them around the house for a while before carefully replacing them in his drawer. Even Laureen would return from the C-suite where she defended billion-dollar lawsuits all day, plunk herself down on the rug next to Simba, and regale him with goofy baby talk.

But like I said, I was the ringleader. I taught Simba tricks that insulted his innate nobility. I taught him to catch little biscuits in his mouth from ten feet across the kitchen. And when I sang, "Who likes to dance? Who likes to dance?" Simba, trained with dog treats, would jump up and place his front paws on my shoulders. Then we would twirl around the kitchen for a while. And probably because I was raised on sixties cartoons and sitcoms, I composed a stupid theme song for Simba that the kids sang all the time and Kara once scored in three-part harmony.

I had time for these shenanigans because Simba and I spent nearly all day every day together. As I worked in my home office writing and designing coffee-table books for Barnes & Noble, Simba was my shadow. When I sat at my desk, Simba lay next to me. When I stood up, he stood up. When I ambled over to the kitchen to make a sandwich or cook dinner, Simba hovered underfoot waiting for a morsel of food to drop (which sometimes happened accidently and sometimes accidently on purpose.)

Simba and I learned to communicate with a fairly extensive vocabulary of words and gestures. If I held my hand parallel to the floor, Simba sat. If I wordlessly pointed to the ground, he lay down. If I opened the back door and said, "Go on, Simba," he ran outside and peed. If I said, "Hey, Simba, wanna go for a ride?" he sprinted out the front door and stood next to my car panting with anticipation. And if I opened the front closet where we hung his leash, he suddenly became the happiest dog on Earth.

Over time, Laureen broke Simba of his maniacal watchdog tendencies. And eventually, whenever somebody yelled, "Simba, go to your spot!" he would reluctantly stop woofing at whoever dared to darken our door and would run instead to a little first floor powder room where he sat quietly on the rug until someone released him. In Simba's mind, this relieved him of his sacred duty to defend the homeland. And only by way of penance will I tell you that we sometimes forgot where he was until someone had to use the toilet or someone else said, "Hey, where's Simba?"

But the conversation wasn't one-way. As I trained Simba, he trained me. When he wanted me to go somewhere or do something, he approached me, looked me straight in the eye, and backed up a few steps. That meant, "Come with me." Then he would lead me to the back door if he needed to pee, or to his water bowl if he wanted me to refill it, or up to Angela's room if he wanted to retire for the evening. (There were some bedtime formalities that required my participation.) If Simba wanted his tummy rubbed, he would lead me to the family room rug, roll over, and give me one of his inelegant "scratch-me" looks.

Simba, no longer the *enfant terrible*, was now unfailingly courteous about all of this. He rarely interrupted me while I worked at my desk or even as I lay on the couch watching TV. He would just wait patiently until I stood up, and then he would respectfully submit his request. If he ever broke that protocol, I knew it meant he really had to pee or that wild animals—usually deer, turkeys, or raccoons—had invaded our yard.

One of Simba's most endearing gestures was pure love. After dinner each evening, I would make my way from the kitchen table to the rug in front of the fireplace and lie down next to Simba—just to let him know that he remained, as always, a cherished member of the pack. Then Simba, in what seemed to be a very human or perhaps just a universal act of affection, would lay one of his huge, white paws on top of my arm as if to comfort me—or maybe just to make a physical connection.

Of course, we never know precisely what dogs are thinking. But if this was Simba's way of saying of saying "I love you," then the feeling was entirely mutual. For none of us could imagine the life of our family without him.

4. OLD DOG

In absolute terms, the time that passed from Simba's arrival on the West Coast until his first serious health crisis was only seven years. But in dog years, it was more like half a century. With dogs you see the human life cycle in condensed form. Simba was a terrible toddler for six months, a wild child for a year, and a rambunctious teenager for a year and a half. He was a strutting young adult for three years, and then a middle-aged gentleman for five or six years after that. But by April 2013, at twelve-and-a-half years of age, Simba could only be described as an old dog—the human equivalent of eighty-five or ninety. Most Labrador retrievers never see their thirteenth birthday. The breed's median lifespan is just over eleven years. But Laureen desperately wanted to believe that Simba's immense strength and stamina would sustain him well past the average. In fact we were all convinced that Simba would be a special case.

For both dogs and people, old age is the slow and relentless stripping away of the things we love. And there was nothing Simba loved more than long walks—particularly his weekend constitutionals with Laureen in Blackie's Pasture on the grassy shores of Richardson Bay. There, Simba enjoyed the magnificent scenery that stretched from Mt. Tamalpais to the Golden Gate Bridge. And he would regally meet and greet other neighborhood dogs. During these weekend promenades, Laureen would often chat with her fellow dog enthusiasts who invariably commented on Simba's imposing size, handsome countenance, and aristocratic bearing.

"Is that a yellow Lab?" they would ask. "He's huge."

And Laureen, ever the proud mother, would tell the inquirer that Simba was the biggest puppy in his litter (this bug had evolved into a feature over the years), that his ancestors were dog show champions, and that Simba was, in fact, not a yellow Lab, but a white Lab with honey-dipped ears. Laureen always topped off the conversation by casually mentioning how old Simba was.

"Wow, he looks great for his age," they inevitably replied—and he did.

Although Simba's walks with Laureen persisted well into his dotage, at twelve and a half, Simba no longer strained the leash like some sort of satanic sled dog. Now he gently strolled beside Laureen like the polite old pensioner he'd become—like Laureen had tried to teach him years ago, but which Simba couldn't quite manage until his life force had sufficiently ebbed.

In his prime, Simba could easily trot seven or eight miles at a clip—and in that regard, fit, outdoorsy Laureen was the perfect companion. But now if Simba walked more than a mile or two, even at a measured pace, his arthritis would flare up. And for the rest of the day, he would lie nearly motionless on his side. When

Simba did finally stand up, it was always very slowly and with visibly painful effort. Then he pitifully limped around the kitchen for a while until we gave him an extra dose of his liver-flavored anti-inflammatory tablets.

We also no longer had to worry about Simba humping other dogs—males to assert his dominance, females out of sheer lust. Despite the fact he was neutered as a puppy—an admittedly barbaric act that was supposed to forefend that sort of behavior—we often had to step in and yank Simba off other dogs. And once, after Laureen and I managed to pry him loose from a particularly beguiling, coffee-colored French Poodle in the parking lot of Lucas's high school, he remained hunched over, back arched and fully aroused, dramatically humping the air.

"Oh, no. Can you do something about that?" asked Laureen, who was truly horrified by the untoward spectacle of her dog simulating a sex act in front of Lucas's school.

"What do you suggest?" I replied.

"There's a water bottle in the car. Can you just get it and pour some water on his head?"

"You mean like a cold shower?" I asked.

"Yes, like a cold shower. Please, David. Just do it."

"No, I don't think so," I replied. "That would just make us look even more ridiculous—if that's even possible. We should probably just let it run its course."

Which it eventually did, but not before a small crowd of parents and children, waiting for the school bus to return from a field trip, were variously amused and horrified by Simba's prurient display.

But now, in his golden years, Simba barely gave the ladies a second look. And when the FedEx guy or the gardeners came to the house, he no longer went berserk. In fact, more often than not, he didn't bother to get up at all. He just lay on the rug and let loose a few half-hearted woofs to let us know that he still understood his duty but now lacked the stamina to execute it.

There was, however, one magical place where Simba regained a measure of his youthful vigor. In February 2011, Laureen bought a vacation home on California's rocky Sonoma Coast. I initially told Laureen that I had no interest whatsoever in owning a second home with all of its attendant expense and time-consuming maintenance.

"For a lot less money," I argued, "we can take vacations wherever we want."

But since her promotion to general counsel of McKesson, Laureen lived—or at least worked—in a world where all of her colleagues owned, in addition to their so-called "primary residence," a timbered ski chalet in Telluride or a charming Napa Valley farmhouse with a few acres of chardonnay.

Laureen's mother, Jane, died from breast cancer when Laureen was nine years old. And for several years thereafter, her previously successful and charismatic father devolved into an abusive alcoholic with a factory job. With ten kids in the house, money was always tight. So Laureen, the youngest of the brood, grew up sharing a tiny attic bedroom with two older sisters and wearing their hand-me-down clothes. When her father told her that there was no good reason for her to go to college "because she could always get a good job as a secretary," Laureen finished high school in three years and then worked full time for a year so she could pay her own way through the University of Wisconsin at Eau Claire. There she became an all-American track star, graduated near the top of her class, and was admitted to the University of Wisconsin Law School in Madison.

During law school, Laureen met her educational expenses by assisting professors, cleaning houses, babysitting, and when straits were particularly dire, by selling her own blood. She didn't have any health insurance, so when she shattered her elbow in a bicycle accident, she quickly blew through her meager savings and nearly had to abandon her lifelong dream of becoming a lawyer. Only the compassionate intercession of the University of Wisconsin chancellor, Donna Shalala, rescued her prospective career.

So to the manor Laureen clearly was not born. And the notion of purchasing a vacation home we might use three or four weeks a year would have been as unthinkable to her parents as buying a private jet or a chateau in France. But up on the thirty-seventh floor of the McKesson Building where the top executives worked, owning only one home was considered vaguely aberrant. And in the upper echelons of corporate America, aberrant is something you definitely don't want to be.

Following our initial conversation, I didn't hear anything more on the subject for several months. I took that as good sign and thought maybe the impulse had passed. But true to form, Laureen had been quietly devoting some of her early hours—she got up at four every morning—systematically analyzing every oceanfront listing within a 150-mile radius of our house. She began her search at the south end of the range near tony Carmel-by-the-Sea and systematically worked her way north until she reached a fascinating, if somewhat obscure, eco-community called The Sea Ranch, about 120 miles north of San Francisco.

Designed by a team of visionary, granola-munching, Birkenstock-wearing (I assume) Berkeley architects in the mid-1960s, this former sheep ranch is a narrow ten-mile-long ocean-side strip that combines a very specific architectural sensibility—the starkly simple wooden houses visually melt into the landscape—with a breathtaking coastal setting. It's not a particularly fashionable spot for a second home—like Tahoe or Napa—so Laureen would still have to live with that petty stigma. But Sea Ranch's rocky ocean-sprayed cliffs, pocket-sized beaches, and wildflower-bejeweled meadows simply take your breath away.

There Laureen found a simple, boxy "mineshaft-style" house perched on a thirty-foot cliff above the gray green Pacific breakers. Built by a childless Ohio couple who suffered a financial setback, the house was only five years old and didn't require much in the way of repairs or improvement. Furthermore, the Ohio couple—who from the look of things had far better taste than we did—wanted to sell the house fully furnished right down to the silverware, dishes, and towels. So it wouldn't take us months to set up second house-keeping.

And as usual, Laureen was right. The entire family loved Sea Ranch right from the start. It was a healthful, relaxing place where you could sit in a weathered wooden rocking chair on the back deck, watching spouting gray whales migrate north and south. Or hike along the magnificent oceanside trail that ran behind our house. Or in twenty-two-year-old Will's case, invite young ladies—usually au pairs from the Nordic nations—up for a romantic weekend.

But nobody loved Sea Ranch more than Simba. He clearly didn't relish the windy gut-twisting drive up the stunningly scenic two-lane coastal highway. But the moment we pulled into the driveway and he heard gravel crunching under the tires, he snapped to attention and panted with anticipation.

As good old Simba leapt gingerly from the back of the station wagon, you could practically see the years melt away. He would always pause in the middle of the driveway for a few minutes, holding his massive head perfectly still as he sniffed the salt air and listened to the breakers crashing rhythmically on the bluff behind the house.

Labrador retrievers were originally called St. John's water dogs. And they likely originated on Newfoundland's rugged Avalon Peninsula, which juts into the icy North Atlantic. So Simba's affinity for rocky seashores and brisk ocean breezes may have been some sort of breed memory. But whatever the reason, Sea Ranch always seemed to breathe fresh life into him.

Whenever he was at Sea Ranch, Simba's appetite sharpened. He could walk farther than usual ,and he would even trot thirty or forty yards across the dark wet sand at nearby Walk-on Beach. And each day when he returned from his jaunt, he would lie regally on a three-by-three-foot area rug left behind by the previous owners. The tan wool rug had a series of black numbers woven into it that allegedly represented the precise latitude and longitude of the house. And it was set squarely in the middle of the big central room that served as our combination kitchen-dining-family room. From that strategic post, his acknowledged place in the house, Simba would placidly observe the life of the family as it swirled around him during the course of the day. And sooner or later, one after another, everyone in the family would kneel down before him and pay homage to the Lord of the Labradors, patting his enormous head and telling him what a good dog he was.

Simba even had his own specialized Sea Ranch duty—barking menacingly at the small gray fox that brazenly employed our back deck as his toilet. And even in the autumn of his life, when he could no longer be bothered to menace the gardeners or bark at the mail carrier, Simba gave that particular duty his all. The Sea Ranch, in short, was Simba's Shangri-la. And he was happier there than he was anywhere else on Earth.

But back home in Tiburon, Simba was an increasingly frequent visitor to nearby Tamalpais Pet Hospital. He was plagued by many of the maladies common to old Labradors and other large-breed dogs. First came the lumps. It began with just one or two. Simba's vet, Dr. Penny Elliott, always biopsied them just to be safe, but she assured us that these soft fatty tumors, called lipomas, were almost always benign and that we really shouldn't worry about them. But then, when Simba was ten, one of his lumps, harder than the others, turned out to be malignant. The cancer wasn't life threatening or anything, just an overnight stay at the pet hospital and a surprisingly large medical bill.

Every three months or so for the next two years, Dr. Elliott methodically palpated, measured, and recorded every one of Simba's many lumps—some as large as small lemons—on a blue chart tucked into his burgeoning file. But then, after a while, the lumps became so large and so prolific—and frankly, Simba got so old—that she simply stopped tracking them. It was kind of like when my father developed a slow-growing form of prostate cancer at age seventy-eight. The oncologist told him that, given his advanced age, no action would be taken because, and I quote, "You're going to die, but not from this." That's when you know that the end of the road, while maybe not just around the next bend, is lurking somewhere out there on the horizon.

Despite his lumps and his cancer and his painful arthritis and his waning strength and stamina, I had almost as much trouble as Laureen accepting the fact that Simba was no longer the hardy athletic dog I had known for more than a decade. Sure, he couldn't walk more than a half hour anymore, but he was as enthusiastic as ever when I grabbed his leash off the hook. And while he no longer loped up the front steps like a young gazelle, he could still climb them at a slow trot. And if Simba had ceased barking maniacally at every sentient being who dared to enter his territory, maybe that was a good thing. "Even cancer couldn't kill him," I always said.

But then Simba contracted an unspecified snout infection. And unlike his previous illnesses, he couldn't just shake this one off. The bug, whatever it was, knocked out Simba's sense of smell, which is pretty serious business for a dog. When Simba couldn't smell his food, he lost his appetite. And when I poured the kibble into his big aluminum bowl, instead of wolfing it down like he usually did, he just glanced at it and shuffled away.

The infection also upset Simba's sense of balance and, like my mother, he began to stumble and fall down from time to time. Falls are nature's way of culling the pack. Before humans settled into permanent agricultural communities ten thousand years ago—and dogs followed close behind—both species hunted nomadically. And when old or infirm members of the tribe, or the pack, stumbled and couldn't get up, they were left to die. It seems heartless now, but with its weakest members culled, the group as a whole stood a better chance of survival. So in both Simba's case and my mother's, I regarded their frequent falls as dark harbingers.

When Simba contracted his snout infection and started falling down, we were having some work done at the house. And there were always two or three construction workers on the premises including Randy Hitchcock, my longtime friend and contractor. Early one morning, Simba and I heard Randy's mammoth Ford F-250 pickup rumble up the driveway. And as we sauntered out to greet him, Simba was all excited to see his old buddy Randy. But then Simba's legs suddenly buckled out from under him, and he collapsed in a heap on the pavers.

Simba desperately tried to pull himself up again, but this time he couldn't do it. And as he tried over and over again, his breath shortened, and his eyes widened with panic. I tried to calm him by saying, "C'mon, buddy. It's okay. You can do it. I'll help you."

But even when I straddled Simba and pulled up on his torso, he couldn't regain his footing. And finally Randy had to help me hoist Simba into the backseat of my car so I could rush him to the vet's.

I liked having Randy and his guys around the house. I enjoyed talking to them about joists and trusses and guy stuff like that. I liked it when they needed an extra pair of hands to hold one end of a beam or a window casement or whatever it was they were trying to install. I mean writing and designing coffee-table books is all well and good, but as the revered former picture editor of the *London Sunday Times*, Michael Rand, once said to me, "It's not what you'd call man's work."

So when Randy and his guys were working around the house, I tended to spend more time than usual away from my computer. And I tried—probably with limited success—to be one of the guys. You know, more gritty western Pennsylvania where I was raised, and less snotty Marin County where I ended up. But after Randy and I loaded Simba into the car and the other guys gathered around to see what all the commotion was about, I started saying to Randy, "Hey, thanks man, I appreciate it. I guess I better get him over to the vet's to find out what's going on. Maybe he …"

And at that point, my voice broke, and I began to cry, damn it. I mean I wasn't bawling or anything, but I was clearly crying. And I couldn't have been more embarrassed. Of course I loved Simba. I knew that. But this was nothing to cry about, and certainly not in front of the guys—who by this time were all staring down at their work boots in embarrassment.

I said "Sorry, sorry" a few times. Then I climbed into my car and drove Simba down Tiburon Boulevard and across 101 to Tamalpais Pet Hospital in Mill Valley. I was barely able to lift him out of the back seat and carry him into the examination room. I set him down on the floor on his feet, hoping he might stay upright. And he did remain standing for a few seconds, looking at me for approval. But then he rocked back and forth, crumpled to the floor, and lay panting on his side.

When Dr. Elliott walked into the examination room a few moments later, I tried to explain what was going on. And, damn it, it happened again. I choked up, my eyes began to tear, and I couldn't speak. This was getting ridiculous. The nurse found my little display of emotion quite touching, which of course only made things worse. But all I could do was sit on the floor and hug Simba's giant head.

After that very awkward display, I was left with the inescapable conclusion that I loved this dog deeply. And not like any other pet I ever had. In my late thirties and early forties, I had a pair of Labradors, Fred and Ginger, who lived a reasonably long life and eventually passed away. And I shed a few tears in their memory. But with Simba, my fear for his life was far more visceral, like something you might feel for a close friend or even a child. Apparently, after spending nearly a decade together, all day, every day, Simba and I were bound together. And sitting on the floor in the vet's office crying, I was afraid that this bond might be broken.

5. DOG DISRUPTED

Tiburon, California
October 2013

With the help of powerful antibiotics and high-calorie dog food, Simba gradually recuperated from his still unidentified snout infection. And over the course of the next two or three months, he regained most of the weight he lost during his illness. But after any serious ailment, very old dogs, like very old people, seldom regain the same level of well-being they enjoyed before their health crisis occurred. And when the next illness strikes, which it inevitably does, they usually rebound to a lower plateau. This pattern repeats itself until the old person or the old dog in question is struck by an infirmity—maybe a broken hip or some sort of sepsis—from which he or she can no longer recover. And at that point, it's game over.

So three weeks after Simba collapsed in the driveway, he began eating his regular food again. But sometimes he left half of it in the bowl. And when Laureen got home from work, he no longer ran to the top of the steps to greet her. He just lay on the family room rug, smiling and thumping his tail on the floor until she came to see him. And once or twice a week, as he arthritically shuffled around the house, he would stumble and slump to the floor. Then he would look terribly sad and embarrassed as he struggled to pull himself up. And he would glance over at me to make sure I still loved him and still wanted him to be part of my pack.

Whenever that happened, I would rub his neck and reassure him as best I could. But Laureen and I both knew that his pattern of decline was now in place. And we girded ourselves for the day, perhaps not that far off, when we would once again drive thirteen-year-old Simba to Tamalpais Pet Hospital, and he would not return.

Laureen also had a pattern, but hers was an upward spiral. She would start a new job—like general counsel of McKesson—and in the early stages of that job, she would live in a constant state of low-grade fear convinced that somehow she'd fail. Harnessing that fear, she would work like a maniac—up to fourteen hours a day, seven days a week—mastering the task at hand. For the next year or two, she would learn the basics, then the subtleties, of her new position. She would become a superstar for five or six years. And finally, near the end of the cycle, beset by creeping boredom, she would scan the horizon for higher mountains to climb.

But seven years into her stint at McKesson, Laureen no longer had to search for higher mountains because the mountains were searching for her. Head lawyers of very large publicly traded companies possess a rare skill set, and there's no substitute for their experience. At any given moment, more than a hundred different individuals, corporations, and government agencies are either suing or threatening to sue the McKesson Corporation, with wildly different prospects of success. The first time the Justice Department slams your company with an $800 million demand or a plaintiff's law firm files a $15 billion bet-the-company class action suit, it's understandably alarming. The third or fourth time it happens, you kind of know what to do. So once you land your first general counsel job at a Fortune 50 company—and if you manage to survive four or five years, which many GC's don't—you tend to get a lot of job offers.

That was certainly true of Laureen. Every three months or so, a corporate recruiter fronting a gigantic corporation with a household name would discreetly contact her and invite her to switch teams. Laureen had genuine affection for her colleagues, and seven years into the job, she remained grateful to the CEO who had plucked her from mid-level obscurity. She also had faith in her company's future. McKesson was a tightly run ship with a gifted skipper. And like most health-care companies, it profited mightily from the twin tailwinds of Obamacare and an aging population. McKesson's surging stock price meant that Laureen's compensation now exceeded her dreams. So even though she was always flattered by the attention and occasionally pictured herself as head lawyer of a more widely known corporation, she would always mull the prospect over for a few weeks and decide to stay put.

But then one day, Laureen took a call from a recruiter representing Manhattan-based American Express Corporation—a company she had always admired in a city where she had always wanted to live.

Actually, it was American Express's second shot at her. Six months earlier, Laureen had politely listened to their headhunter's pitch and briefly considered a more challenging, more prestigious position in the white-hot center of the business universe. But at the time, she was bogged down in a long, complex acquisition, and there was no way she could leave before the transaction was completed.

Laureen assumed that American Express would just jump to the next candidate—which is what usually happened in these cases—and she was occasionally wistful about the lost opportunity. But this time, a top American Express executive convinced his CEO that Laureen was the best person for the job and that they should take one more crack at her. So when the headhunter circled back, Laureen knew it was serious business. And for the first time since she joined McKesson back in 2000, she agreed to engage in a "hiring process."

Needless to say, this turn of events threw our nicely settled household into turmoil. After seven wonderful years in Tiburon, we had finally gotten everything just the way we wanted it—or at least that's how it felt. Only that month, we had finally finished landscaping our Tiburon house. And up at Sea Ranch, we had recently converted our garage into a bunkroom so there would be plenty of room for our theoretical grandchildren.

And of course there was much more than real estate to consider. Over the last twenty-five years, I had developed a wonderful circle of friends in San Francisco and Marin County. We had watched each other's children grow up, graduate from high school then college, and in a few cases, start families of their own. We celebrated holidays and marked the milestones of our lives together. A quarter century of shared history isn't something you just walk away from. And it seemed highly unlikely that I would be able to develop a similar circle of friends in Manhattan—not at my age.

And it wasn't just me. Angela was in her sophomore year at a high school that was a remarkably good fit for her—an institution that nourished her intellectual curiosity, rewarded her diligence, and was full of other proto-intellectual nerds just like her. Hell, we even had season tickets for the San Francisco Giants who had won two of the last four World Series. So the idea of trading our well-settled lives in comfy casual Marin for an amorphous set of scary unknowns in dirty, noisy, dog-eat-dog Manhattan was disconcerting, to say the least.

Even Laureen was conflicted. Deep in her bones, she wanted to climb the higher mountain and finish her career at a globally known company. But she also felt deeply guilty about the disruption her fierce ambition might wreak on the rest of the family. So she decided the only way she could proceed in good conscience was to make her case to the family and take a vote.

Well, it wasn't precisely a vote. As you might expect from a big city lawyer, the referendum was more complex. Since Angela, Grace, and I would actually have to pull up stakes and move to Manhattan, Laureen granted us full veto power. Ostensibly, if any one of us objected to the move, then the whole deal was off. Kara, Will, and Lucas didn't really live with us anymore, and they wouldn't have to relocate. So they were cast in more of an advisory capacity. They could offer their opinions, but they couldn't block the move on their own. As a seasoned trial lawyer who went a career 40–0 in the courtroom, Laureen was probably pretty confident that she would prevail. But her offer to stay put if she didn't seemed substantially sincere.

Laureen approached me first, but I was a pushover. I had made my decision seven years earlier when Laureen ditched her own well-settled life in Atlanta to marry me. I gave her an IOU then. And I felt, if not thrilled, then at least obliged, to redeem it now. Laureen worked incredibly hard. And the rest of us benefitted from that. So if this was something she had to do, then I would support her.

"I want you to be honest with me," Laureen said one evening after dinner. "If I go ahead and take the job and we move to New York, are you honestly going to be okay with it?"

"Well, you know how much I love San Francisco and all my friends here," I replied. "So of course, I'd rather stay."

Laureen's face dropped a bit.

"And I'm not particularly ambitious—at least not the way you are. I was reasonably well-known in my field and set up financially by the time I was thirty-two, so I've had a lot of time to figure out that more money and more prestige don't make you any happier—not at a core level. But that being said, I've always been adventurous. And moving to Manhattan seems like an adventure I can still handle. So, like I told you seven years ago, if this is something you really want to do, then I'm right behind you."

Of course, from that point on, I had to listen to Laureen describe the move as "an adventure" every single time we discussed it. But, hey, once a trial lawyer, always a trial lawyer.

Twenty-six-year-old Kara also backed the move from the start. After graduating from Berkeley with a very impressive if not particularly marketable philosophy degree, she had signed up for some sort of advertising graduate school that I didn't know existed until I was asked to pay for it. Then she landed a job as a so-called "creative" at a hip Manhattan advertising boutique. Kara loved New York, her job, and family life in general, so the prospect of her clan, or at least the greater part of it, joining her in the Big Apple truly delighted her.

"Bring it on," she said.

Will and Lucas didn't seem particularly concerned about the whole fandango one way or the other. Will had graduated with a combination engineering and business degree from Cal Poly and worked in the data security practice of a huge San Francisco business consultancy. Data security was a red-hot space. So as usual, Will had landed in the right place at the right time. He did seek our assurance that we wouldn't offload his bachelor pad up in Sea Ranch. But once that critical issue was put to bed, he gave us his blessing.

Easygoing Lucas was savoring his college years in sunny beachside Santa Barbara and interning at a local tech startup. Lucas had always been a glass-half-full kind of kid. So we weren't particularly surprised when he said that he would be just as happy spending his school vacations in New York as San Francisco.

Grace, of course, had a lot more skin in the game. At fourteen, she was in her final year at a K–8 girls' school in San Francisco. Her classmates were about to scatter off to a dozen different high schools and boarding schools anyway. So for her, the timing was perfect. Plus Grace had always been a big-city girl at heart. She loved visiting New York with her mom. And once a year, she sampled the city's top gourmet fare with her biological father, Guenter the Chef (now rebranded "Günter"), who had moved to Manhattan with his third wife and late-in-life baby a few years earlier. So theoretically at least, Grace would get to see more of him. Grace easily adapted to new situations and was ambitious like her mother. So the prospect of a life lived on a larger stage appealed to her.

And then there was feisty, headstrong Angela.

So to be clear, Angela absolutely, positively did not want to move—uh-uh, no way, not going to happen. Angela is as deeply rooted as they come. And from birth, she has regarded any major change as anathema, particularly if it is imposed upon her from above. She is also a genuine introvert—in some ways still the little kid who trembled at the thought of attending a birthday party. So the idea of starting all over again at a brand new high school in a brand new city as a complete stranger—in the eleventh grade, no less—authentically horrified her. And to be fair, she had a point. But just as Laureen didn't want to be perceived as the hyper-ambitious mother who callously yanked her introverted child out of a high school she truly loved, Angela didn't want to be seen as the ungrateful daughter who stood petulantly between her mother and the job that would crown her career.

So Angela hatched a scheme. First she calculated that this time would be no different from the last several times her mother had contemplated a new job. Sure Laureen would be excited by the shiny new prospect. And sure she would discuss it in animated tones for weeks. But Angela figured that her mother would eventually decide to stay put—just as she always had. So when Laureen asked for her blessing, Angela disingenuously signed off on a plan that in her considered opinion had almost no chance of materializing. That way she would look like a team player but could still stay in Marin. From a sixteen-year-old's point of view, it must have seemed foolproof. But in reality, Angela underestimated just how badly her mother wanted this particular job. And when she failed to exercise her veto, the move to New York became a *fait accompli*.

But it took Angela a very long time to recognize that fact. Every evening when we sat around the dinner table discussing the move, Angela would say dismissively, "We're not really moving, so why are we even talking about this?"

And when we all flew to New York to look at schools, Angela very confidently told me, "Believe me, David. This is *not* going to happen."

And when we cruised around Manhattan looking for an apartment, Angela hung back at the hotel doing her homework because, and again I quote, "We're not really moving, so why should I waste my time?"

But then, after several months of clandestine meetings, Laureen gave her notice at McKesson and formally accepted the position at American Express. Then she packed her outsized wardrobe, bid the family a fond farewell, and boarded a plane for New York. At that point, Angela finally got the picture. And, believe me, she was not happy. Angela was angry at the situation in general and at herself in particular for not putting the kibosh on this whole crazy business back when she had the chance. And although she occasionally made a half-hearted attempt to appear slightly less than miserable in front of her mother, she was clearly terrified by the prospect.

The only way I could talk her off the metaphorical ledge was by making her a promise I hoped I would never have to keep. Namely, that if she sucked it up and moved to New York with a half-decent attitude and a whole lot less complaining, then someday, maybe a year after Simba's eventual demise, we would buy her a pug—a ludicrous breed of tiny dog with which she had become inexplicably obsessed. And by obsessed, I mean she would literally run down the street yelling, "A pug! A pug!" every time she saw one.

"Would that do it?" I asked her one Sunday morning over bacon and eggs in a Sausalito coffee shop. "If we promise to buy you a pug after Simba dies, would that make the move to New York more palatable to you?"

Angela gave me one of her famously skeptical stink-eye looks, and asked, "Are you serious, David?"

"Dead serious," I replied. "Provided, of course, you keep your end of the deal."

A smile spread across Angela's face—one of the few I'd seen in recent months. She looked me straight in the eye, nodded her head and said, "Yep. That would do it."

So even though I didn't really need one, I now had yet another reason to hope that Simba would live on—at least for two more years when Angela would leave for college and she could get her own damn pug. In the meantime, I hoped the mere prospect of a pug puppy in the big city would help Angela make peace with her plight—and to a large extent, it did.

Of course, we didn't tell Simba about the pug. Nobody wants to contemplate his own demise, let alone his successor. Plus the idea of replacing a big strapping hound like Simba with a twenty-pound gargoyle that resembled a cross between a pot-bellied pig and a rhesus monkey seemed like nothing short of blasphemy.

Nor could we discuss with Simba his imminent relocation from our sunny wooded acre in Marin to a comparatively small apartment in the concrete heart of a cold, noisy city. All Simba knew was that Laureen left home after the long Fourth of July weekend and never returned. Then the girls took off a month later, and they didn't come back either.

Despite his conspicuous courage in nearly all other arenas, Simba had always suffered from separation anxiety. Fortunately it was seldom an issue. With seven family members, extended family, and the kids' friends running in and out of the house all day—not to mention the fact that I worked at home—Simba was almost never alone. And whenever he did find himself unattended for a few hours, he seemed to embrace the notion that occasionally it would be his duty to hang back and guard the fort.

Still, Simba became visibly upset every time he saw suitcases in the front hall, because he knew that meant one or more of his pack members would be leaving for a while. And once a year, when the whole family traveled to Tahoe, and we all went out to dinner, leaving him alone in a strange rental property, Simba would sometimes brood for a while and then vomit on the rug. One of the few insoluable glitches in the glorious human-canine relationship is that there's simply no way to tell a dog how long you'll be gone or to reassure him that you will eventually return. So when you walk out the door with a suitcase in your hand, dogs tend to worry.

Simba didn't throw up when Laureen and the girls left for New York. But he did seem a bit depressed that his pack had dwindled down to just the two of us. Laureen and I had decided to keep our home in Tiburon for a while—just in case things didn't work out as well as expected. So when Laureen and the girls took off, Simba and I stayed back to close up the house and clean out all the closets, cupboards, and drawers. I also had to deal with several sets of movers who came by to pick up all of our clothes, ten cases of California wine, and three or four paintings we wanted to hang in our big city apartment. All of that involved moving dozens of suitcases, boxes, and crates out of the house, which was exactly the sort of commotion that upset Simba. That mental stress, combined with a sleepover at the vet's when I went out of town for four days, likely caused Simba to contract an ailment called kennel cough.

Simba had been inoculated against kennel cough, which is essentially the canine version of bronchitis. But he got it anyway. And that was worrisome for two reasons. First, Simba's advanced age and recent snout infection made what is usually a manageable illness significantly more dangerous. And second, Simba might not be healthy enough to fly to New York in two weeks when we were scheduled to join Laureen and the girls.

Simba's longtime vet, Penny Elliott, had recently retired from Tamalpais Pet Hospital. So when I brought him in for his appointment, we met her replacement, a slim middle-aged Australian woman named Shay Redfield. That particular afternoon, every canine examination room was occupied, so Simba and I conferred with Dr. Redfield in a small cinderblock cubicle on the feline side of the practice. I'm acutely allergic to cats—nine on a scale of ten, one allergist told me—so to avoid the onset of asthma, I wore a blue surgical mask during the entire course of the consultation. That made the conversation we were about to have even more difficult.

"So how's he doing," I asked Dr. Redfield after she examined Simba with a stethoscope, peered down his throat, and drew some blood.

"Well, he does have bordetella," she replied, using kennel cough's official name, "But there's another more serious problem. Have you noticed any labored breathing?"

"Definitely." I replied, "Not all the time, but sometimes when he's just lying on the family-room rug he starts panting like this." I imitated a dog panting hard through the surgical mask. "I kind of wondered what that was. I thought maybe he was just excited about something."

"No. That's laryngeal paralysis," Dr. Redfield replied. "It's fairly common in old Labradors and other large-breed dogs. Basically, the larynx constricts and becomes inelastic, and that makes it difficult for the dog to breathe—more so with the bordetella."

"Is there anything you can do for him?" I asked.

"For the bordetella, yes. We can give him a course of antibiotics that should clear it up in three or four weeks. And there is a surgical procedure that can permanently open up the larynx. But at Simba's age, it doesn't make sense. Just putting him under would be dangerous."

So apparently this was like Simba's lumps. There was a simple fix, but he was too old to benefit from it.

"There's another wrinkle," I said. "Simba and I are moving to New York soon. My wife recently took a new job there, and she's already in Manhattan with the girls. Simba and I are supposed to join them in two weeks. Will it still be okay to put Simba in his crate and fly him to New York?"

"I wouldn't," Dr. Redfield replied. "That's a stressful situation for any dog, let alone a dog as old as Simba. And if you factor in the paralyzed larynx and the bordetella, it's doubtful he would survive the trip. In fact, you should probably get used to the idea that Simba won't be around very much longer." She glanced at his chart and added, "He's nearly fourteen. That's pretty ancient for such a big dog."

"So how much time does he have?" I asked, not really wanting to know the answer.

I expected her to say something vague like, "Well, there's no way to know for sure," or "It depends upon various factors," like doctors usually do. But I guess veterinarians are more straightforward than the doctors who treat humans because Dr. Redfield replied very plainly—though not unkindly—saying, "Honestly, it could happen any day now."

I lowered the surgical mask and thanked her.

"Alright," I said, "I understand. I need to talk to my wife. I'm sure we'll figure something out."

6. DOGGED DETERMINATION

That evening I called Laureen, who was staying with Angela and Grace at a midtown hotel while our new apartment was being repainted.

"Bad news," I began.

"What is it?" asked Laureen, unflappable as usual, because in her line of work she gets at least some bad news every day.

"So, as you know," I continued, "Simba has been under the weather again. There's a new vet at the pet hospital. And she says Simba has kennel cough—which is already a problem. But there's another more serious issue. Apparently, he also has a paralyzed larynx, which I guess is fairly common in old Labs."

"What does that mean exactly?" asked Laureen.

I recounted what Dr. Redfield told me as faithfully as possible and then added, "The bottom line is that we can't put Simba in a crate and fly him to New York. The vet says it would kill him."

Laureen sighed. Yet another reason to feel guilty about the move.

"So I've been looking into alternatives," I continued. "And realistically, there are two. We can hire a commercial pet transportation service that will drive Simba from San Francisco to New York in three days. It costs around $3,000. But I checked with your new employers, and apparently they will reimburse you for that. The downside, of course, is that Simba would have to ride all the way across America in the back of a van with someone he's never met and who probably won't take care of him the same way we would."

Laureen paused for a moment and said, "That doesn't feel right to me. Separating Simba from everyone in his family right now is probably the worst thing we could do. If he's as sick as you say he is, he'll need a lot of attention, which he probably won't get from the driver."

"I agree. So here's the other alternative. You told me that you wanted to bring your station wagon to New York. So instead of shipping it across the country on a truck or a train, or whatever it is they do, why don't I just drive it to New York? And Simba can lie on his bed in the back with his food and water and all of his stuff. And I could pull over whenever he gets nauseous or looks like he needs a break. Basically, I would be with him 24/7, and we'd get to New York in a week or so."

Then I had to deliver the really bad news. "But here's the thing, Laureen. The vet said pretty clearly that Simba could die any time now. So if I do drive him to New York, he might make it, and he might not. So you have to prepare yourself for that."

In Laureen's mind, neither option was great. She obviously didn't want Simba to die all alone in the back of a van driven by a stranger. But she also didn't love the idea of me cruising across America with only Simba for company.

In my early forties—about a decade after I sold my little publishing company—I took my first wife and three young children—nine, eight, and three at the time—on a yearlong trip around the world.[2] During the course of that journey, I drove my family across several fairly large countries including France, Greece, Italy, and Australia. We also drove across India, but that actually did scare the crap out of me, so I hired a local driver. But the point is, Laureen didn't know me back then. So she didn't really see me as the entirely competent long-distance driver I was. She saw me more as the absent-minded suburban motorist who occasionally got into a close scrape in the Whole Foods parking lot and was once responsible for a rather expensive fender bender on Tiburon Boulevard.

So if Simba and I did drive across America, Laureen would likely worry the entire time. And since she was already worried about whether she would succeed in her new job, whether our apartment would be ready before school started, whether the girls were adjusting to their new life in Manhattan, and now thanks to me, whether Simba was going to live or die, pretty much the last thing she needed was an additional source of anxiety. It might just push her past her breaking point, which is exceedingly high but certainly not infinite.

"Let me think about it," said Laureen. "We still have two weeks before you leave. So we don't have to decide right now."

---

[2] The journey is recounted in my 1999 book, *One Year Off: Leaving It All Behind for a Round-the-World Journey with Our Children*.

The next morning, I drove ten miles north to the little nine-hole golf course where my old friend Erick Steinberg and I played every Sunday morning. One of the many wonderful things about the sublime game of golf is that you always have plenty of time between strokes to discuss whatever's on your mind. And in my case, there are always lots of strokes.

"You nearly packed?" Erick asked as we strolled down the seventh fairway.

"Yeah, pretty much," I replied, "and I'll tell you, Erick, I'm really going to miss our Sunday morning golf games. I have no idea how I'm going to play golf when we live in Manhattan."

"I'll miss it, too," said Erick. "But whenever you come back, we can always shoot a few rounds."

"I have run into one major problem," I replied. Then I explained the whole Simba dilemma, including the fact that Laurcen didn't really trust me to drive across America by myself. Erick expressed sympathy for Simba. Then he paused for a beat and a big grin spread across his face.

"What are you smiling about?" I asked.

"Road trip," he replied.

"What do you mean?"

"Road trip!" he repeated more emphatically.

"Are you saying that you'd be willing to drive three thousand miles to New York with Simba and me?"

"Hell, yeah!" said Erick, "You and I have been talking about a boys' road trip for more than ten years. So why don't we just do it? And we'll get Simba to New York in the process."

"I guess we could head south and follow the old Route 66, which is essentially I-40 now."

"Exactly," said Erick.

We were on the same page.

"But you do realize, Erick, that Simba is on his last leg. The vet basically told me it was even money whether he'd make it to New York. And if he kicks the bucket out in Oklahoma or Kansas or somewhere, it won't be pretty."

"Then that will be our mission," Erick replied. "Come hell or high water, we will get Simba to Manhattan."

Erick was right. First Simba had to say goodbye to Will and Lucas in California. Then Erick and I had to get him to New York so he could see Laureen and the girls before he died. Simba had lived with Angela and Grace since he was an eight-week-old puppy and the girls were only two and four years old. Now Angela was a bright, articulate seventeen-year-old, and Grace, at fifteen, was an athletic, six-foot-tall beauty.

For as long as the girls could remember, Simba had been a source of immense joy and comfort to them. He enhanced their lives in countless ways. When they were sad, they hugged Simba. When they were happy, Simba jumped around with them. He was like a brother to them, only nicer. And if he died before they could say farewell, they would always regret it. And Simba wouldn't understand why his family wasn't there for him in his final moments.

And Laureen, raised on Catholic guilt, would of course blame herself for everything.

Plus, there was another more metaphysical consideration. At the end of the day, we all die, and there's nothing we can do about it. The vet already told me she couldn't help Simba anymore. And there was probably nothing I could do to forestall his death. But with Erick's help, I could at least reunite Simba with his family before he bid this world adieu. It would be an admittedly small victory in the face of a heart-rending loss. But if I succeeded, I could at least console myself with the thought that I did everything I could to give my old friend the best possible death. If the King of the Canines had to die—which he certainly did and probably soon—then he should at least do so in the loving arms of his family, not alone and terrified in the back of a dog-moving van. Making sure that happened was my sacred duty as his friend and companion. It was a simple matter of respect and, of course, love.

Erick not only framed the mission, he also made it possible. It was a well-established fact that Erick's wife, Lisa, would let him do pretty much anything he wanted provided he did it with me. And it was also true that Laureen cut me a lot more slack when I was with Erick. I haven't the slightest idea why Lisa would put so much confidence in me. It honestly seemed misplaced. But I do know why Laureen trusted Erick.

Erick is what you call a *mensch*, which in German just means "human being," but in Yiddish connotes a man of integrity, someone you can count on. The closest English equivalent is probably "stand-up guy." What's more, Erick is amazingly competent in the physical world. For most of his career, Erick designed, built, and maintained the sort of broadcast equipment used by commercial radio stations. And he loved everything about radio transmission, right down to the last kilowatt. In fact, one of his many nerdy hobbies was yakking on a state-of-the-art ham radio set with other ham radio nerds around the world. And for fun, he rebuilt old vacuum tube transmitters that he found online or at specialized flea markets.

But with the decline of commercial radio and the rise of all things digital, Erick was compelled to switch careers in his late fifties. And for the last several years, he had designed and engineered smart power grids for electric utilities around the world. That was impressive in its own right. But what it meant in terms of a road trip was that Erick could fix an engine or a flat tire or pretty much anything else that might conceivably break on a car. He could drive and navigate well, and I knew he was 100 percent dependable. I always called Erick "the world's most competent person." And although he's modest by nature, he never really objected to that characterization.

But even more essential on a three-thousand-mile road trip, Erick was pretty good company—this despite the fact that he didn't really talk that much—or maybe it was because of that. Either way, I knew that Erick wouldn't drive me crazy when we were stuck in a car together nine or ten hours a day for seven or eight days straight.

Now it was true that whenever you drove somewhere with Erick, he felt compelled for some reason to point out every single AM, FM, cellular, microwave, or any other type of cockamamie radio tower he happened to see along the way. And on a trip across America, that could mean hundreds, maybe even thousands, of such radio towers. But I figured that was a reasonable price to pay for Erick's companionship.

So with reliable, old, tried-and-true Erick onboard, Laureen was satisfied that I would have adequate adult supervision, and she approved the expedition. I gave Erick the good news. Then I spent the next several days tying up loose ends, buying provisions, and plotting our course.

Unlike the commercial dog van, we wouldn't sprint across America as quickly as possible. At first flush, a quick trip made sense. We were, after all, racing death. And if Erick and I just put the pedal to the metal and took turns at the wheel, we could probably make it to Manhattan in just over two days. But driving twenty-four hours a day—or even twelve hours a day—would likely take its toll on Simba and might hasten his demise. In my experience, Simba was good for three, maybe three-and-a-half hours at most in the back of a station wagon. After that, he needed a bathroom break and ten or fifteen minutes of just walking around in order to regain his equilibrium. Otherwise he would get carsick and make very disturbing gagging noises. And in his frail condition, I didn't want to push his limits.

And because we can't help but anthropomorphize our pets, I initially told myself that this journey would also be a wonderful opportunity for Simba to see America before he kicked the bucket. And oddly, whenever I mentioned that notion to family or friends, they would always say something encouraging like, "Yeah, Simba's going to love seeing all those amazing sights."

But if you actually think about it for more than a few seconds, you realize that dogs probably don't care very much about seeing America. To Simba, a roadside field in Tennessee or Kentucky—or Outer Mongolia for that matter—was probably pretty much the same as a roadside field in California. And I sincerely doubted that Simba—or any other dog for that matter—had a bucket list. But, hey, Labradors always like to sniff new smells and meet new people. So maybe Simba, who had always been gregarious and intrepid by nature, might enjoy spending his final days meeting the nice folks in Arizona or strolling through a cow pasture in Texas or pissing on a tree at Graceland.

In 1960, the celebrated American novelist John Steinbeck drove from Long Island to Salinas, California, and back in a camper truck with only his brown standard poodle, Charley, for company. Most of America's interstate highway system didn't exist in 1960. So Steinbeck drove, for the most part, along two-lane roads lined here and there with fruit and vegetable stands, antique shops, local bars and restaurants. In *Travels with Charley*, his popular memoir of the eleven-week journey, Steinbeck predicted that, "When we get these thruways across the country, as we will and must, it will be possible to drive from New York to California without seeing a single thing."

Needless to say, Steinbeck's prediction came true. And fifty years later, Erick and I could easily drive from San Francisco to New York without seeing very much at all—except, of course, hundreds of radio towers. But that seemed like a wasted opportunity. So as long as we were making the journey—and as long as we had to stop every three hours for Simba anyway—we might as well see some of what was out there. And if Simba lacked the capacity to appreciate our grand tour, he probably wouldn't mind it either.

Based on those considerations, the trip began to gel. Erick and I would loop across America's southern tier for seven or eight days depending how it went. We would overnight in Las Vegas, Nevada; Gallup, New Mexico; Amarillo, Texas; Little Rock, Arkansas; Nashville, Tennessee; and Pittsburgh, Pennsylvania, where, after a guilt-ridden six-month hiatus, I would finally visit my ailing parents. These cities were all between six and nine hours apart—so a decent day's drive, but not an endurance test and probably a comfortable pace for Simba.

Then on the last day of the journey—at least the way I imagined it—Erick, Simba, and I would bid Pittsburgh good-bye, ramble across Pennsylvania and New Jersey, triumphantly cruise into Manhattan, and pull up in front of our new apartment building on New York's Upper East Side. I would phone Laureen from the street. She and the girls would run out the front door of the building and joyously clasp Simba to their bosoms before he met his maker. And at that point, my duty to Simba would be fulfilled. According to this plan, we would leave San Francisco on Sunday, August 17th, and if all went well, we would cross the finish line on Saturday, the 23rd, or Sunday, the 24th.

Six days before our departure, I heard a helicopter hovering just above my house, then another helicopter, then a third, and a fourth.

I was used to seeing small planes flying low over our property. It's a scenic area, and private pilots like the view. But I couldn't remember seeing a helicopter up there before, let alone four helicopters at one time. I knew it couldn't be anything good—maybe a big brushfire up in San Rafael or a pileup on 101. I switched on the television, and the answer was on at least seven different channels. The iconic sixty-three-year-old comic actor Robin Williams, who lived just north of us, had passed away. The helicopters were news choppers taking live shots of his house, which now had several police cars parked outside.

Watching those initial news reports, I didn't know yet that Robin Williams had taken his own life or why. In retrospect, I guess it makes sense that so much high-voltage mania would have to be offset by some sort of compensating depression. Plus there were rumors circulating that he might have a degenerative brain disease. But even so, the fact that a human dynamo like Robin Williams could be switched off just like that, leaving only a black void in his wake, sharpened my current preoccupation with the fragility of life. I knew, of course, that Robin Williams and my old dog Simba had nothing in common except in my own mind. One just died. One would probably die sometime soon. But Robin Williams's sudden demise—so unexpected and so close to home—seemed to lend our journey a new urgency.

7. ROAD DOG

Our first day on the road would also be our longest. According to Google Maps, our Las Vegas hotel was 580 miles from my house in Tiburon. At an average speed of sixty-five miles per hour, that meant nine hours of driving. And of course we would have to stop every three hours for Simba. Lunch would probably take another hour. So bottom line, if Frick and I wanted to eat a decent dinner in Las Vegas that evening, which we certainly did, then we would have to hit the road by 7:00 a.m., 8:00 at the latest.

When the odious little alarm on my iPhone began chirping at five in the morning, I woke with a shudder and a nervous stomach. Despite the fact that I had traveled internationally for decades as part of my job, the simple act of locking up and leaving home has always flummoxed me. Maybe I have some sort of low-level OCD or something, but I always feel like I'm forgetting some crucial but unspecified detail. So I end up running around the house like a chicken with its head cut off double- and triple-checking thermostats, door locks, the alarm system, every window in the house, the stove, the toaster oven, the coffeemaker, and any other electrical appliance that could conceivably spark the calamitous house fire that always lurks in the back of my mind. Maybe it's because my boyhood home in Erie, Pennsylvania, actually did catch fire in the middle of the night—back when I was thirteen. And a dozen firemen tramped through the house and ripped out a wall with their axes before they got the blaze under control. I should probably talk to a shrink about that.

Anyway, this particular morning was much worse than usual, because in addition to the confounding mechanics of departure, I was disoriented by the notion that this time when I closed up the house and took off for New York, I had no concrete plans to return. Today it wasn't just a five-day business trip or a ten-day vacation. This time the locus of our family life would shift from one side of the continent to the other.

That realization sparked an unanticipated wave of nostalgia. And I started thinking about the fact that our blended family had celebrated eight Thanksgiving dinners in this house, eight Christmas mornings, eight New Year's Eves and fifty-six birthdays—sixty-four if you counted Simba. I started thinking about the big fights we had here and how we made up. How we celebrated good report cards, college acceptances, and middle school sports victories. How we cried when someone was mean to us at school or work. Or when a boyfriend or girlfriend fell out of love with us.

I remembered the stormy night when the thirty-foot plum tree in the backyard toppled over and we had to hoist it back up with a winch; the time the garage flooded and we had to rip up the concrete floor; and of course the time the drapery hangers pierced the fire sprinkler line in the dining room with an electric drill (and a torrent of pressurized water shot across the room and splashed off the opposite wall until Angela climbed a ladder and stuck her finger in the hole like the little Dutch boy.) In fact I remembered all manner of minor calamity that bedeviled this house over the last eight years. And now that I was locking up for good, I found myself weaving all of those wretched little mishaps—irritating, maddening, even frightening when they occurred—into a warm and wistful tapestry.

But most of all, I remembered a brief shining chapter in our lives when five beautiful children and their faithful hound, Simba, filled every room in this house with laughter, shouting, barking, blaring music, and slamming doors. A time when there was always someone at home so we never locked our doors. A time when no one ever returned to an empty house. A time that overflowed with the fullness of life. And I mourned the passing of that luminous episode.

Kara had been gone for six years now—first across the bay in Berkeley, now across the country in Brooklyn. Maybe we'd see more of her in New York—maybe not. Every two weeks or so, Will used to drive across the Golden Gate Bridge from San Francisco to have dinner with us. But now we might go months without seeing him. And this year for the first time, Lucas stayed down in Santa Barbara for the summer instead of coming home because now he had a year-round internship. A fuzzy image of Lucas as a cherubic, curly-haired, slightly cross-eyed two-year-old popped into my mind. Then with a burn in my gut, I felt him drifting away.

Nearly every person who has ever met my mother has used the same phrase to describe her—"a force of nature." But now that force had waned. My mother—still brilliant and articulate on the days when her brain got enough oxygen—was, for the most part, a feeble invalid, bedridden twenty-two hours a day with an oxygen tube stuck up her nose because her heart was slowly dying.

When my mother was first confined to her bed—after several bad falls and a mitral valve replacement that didn't really work because she refused to do the rehab—she asked me to call her every day. And I did that religiously. And nearly every day she would tell me in her raspy, gasping voice that as soon as she felt better she was going to hop on a plane and fly to San Francisco so she could visit this wonderful house one more time. And every time she said that, I enthusiastically agreed that when that day finally came we would all have a magical time. But we both knew in our hearts, hers slowly failing, that she would never come here again. And closing up the house and stashing away the wheelchair she used when she was here only put a period on that sentence.

Simba and I, both a little stiff so early in the morning, tottered down the bluestone steps to the driveway. Simba sat patiently on the concrete pavers while I backed Laureen's mom car, a gray Mercedes station wagon, out of the garage. I wore my khaki-green Elm Forks Shooting Sports cap, which I bought at this crazy five-hundred-acre gun range outside Dallas a few years earlier. I figured the cap might offset some of the soccer mom vibes emanating from the station wagon. And in my rich fantasy world, the bad guys out there on the road who saw me as an easy mark because of the mom car would think twice when they saw my shooting-range cap. I knew, of course, that all of that was complete idiocy. But I wore the cap anyway.

Six months earlier, Simba could still jump up into the back of the station wagon under his own steam. But that time had also passed. And Simba knew the drill. I opened the tailgate. He stood still as I lifted his front paws up onto the deck. Then he held fast as I boosted his hindquarters and pushed him forward into the car. Simba circled his bed three times as dogs always do. Then he lay down with a long, low groan, reminding me how much he suffered from arthritis. When the pain subsided, he let out a big sigh and looked up at me with his big brown eyes.

"Don't worry, buddy," I said, "I'm taking you to see Laureen and the girls."

Simba smiled and panted, just delighted we were taking a ride together. His pure guileless joy instantly offset all the maudlin thoughts crowding my head, and I thought to myself, "Is it any wonder we love dogs?"

I buckled my seatbelt, put the station wagon into gear, and didn't look back.

When I first resolved to drive Simba across America, I failed to consider certain fundamental aspects of the journey. For example, pretty much everyone knows or would at least guess that only a small fraction of America's finer hotels and inns would be willing to board a very large dog for the evening. But somehow that thought never occurred to me—not, that is, until I tried to book our first night's accommodation in supposedly-anything-goes Las Vegas.

I began by calling the Bellagio Hotel since I had stayed there before. The conversation began amicably enough. I booked two rooms—one for me, one for Erick. I gave the reservationist—that's what they're called—my credit card information. And at the conclusion of the transaction, I casually mentioned that I would be sharing one of the rooms with my faithful hound and I presumed that wouldn't pose a problem. But it did pose a problem—not only at the Bellagio but also at every other Las Vegas hotel I called. It wasn't long before I began each such conversation not with, "Hello. Do you have two rooms available the evening of August 17th?" but rather with, "Hello. Do you take dogs?"

I did speak to a few nice folks who responded with a cheerful "Yes, sir, we do." But eventually they all got around to the same unexpected question: "How much does your dog weigh?"

Apparently, the bright line between acceptable and unacceptable canine guests is precisely fifty pounds, which seems entirely arbitrary to me. I mean why would a scrappy forty-five-pound pit bull or a yappy ten-pound shih tzu be okay, but an elderly eighty-five-pound gentleman like Simba wouldn't? It didn't make sense. It made even less sense that some of these places would accommodate not one, but two, dogs provided their combined weight didn't exceed the magical fifty-pound limit.

Instead of asking, "How much does your dog weigh?" shouldn't they be asking, "Does your dog bark for hours on end every time you leave the room?" or "Will your dog attack the cleaning staff? Or crap on the rug?"

Anyway, I spoke to at least five reservationists and three of their supervisors, and I politely asked each of them how they could presume to discriminate against a sweet old dog like Simba. And each time I argued my traveling companion's case with a heartfelt eloquence that failed to sway even one person's opinion.

But then, on a website called BringFido.com, I found The Vdara Hotel and Spa. (I mean, seriously, who names these places?) Located in the heart of Las Vegas's relatively new and entirely gargantuan CityCenter development, The Vdara is a cozy little inn with 1,495 guest rooms spread over fifty-seven floors and 1.6 million square feet. But for me, the hotel's fundamental allure was its comparatively liberal seventy-pound canine weight limit. And that, I figured, was close enough. I mean it's not as if they were going to pull out a scale and weigh Simba—or at least I hoped not.

"He might be a little over seventy pounds," I told the reservationist in an entirely unnecessary outburst of quasi-honesty. And when she didn't object, I moved on.

Needless to say, certain conditions applied. Simba and I would have to stay in one of the hotel's "Deluxe Vdog Suites," which didn't appear—at least on the website—to be precisely what you'd call a suite. And if you factored in the $50 "Dog Fee," and a separate $75 "Dog Cleaning Fee," it also wasn't precisely what you'd call cheap.

On the other hand, the Vdara did promise to welcome my big fat Lab with a generous array of canine amenities that included a handsome black acrylic dog blanket embroidered with the hotel's ridiculous name, a plush doggie bed, and a goodie bag packed with some pretty fancy-looking dog biscuits and a cutesy chew toy. They also had an optional dog crate that wouldn't come anywhere close to fitting Simba—although I wouldn't want to draw attention to that fact. And there was an "In-suite Dog Dining Menu," which, if you think about it, might confuse guests from certain Asian nations. But honestly, I was so relieved that Simba and I wouldn't have to sleep in the car that I fairly leapt at the opportunity to fork over whatever sum of money these good folks deemed appropriate.

Then there was another issue. During the course of the last quarter century, I have been fortunate enough to reside in a scenic locale blessed with a remarkably temperate climate. San Francisco's average daily high temperature is fifty-seven degrees in January and sixty-seven degrees in August. And where I live, in southern Marin, no one has air-conditioning because there's rarely any need for it. So even though I absolutely should have anticipated the dog in the hotel problem, I might be excused for overlooking another crucial question, namely: What do you do with your dog while you eat lunch at a restaurant during the torrid month of August when a parked car quickly becomes fatally hot?

I know your dog can't sit next to you at the table like they do in some Parisian restaurants—God, I love the French—and I've seen enough local news broadcasts to know that the correct answer is not "crack the window." But I'm embarrassed to tell you that this predicament only occurred to me—or to "the world's most competent person" for that matter—when Erick and I stopped to eat our very first meal of the journey in Bakersfield, California, a workaday city of 350,000 residents at the southern end of California's agrarian Central Valley.

Bakersfield, gateway to the Mojave Desert, was exactly halfway between Tiburon and Las Vegas—so a natural stopping point. And we knew there wouldn't be much in the way of amenities—or civilization really—once we drove into the desert. But the preeminent reason we decided to enjoy the first meal of our very long journey in Bakersfield was that Erick fondly remembered a dish he once ate there called Buck's Chicken-fried Steak. And you can only get Buck's Chicken-fried Steak at Buck Owens' Crystal Palace—an elaborate restaurant-cum-music hall on Buck Owens Boulevard in Bakersfield, California. Chicken-fried steak combines two things I really like—pounded beef and deep-fried breading—so when Erick suggested it as a lunch option, I pounced all over it.

Apparently Bakersfield once was—and probably still is—the home of "the Bakersfield Sound," a down-home genre of country music that arose in reaction to Nashville's increasingly slick orchestrations in the late 1950s. The idea was that even if Nashville decided to go all Percy Faith with its lush arrangements and syrupy strings, Bakersfield would stay true to its twangy Okie roots.

The Bakersfield Sound's foremost practitioners, Merle Haggard and Buck Owens, were country music superstars in the late fifties, sixties, and early seventies. Haggard was born in a repurposed boxcar in neighboring Oildale, California—a remarkably on-the-nose provenance for a self-described country outlaw. And Owens was reared on a Dustbowl dirt farm on the Texas-Oklahoma border. But they joined forces in Bakersfield. And they made beautiful music, both separately and together. They also married the same woman, Bonnie Campbell—at different times, of course. But since they lived in a relatively small city and had no fewer than nine wives between them, there was bound to be some overlap.

Anyway, when old Buck shuffled off to country-western heaven in 2006, he left behind the Crystal Palace as a physical manifestation of his musical legacy. It was a clean, happy, family-oriented venue where practitioners of the Bakersfield Sound and other similar-minded country acts could sing their hearts out on a state-of-the-art stage while their fans scarfed down Cryin' Time Onion Rings, Oklahoma Nachos, and, of course, the aforementioned Buck's Chicken-fried Steak.

Why it's called the Crystal Palace I have absolutely no idea, because there didn't seem to be any crystal in evidence. Nor did it in any way resemble its Victorian London namesake. It looked instead like a handsome nineteenth-century western village—or at least a pink and blue Disney version of that. And it was set beside a remarkably large parking lot that was practically empty—which didn't strike me as a very good sign.

That whole summer, Bakersfield—and pretty much all of California—had suffered record drought and scorching heat—a point driven home by the dust devils Erick and I saw spinning across the Central Valley's fallow fields and a massive brushfire we witnessed as we pulled into Bakersfield. So when we rolled to a stop in the Crystal Palace's huge empty parking lot and threw open the car doors, it of course felt like a blast furnace. And at that point it became instantly clear, even to a moron like me, that leaving Simba in the car would be a highly irresponsible decision.

"Hey Erick," I said as the lightbulb finally snapped on, "what are we going to do with Simba while we eat?"

"Now that's a good question," Erick replied. "Why don't we go inside and ask them what people usually do with their dogs?"

The answer to that question, I quickly found out from a pretty young hostess in a cowgirl dress, is that they leave their dogs at home.

"Just how badly do you want this chicken fried steak?" I asked Erick.

Erick's mouth said, "Honestly, it's really not that important to me," but his eyes said, "I've been dreaming of Buck's scrumptious chicken-fried steak all week." So I determined to make this happen.

I strode back across the sweltering asphalt and retrieved Simba's big aluminum bowl from the back of the car. Then I popped inside, found the men's room and filled the bowl with cold water. I located a wooden bench set in a shady section of the front veranda. (It could only be called a veranda.) Then using the compass app on my iPhone, I calculated the likely arc of the sun over the course of the next hour—just to make sure that Simba would remain safely in the shade while we were inside. I lifted one leg of the wooden bench, put the loop of Simba's red leash around it, set it back down again, placed his water bowl next to him, and told him I'd check up on him every fifteen minutes—as if that meant anything to him. Then

I marched back inside and triumphantly informed the pretty young hostess in the cowgirl dress that I had expertly managed the whole dog situation and that we now required a table for two and, more to the point, two orders of Buck's Chicken-fried Steak. To which she sweetly replied, "Oh, I'm sorry. We stop serving brunch at one."

I pulled out my iPhone again. It was 1:10. This was information I could have used ten minutes earlier. So I asked the pretty young hostess very politely—honestly, I did—why she hadn't bothered to impart that information when first we met.

"Well, you can still go inside and look at the museum next to the restaurant," she replied as sweet as pie.

And you know what? That's exactly what we did. And to tell you the truth, there was a whole lot of very cool stuff in there, including a life-size bronze statue of Buck Owens, one of Buck's trademark red, white, and blue Mosrite guitars, and what had to be the world's largest collection of *Hee-Haw* memorabilia—since Buck famously co-hosted that country-western TV variety show for more than two decades. And this being Buck Owens' elaborate shrine to himself, there was also a colossal trophy case filled with every one of his music awards, which let me tell you, was a whole lot of music awards.

Perhaps most impressively, there was a Cadillac convertible ingeniously mounted to the wall above the music hall's long bar—its tires pressed to the wall and its open top facing the stage. The 1973 Grand Ville had apparently been pimped out by a once-renowned Ukrainian madman named Nudie Cohn (né Nuta Kotlyarenko.) A former shoeshine boy and professional boxer, Nudie found his true métier wildly overdecorating both Cadillacs and glittery "Nudie

Suits" worn by country music royalty and the occasional rock star back in the day. Remember the garish lit-up cowboy suit Robert Redford wore in *The Electric Horseman*? Well, that was a Nudie Suit, and not even his most flamboyant effort.

The wall-mounted Caddie featured a huge pair of chrome-tipped longhorns above the grill and door handles fashioned from real pearl-handled six-shooters. And the car's buckskin seats were embossed with nostalgic tableaux of Conestoga wagons traversing the Western prairie and caricatures of Indian chiefs in feathered headdresses. Legend has it—and the legend may well be apocryphal—that Buck Owens won this charming grotesquery from Elvis Presley in a poker game or possibly on a bet. Maybe the bet was about who had the classiest Cadillac.

At any rate, we were only inside Buck Owens's fantastical Crystal Palace for maybe twenty minutes, and even then, I popped out once to see how Simba was faring. But now it was one thirty. And according to the Yelp app on my iPhone, Bakersfield was not the Sunday brunch mecca one might expect. So that left fast food.

I watch a lot of television. There, I said it. And I won't try to justify my déclassé penchant by telling you that this is the "golden age of television" or that some of the best dramas are now written for the tube. Because, honestly, I also watched a lot of television back when it was mostly crap. More specifically, I've always loved sitcoms. It's probably because when I was a kid my mom and dad both worked at our family furniture store and didn't get home until six or seven each evening. So instead of sharing my day with them, I turned instead to my very amusing television friends—Gilligan and the Skipper, Major Nelson and Jeannie, and those zany POWs at Stalag 13. Anyway, as a result of this shameful addiction, I've been pummeled with literally thousands of commercials for a chain of fast food restaurants called Sonic Drive-Ins.

Despite the fact that there are more than 3,500 Sonic Drive-Ins nationwide, there are no Sonics Drive-Ins at all in either San Francisco or Marin County, California—just as there are no Walmarts or Dunkin' Donuts—at least not yet. Years ago, when my oldest daughter Kara was fourteen, we sent her off to French camp in Minnesota. (Don't ask.) And one fine day, she and her fellow campers dropped by the local Walmart to purchase some French camp provisions, whatever those might be. Kara casually mentioned that she'd never been to a Walmart before. And based on that offhand assertion, her fellow campers concluded that she must be vastly wealthy—which she certainly was not, although she did revel in the notoriety for a little while.

But my point here is that Sonics, Walmarts, Dunkin' Donuts, Dairy Queens, and the like can only be found in The Real America, which, as any Real American can tell you, specifically excludes the city of San Francisco and the adjacent county of Marin. And since, like the immortal Steinbeck, I wanted to see some of "The Real America" during the course of our cross-country journey, I asked Erick if he wouldn't mind dining at a Sonic Drive-In. And as always, Erick was amenable.

According to their round-the-clock fusillade of commercials, Sonic serves plump juicy hot dogs topped with a vast selection of condiments, some very oddly flavored milkshakes (Oreo cheesecake anyone?), and a nearly infinite variety of super-sugary soft drinks that include, for example, Green Apple Slush with Nerds-brand Candy. That's right. They spike their slushies with candy. Sonic obviously didn't serve Buck's Chicken-Fried Steak, so a modicum of disappointment was inherent in the venture. But with so many thousands of locations across America, I figured, how bad could it be?

Well, it is conceivable that Erick and I stumbled upon the worst Sonic Drive-In in the forty-four states where the chain operates. And if that's the case, I formally apologize to what must be tens of thousands of Sonic employees for drawing a universal conclusion from one bad experience. But it has always been my understanding that a bedrock principal of every fast food franchise is nationwide uniformity. And if that's the case, I will henceforth hurl caviar and foie gras at the screen every time I see a Sonic commercial. Because the grub at this place made the simple fare proffered at our local In-N-Out Burger seem like the pinnacle of haute cuisine.

Sonic's one saving grace was its shaded outdoor eating area. And that's precisely what we needed for Simba. So Erick and I jumped out of the car and found a dirty metal table that we tidied up with a handful of single-ply napkins. Then I plunked Simba down next to us without asking anyone's permission and tried to very quickly and discreetly pour a cup of dry dog food into his bowl from a twenty-pound bag before anyone could tell me to stop. In my haste, I missed the bowl entirely, and hundreds of little brown Science Diet Active Longevity Senior Dog Food nuggets rattled noisily across the patio, which, needless to say, attracted a good deal of unwanted attention from our fellow diners.

"Oh, shit!" I said to Erick. "Is anyone looking?"

Erick just shook his head and smiled because it was pretty obvious that everyone was looking.

"Can I help you with that?" Erick asked as I bent over and attempted to scrape up a zillion tiny nuggets with my hands.

"No. I think I can clean this up pretty quickly," I replied. "Why don't you run interference if the manager comes out."

"I can do that," said Erick, who fortunately finds it amusing when I do really stupid things.

After I recovered most of the kibble—amazingly, without being ejected from the premises—Erick and I shouted our orders into a crackly intercom that apparently had an ESL student at the other end. And eventually we received our "food." It's rare that Simba gets a better lunch than I do, but as I consumed something vaguely resembling a cheeseburger and onion rings, I regarded his kibble with envy.

"I'm sorry, Erick," I said. "Maybe I've been spoiled by a bunch of fancy-ass San Francisco eateries, but does this stuff taste like crap to you?"

"No, it's fine," said Erick, who probably didn't want me to feel bad about bringing him to Sonic in the first place. "I'm sure we'll do better in Vegas."

"That I promise you," I replied confidently. But then I realized that I hadn't made our dinner reservations yet, so I would have to do that as soon as we got back in the car.

Honestly, I'm normally a pretty confident guy. And before we embarked on this journey, I never doubted my ability to get Simba to New York in a safe, comfortable fashion—particularly with the world's most competent person by my side. But if our very first meal on the road—which really should have been a simple, straightforward affair—was any indication of how the rest of the journey might go, I knew I would have to up my game.

8. DOG STAR

After our regrettable lunch and a brief sweaty walkabout with Simba, Erick and I scrambled back into the air-conditioned station wagon, pulled onto CA-58, and headed east into the Mojave Desert. We were still four hours and 280 miles from Las Vegas, and Laureen's unspoken doubts about my basic fitness to manage this enterprise were slowly creeping into my head.

Shake it off, I told myself. Sure, we bungled our first meal on the road. We arrived at Buck Owens' Crystal Palace too late for brunch. Then I may have put Simba at risk by tying him to a bench in ninety-five-degree heat. I scattered dog food nuggets all over Sonic's outdoor patio. And I made Erick eat truly appalling fast food instead of the one meal he most looked forward to during the entire course of our journey. So all in all, not a great start.

But, hey, this was only the first half of our first day on the road. And we probably just hadn't hit our stride yet. Admittedly we didn't have a lunch plan that wouldn't require us to eat fast food in the car every day. And I still had no evidence whatsoever that any hotels beyond Las Vegas would admit Simba. But, hey, we could figure all that out as we went. And the important thing was that Simba was tolerating the drive remarkably well—maybe even enjoying it—and he didn't seem to be getting any sicker. So I just needed to clear my head. And, honestly, the Mojave Desert seemed like a great place to do that.

I've always loved deserts. Back when I was doing my *Day in the Life* books in different countries around the world—and later when I circled the globe for a year with my first wife and our three children—I made it a point to visit at least nine different deserts on four continents. Admittedly I only drove a car through most of those deserts or at most hiked around for a few hours. (I'm not really the hiking type.) But from that limited perspective, I've always found deserts to be serene, unsullied places with huge azure skies, rock formations that shift hues with the angle of the sun, and otherworldly flora you can't see anywhere else. Remember the epic 1962 David Lean film, *Lawrence of Arabia?* Well, at one point in the movie, a journalist asks Lawrence why he loves deserts. With a maniacal glint in his eye, he hisses, "It's clean."

And that's sort of how I feel.

At any rate, if you like deserts, you'll love the Mojave with its low-slung, pewter-gray mountain ranges, wide-open vistas, and thousands upon thousands of gnarly Joshua Trees. No wonder Jim Morrison and the rest of the Doors puttered out here in a VW microbus seeking enlightenment with a baggie full of peyote buttons. The desert gives you room to think. Or as the 1970s rock band America put it, in perhaps the most inelegant song lyrics ever penned, "In the desert, you can remember your name, 'cause there ain't no one for to give you no pain." And now that Erick and I were cruising across the Mojave, there weren't no one for to give us no pain either.

As we whisked eastward on CA-58, then northeast on I-15, it was comfortably cool inside the air-conditioned station wagon. But when I touched the passenger side window, it was nearly hot enough to burn your fingers. It was obviously sweltering outside, but we didn't know precisely how sweltering until we reached the aptly named hamlet of Baker, California (pop. 735).

The tallest structures in most communities usually offer clues to their defining characteristics or centers of power. Until the last century, the tallest structure in many European cities was the local Roman Catholic cathedral because the Holy See was much of Europe's dominant institution for centuries. In New York—a town more inclined to worship filthy lucre—the tallest buildings house mighty financial firms and, in recent years, the sprawling aeries of the rich and famous. But the tallest structure, by far, in tiny Baker, California, was a 134-foot-high thermometer erected in 1991 to celebrate the town's torrid climate, and more specifically, the world record 134-degree temperature recorded in nearby Death Valley just over a century ago. (Baker's own record high, notched in 2007, is a paltry 125.)

Apparently, what's billed as the "world's tallest thermometer," and very likely is, had been switched off for the past two years because the electricity needed to illuminate it had proven too costly. (If there was ever a case for solar conversion, this had to be it.)

But luckily for Erick and me, the widow and daughter of Willis Herron, the thermometer's visionary creator, had recently plunked down enough scratch to repaint the local landmark, replace its incandescent bulbs with cost-efficient LEDs, and switch this towering testament to torridity back on again. And that's how Erick and I knew that it was precisely 111 degrees Fahrenheit when we pulled into Baker to refill our tank and tend to Simba.

I thought it was hot in Bakersfield. But there's a palpable difference between 95 degrees and 111 degrees. In fact, it was so shockingly hot outside we weren't sure we should let Simba out of the air-conditioned car at all. After we topped off the gas tank, Erick and I bent over and felt the asphalt with our hands to determine whether it might burn Simba's pads. It clearly would. But one look into Simba's rheumy brown eyes told us that the dog had to go— and sooner rather than later. So we handled it like an Indy pit stop.

I drove the station wagon onto a patch of dusty ground adjacent to the gas station. Then we lifted Simba out of the car straight onto the dirt, which was hot, but not nearly as hot as the asphalt. At first Simba looked stunned. His eight years in Tiburon had been a balmy cavalcade of warm days and cool nights. So he had never felt anything like this, even during his sultry Georgia puppyhood. I was initially worried that the sudden surge of heat might overwhelm old Simba and cause him to faint. But after the initial shock subsided, he literally shook it off and promptly took care of business. Then Erick and I lifted him back into the car in the usual fashion. And the whole process took less than a minute. Simba still needed a proper walk, but that would have to wait until Las Vegas, which made me wonder how hot it might be there.

In addition to the "world tallest thermometer," there were two other notable points of interest on the road from Bakersfield to Las Vegas. The first was a standard green and white highway sign that marked the exit for the fabulously named Zzyzx Road (pronounced "Zy-ziks"). If taken, the road terminates in the tiny settlement of Zzyzx, California. You may be asking yourself now, as we did then, why any place on Earth would be named Zzyzx. And I now know the answer to that question.

It seems that back in 1944, an enterprising radio evangelist and itinerant Alabama con man named the Reverend Curtis Howe Springer filed a mining claim here with the Bureau of Land Management. And on the strength of that slender assertion, he took it upon himself to change the name of this former wagon stop from Camp Soda Springs to the much more memorable Zzyzx— his thinking being that Zzyzx would always be the last place name listed in any atlas ever published. Then Springer bused in a work crew of semireformed drunks and derelicts from a skid row mission he operated in Los Angeles. And they very quickly and altogether illegally erected the Zzyzx Mineral Springs and Health Resort— an institution that Springer touted as "The Last Word in Health." (Get it?)

Springer prospered in his remote desert outpost for three full decades, selling drinks to thirsty travelers, advertising a "natural hot springs" that was only hot because Springer heated it with a large hidden boiler and, most of all, by peddling Zzyzx-brand patent medicines that claimed to cure everything from baldness and hemorrhoids to various types of cancer. By the early 1970s, Zzyzx could boast a sixty-room motel, an airstrip (called the Zyport, of course), an AM radio station, and an evangelical church where Springer preached the gospel and, needless to say, solicited contributions from the faithful.

But then as con artists, even talented con artists like Springer, are wont to do, he took things one step too far, selling building plots around the health spa to some of his wealthier patrons. As you might imagine, selling government-owned land to well-heeled marks tends to attract the wrong sort of official attention—particularly when the marks in question tried to record their deeds at the local courthouse. And once the feds wised up to Springer's assorted scams, they seized his beloved Zzyzx and tossed Springer in the hoosegow on charges ranging from false claims and fraud to squatting on federal land.

Springer must have had a very good lawyer because in addition to the land seizure, he drew only a sixty-day jail term. And in the end he served only forty-nine of those days. Upon his release, Springer retired to Las Vegas—a town that has always appreciated a good con man. And until his death in 1985, he proudly maintained to all who would listen that he was and ever would be the rightful Lord of Zzyzx.

It's a good story. But I do realize that the Reverend Curtis Howe Springer bamboozled thousands of hardworking folks with his radio ministry, his fake hot springs, and, worst of all, with his worthless elixirs. But every swindle has a silver lining. And in this case, the payoff was three-fold. First, the compound that once housed Springer's "health resort" has now been put to much better use by the California State University's Desert Studies Center.[3]

More remarkably, a series of man-made ponds that Springer dug and stocked with fish for his guests' enjoyment turns out to be one of the last remaining habitats of the critically endangered Mohave tui chub—a species of small fish that would have vanished from the planet had it not been for Springer's elaborate three-decade scam. And of course, there's the marvelous green highway sign that still bears Springer's magnificent neologism—a sign that incites a smile from nearly everyone barreling along I-15, including Erick and me.

The other astonishing vision Erick and I witnessed on the road to Las Vegas was splayed out across five square miles of barren scrubland in a wide desert valley just west of the highway. The recently opened Ivanpah Solar Electric Generating System, a so-called thermal farm, consists of 350,000 mirrors—you heard me—each the size of a garage door. The mirrors are arrayed concentrically around three forty-five-story towers topped with black cube-shaped water tanks. Apparently, the mirrors reflect and concentrate the desert sun in order to boil water inside the tanks. And the steam they produce drives turbines that generate enough electricity to power 140,000

---

[3] In a truly stunning display of *chutzpah*, Springer showed up uninvited to the inaugural ceremony, spoke to reporters, and vaguely took credit for his "donation."

homes—which seems like an awful lot of homes to me, but apparently doesn't justify the $2.2 billion ponied up by investors like Google and the U.S. Department of Energy.

As Erick and I gazed down upon the sprawling thermal farm at five in the afternoon, it was still pretty bright in the Mojave Desert. But the fiery desert sun reflected in a third of a million mirrors created a luminous aura called a "solar flux" that was another order of magnitude brighter.

The atmosphere above the mirrors looked as if it might ignite at any moment. And that concept is not as far-fetched as you might think. Because only a few days later, as Erick and I drove through Oklahoma, we learned from an NPR report that the solar farm's employees had begun to notice a truly disagreeable phenomenon. Namely, that birds inadvertently flapping their way through the 900-degree solar flux were abruptly bursting into flame and plummeting to Earth trailing plumes of dark smoke. The employees had taken to calling these unfortunate creatures "streamers." And depending upon whom you believe—the plant's operators or incensed environmentalists—Ivanpah's solar flux will incinerate somewhere between 2,000 and 28,000 birds annually.

Every form of energy generation and extraction—even so-called green energy—comes with an ecological price tag attached. But rarely does the bill present itself so flamboyantly— actually I'd say biblically—as flaming birds raining down from the sky.

At any rate, from Ivanpah it was less than an hour's drive across the southern Nevada desert to Las Vegas. And it wasn't long before we spotted, off in the distance, Sin City's enormous hotel-casinos rising like phantasms from the desert. Our destination for the day was finally in sight. And after our ghastly lunch, Erick and I were more than ready for dinner.

Before we embarked on our cross-country mission, I assumed that Simba would enjoy, or at least abide, cruising down the highway all day in the back of a station wagon. And I knew he would relish the round-the-clock companionship implicit in such a journey. But as I mentioned earlier, I didn't think he would care much one way or the other about the various points of interest we might encounter along the way. And of all the points of interest that we might encounter during the course of our three-thousand-mile trek, the last place I thought Simba would enjoy was glitzy, libertine Las Vegas. As I quickly learned when I tried to book our first night's accommodations, the Las Vegas Strip isn't really set up for family pets.

But what I failed to consider is this: so few people actually bring their dogs to the Las Vegas Strip that the few intrepid mutts who do turn up tend to attract the sort of attention normally reserved for yetis and unicorns. Bringing Simba to Las Vegas was like bringing a baby to an old age home, or a Dallas Cowboys cheerleader to a mining camp. From the moment his paws hit the pavement—which was hot, but not Baker hot—Simba was the star of the show and King of the Strip. Dozens, nay scores, of people we met during our brief Vegas sojourn were pleased, nay, thrilled to make Simba's acquaintance. And in a setting otherwise rife with artifice and illusion, scruffy-faced young men with their shirttails hanging out, twenty-something women in platform shoes and spandex mini-dresses, and grizzled old duffers in sandals and baseball caps were all delighted to meet a big, tail-wagging reminder of the humdrum life they came here to escape.

And every one of these folks seemed to have a beloved pooch they left at home when they packed their roller bags and jetted off to Vegas. And within ten seconds of meeting Simba, they would all rummage through their purses or shimmy smart phones out of their jeans so they could show me photos of Jake the beagle or Fluffy the Maltese or Brutus the Great Dane who faithfully awaited their returns.

"Check this out," they would say. "This is *my* dog back in Cleveland (or Kansas City or Sacramento). He's a cockapoo (or a Labradoodle or a German shepherd). She's staying with my mother (or my sister or...)." Anyway, you get the idea.

It was a poignant and revelatory experience. And the upshot was this: if ever you doubt the vast and benevolent role dogs play in America's family life, just bring your pooch to Las Vegas, walk him down South Las Vegas Boulevard, and let the love flow. If you bring him, I promise they will come.

And Simba, who was an aristocrat by nature and extroverted even for a Labrador, basked in the warm glow of their adoration—sitting, smiling, and wagging his tail for all comers. For Simba, it must have been like when movie stars or politicians first become famous. And they can't quite believe that everyone they meet wants to shake their hand or take a selfie with them—or in Simba's case, scratch his neck and commend his rugged good looks. During those first ambrosial days of fame, before it all becomes tedious and creepy—which I imagine it does fairly quickly—it's probably gratifying to know that everyone loves and adores you and yearns to make a connection. And it's even more wonderful if you actually like that sort of thing, which Simba clearly did. And it's most wonderful of all if, again like Simba, you are old and infirm and your days are dwindling to a precious few and everyone still wants to lavish you with love and affection. In Las Vegas, Simba was a god.

In the preceding chapter of this small book, I penned a few harsh words about the Vdara Hotel and Spa. How they had a stupid name. How they were going to make Simba and me stay in an overpriced Vdog Suite. And how they were going to foist an array of tacky dog-related amenities on me—that sort of thing. I now wish to retract every last word. Because I don't care if management decides to rename this place the Shit-dara Hotel and Spa and charge me double what they did. Because in a town not always characterized by generosity of spirit, the staff of the Vdara could not have welcomed Simba more warmly had he been the queen of England's prize corgi.

I do realize that some of their gushy hospitality was probably attributable to the unicorn effect. But if it was, I don't care. Because from the moment we rolled our dusty, bug-bespattered station wagon up to the hotel's front entrance and released the hound, every parking attendant, doorman, and security guard greeted Simba with a big smile and heartfelt joy. And then, as we waited in line at the check-in desk, each passing bellman—and there were many employed by a hotel this size—paused long enough to babble some baby talk at Simba and rub his big furry head. The polite and amiable desk clerk graciously ignored the obvious—namely, that Simba clearly exceeded the hotel's officially stated canine weight limit. And cynical me, the Vdog Amenity Package that I previously ridiculed actually turned out to be a useful and thoughtfully assembled gift.

But perhaps best of all, the Vdara Hotel and Spa maintained a well-groomed dog park across from the front entrance—a lovely patch of well worn grass where Simba could relieve himself day or night. I hadn't noticed this particular frill when I scanned the Vdara's website back in Tiburon. But I couldn't miss it when we actually arrived because no fewer than a dozen hotel employees upon spotting Simba cheerfully cried out, "Hey, you know we have our own dog park."

Since Simba had so recently watered the scorched earth of Baker, we didn't take advantage of this amenity until after we checked in. But after that and before we went up to our room I used my newly acquired plastic key card to gain entrance to a verdant postage-stamp-sized paradise ringed by fifty-story hotels. Simba was still a bit stiff from lying in the back of the station wagon all day. So he limped around on the grass for a while and sniffed here and there before he let loose. Once that was accomplished, I took him on his Las Vegas walk of fame. And then we headed up to our Vdog Suite on the thirty-third floor.

The Vdara Hotel was only four years old, so the accommodations were clean and modern and as warm and tasteful as a 1,500-room hotel can be. But more to the point, a comfortable dog bed was already in place. So I gave Simba one of his chewable arthritis pills and the antibiotic he was still taking for his kennel cough. Then I poured kibble into his bowl and watched carefully to make sure he ate it. After that I dressed up for my own much-anticipated dinner with Erick. I pulled down the shades, turned off the lights, and led Simba to his bed. I gently spread the black acrylic V-dog blanket over him. And finally, with the earnest hope that Simba wouldn't become lonely or anxious while I was gone, I lay down next to him and stroked his furry back until he began to snore—at which point I tiptoed out of the room and very quietly closed the door behind me.

I met Erick in the lobby, and we took a cab over to the Venetian Hotel where—after a brief phone consultation with Günter the Chef—I had booked a table for two at Daniel Boulud's DB Brasserie. In my mind, this would be the one evening during the entire journey when I would be able to treat Erick to a few tattered vestiges of the epic road trip he had once envisioned—before it turned into a mission of mercy. I knew I only had three or four hours before I had to get back to Simba. But during that interval, I hoped that Erick and I would be able to enjoy a proper dinner, polish off a decent bottle of Burgundy, hit the blackjack tables for as long as my customary hundred-dollar venture fund held out. And then who knows what might happen because, hey, it was Vegas, baby!

Anyway, that was the dream. But in reality, when we sat down at our little table in the DB Brasserie, I couldn't help but notice that, like several other Vegas outposts bearing the names of celebrated chefs, the sparsely patronized restaurant was excessively large and decidedly over-lit—more like a gourmet cafeteria. Chef Daniel's eponymous flagship restaurant on New York's Upper East Side serves up, by nearly everyone's estimation, one of the finest dining experiences on Earth. But the Vegas branch was more of a mass-market enterprise, which I should have anticipated but found disappointing nonetheless.

And to be fair, my perception of our very competently prepared meal conscientiously served in a clean, well-lighted place was likely colored by my slowly but inexorably mounting sense of abject guilt. As Erick and I engaged in a pleasant conversation about our various children and how they were doing in school or at work and whether or not they had boyfriends or girlfriends, etcetera, the monologue in my head was running something like this:

How could I have left Simba all alone in a strange hotel room our first night on the road?

Does he feel abandoned up there on the thirty-third floor?

I wonder if he threw up on the rug.

What if he gets sick and dies while I'm sitting here blithely nibbling duck confit?

What would I tell Laureen and the girls?

How could I forgive myself?

*I need to get back to the room **right now**.*

This spiral of self-recrimination persisted through dinner and dessert. And when Erick and I finally plunked ourselves down at one of the Venetian's bottom-end ten-dollar blackjack tables, it was almost as if I were trying to blow my hundred-dollar grubstake as quickly as possible so I could return to Simba's side where I rightfully belonged.

Whether it was self-sabotage or my complete lack of gambling skills, I'll never know, but I successfully relinquished my whole wad in less than fifteen minutes. Then I turned to my traveling companion and said, "Erick, you know I wanted this to be a great boys' night out so I could thank you for helping me with this trip and all. But honestly, I feel like I should be back in the room with Simba. I'm sorry to be a spoilsport, but I think I gotta bail."

Erick, ever the gentleman, understood or at least said he did. So we abandoned our theoretically epic night in Las Vegas and grabbed a cab back to our hotel.

When we pulled up in front of the Vdara ten minutes later, I jumped out of the taxi and trotted across the lobby to the elevator leaving Erick in my dust. I pushed the call button repeatedly and then fumbled with the keycard outside my room. With each passing second, I became further convinced that Simba was either in distress or already dead.

When I finally pushed open the door to my room, I could see from the light in the corridor that Simba was right where I left him. Then I heard him snoring, and a wave of relief washed over me. A thorough search of the carpet on my hands and knees in the dark failed to turn up any anxiety-induced dog vomit. So apparently my entire guilty panic episode was completely unfounded and actually pretty ridiculous.

I woke Simba up with a gentle nudge just to let him know I was there. He gazed up at me with his big brown eyes and smiled lovingly before he drifted back to sleep. Apparently the long car ride from San Francisco and his Vegas walk of fame had exhausted the old dog. And he hadn't even noticed I was gone.

9. RAINING CATS AND DOGS

Simba shook himself awake, dog tags jingling, just before five the next morning. He roused me in the process, and my first thought was, "Thank goodness. He's still alive."

I gave Simba a big hug and told him what a good dog he was. Then I fed him breakfast and snapped the red leash onto his leather collar. We took the elevator down to the Vdara's colossal lobby. The doormen greeted us in their usual chummy fashion. Then we shuffled outside in the predawn gloaming for Simba's morning constitutional.

On the way back to the room, I popped into the lobby snack bar for a tall coffee and a breakfast sandwich. Needless to say, one of the counter guys working the dawn shift had two Labradors at home. And the moment he saw Simba, he fairly leapt out from behind the counter so he could share a few dozen cell-phone photos and some riveting tales of their shenanigans. (I know. I do it too.) Erick, Simba, and I were back in the car by eight, and Erick took the first shift driving east out of Las Vegas on U.S. 93.

Our ultimate destination that day was Gallup, New Mexico, 435 miles due east. At just over six hours, it would be one of our shortest one-day drives. And the larger, more cosmopolitan city of Albuquerque was only two hours further down the road. But I wanted to bunk in Gallup for two somewhat dubious reasons: first, I loved its evocative name; and second, a hot tip. Honestly, I didn't know the first thing about Gallup—and as it turned out, I should have taken the time to find out. But doesn't the name Gallup, New Mexico, fairly reek of historical romance—like Tombstone, Arizona, or Deadwood, South Dakota? And doesn't it seem as if it would be a classic Old West town with three or four swinging-door saloons, a limestone-clad bank with Ionic columns, and a rough-hewn wooden railroad depot, circa 1894?

I had no idea whether any of that was true. But I've always been a big believer in serendipity, particularly as it pertains to travel. And picking a place to visit solely on the basis of its name has worked out pretty well for me in the past. Elegant Spoleto, Italy, nestled in the Umbrian foothills; the colorful Mekong River town of Luang Prabang, Laos, and the South Pacific paradise of Bora Bora immediately come to mind—and all three were enchanting.

The second reason I wanted to lay my head down in Gallup that evening was somewhat more substantive. When I immodestly posted a Facebook item mentioning that Erick, Simba, and I would be more or less retracing the old Route 66—the fabled "Mother Road"—from Kingman, Arizona, to Oklahoma City, a Time-Life photojournalist I knew from back in the day posted an intriguing response. He said that whatever other kicks we got on Route 66, we should definitely spend a night at the historic El Rancho Hotel in Gallup, New Mexico.

Apparently, old-time icons of the silver screen such as John Wayne, Spencer Tracy, and Ronald Reagan once bunked at the El Rancho while filming classic Hollywood Westerns in the picturesque environs. And like Buck Owens' Crystal Palace, the El Rancho was supposed to be a living museum packed to the rafters with vintage Navajo rugs, ornate Victorian furniture, autographed publicity photos from the forties and fifties, and the sort of obscure memorabilia that's always been catnip to me.

Again, taking travel tips from globe-trotting photojournalists has always paid off in the past, landing me in any number of offbeat locales. The best, I think, was a lovely farmstead off South Africa's spectacular Garden Route between Port Elizabeth and Capetown. There the kids and I were met at the front door by the estate's grande dame, who was improbably attended by a baby baboon in disposable diapers… and the little fellow was casually sitting astride a remarkably patient Golden retriever! Now that's something you don't see every day. And the kids and I wouldn't have seen it at all if I hadn't been susceptible to random advice from my photojournalist friends. So if you put the two together—romantic moniker plus well-informed travel tip—then Gallup, New Mexico, seemed like a no-brainer—at least until we got there.

As the Las Vegas skyscrapers receded in the rearview mirror, I was pleased we had selected Sin City as our first overnight stop of the trip. Honestly, it was fifty miles out of the way. And if the truth be told, putting Vegas on the agenda had very little to do with

Simba or our core mission. It was just a selfish desire to have one great boys' night out before we resumed our dash across America. But thanks to my guilty panic episode, our boys' night out had been a total bust. But good old Simba had one of his best days ever soaking up the tourist love on the Las Vegas Strip. So score one for serendipity.

Twenty-six miles down the road—Just over the Nevada–Arizona border at a speck on the map called Last Stop—Erick and I couldn't help but notice a long, low-slung compound painted fluorescent yellow and ringed by a dozen large, brightly colored signs. It was apparently a combination restaurant, gas station, ATV rental office, and gun range—but mostly a gun range. And the largest of its many flashy billboards read:

BULLETS & BURGERS
SHOOT A 50 CAL. MACHINE GUN

Apparently, Las Vegas tourists who want to add a dash of violence to their sex and gambling can cruise out into the desert aboard a lavishly illustrated Bullets & Burgers van and engage in four or five hours of exuberant gunplay.

And they don't play with just any guns. Bullets & Burgers stocks more than thirty varieties of high-caliber weapons including .44 Magnums (when a .357 just won't do), the globally popular AK-

47 assault rifle, a Browning .50 caliber machine gun on a tripod (which, judging from the sign, is the main attraction), and, I kid you not, a fully operational grenade launcher mounted to the business end of an M16. The Browning, by the way, can pierce lightly armored vehicles and blow low-flying aircraft out of the sky—so not what you'd call a sporting weapon.

Bullets & Burgers also boasts a large collection of submachine guns, including gangster-style Tommy guns with their distinctive round magazines, and compact Israeli Uzis, the most ubiquitous submachine gun in the world for more than two decades. And just in case you think this heavily-armed playground only attracts gun nuts and Second Amendment enthusiasts, you should know that in terms of popularity, Bullets & Burgers ranks number two—I'm tempted to say with a bullet—amongst all 199 Las Vegas-area "Fun & Games" activities listed on the popular TripAdvisor website. And it's apparently considered good, clean fun for the entire family, including children as young as eight.

Unfortunately, some children as young as eight can't be fully trusted with a submachine gun. And about a week after Erick and I blew past Bullets & Burgers—me still wearing my stupid Elm Forks Shooting Sports hat—I was chagrined to learn that a sweet nine-year-old girl in a pink shirt and ponytail had lost control of her Uzi and shot her instructor—a father of four—in the head at point-blank range.

Don't get me wrong. As my hat clearly indicates, I occasionally patronize gun ranges myself. And I grew up in a blue-collar western Pennsylvania town where the first day of deer season was a school holiday. I'll further admit that I've taken both Lucas and Grace to an indoor shooting range near our house in Marin County. But they were fourteen or fifteen at the time, not nine. And they took a half-hour lesson from a trained professional before they squeezed off their first round. But far more germane to this discussion, they fired a dinky .22 caliber revolver, which has almost no recoil, not a nine-millimeter automatic that, despite what you see on TV, generally requires two adult hands to control it.

When it comes to guns and the Second Amendment, I guess we all draw our own lines. But putting a powerful automatic weapon in the hands of a nine-year-old child seems to violate, if not the laws of Arizona, then certainly the dictates of common sense. When I first saw the story on television, and then all over the Internet, I initially thought, "Hey, I know that place." But then, of course, I felt deeply sorry for the instructor's wife and his four teenage children. But most of all I felt sorry for the nameless young girl in the pink shirt and ponytail who will probably spend the rest of her life reliving a horrific incident she couldn't prevent.

I'm pretty sure you're still reading this book to find out what happens to Simba, not to be subjected to a random tirade about gun control. But as a father of five who occasionally enjoys shooting pistols at paper targets and shotguns at clay pigeons, may I humbly suggest—I'm talking to you National Rifle Association—that keeping automatic weapons out of the hands of small children is not quite the same thing as depriving all red-blooded Americans of their God-given right to bear arms—in well-regulated militias or otherwise.

Hey, I realize that all governments, including our own—sometimes especially our own—overreach from time to time. But honestly, NRA, the slope isn't quite as slippery as you incessantly make it out to be. And, like it or not, common sense actually has a place in this discussion. So you can pry that little nugget of truth out of my cold dead hands.

Okay, now that I got that out of my system—and likely alienated half of my tiny population of readers—let's return to the story. Because a little past Bullets & Burgers, Erick, Simba, and I left the low desert behind and began our climb into the northern Arizona high country that eventually reaches an altitude of a mile and a half above sea level.

Our first day on the road, including the Mojave Desert run, had been about as hot as possible—always above ninety degrees and well into triple digits in the desert. And except for the Central Valley's patchwork of irrigated farm fields, the drought-parched western landscape had been a desiccated shade of brown all the way from San Francisco's East Bay to Las Vegas.

But now that we were gaining altitude, the temperature gradually cooled into the low seventies, and the scenery grew progressively greener. Eventually the highway ran through vast stands of ponderosa pine in the Tonto National Forest. And I could occasionally spot a few tiny lakes—or maybe they were just ponds—off the side of the highway. There was obviously a lot more annual rainfall up here than there was anywhere we'd been thus far. But I didn't expect to see it all at once.

When Erick and I stopped for gas in Kingman, Arizona, I took the wheel. So I was driving when the sky turned an ominous shade of gunmetal gray. Then, ten minutes later, the heavens let loose. Since there's little if any precipitation in San Francisco between May and October—even in non-drought years—Erick and I were initially delighted to see fat splashes of rain slapping the windshield and rinsing the Mojave dust off the hood of our car.

But then, minute by minute, mile after mile, the rain fell progressively harder. And it wasn't long before the windshield wipers, even at their highest setting, couldn't keep up with the downpour. I'd only seen this sheer volume of rain twice before—once in my early twenties when I was caught in a hurricane on the west coast of Africa; and again, two decades later, when I drove into Oklahoma City during a terrifying thunderstorm that featured thousands of lightening strikes and 110-mile-per-hour winds.

I tried slowing the car down from sixty-five to forty to see if that might improve the visibility. But even then it was like trying to see the highway ahead through a waterfall. Other vehicles on the road were just colorful blurs, and it sounded as if someone were playing a drum solo on the roof of the car. This, I concluded, was a dangerous situation. But being a guy and all, I didn't want Erick to think that I lacked either the proficiency or the intestinal fortitude to press forward—even in the face of this apocalyptically proportioned deluge.

But then, after ten or twelve more miles of squinting through the windshield and not being able to see very much at all, my bravado frayed. And I began hoping that Erick might say something to the effect of, "Hey, maybe we should pull over for a while." So that it would be him, not me, who was throwing in the towel.

But, alas, when I glanced over at my traveling companion, he seemed entirely at ease with the whole 'Noah and the Ark' situation. And I knew he would never capitulate. So in an act of cowardice, I glanced back over my shoulder at Simba to see whether he might be upset by the storm—you know, like dogs are supposed to be. Because if Simba were scared, that would be a perfectly valid excuse—I mean reason—to pull over and comfort the poor old hound until the tempest passed. (Sadly, this is how some men think.)

But, nope, brave old Simba was just as relaxed as Erick, casually sprawled across his bed and seemingly oblivious to our imminent demise. And when I briefly caught his eye, he just smiled at me and panted. And I knew that the panting was due to his paralyzed larynx rather than any sense of dread.

When that craven plan collapsed, I gripped the wheel even harder and stared straight into the monsoon. And as I did, I began to tell Erick a few poignant details of my epic Oklahoma thunderstorm adventure. How the fierce gale blew big green highway signs right over backward. How marble-size hailstones followed hard on the rain. And how I was eventually forced to seek refuge under a highway overpass in order to avoid certain death—you know, that sort of thing. I did that not only to establish my foul-weather credentials but also to let Erick know just how bad it might get out here if the storm persisted and we failed to respect its majesty. After I made my case, I turned to Erick and said as casually as possible, "You know, Erick, maybe we should pull over. I mean just until this lets up a bit."

And that, I figured, should do it.

Erick pondered my suggestion for a moment, peered up at the angry skies through the moon roof, contemplated the road ahead, and I suppose did a few calculations in his head. Then he replied, just as casually, "Nah, I think we should keep moving. The storm seems to be blowing from east to west. So if we maintain our speed, we'll probably come out the other side of it fairly quickly."

"How could you possibly know that?" I asked, trying not to sound exasperated.

"Well," Erick said. "Sometimes I study weather patterns to determine how radio towers will be affected by various atmospheric conditions."

Oh, no. Not the fucking radio towers again.

"And I'm pretty sure," Erick continued, "that we're not in any real danger here. It'll blow over soon."

Which forced me to say, "Well, better safe than sorry."

And before Erick could utter one more logical, science-based word, I jerked the car off the highway and onto the shoulder.

At first, I was relieved to see that we'd ended up right behind another vehicle—a big gray SUV presumably piloted by a similarly gutless, I mean sensible, motorist. Cowardice, after all, loves company. But then it struck me. I hadn't been able to see the gray SUV at all until I zoomed up right behind it at a fairly high rate of speed. And I could have easily crashed into it. So maybe it would have been safer to keep driving after all—like Erick said.

But now the deed was done. So I switched off the engine. And Erick, Simba, and I waited in near silence for the storm to pass, which I'm chagrined say, happened no more than ten minutes hence—exactly as Erick predicted.

So, basically, there had been no reason to push the panic button. And I realized that my reaction to the rainstorm along with my hasty flight from the Venetian Hotel Casino the previous evening made not one, but two, unnecessary panic attacks in the course of a single twenty-four hour period.

"Jesus, " I thought. "You really need to get ahold of yourself."

10. WONDER DOG

Erick being Erick, I guess I shouldn't have been surprised. But it seems that prior to our departure my traveling companion had compiled a list of fascinating roadside attractions that we could visit whenever time allowed and the spirit moved us. But rather than share this touristy lineup at the outset of the journey, as one might expect, Erick demonstrated a real showman's flair by revealing the prospective stops only as they came into range.

It took me a little while to figure out what Erick was up to. But once I did, I realized that his system perfectly suited our cross-country partnership. Since Erick was sole keeper of the Wonder List, I never knew what the next stop would be or when it might occur. And that appealed to my spontaneous nature. Erick, on the other hand, knew exactly what was coming and when. And that gratified his engineer's heart.

So every time Erick smiled his slightly crooked smile and got a particular twinkle in his eye, I knew that he was about to reveal his next all-American wonder. And each time, just before he did, I raised my hand like a kid in school and made the same tired joke, crying out, "I know! I know! It's the world's largest ball of twine!"

In point of fact, the world's largest ball of twine is in Branson, Missouri[4], a full 140 miles off our charted course. So we probably wouldn't go there, even to justify the joke. But on a road trip this long—on Route 66 no less—it did seem somehow imperative to visit as many of the world's largest doodads and gewgaws as possible.

And in that regard, we were more or less successful. Simba did, after all, take a piss in the shadow of the world's tallest thermometer. And at one point, in the tiny Texas panhandle town of Groom, we were privileged to witness what Erick claimed was "the largest cross in the Western Hemisphere." Although maybe that shouldn't count because, (a) by definition, the Western Hemisphere is only half the world, and (b) the claim itself is hotly contested by at least four other very tall Western Hemisphere crosses. One of these crosses, the 198-foot-tall "Cross at the Crossroads" in Effingham, Illinois, was built only seven years after our Groom, Texas, cross, apparently just to grab the title—which, by the way, doesn't strike me as particularly Christian.

But whatever the actual facts of the case are, I vote for Erick's giant Groom, Texas, cross because

a. to the best of my knowledge, none of those other giant crucifixes are ringed by life-size bronze figures depicting all

---

[4] To be as evenhanded as possible, I really should mention that while "the world's largest ball of twine" is in Branson, Missouri, "the world's heaviest ball of twine" is in Lake Nebagamon, Wisconsin, and the largest ball of sisal twine (as opposed to nylon twine) is in either Cawker City, Kansas, or Darwin, Minnesota, depending upon whom you believe.

fourteen Stations of the Cross (not to mention a full-size replica of Christ's empty tomb);

b. no other cross is anywhere near the "Leaning Water Tower of Groom," which is exactly what it sounds like, but which, for some reason, hasn't garnered the same global acclaim as its famous leaning cousin in Pisa; and

c. it's nowhere near as creepy as the 1,056 wooden crosses—grouped in Calvaryesque threes—that line the highways of West Virginia. (And by the way, I'd be just as creeped out if someone had erected a thousand crescent moons or a thousand six-pointed stars.)

Anyway, after the somewhat-less-than-apocalyptic Arizona cloudburst, I manfully admitted to Erick that maybe his foul-weather strategy might have been superior to my own. And I vowed that going forward I would not lightly dismiss any advice emanating from the world's most competent person.

I revved up the car, pulled back onto I-40, and within a matter of minutes, Erick gleefully revealed the first of his three wonders of the day. It was… drum roll, please… Meteor Crater, approximately fifty miles east in… okay, one more drum roll… the middle of freakin' nowhere.

The reason it's called just Meteor Crater, instead of Meteor Crater State Park or Meteor Crater National Monument or some other equally august appellation is that this particular natural wonder is privately owned and operated—by the Barringer family of Arizona.

So, how does one family end up owning a 500-foot-deep, nearly-mile-wide meteor crater? It's a great story, actually. And it all begins in 1906 with one Daniel Moreau Barringer, Jr., a Philadelphia lawyer and Princeton-trained mining engineer who had already made his fortune in Arizona silver. That year Barringer publicly challenged the generally accepted wisdom—championed by the preeminent geologist of the day, G. K. Gilbert—that the crater in question was the caldera of an ancient volcano. Barringer was convinced that only a very large meteor crashing into the earth at thousands of miles per hour could have made this particular hole in the ground. More specifically, he calculated that the meteorite in question would have a mass of ten million tons. And based on fragments littering the crater rim, that it would consist almost entirely of extraterrestrial iron with a little space nickel thrown in.

That, by the way, is enough iron to build more than a thousand Eiffel Towers. And once processed, it would yield the modern-day equivalent of $6 billion in profits. So the meteorite was well worth finding—particularly back in 1906 when it was apparently acceptable to dig up, melt down, and monetize a giant natural wonder from outer space. And since a ten-million-ton hunk of iron can't just disappear in a puff of smoke, Barringer figured it had to be down there somewhere—either deep beneath the crater floor or maybe a little off to one side if the meteor had struck at an angle.

So like the Reverend Curtis Howe Springer of Zzyzx, California, Daniel Moreau Barringer, Jr., filed a mining claim with the U.S. Bureau of Land Management. But unlike the grifting Reverend Springer, Barringer was already a wealthy man and the scion of a prominent North Carolina family—not to mention Teddy Roosevelt's hunting buddy. So he was able to procure what Springer never did: a "land patent" granting his newly incorporated Standard Iron Company full right and title to the entire mile-wide crater and a good deal of surrounding acreage. So with official federal paperwork in hand, but apparently without a simple magnetometer—which was certainly available at the time and would have told Barringer that there was no colossal mass of iron anywhere in the vicinity—he proceeded to spend the next twenty-three years digging for his six-billion dollar meteorite.

As it turned out, Barringer was right, but only partially so. What is now known as Barringer Crater was indeed formed by a giant meteor that collided with the earth approximately fifty thousand years ago. And just as Barringer predicted, the meteor was made almost entirely of iron. But, unfortunately, Barringer and his mathematically inclined colleague, Benjamin Chew Tilghman, overestimated the meteor's mass by a factor of thirty-three. Which meant that upon impact the meteor weighed a mere 300,000 tons, not 10 million tons as they had calculated. And the key phrase here is "upon impact." Because when the meteor slammed into the earth's surface at more than 25,000 miles per hour, it released 2-½ megatons of energy—roughly 125 times as much energy as the Nagasaki A-bomb—and the giant meteor pretty much vaporized, spreading a fine iron-nickel mist and the occasional chunk of iron across the high-desert floor.

So Barringer squandered more than two decades of his life, nearly his entire silver fortune, and virtually all of his investors' money rooting around for an enormous hunk of iron that was never there. Eventually—and some might say belatedly—Standard Iron's board of directors consulted one F. R. Moulton, a renowned University of Chicago astronomer. They asked Professor Moulton where their ten-million-ton meteorite might be. And at what must have been a very uncomfortable board meeting, Moulton explained the whole meteorite vaporization phenomenon. At which point, the directors pulled the proverbial plug. Daniel Barringer died shortly thereafter—a disillusioned man of substantially reduced means.

But as with Reverend Springer's beloved Zzyzx, Barringer's Folly had a silver lining (as opposed, I guess, to an iron lining). Daniel Moreau Barringer did not save an endangered species of fish like Reverend Springer, but he did significantly advance humankind's understanding of meteor impact sites. In fact Barringer was the first person to conclusively prove that meteor impact craters existed here on planet Earth. And he is still widely recognized for his contributions to the field. In 1970, NASA even named an impact crater after him—albeit on the dark side of the moon.

Furthermore, Barringer's heirs—and he sired no fewer than eight children—ended up owning a rather large swathe of remote Arizona scrubland that featured by nearly anyone's estimation a pretty spectacular hole in the ground. So with an eye toward posterity, they decided to preserve the crater—both as a scientific research site and as a fascinating tourist attraction that now includes what's supposed to be a pretty good RV park and the sort of carefully contrived visitor center one might find at a real national park.

Erick thought that Meteor Crater might be a great first stop of the day for two reasons. First, even though Meteor Crater was nowhere close to being the world's largest impact crater—that would be the two-hundred-mile-wide Vredefort Crater in South Africa by the way—it was still "the world's best preserved meteor impact site" and therefore an authentic Route 66 superlative, admittedly an obscure one (or maybe they're all obscure). More importantly, Meteor Crater was a spectacular outdoor attraction that could be thoroughly enjoyed by humans and canines alike. Erick envisioned a leisurely forty-five-minute hike around the rim so we could see the crater up close and give Simba a proper walk in the process.

That all sounded good to me. So we took the Meteor Crater Road exit off I-40 and drove seven miles along a picturesque two-lane byway through the high desert. We pulled into the Meteor Crater parking lot, scrambled out of the station wagon, and snapped Simba's leash onto his collar. Then we strolled across the parking lot toward the visitor center where we were met by a discreet little sign that read, "No Pets Allowed."

I was naturally incensed. I mean what possible damage could Simba inflict upon a mile-wide meteor crater that old Daniel Moreau Barringer himself hadn't wreaked during his misbegotten two-decade-long mining effort? I supposed Simba might take a dump on their precious meteor crater. But if he did, I had poop bags at the ready. That being said, I knew from bitter experience that it would likely be useless to reason with whoever was guarding the entrance. So, instead, I decided to evade this petty edict by finding an alternate route to the crater rim.

The only other time I had attempted this particular sort of trespass was in my early thirties at Hearst Castle, on California's Central Coast. Thoroughly disappointed when I pulled into the parking lot only minutes after closing time, my traveling companion and I found an unlocked gate, swung it open and attempted to drive our rental car up the long winding road to press baron William Randolph Hearst's grandiose mish-mash of a house.

I wasn't going to break in or anything. But I'd just driven forty miles out of my way to see this celebrated pile, so I figured I should at least take a quick peek at the exterior and maybe a brief stroll around the formal gardens. Needless to say, I was apprehended well short of my goal—and mercifully released with only a warning. Anyway, I figured Meteor Crater was a much larger target with a much smaller security detail. So it was at least worth a shot.

"Hey, Erick," I said, not too loudly, "I'm going to try to find a way around the visitor center. I'm pretty sure we can get Simba to the crater rim without anyone spotting us."

Erick just shook his head and said, "Okay, do what you have to."

So Simba and I sauntered as nonchalantly as possible around the perimeter of the parking lot. Then I glanced furtively out the front gate searching for a hidden access road or a path that might lead to the main attraction. But needless to say, Barringer Crater Enterprises didn't really want idiots like me ducking their eighteen-dollar admission fee and tramping willy-nilly over their so-called scientific research site. So there were chain-link fences and a high berm—or maybe it was just the crater rim—between the parking lot and the main attraction. And without significantly more local knowledge, it looked as if the only way Erick and I would get anywhere near the meteor crater—or even glimpse it for that matter—was by paying the posted tariff and passing through the visitor center *sans* pooch.[5] Clever, these Barringers!

That, of course, meant that Simba's walk would be limited to a fifteen-minute stroll around the big boring parking lot. And that he would live the rest of his life—however long or short that might be—without ever seeing the world's best-preserved meteor impact site. It also meant that he would be confined to the station wagon with a bowl of water, a hunk of braided rawhide for chewing purposes and an open moon roof while Erick and I ran up for a quick look at the crater. Fortunately, we were now more than a mile above sea level and it was cool enough to leave Simba in the car without fear of heat prostration.

And I have to admit that the visitor center with its huge canti-levered observation decks did afford a magnificent view of the vast crater. It also had two full floors of genuinely informative exhibits about meteors, meteorites, and meteor strikes, not only in the great Southwest but also all around the world. And to pad things out a bit, there were several exhibits about the Apollo space program—including a full-scale reproduction of the Apollo capsule—because NASA astronauts, for apparent reasons, used the crater for training purposes before they blasted off for the moon.

The visitor center's very straightforwardly named Rock Shop had a full range of excellent fossils, which I collected as a boy. So I can tell you these were really good ones. And true to its claim, Me-

---

[5] I have since emailed Brad Andes, president of Meteor Crater Enterprises and a very nice man who adores dogs. I asked him about the security setup at Meteor Crater. To make a long story short, they have remote sensing equipment that alerts a central guardhouse whenever morons like me try to encroach upon nonpublic areas of the crater. So there—you've been warned.

teor Crater itself was very well preserved with almost no evidence of the futile mining operation mounted here a century ago. Naturally, we were disappointed that we couldn't share the first entry on Erick's Wonder List with good old Simba. But fortunately, the next two stops were right up his alley.

In order to fully appreciate the second entry on Erick's Wonder List for the day, you have to be, as they euphemistically say, "of a certain age." Because if you are of that age and you ever hear anyone even casually mention Winslow, Arizona, pretty much the only thing you can think of, no matter how hard you try is, maestro please:

> I was standin' on a corner in Winslow, Arizona
> And such a fine sight to see.

Which are, of course, the first two lines of the second verse of the venerable Eagles anthem, "Take It Easy."

"Take It Easy" was the very first cut on the very first Eagles LP. So it set the tone for what would eventually become one of the best-selling musical acts of all time. It was composed back in 1971 when Eagles front man Glenn Frey lived in a modest first floor apartment in the Echo Park section of Los Angeles directly above singer-songwriter Jackson Browne, who lived in the basement. Again, if you're old enough, you might remember Jackson Browne from his 1977 hit, "Running on Empty" or maybe "Doctor My Eyes," which was a top ten tune in 1972.

So apparently Jackson Browne was sitting at his keyboard day after day trying to compose "Take It Easy." But he always got stuck right after, "and such a fine sight to see." Glenn Frey heard Browne singing the same musical phrase over and over through his floorboards. And eventually he marched downstairs and handed Browne the next few lines of the song, which are, of course:

It's a girl, my Lord, in a flatbed Ford
Slowing down to take a look at me.

Frey's contribution apparently broke the creative logjam and the two front men quickly finished the composition side by side. Then Browne graciously allowed the Eagles to record "Take It Easy" on their eponymous debut album. And the rest, as they say, is rock 'n' roll history.

Why this particular song exerts such a visceral pull on decrepit geezers like Erick and me I cannot tell you. But it does. When I was cruising through this same stretch of northern Arizona with my first wife and three young children back in 1996, I practically insisted on pulling off the interstate and rolling into Winslow just so I could stand on a corner, any corner really, and croon a few verses of "Take It Easy"—much, of course, to my children's dismay. And to this day, when I can barely remember my home phone number or what I ate for lunch, I can still recall every lyric in the song.

Winslow's town fathers decided to cash in on this generational peccadillo. And only a year after I butchered "Take It Easy" on a random Winslow, Arizona, street corner, they acquired their own random corner—West Second Street and North Kinsley Avenue—so they could build Standin' on the Corner Park. (Shouldn't it be Standin' on *a* Corner Park? Oh, well.) Funds were quickly raised, and the little pocket park was completed in less than two years. It now features a brick patio—each brick bearing the name of a donor—a life-size metal statue of a generic 1970s singer-songwriter dude in bell-bottom jeans—meant, I suppose, to be the protagonist of the song—and most prominently, a forty-foot *trompe l'oeil* mural depicting, you guessed it, "a girl, my Lord, in a flatbed Ford slowing down to take a look at me." And if you look at the mural carefully, you'll see an eagle perched on a *trompe l'oeil* windowsill—a richly deserved, though likely unauthorized, nod to the boys in the band.

But here's the really sweet part. Once upon a time, when busy Route 66 ran through the middle of town, Winslow, Arizona, was a popular stopover for bleary motorists shuttling between Chicago and LA. But when the newly constructed Interstate 40 bypassed Winslow in the late 1970s, tourist traffic slowed to a trickle and the town's economy slowly withered.

Standin' on the Corner Park changed all of that. In terms of foot traffic, Winslow isn't Grand Central Station or Disneyland or even what it was fifty years ago. But Erick and I aren't the only old fogies drawn off I-40 by nostalgic yearning. Lots of other duffers come here, too—more than two hundred a day in fact. And some of them drop a few tourist dollars in the process. So if a well-crafted song by Jackson Browne and Glenn Frey didn't restore Winslow to its full former glory, then it certainly stemmed its decline—which kind of gives you faith in the power of popular song.

Simba, of course, was entirely unfamiliar with "Take It Easy," or any of the Eagles' songbook really. But he did recognize a nice place to pee when he saw one. Out of respect for the song, we made that happen on West Second Street itself, rather than the donor bricks. And as you might guess, Erick and I took an inordinate number of cell-phone photos next to the hokey bronze statue of the jeans-clad guitar player and in front of the equally hokey mural of the girl in a flatbed Ford. And we did visit the souvenir shop just across North Kinsley Avenue. And, yes, my friends, we did stand on the now officially designated corner in Winslow, Arizona, and belted out the greater part of "Take it Easy."

And standin' on that corner, artlessly crooning the soundtrack of our youth, Erick and I were transported back to a simpler, freer time in our lives—a time before mortgages, colonoscopies, college tuition payments, alimony, Lipitor, and elderly mothers slowly dying from congestive heart failure. A time when the world was full of promise and anything seemed possible. A time, I thought, when life wasn't so goddamned complicated.

But then I reconsidered the lyrics, and I realized that this entire anthem to just takin' it easy, man, is really about a guy who—in the words of the song itself—has "a world of trouble on his mind"… and four women who want to own him… and two who want to stone him… and the sound of his own wheels driving him crazy— whatever that means.

"Take it Easy," I realized, is about a guy who's pretty stressed out, just trying to calm himself down and hoping that the love of the next pretty girl who drives by will somehow save him. Yeah, well, good luck with that, buddy.

So maybe our youth is only a simpler, freer time in retrospect—just a different set of problems that only seem less perplexing now because we eventually figured out how to solve those problems—or better yet let them go. And maybe twenty years from now, when I'm in my late seventies—if I'm lucky enough to survive that long—I'll look back on my life way back when I was fifty-nine and think, "Wow, those were the good old days—a simpler, freer time when I didn't have to visit the cardiologist every week or wear adult diapers or attend my friends' funerals."

I suppose it's a testament to the human spirit that most of us gaze back upon the serpentine course of our lives and mostly remember the good stuff. I guess that's healthy because people who dwell on old slights and missed opportunities tend to become bitter over time. Still, it probably wouldn't hurt to go one step further and appreciate our lives just as they unfold rather than only in retrospect. Nostalgia for the present! Yeah, that's the ticket! So standin' on a corner in Winslow, Arizona, I resolved to roundly enjoy the here and now—at least, that is, until one of my idiot children wrecks another car or I get a certified letter from the IRS saying they're going to audit my last three returns.

At any rate, I can't imagine how sick and tired the good citizens of Winslow must be, having to listen to aging Baby Boomers like Erick and me butcher the same great song day after day. But they'll just have to deal with it because (a) that song put Winslow back on the map and (b) singing that particular tune in that particular place was a sweet moment for a couple of old guys schlepping a dying dog across America.

Song sung, Erick and I lifted Simba back into the station wagon in the usual manner and resumed our cross-country journey with smiles on our faces and love in our hearts, as happy as Labradors—which, I presume, have a substantially less-developed sense of their own mortality, although it's difficult to know for sure.

If Standin' on the Corner Park hearkened back to an earlier era in our lives, then our next stop, fifty miles further east, evoked a much, much earlier time on planet Earth—the Triassic period of the Mesozoic era to be precise.

So for all of you non-paleontologists out there, the Triassic period was the 50-million-year-long span that immediately preceded the 56-million-year-long Jurassic period, which is familiar to nearly everyone from the wildly popular *Jurassic Park* movie franchise. Or to put it another way, it was between 200 and 250 million years ago in the age of the early dinosaurs.

Back then this stretch of land, now known as the Painted Desert, was a very different place. First of all, it was a low plain, not a mile-high desert plateau. And due to continental drift, it was much closer to the equator—near the southwest shore of Pangaea, the supercontinent that comprised nearly all of Earth's dry land before it eventually broke up into the six continents we know today.

The climate in southern Pangaea was hot and humid. In fact, the entire Earth, on average, was five-and-a-half-degrees Fahrenheit warmer than it is now—even with our justifiably alarming carbon-induced climate change. There were volcanoes to the south and an ocean to the west. And a multitude of rivers and streams flowed lazily across the loamy plains nurturing a rich variety of life.

When it rained, which it did quite often, fallen tree trunks would sometimes wash off the mountains and down into riverbeds where they sank into the primordial ooze. Most of these logs did the usual thing, rotting away over the course of a few decades. But some were so deeply buried in the muck that they were sequestered from the oxygen necessary for decomposition. These logs remained intact. And when water carrying volcanic ash seeped into the sediment, the silica and colorful metallic elements in the ash gradually replaced the organic material in the logs, molecule by molecule, until the fallen tree trunks were wondrously transformed into perfectly log-shaped masses of multicolored quartz crystal.

Some 165 million years later, tectonic forces lifted the low Triassic plain 5,400 feet above sea level. Wind and rain gradually eroded the sedimentary rock laid down in the interim. And that left what Erick, Simba, and I witnessed upon our arrival at Petrified Forest National Park—namely sandstone and siltstone hills, buttes, and mesas gorgeously banded in warm tones of red, ochre, and rust in the ineffably beautiful Painted Desert. And in this section of the

Painted Desert were thousands of fantastical petrified tree trunks strewn haphazardly across the prospect.

Needless to say, large masses of semiprecious stone scattered prolifically across an unprotected plain tend to attract fortune seekers. The first U.S. military surveyors who rode across the Painted Desert in the mid-1850s filled their saddlebags with chunks of petrified wood. And when word of the incredible crystallized logs leaked out, enterprising prospectors flocked to the Painted Desert and hauled them away by the wagonload. In the 1890s, gem collectors dynamited the petrified logs In order to loot chunks of crystal more conveniently. And in 1905, the pioneering environmentalist John Muir gravely informed President Theodore Roosevelt that pillagers were shipping railroad cars full of petrified wood "back East to make jewelry, book ends, table tops, mantel pieces, and curios." For a while, there was even talk of setting up a stone mill here that would grind petrified wood into the sort of grit used in the manufacture of sandpaper. Happily that spectacularly bad idea never gained traction.

It wasn't until 1906—when our most outdoorsy of presidents, Teddy Roosevelt, signed into law the so-called Antiquities Act—that this natural wonder was finally protected as the Petrified Forest National Monument. The national monument became a national park in 1962. And in 2004, the second President Bush more than doubled its size to 341 square miles.

But even though this is now government-protected land, there aren't that many "protection employees" here—sometimes as few as two at a time. So each year, tens of thousand of tourists take advantage of the situation. And perfectly nice folks who wouldn't dream of shoplifting a candy bar from a convenience store or pilfering lumber from a construction site seem entirely at ease grabbing pocketfuls, even the occasional trunk full, of petrified wood and taking it home. There is no way to know exactly how much of the semiprecious stone they take, but one ranger told me that approximately 5 percent of all visitors—so about thirty thousand tourists a year—pilfer at least some. And their annual haul can be measured in tons.

That's the bad news. The good news is that, even after a century and a half of gratuitous looting, there's still an awful lot of petrified wood here—millions of tons, in fact. The other reasonably good news is that remorseful pillagers actually return up to a hundred pounds of petrified wood each month—mostly by mail. Some looters are merely guilt struck. But a surprisingly large number are convinced that their petrified booty precipitated a streak of bad luck that couldn't otherwise be explained. These restituted rocks—which the rangers stack in big piles because they don't know which part of the park they came from—are often accompanied by so-called "conscience letters" that apologize for the larceny.

When Erick, Simba, and I pulled up to the Petrified Forest National Park entrance station and paid the very reasonable ten-dollar admission fee, a friendly Park Service employee handed us a brochure with a map. The map indicated that there were approximately forty miles of paved road running through the preserve, built mostly by Franklin Roosevelt's Civilian Conservation Corps during the Great Depression. And all along these roads were attractions with fairy-tale names like Jasper Forest, Agate Bridge, and Blue Mesa.

Erick and I wanted to see as much of the Petrified Forest as possible. But the brochure also mentioned that the park closed at seven. And, unfortunately, we were a little late to the party.

We had left Las Vegas at eight in the morning. And if we had driven straight through to the Petrified Forest, we would have gotten there at around two in the afternoon. But first the Arizona rainstorm slowed us down. Then we stopped at Meteor Crater and Winslow. And now it was four thirty in the afternoon, which meant that Erick, Simba, and I would have only a couple of hours to explore what promised to be Erick's premier wonder of the day. Luckily, unlike Meteor Crater, the Petrified Forest was only too happy to admit Simba. "Please take your furry friends on trails and even backpacking in the wilderness area," proclaimed the brochure. Now this was my kind of natural wonder.

I have been fortunate enough to view some pretty spectacular vistas over the course of my long life. The Grand Canyon never disappoints. South Africa's Garden Route is a wild medley of scenic surprises. And Big Sur's oceanfront escarpments define the word *dramatic*. But when Erick, Simba, and I pulled into the small parking area at Chinde Point, a few miles past the entrance station, we witnessed a spectacle we'll never forget.

When Erick and I jumped out of the car and helped Simba climb down from the back, we all gazed northward over the Painted Desert and gasped. It was cool and dry where we stood. But off in the distance cumulonimbus clouds—perfectly flat and midnight blue on the bottom, fluffy white on top—were drifting across the high-desert plateau discharging visible sheets of gray rain at a forty-five-degree angle. The landscape was sand-colored in the foreground with brown and gray-banded buttes in the middle and then shockingly beautiful pink, rose, and salmon-colored hills rolling off toward the horizon. Painted Desert, indeed! The one advantage to our last-minute arrival was that the late afternoon light lent the pink hills an otherworldly glow that would have been lost in the midday sun.

"Holy shit," I said to Erick. "This is one of the most beautiful places I've ever seen."

"Yeah, it's pretty spectacular," said Erick, who, unlike me, rarely swears. Also, unlike me, Erick had been here before. And he seemed delighted that I was as entranced with the Painted Desert as he was. Erick, Simba, and I stood at Chinde Point peering out across the vast plain for maybe ten or fifteen minutes before we climbed back into the car to see what else we might find. Since time was short, we rolled past Blue Mesa and Agate Bridge—both now added to my bucket list—so we could spend more time in Jasper Forest, which of course wasn't a forest at all, but rather a forest's worth of crystalline tree trunks strewn across the desert like enormous Pick-up Sticks.

In Jasper Forest, at five thirty in the afternoon, Simba finally got a proper walk in a setting that both delighted and bewildered him. Simba seemed to like the idea of fallen tree trunks lying all over the place. But when he stopped to sniff them, they didn't seem quite right to him. We sometimes forget to what extent dogs rely on their noses to make sense of the world. And these tree-shaped objects that looked like wood but smelled like stone obviously confused him. To Simba, they were probably like those lovely little pieces of plastic sushi you see in the front windows of Japanese restaurants—fun to look at, but a disturbing simulacrum nonetheless.

Erick offered to take a cell-phone photo of Simba and me that would turn out to be one of Simba's last portraits and certainly one of his best. In the photo, Simba and I are standing behind a massive reddish-brown petrified log laid out on the ground. The log, which closely resembles a modern-day redwood tree right down to its stone "bark," is cracked through in a few places but otherwise looks much like it did when it burbled down into the Triassic muck 200 million years ago.

I am looking straight into the camera and smiling, as happy humans do. And Simba is peering out across the landscape and smiling, as happy Labradors do. The flat-bottomed clouds are dark behind us. And they are dark above my head. But directly over Simba is a perfect little hole in the clouds—a small round patch of bright clear blue sky that looks like nothing so much as a portal to heaven.

11. IT'S A DOG'S LIFE

Erick, Simba, and I reluctantly quit the sublime Petrified Forest at six thirty in the evening. It had been a magnificent sojourn—a balm for the soul and a splendid outdoor adventure—particularly for Simba who had joyously sniffed the high-desert air, savored the sweet breeze in his face, and happily rambled around Jasper Forest—to the extent his arthritis allowed. Along with Meteor Crater and Winslow, Arizona, that made three great stopovers during our second day on the road. So kudos to Erick and his Wonder List!

But now it was time for my own modest contribution to the day's itinerary: the frontier charm of Gallup, New Mexico, and the historic El Rancho Hotel—self-proclaimed "Home of the Movie Stars." When Erick pulled the station wagon back onto I-40, I tapped Google Maps and saw we were only fifty miles from the Arizona–New Mexico border. Gallup was only twenty miles beyond that, and the summer sun wouldn't set until quarter past eight. So we'd definitely make it to Gallup before nightfall. And that was great, because I wanted to see for myself in the clear light of day just how real-life Gallup, New Mexico, stacked up to my romantic Old West vision of it.

When we pulled into Gallup fifty minutes later, I got my first good look at the place. And I could see right away that I would now have to completely rethink my happy-go-lucky policy of visiting random locales merely because I liked the sound of their names. Because in sharp contrast to elegant Spoleto, Italy; bucolic Luang Prabang; and the South Seas paradise of Bora Bora; shabby old Gallup, New Mexico, looked far worse than it sounded. Gallup's retail economy seemed to be founded largely upon its dozens of bars, taverns, and liquor stores, its many Native American craft emporia, and a shockingly large number of pawnbrokers and payday loan shops.

As it turns out, Gallup inherited its lyrical moniker from one David L. Gallup, local paymaster for the short-lived and long-defunct Atlantic and Pacific Railroad. Mr. Gallup established the railroad's regional headquarters here in 1880. And back then, whenever railroad employees wanted to collect their wages they would say, "I'm going to Gallup." When the town was officially founded in 1881, the name stuck.

These days, Gallup's population is more than 40 percent Native American. And it is surrounded on three sides by Indian reservations.[6] The Navajo Reservation, the largest Native American homeland in the United States, is located to the north and west. The smaller Zuni Pueblo is twenty-five miles south. And the Hopi

---

[6] In case you were wondering, both "Native American" and "Indian" are considered politically correct. According to "'American Indian' or 'Native American?'" by Dennis Gaffney, www.pbs.org, April 4, 2006, "A 1995 Census Bureau survey that asked indigenous Americans their preferences... found that 49 percent preferred the term *Indian* and 37 percent *Native American*."

Reservation, a separate enclave within the Navajo nation, is within easy driving distance. So Gallup is sometimes called a "border town," or more grandly, "The Indian Capital of the World."

But it wasn't that long ago that Gallup had some other less flattering nicknames. At least until the late 1980s, it was widely known as "Drunk City" or "Drunk Town, USA." That's because alcohol has been banned on the surrounding Indian reservations since the mid-nineteenth century, but it's always been legal in Gallup. So every weekend, a substantial number of Navajos, Hopis, and Zunis would jump in their pickups and drive into Gallup—often to sell handicrafts and jewelry and then, as often as not, to purchase and consume prodigious quantities of liquor, beer, and fortified wine.

The consequences were predictable. Every weekend brought flagrant displays of public intoxication. Every winter dozens of passed out Indians froze to death in the fields and ravines surrounding Gallup. And a calamitous number of fatal auto accidents occurred when drunken revelers tried to drive themselves home after a big night out. In 1985, the National Institute on Alcoholism and Alcohol Abuse made it official. When it came to heavy drinking, Gallup and surrounding McKinley County lead the nation by a large margin.

Change was a long time coming. But over the course of the 1990s and 2000s, state and local officials gradually addressed Gallup's egregious alcohol problem. They shuttered the town's bustling drunk tank and opened the Na'Nizhoozhi[7] Alcohol Treatment Center. Local law enforcement cracked down on bars and liquor stores

---

[7] Navajo for "Gallup."

that peddled their cut-rate hooch to intoxicated patrons. And they boarded up the entirely-too-convenient drive-up windows at Gallup's copious liquor outlets.

These steps mitigated the problem but didn't really solve it. McKinley County still has the highest alcoholism and cirrhosis rates in New Mexico—a state not noted for its sobriety. Winter still brings an unconscionable number of deaths from exposure. And not everyone is comfortable with a public safety system that empowers generally white "Community Service Aides" to throw generally Native American inebriates into "protective custody." But like I said, it's better than it used to be. And perhaps it was only because we rolled into town on a Tuesday night instead of a weekend, but Erick and I didn't see a single drunk careening along the nearly deserted streets of Gallup.

We did, however, see telltale signs of Gallup's other major affliction, which is, of course, poverty. Because in addition to its alcohol issues, McKinley County has the lowest per capita income in New Mexico. And in 2013, U.S. Census Bureau figures pinpointed Gallup as the second-poorest community in the entire United States.[8] So along with Gallup's ubiquitous pawnbrokers and loan shops, Erick and I couldn't help but notice a few presumably homeless guys looking for a place to bivouac and some reasonably well-dressed folks tramping along the side of the highway who probably would have been driving if they could afford a car. And, oh yeah, Gallup's violent crime rate is five times the national average. But, thankfully, Erick and I didn't experience that scourge either.

---

[8] The poorest town in the United States that year was Lumberton, North Carolina.

Of course, every town has its charms, even Gallup, New Mexico. There are nine or ten beautiful murals in the downtown area that depict local history and various Native American themes. Gallup's tastefully renovated railroad depot houses an impressive cultural center. And of course, you can buy all the decorative silver, turquoise jewelry, woven rugs, and other Indian handicrafts you'll ever need at Gallup's umpteen craft shops and "trading posts."

It's also probably worth noting that in 2013, map and atlas publisher Rand McNally tapped Gallup as "America's Most Patriotic Small Town"—although that distinction may have been largely based on historical considerations such as the brave and effective Navajo code talkers of World War II and Gallup's immensely popular Korean War Congressional Medal of Honor winner, Hiroshi "Hershey" Miyamura.

But honestly, I'm not sure why the nearly 50 percent Native American population of Gallup would feel particularly patriotic. In the mid-1860s, the commander of the Department of New Mexico, General James Henry Carleton, ordered the celebrated frontiersman Kit Carson to wage a scorched-earth campaign against the Navajo nation that effectively destroyed its food supply. Then the astoundingly racist general[9] followed that up with a series of three-hundred-mile death marches to Bosque Redondo, New Mexico, that were collectively dubbed "The Long Walk." Nearly a third of all Navajo men, women, and children perished from starvation and exposure before they were finally allowed to return to their ancestral

---

[9] Carleton's written orders to Carson included the following: "The [Navajo] men are to be slain whenever and wherever they can be found. The women and children may be taken prisoners." politicalquotes.org.

lands in 1868. So Navajos feeling patriotic toward America is sort of like Jews feeling patriotic toward Germany—although at least the Navajos put up a good fight for a while.

Okay, now that I got that off my chest, let's get back to our story. Because smack in the middle of all this alcohol-fueled, poverty-stricken, crime-ridden sadness was—ta-dah!—the El Rancho Hotel, self-proclaimed "Home of the Movie Stars." When Erick and I pulled into the El Rancho's parking lot, we didn't quite know what to make of the place. I had already phoned ahead to make sure that Simba would be welcome here. And whoever took that call made it clear that what I did with my dog was of absolutely no interest to him. So I guessed that was handled.

But the "Home of the Movie Stars" had some other puzzling aspects to it. First of all, there were eight or nine Harley Davidson motorcycles parked outside, which might or might not indicate that we would be sharing our accommodations not with old time luminaries of the silver screen but rather with a marauding band of Hell's Angels—or this being the great Southwest, maybe a Bandidos M.C. chapter roaring down the Mother Road. So that might not be good. Secondly, the building itself was a curious mash-up of half-timbered Tudor balconies, a large Georgian portico, and some lumpy Spanish colonial stonework with a bit of ivy-covered stucco thrown in. There was also an impressively large bronze eagle poised to take flight from one of the railings. And there were two somewhat redundant signs hanging over the entrance.

The larger neon sign on top read "Hotel el Rancho." The smaller sign directly beneath it read, "El Rancho Hotel." And then there was a third lit-up sign on the shoulder of Route 66 that read "Hotel & Motel El Rancho." So apparently consistent branding wasn't a corporate priority. Finally, there was another sign above the front door that sported what I took to be the hotel's auxiliary motto (after "Home of the Movie Stars.") It read "Charm of Yesterday... Convenience of Tomorrow." Now that sounded good, at least in theory. But as Erick and I yanked our suitcases out of the backseat and gently offloaded Simba, both claims seemed dubious.

But as it turned out, I was at least half wrong. Because the front doors of the El Rancho Hotel or the Hotel el Rancho or the El Rancho Hotel and Motel or whatever this place was called were, in fact, magical portals to a bygone era. For while the El Rancho's exterior had clearly evolved on an ad hoc basis, its spacious two-story lobby was a lovingly preserved vestige of the hotel's glory years. And yes, my friends, it fairly oozed the charm of yesterday.

Imagine, if you will, a cavernous two-story room with lustrous brown ceramic floor tiles covered here and there with gorgeous Navajo rugs. The white stucco ceiling is supported by dark wooden posts and hand-hewn rafters. And at the far end of the room—which manages to be both impressively large and comfortably cozy at the same time—is a hearth surrounded by pearly white tiles. On either side of the fireplace are two massive semicircular staircases constructed from gray fieldstones, split-log stair treads, and varnished handrails crafted from tree branches. The treads are covered with blood-red carpet runners that lead up to a large open gallery running along three sides of the room. The gallery's exposed brick walls are hung with six-foot-high framed black-and-white photos depicting Navajos in traditional garb. And between these larger prints are dozens of eight-by-ten publicity photos, each inscribed with a heart-felt message from one of the many glamorous movie stars who bunked at the El Rancho back in the day.

The lobby is furnished with sofas and lounge chairs sporting a wagon-wheel motif and brown-and-white cowhide seat cushions that might be considered tacky somewhere else but are right on the money here. Throw in a few mounted deer heads and some stained-glass pendant lights and you've got yourself one heck of a lobby. In fact, you can easily imagine Gary Cooper, Jane Wyman, John Wayne, and maybe Rosalind Russell lounging around this gorgeous old-school lobby languidly puffing their Lucky Strikes and sipping Rob Roys from lowball glasses. And apparently every one of those stars and quite a few others actually did that—or something very similar.

After admiring the lobby for a few minutes, Erick and I moseyed over to the check-in desk, which was manned by a short, slight, middle-aged man who looked as if he might have lived life pretty hard at some point.

"Good evening," I said, "My name is Cohen, and I reserved two rooms for this evening."

"What kinda rooms ya want?" the desk clerk asked.

Hmmm. I thought I'd settled that when I made the reservation.

"It doesn't really matter," I replied. "We're only stayin' over fer one night, so any a' yer single rooms'll do just fine."

Crap! I was unconsciously mimicking his New Mexico accent, which is a truly annoying habit of mine. Fortunately, the desk clerk didn't seem to notice. He pulled out a laminated rate card and said, "Okay, we got singles for $109. And if you got triple-A, then it's $98 plus tax."

"That's fine," I said using my everyday non-New Mexico accent. "And, yes, I do have triple-A. Do you take American Express?" (Ever since Laureen landed her new job, I have endeavored to be loyal to her employer.)

The check-in clerk ran my card and then said to Erick, "Okay, you got the Katharine Hepburn room. And you," he said turning to me, "got the Betty Hutton." Then he handed us two old-fashioned brass keys—not the plastic keycards you usually get these days.

"Does that mean Katharine Hepburn actually stayed in Erick's room?" I asked with boyish enthusiasm. I instantly knew it was a stupid question. The check-in clerk confirmed that with a sideways glance and didn't bother to respond.

"Okay, then," I continued. "Where would we find the elevator?"

"Stairs over there," he said, pointing at the massive semicircular staircases.

"Do you happen to have an elevator?" I asked. "We have these big rolling suitcases, and old Simba here has arthritis. So he has trouble with stairs." Simba, hearing his name, smiled and panted in agreement.

"Yup," he said, and without another extraneous word, he stepped out from behind the counter and led us to an ancient manually operated elevator. So much for "The Convenience of Tomorrow." The elevator slowly creaked its way up to the second floor. And when it shuddered to a stop, the desk clerk/elevator operator opened the door and pointed down a long and narrow, dimly-lit corridor with compact fluorescent bulbs, exposed water pipes, and assorted electrical wires running along its ceiling.

As Erick, Simba, and I made our way down the shadowy hallway, I squinted to read the names of the movie stars printed on little plaques mounted to each guest room door. I'm sort of a classic film buff. So most of the names—like Errol Flynn, Jean Harlow, and Joseph Cotten—were entirely familiar. A few others—like Jack Oakie and Irene Manning—were a bit more obscure. But eventually we found a door marked Katherine Hepburn where we dropped off Erick. Then Simba and I proceeded to the Betty Hutton Room.

Betty Hutton, *nee* Elizabeth June Thornburg of Battle Creek, Michigan, is probably best known for replacing a very uncooperative Judy Garland in the role of Annie Oakley in the 1950 film version of *Annie Get Your Gun*. But she also played the wonderfully zany Trudy Kockenlocker in one of my favorite films of all time, the 1944 Preston Sturges satire, *The Miracle of Morgan's Creek*. The preternaturally perky Ms. Hutton was actually Paramount Pictures' top female box-office draw for a ten-year span beginning in the early 1940s. And despite the fact that she was young, beautiful, prodigiously talented, and globally famous for a time, Betty Hutton was not one of your snooty Hollywood prima donnas—not if she was willing to stay in this room.

I do realize that I had specifically requested a bargain-rate $98 single, but the Betty Hutton Room was small, very small—so small, in fact, that when I pulled the bedspread off the double bed, folded it in four, and laid it over the well-worn carpet to make a bed for

Simba, there wasn't much left in the way of useable floor space. And the bathroom was even smaller, like something you might find on a boat or an airplane. It did have a pint-sized shower. But, by all appearances, neither the bathroom nor the room itself had been updated since... well, maybe since Betty Hutton stayed here in the 1950s.

But, honestly, none of that really mattered because (a) Simba was all about coziness when he slept—which was most of the time these days—and (b) we were only staying one night. Plus the El Rancho's fabulous lobby and nostalgic photo gallery more than compensated for any shortcomings in our room.

Before I changed for dinner, I called my dad to find out how my mother was holding up. Long story short, she wasn't holding up well.

"Did something specific happen?" I asked.

"Well, first we went to Dr. Kross's office, and he said that even with the oxygen concentrator running twenty-four hours a day, her blood oxygen level is way too low."

"Do you know why it's getting worse?" I asked.

"It's the same thing that's been happening for the last two years," he said. "Only now it's speeding up. Basically her heart has gotten to the point where it can't clear enough fluid from her lungs for the air to get it. So, in effect, she's drowning."

"Does it help to turn the oxygen up?" I asked (as if he wouldn't think of that).

"It's already up to eight," my dad replied, "and it only goes to ten. So we don't have a lot of headroom here. Also, last night she tried to get up at three a.m. to go the bathroom, and she didn't use her walker, so she fell on the floor. And normally I would have called your brother to come over and help me lift her up, but he's out of town this week, so I had to call 911. They were very nice and all, but I was kind of embarrassed that I couldn't get her back into bed on my own."

Oh Christ! I thought. This was getting much worse, much faster than I expected. But there wasn't much I could do at the moment because I was in frickin' Gallup, New Mexico.

"Well, hang in there," I said to my dad. "For what it's worth, I should be in Pittsburgh in about three days. I'm not exactly sure what I can do to help you, but I'll do whatever you want."

"You're already doing something," said my father, who always put the best possible spin on everything I had ever done in my life, even when it wasn't entirely warranted. "Your mother's very excited to see you. And I know it sounds crazy, but when she has something like that to look forward to, it really keeps her going. In fact it's all she's been talking about for the last week."

"Okay, thanks Dad," I said. "I love you."

I lay back on the bed and tried to sort out my priorities, "Okay," I thought, "Simba's slowly dying—at least I hope it's slowly—and I need to get him to New York to see Laureen and the girls as soon as possible. And my mother is slowly dying, and I need to get myself to Pittsburgh to see her as soon as possible. Simba can only take so many hours a day in the car. So we can't go much faster. I guess we just need to keep pushing forward."

I got up from the bed and squeezed into the micro-bathroom to wash my face and brush my teeth. I called Erick on his cell phone to see if he was ready for dinner. And then to avoid a replay of the whole Venetian Hotel Panic Incident, I brought Simba down to the car with me so he could sleep in the back of the station wagon while Erick and I ate.

Once we were in the car, I found a four-star restaurant on Trip-Advisor. (The local Taco Bell had been awarded five stars by the way.) I dropped the address into Google Maps. Then we set forth to find it. We followed Google's step-by-step directions to a modest residential neighborhood with no streetlights. Then we circled around in the car for a while before concluding that either Google was wrong or, more likely, that the restaurant had ceased to exist. So we admitted defeat and headed back to the El Rancho, which had its own small-but-charming restaurant just off the lobby.

Erick and I scarfed down some decent Mexican food. And, honestly, it was nice having Simba right upstairs where I could check up on him any time I wanted. It was also nice bedding down with my old buddy in such tight quarters—especially after the very unsettling conversation with my father. Thanks to Simba and his soft rhythmic snoring, I managed to sleep straight through the night entirely undisturbed by carousing Navajos, imaginary motorcycle gangs, or the restless shade of Betty Hutton, whose three estranged daughters skipped their own mother's funeral. But that's another story.

12. JUNKYARD DOG

Simba was now our virtual alarm clock, always set for dawn. So we were able to wake up, pack our bags, take the old dog for a sunrise stroll, and still decamp from the El Rancho well before the stroke of seven. Then Erick and I pulled onto Route 66 and began an earnest search for a decent cup of coffee. Less than a half mile down the road, we spotted a little, white clapboard shed with neat red trim and a black-and-white sign that read Blunt Brothers Coffee.

"What do you think?" asked Erick.

"I'm not sure we have a lot of options," I replied.

"Okay. Then let's do it."

We pulled up to the drive-in window and read the bill of fare, which was posted on a chalkboard hanging from the side of the shed. Blunt Brothers' hot beverage menu was unexpectedly comprehensive, including everything from espresso, chai tea, and organic macchiatos to a "coconut and macadamia mocha," whatever that was. Being the elitist San Francisco jerks we are, Erick and I both ordered cappuccinos—often a dubious choice in a town this small. But as I keep learning every day, you don't know what you don't know. The cheerful young guy manning the drive-in window turned out to be a master of his craft. And the two sublimely brewed beverages he tendered put Starbuck's, maybe even Peet's, to shame.

"Wow," I said after my first hot foamy sip. "This is a damn good cappuccino." Erick concurred. And with that, shabby old Gallup, New Mexico—which may have had a lot of other problems but still served a magnificent cup of joe—rose a notch in our estimation.

Amarillo, Texas, our ultimate destination that day, was another relatively short hop—only six hours and 424 miles due east. And in Erick's considered opinion, there weren't that many points of interest worth visiting on the barren New Mexico plains or the flat, nearly treeless Texas Panhandle. There were some vaguely famous ice caves about an hour east of Gallup. But ever since I was knocked for a loop by heart-pounding claustrophobia deep inside the Roman catacombs, I've generally tried to avoid caverns, caves, and other subterranean burrows. And ice caves, at least to me, seemed like the worst possible type of subterranean burrow.

Unfortunately, when I vetoed the ice caves for valid psychological reasons, that left only one other entry on Erick's Wonder List for the day, which is probably why he was so darn dramatic about it. As we drove eastward on I-40 all morning, losing three thousand feet in altitude and gaining thirty degrees in temperature, I periodically asked Erick what was on the agenda. But of course, he wouldn't tell me. He just smiled and said, "Wait for it. You'll see."

But then we drove more than 400 miles, stopping only once for gas and dog-pooping purposes, and Erick still hadn't gotten that telltale twinkle in eye.

"Hey, Erick," I finally said. "We're only ten miles from Amarillo, and we haven't seen any wonders of the day yet. What gives?"

"Be patient," he said. "We're almost there."

Another five minutes passed, and I saw an exit sign for Arnot Road coming up on the right.

"Okay," said Erick. "We're here. Take this exit. Then turn left."

After a short drive along the frontage road, we rolled to a stop behind a long line of vehicles improbably parked next to a very large cow pasture. Entire families were clambering out of their cars and squeezing sideways through a narrow gap in the livestock fence. And some of the visitors, mostly kids and teenagers, were rattling cans of spray paint as they gamboled into the field.

At first I couldn't imagine why all these people would make a pilgrimage to a nondescript Texas Panhandle cow pasture or why on Earth they would bring spray paint. But then I saw it. Two or three hundred yards from the road was a long row of ancient graffiti-covered automobiles half-buried nose first in the earth. Erick smiled broadly, proud to present yet another wacky Route 66 oddity.

Without sufficiently considering Erick's sensibilities in the matter, I quickly blurted out, "Hey, I know what this is. It's Cadillac Ranch!"

And Erick said, with a touch of dejection, "Oh, okay, so you already know about this. I thought it would be a surprise."

"No, no, Erick," I replied, "this is great. The only reason I know about Cadillac Ranch is that I had this amazing history of art teacher named Vincent Scully who talked about it in class and showed us a bunch of slides. But, honestly, I didn't remember where it was. And I've always wanted to see it. So this is actually a great surprise. Plus, look. People are bringing their dogs in there."

That seemed to make Erick feel better. So we all climbed out of the car and shimmied through a narrow cattle stile that had no Cadillac Ranch sign, no ticket taker, no posted rules or regulations of any kind, nor any other indication that the general public was in any way welcome here. But since there were already fifty or sixty art enthusiasts milling around the half-buried cars, it seemed like it would be okay to join them.

So, if like most people, you didn't take Vincent Scully's history of art class and don't live in the Texas Panhandle, here's the scoop: Cadillac Ranch consists of ten ancient Cadillacs, each from a different model year between 1949 and 1963. These vehicles are buried nose-first from the front bumper to the top of the windshield at a 51.5-degree angle—supposedly the same angle as the four sides of the Great Pyramid of Giza, but who knows if that's true. And that leaves the passenger compartments and trunks—and since they're vintage Cadillacs, tailfins of various shapes and sizes—proudly protruding into the azure Texas sky. Cadillac Ranch was created in 1974, originally in another cow pasture a few miles away. And it has somehow defied the vicissitudes of time and taste to become an enduring, if somewhat eccentric, classic.

So who would do such a thing? And why? And who would be crazy enough to pay for it? Well, like so many trippy 1970s concoctions, Cadillac Ranch was originally dreamt up in the San Francisco Bay Area. Back then Chip Lord, a recent Tulane School of Architecture graduate; Doug Michels, a Yale architecture grad; and Hudson Marquez, another Big Easy transplant with a Tulane art degree, formed what they termed "a radical art and design collective." At first the trio didn't know what to call their new enterprise. But when they told a friend they wanted to do "underground architecture," the friend, who was likely high at the time, replied, "Oh, you mean like ants?" So they dubbed their new venture Ant Farm.

One day, Marquez, the graphic artist of the group, was sitting with Chip Lord in a rustic NorCal tavern in the Marin County hills. There, Marquez found a kids' book, entitled *The Look of Cars,* sitting on the bar. As he thumbed through the book, he noticed a series of drawings that documented the rise and fall of Cadillac tail fins during the nineteen fifties and sixties. Marquez had a straight up 'Eureka' moment, and on the spot, he sketched out his idea for Cadillac Ranch.

Then, armed with Marquez's zany zeitgeisty concept, the Ant Farm guys set out to find a patron with enough cash and whimsy to purchase and half-bury ten old Cadillacs—and ideally, a spacious patch of land where they could do that. Enter eccentric former banker, local Amarillo TV mogul, and oil heir Stanley Marsh 3.

(Marsh told people—unconvincingly, I think—that he used "3" not "III," because he considered Roman numerals pretentious.)

The Ant Farm guys sent Marsh a plaintive letter requesting funds for their outré scheme. And on March 8, 1974, Marsh wrote back saying he would give them an answer on April Fools' Day, since "it's such an irrelevant and silly proposition that I want to give it all my time and attention." Marsh apparently concluded that Cadillac Ranch was just irrelevant and silly enough, because he put up the requisite cash and lent Ant Farm one of his Amarillo-area cow pastures. Upon hearing the happy news, the Ant Farm guys scoured the great state of Texas for used Cadillacs. And they very quickly—by the end of the year in fact—completed their installation.

So if you think about it, Cadillac Ranch was a pretty arbitrary, spur of the moment conceit—literally back-of-the-napkin stuff. But forty years on, it's still considered the defining artistic achievement of everyone involved. Cadillac Ranch is mentioned in the very first sentence of Stanley Marsh 3's 2014 *New York Times* obituary—prior to several other fascinating tidbits about his life, including the fact that he kept a pet lion and erected dozens of whimsical street signs around Amarillo (e.g. "Road Does Not End"). Also that he secured a coveted spot on President Richard Nixon's infamous "Enemies List" when he wrote Tricky Dick a letter offering to display one of Pat Nixon's Sunday bonnets in a proposed "Museum of Decadent Art." Cadillac Ranch is also mentioned before the far-less-amusing fact that Marsh's "reputation was badly tarnished by accusations that he had sexually abused teenage boys." Lots of teenage boys, actually, but let's stick to the art here.

When asked what Cadillac Ranch meant to him, what its significance was, Marsh replied, somewhat high-mindedly, that it was "a monument to the American dream." And then somewhat less high-mindedly that to him Cadillacs represented money, sex, and "getting away from home for the first time."

The Ant Farm trio was less forthcoming in its exegesis, preferring to let the art speak for itself. Or as Hudson Marquez very plainly put it in a 2013 LA Weekly interview, "Anybody who talks about their own art is full of shit."

Ant Farm's 1975 follow up project, "Media Burn," was significantly less subtle in its semiotics. That short-lived performance piece consisted of two guys dressed as crash-test dummies ramming a tricked-out '59 Cadillac El Dorado Biarritz through a twelve-foot-high pyramid of flaming television sets. Ant Farm mounted this "media event"—it was a new term back then—on the Fourth of July in the parking lot of the Cow Palace, a venerable San Francisco event center that had hosted the 1956 and 1964 Republican National Conventions. And they mischievously invited every television news director in Northern California to send a reporter and camera crew.

The reporters knew, of course, that they, themselves, were the butt of this high-concept joke. But they had to cover it anyway because an enormous white Caddie plowing through a pyramid of flaming televisions is practically the definition of must-see TV. Even Nudie Cohn, the Ukrainian shlockmeister who tricked out Buck Owens' wall-mounted Grande Ville back in Bakersfield, never did anything that flamboyant with a Cadillac.

When Erick, Simba, and I finally made our way out to the ninety-foot-long row of half-buried cars, we could see that they were slowly rusting away and that every square inch of every vehicle was covered in graffiti. Visitors aren't normally encouraged to deface semifamous monumental sculptures. I'm sure Christo or Richard Serra wouldn't appreciate it. But given their distinctly antiestablishment bent, I feel certain the Ant Farm guys wouldn't object. Chip Lord did have all ten Cadillacs repainted matte black when his old friend and partner Doug Michels died in a hiking accident in 2003. But then he let them revert to their natural graffiti-covered state.

Out in the middle of a Texas cow pasture, our fellow art lovers were not only vandalizing the rusty old Caddies, they were also clambering all over them with little regard for their fragile condition. So while this droll monument to the futility of the American Dream or the freedom of the open road or maybe just absurdity for absurdity's sake had survived forty years, it didn't look as if it would last forty more. So Erick and I memorialized this moment in art history with a raft of cell-phone photos that all featured our old buddy Simba lying in the dusty foreground. And for the first time since we left Tiburon, Simba had the opportunity to meet and greet fellow dogs from the Lone Star State and all around this great nation, and to ceremoniously sniff their butts in the shadow of arguably important art.

After an hour or so, we all climbed back into the station wagon. And with a little help from the TripAdvisor app, we were lucky enough to find Tyler's, a terrific little barbecue joint on the outskirts of Amarillo. Happily, Tyler's had two outdoor picnic tables, so Simba was able to join our luncheon. And over heaping plates of top-notch ribs and brisket, Erick and I decided to push past Amarillo and drive another four hours to Oklahoma City, where Simba would suffer his first major health setback of the journey.

13. PRAIRIE DOG

Erick, Oklahoma
Still August 19, 2014
1,751 miles to go

About halfway between Amarillo and Oklahoma City, about ten miles over the Texas–Oklahoma border, Erick wanted to pull off the interstate again, so he could make a childhood dream come true. Apparently, when Erick was a lad of seven or eight, back in Norfolk, Virginia, he kept an atlas in his room. And from that atlas, he learned that there was only one municipality, large or small, in the entire U.S. of A. named Erick with a *k*.[10] And that municipality, my friends, was Erick, Oklahoma, pop. 1,052. And guess what? Despite the fact that Erick had lived in six or seven different states over the course of his life—and at one point or another, had visited nearly all the others—he never quite made it to Erick, Oklahoma. And he had always wanted to see it. So now, in his sixty-third year, he would finally get that opportunity.

[10] On the United States Board on Geographic Names website (http://geonames.usgs.gov) I found a tiny hamlet in Wheeler County, Georgia, that is also named Erick. It even has an Erick Road and an Erick Church—but please don't tell our Erick about it, because first of all, it would take the blush off Erick, Oklahoma, and secondly, I have no strong desire to visit Wheeler County, Georgia.

So we pulled off I-40 again at the North Sheb Wooley Avenue exit. And lo and behold, the very first thing we saw was pretty much the best thing we could have seen—at least for Erick's purposes. It was a big billboard set low to the ground. And it featured an energetic illustration of a cherry-red 1957 Chevy roaring out of a sunset—or maybe a sunrise—its headlights blazing and some retro Route 66-style type that read, "Welcome to Erick, Oklahoma." It looked like a giant postcard, and it was the perfect backdrop for a photo op. So out came the cell phones.

First I shot Erick, arms akimbo, in front of the Erick sign, then Erick and Simba in front of the Erick sign from a low angle, then Erick giving the thumbs up in front of the Erick sign, then Erick crossing his arms and leaning back in front of the Erick sign—click, click, and done. Then we hopped back into the station wagon and drove a mile or so south on Sheb Wooley Avenue toward Erick, Oklahoma's tiny business district to see how things were going there. And to me, at least, it didn't look as if things were going all that well.

Like Winslow, Arizona, the hamlet of Erick, Oklahoma, sits astride the old Route 66. Also like Winslow, it has legitimate musical roots—probably more legit than Winslow. Because while tiny Erick, Oklahoma, isn't mentioned in any classic rock lyrics I know of, it is the childhood home of the prodigiously talented country-western songsmith, the "King of the Road" himself, Roger Miller. A consummate entertainer, Miller snagged six Grammies on a single, luminous night back in 1966—still the biggest sweep ever for a country-western artist. Then, two decades later, he won a Tony award for scoring the folksy Broadway smash *Big River*, a toe-tapping musical version of *Huckleberry Finn*.

Miller, a lifelong smoker, died from lung and throat cancer at age fifty-six. And these days, Erick honors its favorite son with a homey little Roger Miller Museum at the corner of Roger Miller Boulevard and Sheb Wooley Avenue. Erick also hosts a Roger Miller Festival every October. The festival features three or four concerts, a "King of the Road Classic Car Contest," that apparently pits Oklahoma against Texas, a Little-Miss-type beauty pageant, and in more recent years, a wild hog hunt.

And if that weren't enough celebrity cred for one tiny dot on the map, Erick is also the birthplace of actor-singer-songwriter Sheb Wooley—hence, Sheb Wooley Avenue. I know that right now you're probably asking yourself, "Who the hell is Sheb Wooley?" And honestly, I didn't remember myself until Erick reminded me that he played Pete Nolan opposite Clint Eastwood's Rowdy Yates on the classic 1960s TV series *Rawhide*. And perhaps more importantly, he topped the charts in 1958 with his ubiquitous novelty hit, "The Purple People Eater," which pretty much everyone has heard at some point in their lives. (Oh, come on, you remember: "It was a one-eyed, one-horned, flying purple people eater.") "The Purple People Eater," is either a canny allegory about the vagaries of rock 'n' roll stardom or just an incredibly stupid song. But either way, it's pretty darn catchy. Plus Sheb Wooley taught Roger Miller, his wife's young cousin, how to strum a gee-tar in the first place, so he deserves some credit for that.

But like I said, Erick, Oklahoma, didn't look as if it was particularly thriving in the post-Route-66 era. There seemed to be a few empty storefronts and a couple of marginal enterprises like second-hand stores that tend to pop up when rents drop sufficiently. And, of course, there wasn't much in the way of foot traffic—or really any traffic for that matter.

But looks can be deceiving, particularly to a big-city slicker like me, because I later learned that in 2014, Erick, Oklahoma, boasted an unemployment rate of 2.2 percent, which is pretty much no unemployment at all. And according to a website called "Sperling's Best Places," which apparently tracks such things, Erick's median home price is a spectacularly affordable $64,200, which, if you live in San Francisco or New York, seems practically incredible.

So if you've ever thought about making your home, home on the range, you might want to take a hard look at Erick, Oklahoma, where you can live pretty well very cheaply. And you can definitely get a job there. And every October, you can take in the Roger Miller Festival, show off your classic car, and chow down on some wild hog, which, if you've never had the pleasure, is like the tastiest *treif*[11] ever.

But for the time being at least, I was personally committed to wildly overcrowded, wildly overpriced, wild-hog-free Manhattan. And, unfortunately for Erick and me, the Roger Miller Museum was closed on Tuesdays. So we made a U-turn on Sheb Wooley Avenue and bid Erick, Oklahoma, a fond farewell. And with Erick's fifty-five-year-old dream finally realized, we hopped back onto I-40 and headed east toward Oklahoma City.

---

[11] Yiddish for nonkosher food.

I had been to Oklahoma City only once before—in 1995—and that was under difficult circumstances. Two months prior to my visit—on April 19, 1995, at 9:02 a.m. to be precise—a disgruntled First Gulf War veteran, Special Forces washout, and right-wing sociopath named Timothy McVeigh exacted his revenge on the federal government by bombing the Alfred P. Murrah Federal Building in downtown Oklahoma City. Twenty-six-year-old McVeigh rented a yellow Ryder truck, packed it with nearly three tons of ammonium nitrate fertilizer, nitro-methane fuel, and 500 blasting caps. Then he parked it in front of the Murrah Building, lit a two-minute fuse, popped in his earplugs, and walked away.

The massive explosion ripped the entire north wall off the nine-story federal building, damaged or destroyed 347 other downtown structures, and killed 168 innocent people, including nineteen babies and toddlers just starting their day at the America's Kids Day Care Center on the Murrah building's second floor. McVeigh, who apparently learned some self-serving jargon in the military, later characterized the dead babies and toddlers as "collateral damage," so not worthy of his remorse.

So what exactly was Timothy McVeigh avenging? And why did he target the Murrah building on April 19?

Well, McVeigh, who claims to have been bullied as a child, became convinced over time that the federal government was "the ultimate bully." And as proof of that conviction, he pointed to a disastrous 1993 raid mounted by the Bureau of Alcohol, Tobacco and Firearms in concert with the FBI and, eventually, several other federal and state agencies. What's now called "the Waco Siege" or "the Branch Davidian Massacre," began as a fairly straightforward incursion designed to confiscate a cache of weapons hoarded by an end-of-days religious sect called the Branch Davidians. But when the ATF breached the sect's Mount Carmel compound, the Davidians opened fire, slaying four agents and wounding sixteen others. The agents shot back killing six cult members before they ran low on ammo and retreated.

Then, what was supposed to be a quick in-and-out sortie devolved into a fifty-day nationally televised siege. On the fifty first day, April 19, 1993, the feds finally lost patience with cult leader David Koresh. And with the reluctant blessing of Bill Clinton's rookie attorney general, Janet Reno, they massed more than 800 law enforcement personnel for a final showdown —a scenario that played right into the Davidians' apocalyptic worldview.

Armed with nine Bradley Fighting Vehicles and five M728 Combat Engineering Vehicles—basically Patton Battle Tanks with bulldozer blades and booms—the feds pierced several buildings in the compound and filled them with tear gas. Then, when the Branch Davidian men, women, and children didn't stream out as expected, they mounted a massive frontal assault.

A fire started—almost certainly set by the Davidians—and it quickly became an inferno. Four hours later, the compound was more or less leveled, and seventy-five more cult members, including nineteen children under the age of six, lay dead in the ashes. Although exactly who killed them—the feds, the Branch Davidians, or both—still remains a matter of controversy.

By nearly anyone's reckoning, the ATF and FBI botched the Waco raid with horrific results. But for the militant antigovernment crowd, the incident had deeper meaning. Along with another bungled raid in Idaho called the Ruby Ridge Incident, the Branch Davidian Massacre confirmed their worst fears. Namely, that the Second Amendment was under federal attack and the century-old doctrine of *posse comitatus*—which prohibits the federal government from using the army against its own citizens—was now a thing of the past.[12] Not one to abide that sort of tyranny, Timothy McVeigh "decided to send a message to a government that was becoming increasingly hostile."

McVeigh got the specific idea to bomb a federal building housing law enforcement agencies from a wildly anti-Semitic, virulently racist novel called *The Turner Diaries*. A perennial bestseller in white supremacist circles from sea to shining sea, *The Turner Diaries* was penned under the pseudonym Andrew Macdonald in 1978. But lurking behind that nom de plume was one William Luther Pierce, III, a former Oregon State physics professor and grand poobah of a now blessedly defunct neo-Nazi network called the National Alliance. Dr. Pierce's lurid race-war fantasy breathlessly imagines America—and eventually the world—as a white Protestant utopia where all the cunning Jews get their just desserts, "inferior races" such

---

[12] The Posse Comitatus Act of 1878—updated in 1956 and 1981—prohibits the federal government from deploying either the Army or the Air Force (which was once part of the Army) domestically. The Navy and Marines are not bound by posse comitatus, but have parallel internal regulations. The National Guard, on the other hand, acts under the authority of individual states and is often used in domestic conflicts.

as "black cannibals" and "repulsive mongrel Puerto Ricans" are either massacred or deported, and every man, woman, and child in sub-Saharan Africa is annihilated—to name just a few of the more loathsome plot points.

But one section of *The Turner Diaries* particularly spoke to young Timothy McVeigh. After the Jewish-controlled U.S. Congress passes the insidious Cohen Act (hey!), federal agents and their black radical henchmen fan out across America in an effort to seize all privately owned firearms—like the ATF did in Waco. And in response, the novel's protagonist, Earl Turner, sparks a glorious white-folks revolt by blasting FBI headquarters in Washington with—you guessed it—three tons of ammonium nitrate fertilizer packed into a truck.

So basically, Timothy McVeigh took a page from *The Turner Diaries*—the part where Turner and his band of not-so-merry men build and detonate their truck bomb. And on the second anniversary of the Branch Davidian Massacre, he emulated his fictional hero right down to the type, size, and delivery method of the explosive.

In this case, "take a page" is not a figure of speech. When Charlie Hanger, an on-the-ball Oklahoma state trooper, pulled over McVeigh's yellow Mercury sedan less than two hours after the blast, he spotted a manila envelope on the front seat. And inside that envelope were seven photocopied pages from *The Turner Diaries*, which McVeigh employed both as a how-to manual and a message.

Timothy McVeigh died what he hoped would be a martyr's death at the Federal Correctional Complex in Terre Haute, Indiana, on June 11, 2001—the first federal execution in nearly four decades.

Since his vile act had failed to incite a *Turner Diaries*-type white people uprising, McVeigh wanted his execution to be nationally televised thinking that might do the trick. But the federal court would approve only a closed-circuit feed to the victims' families. And that wasn't what you'd call a sympathetic audience.

At the time, the Oklahoma City bombing was the deadliest act of terrorism committed on U.S. soil. But McVeigh's grisly record wouldn't stand for long. Three months to the day after McVeigh's execution, the grim Saudi barbarian Osama bin Laden significantly upped the ante.

But what does all that have to do with my 1995 visit to Oklahoma City? Well, like most people, I was repulsed to the core by both the carnage and its inspiration. And I wanted to do something to help. So since my occupation was creating photo books, I decided to publish a slim volume that documented the heinous event and donate the proceeds to a scholarship fund set up for the 219 children who lost one or both of their parents in the blast. I did something similar to benefit migrant farm workers who lost their housing in the 1989 San Francisco earthquake so I knew it would work.

With so-called "instant books" or "disaster books"—that's what publishers call them—the key to success is getting the product onto bookstore shelves as quickly as possible. Basically, you have a week or so to gather and edit the photos, design the book, and write the captions, then another week to get the book printed and ten days to distribute it. Not long after that, the gruesome event fades in the public mind and sales dry up. So if I wanted to raise as much money as possible for the scholarship fund, I had to get the book out quickly. And as a result, I spent fifteen or sixteen hours a day for six days straight poring over thousands of grisly slides with a magnifying loupe—this was pre-digital—trying to make sure the pictures we used were well-framed, well-composed, and sharply focused.

There is, of course, a world of difference between experiencing a large-scale disaster firsthand and perusing photos of that disaster a few days later. I know, because I've done both. But up to that point in my career, nearly all my books had been lighthearted celebrations of everyday life as it's lived in various countries around the world. So I wasn't mentally prepared to examine thousand of photos of bloody corpses, the dazed faces of devastated family members, exhausted soot-caked first responders, and, worst of all, the slaughtered babies and children.

And traveling to Oklahoma City to launch the book several weeks later brought all of those disturbing images to life. First of all, I arrived in the middle of that crazy lightening storm with 110-mile-per-hour winds that I described to Erick back in Arizona. Then I was privileged to meet some of the heroic first responders and incredibly decent people of Oklahoma City who lost family and friends in the blast. Those encounters took all of those thousands of photos I edited right out of the sphere of dispassionate photojournalism into a far more personal realm.

So the upshot was this: as we drove across the prairie from tiny Erick, Oklahoma, to Oklahoma City on a sunny Tuesday afternoon, I thought it would be a great idea to visit the Oklahoma City National Memorial, which opened its doors five years after my little book was published. And since much of the memorial is outdoors, I hoped Simba might be able to accompany us. But when we actually reached OKC and I began to recognize some of the landmarks I had seen in the photos, the stomach-churning revulsion I felt back in 1995 resurfaced. And I decided to put off the visit, at least for the time being. So I told Erick I was sorry, but I didn't want to see the memorial quite yet—and I do realize that "quite yet" in this case was two full decades after the event.

But, hey, don't get me wrong. By all accounts the Oklahoma City National Memorial is one of the most beautiful, dignified, and tasteful monuments on Earth. It has a graceful block-long reflecting pool bounded at both ends by thirty-foot-high rectangular bronze arches called "the Gates of Time." One arch is inscribed "9:01," the minute before the blast; the other, "9:03," the minute after. And it is a refined and thoughtful representation of the tragedy. And next to the reflecting pool are 168 oversized empty chairs—one for each victim. There is also a lone elm, called "the Survivor Tree," that miraculously withstood the blast and then surprised everyone by sprouting hopeful green buds the following spring. And everyone says that the on-site museum is both informative and moving. But I'm telling you all of this as someone who hasn't seen any of these things. I've only seen them the same way I saw the incident itself— through photographs and videos.

So even though I knew I should visit the Oklahoma City National Memorial, I didn't. And honestly, I felt guilty about that. But it is a measure of Erick's discretion as a stand-up guy on a road trip that when I said I didn't want to go and didn't offer any explanation, he didn't try to discuss it with me or even ask why. He just shrugged and said, "Okay. If that's what you want." And that reminded me what a discerning friend he was.

Huzzah! The dog in the hotel problem has been solved! After making ten freakin' phone calls to find one lousy place in Las Vegas that would admit Simba as a guest, then more or less lucking out at the loosey-goosey El Rancho, I finally stumbled upon a nationwide chain of relatively inexpensive hotels that seemed to welcome canine companions—regardless of weight—at most of its two-thousand-plus locations (or at least the ones we needed.) So, thank you, Hampton Inns by Hilton. And thank you Hampton Inn & Suites Oklahoma City-Bricktown.

After pulling up in front of the hotel, Erick and I took Simba for a brief stroll. Then we checked into our rooms. And since Simba had successfully braved two consecutive dinners, more or less solo, I figured it would probably be okay to let him veg out in front of *Wheel of Fortune* while Erick and I ventured out to find some dinner.

I bid Simba adieu while he was still crunching his kibble. Then Erick and I took off on foot down East Sheridan Avenue. When we hit North Mickey Mantle Drive—the Yankees slugger was a proud

Sooner—we happened upon Nonna's Euro-American Ristorante and Bar, which looked as if it might be a pretty good place to eat. And it was. Erick and I enjoyed an Italian-themed repast and left a generous tip for the young single mom who, entirely at our prompting, recounted most of her life story as she served us dinner.

We returned to the Hampton Inn only an hour and a half after we left. But that turned out to be too long. And it also turned out that all of those ridiculous rituals I performed with Simba before I took off for dinner in Las Vegas weren't that ridiculous after all. Because when I didn't watch over Simba as he ate his dinner... and I didn't lie down next to him and babble baby talk at him... and I didn't stroke his giant furry head until he fell asleep and started snoring... and I didn't sneak out of the room so he didn't realize I was gone, Simba panicked and let loose at both ends. And he repaid the Hampton Inn's hospitality with a small pile of dog vomit and a somewhat larger pool of urine that had soaked into the carpet. What's more, Simba didn't really look that good. He wasn't smiling like he usually did, and his panting was more pronounced.

When I saw—or more accurately, smelled—what happened, I sat on the floor and held Simba in my arms for a while, stroking his neck until he fell asleep. Then I set to work with two wet washcloths, two bath towels, a little bar of soap, and a tiny bottle of shampoo trying to clean up the mess he made.

The next morning Simba failed to rouse me at five like he had the previous two mornings. So when I got up on my own at seven, I had to gently shake him awake. And again, he looked subdued. At first I thought I might be overreacting. After all, he had only peed on the rug and thrown up a little from separation anxiety—so maybe it wasn't the end of the world. And he might be melancholy now because he was still embarrassed over the previous evening's faux pas. But then when I poured his breakfast, Simba just looked at it and shuffled away like he did when he first contracted his snout infection. And that, I figured, was a very bad sign.

My first instinct was to call Laureen in New York so I could share my anxiety and solicit her advice. But then I remembered how much pressure she was enduring in her new job. So I decided not to make things worse. I mean, I called Laureen anyway, but when I spoke to her, I told her that everything was fine. And that Erick and I were having a great time on the road and that we were actually slightly ahead of schedule. And when she asked how Simba was doing, I only vaguely alluded to his condition, saying, "Well, he does seem a little tired."

"That makes sense," Laureen replied. "It's probably hard for him being stuck in the back of the station wagon all day."

"Yeah, that's probably it," I said. Then I deftly steered the conversation away from Simba by asking her about her new job—a tactic that always works. Fifteen minutes later, I closed the conversation by saying, "So in terms of distance, we're now more than halfway to New York. So if all goes well, we should be rolling into town right on schedule—maybe even a day early if we don't spend two nights in Pittsburgh."

"Can't wait," said Laureen. "I love you."

I told Laureen that I loved her, too, and that I missed her, which I did. And after I hung up, I didn't feel particularly guilty about withholding bad news from her because it was basically for her own good. And besides, I could always fill her in later—when Simba felt better and she wouldn't have to fret. I was much more straightforward with Erick, who was integral to the mission. After we climbed back into the station wagon, I told him about Simba's accident and how he wouldn't eat breakfast, and I asked him what he thought we should do.

"Whatever you think is best," said Erick "But to me this seems like a wait-and-see situation. Maybe Simba really is sick. Or maybe he just got lonely while we were out for dinner. That's happened before, right?"

I nodded and said, "Yeah, sometimes it happens when we go up to Tahoe."

"So why don't we just drive to Little Rock today as originally planned. And if Simba seems okay when we get there, we can check out the Clinton Library. Then we can spend the night in Memphis, and take a two-hour Graceland tour tomorrow morning. After that, we'll head straight to Pittsburgh."

"The only problem with that," I replied, "is that I don't think we should leave Simba alone anymore. Not even for a few hours. And I'm pretty sure they're not going to let him inside the Clinton Library. And he definitely won't be able to traipse around Graceland."

Then Erick got that telltale twinkle in his eye again, and I thought, "Really? What could he possibly have up his sleeve that would address *this* problem?"

"So I was poking around the internet last night," Erick said. "And I found a place called the Raines Road Animal Hospital in

Memphis. They take care of dogs while their owners visit Graceland. And you don't have to feel guilty about leaving Simba there because, hey, it's a vet's office. And that's probably the best place for him right now."

"Thanks, Erick. That's a great solution," I said. "I should probably call them now and make an appointment. And they can check Simba out and see if there's anything seriously wrong with him—I mean, aside from all the stuff we already know about.

"By the way," I asked, "how much does it cost?" I figured Graceland was a popular tourist destination, so I'd be paying top dollar.

"That's the best part," said Erick. "It's only ten bucks."

"So maybe three hours at ten bucks an hour plus the check-up will come to what? A $100 . . . $125. That's not too bad."

"No," said Erick. "It's ten bucks for the entire day."

That seemed beyond fair. So while Erick drove toward Little Rock, Arkansas, I booked an appointment for Simba at Raines Road Animal Hospital, which was less than a mile up Elvis Presley Boulevard from Graceland.

When we got to Little Rock, it was hot—Bakersfield hot—maybe ninety-five degrees, maybe a hundred, but with a lot more humidity. Basically, it was a sauna. So when we pulled into the big parking lot outside the Clinton Presidential Center at one thirty in the afternoon, Erick and I knew we had to somehow bust Simba into its big air-conditioned lobby.

The massive cantilevered glass-and-steel structure that housed the Clinton Library looked sort of like an alien spaceship that had inadvertently landed in a small southern town. (I know it's supposed to look like a bridge, but I'm going to go with spaceship here.) And as we walked toward the spaceship's front hatch, I mentally rehearsed my arguments for letting Simba inside. "He's old. He's sick. Don't worry. He'll just lie quietly on the floor. Believe me: he won't cause any trouble. Hey, he's a Democrat." Y'know, that sort of thing.

And to my great surprise, when we attempted to board the spaceship with Simba in tow, my charming line of crap actually seemed to work. The kindhearted older lady who was guarding the front door was just about to let Simba and me sit on a bench in a remote corner of the lobby when a stocky fellow in a blue blazer—or maybe it was gray, I don't remember—strode over, wagging his finger, and he laid down the law, the big jerk. And the law, simply put, was: No dogs allowed. So first I sat on a bench in a shady spot outside the front door with Simba and his water bowl while Erick toured the spaceship. Then Erick stayed with Simba while I went inside.

The Clinton Presidential Center was much larger and far slicker than I expected. I guess the Clintons have never really had much trouble raising money. But in terms of content, there were no major surprises. In 2012, I put together a book called *The Clintons: Their Story in Photographs* for Barnes & Noble's in-house publisher, Sterling. And the Clinton Presidential Center was kind enough to provide a few dozen images that appear in the book. So I was grateful for that. And while I was producing the book, I spent three or four months researching the Clintons' life and times. So I had a reasonably good frame of reference for the many interesting exhibits I saw inside the spaceship. And honestly, it was fun peering into the world's only full-size replica of the Oval Office and then walking around a reproduction of Clinton's cabinet room.

But I didn't want to leave Erick and Simba steaming outside in the Arkansas sauna too long. So I practically ran from exhibit to exhibit. I only glanced, for example, at the six or seven saxophones world leaders bestowed upon our forty-second president. And I spent a mere five or six minutes scanning the very long, lavishly illustrated timeline of the Clinton presidency that ran the length of the spaceship and was cast, as you might imagine, in the best possible light.

After about twenty minutes, I disembarked from the spaceship with the same general feeling about the Clintons with which I entered it. That is, that the Clintons are a remarkable larger-than-life combination of mostly good intentions and truly remarkable achievements—all richly chronicled in the presidential center—along with a whole mess of vaguely shady stuff—not nearly as well chronicled in the presidential center—constantly bubbling beneath the surface.

And every so often the shady stuff—Gennifer Flowers (1992), Travelgate (1993), Vince Foster (1993), Whitewater (1994), the missing Rose Law Firm billing records (1996), Paula Jones (1997), Monica Lewinsky (1997–1998), the Marc Rich pardon (1999), and in more recent years, fishy contributions to the Clinton Foundation and Hillary's secret email account—every so often some of that shady stuff percolates out of the muck and trips the Clintons up for a while. But then—Alakazam!—every single time (at least thus far) the Clintons manage to stand up, brush themselves off, and move forward with aplomb. Then they achieve even more remarkable things.

And believe me, if you put all of the shady stuff off to one side, Bill Clinton's eight years in the White House constitute a glorious cavalcade of remarkable achievement—economic expansion, reduced unemployment, sharply reduced crime rates, welfare reform, curtailed government spending, and the biggest budget surplus in American history—to name just a few of the biggies. And to those of you who say that President Clinton doesn't deserve credit for all of that—that it was just an historical anomaly—let me remind you that if all of those things had gone south instead, you would have been the first to cast blame.

Actually, the story of the Clintons is sort of like a Greek tragedy that almost, but never quite, reaches its *catastrophe*—and I use that word in its formal sense to mean the inevitable bad ending of all Greek tragedies. I'm probably not the first person to draw this analogy, but consider the following: our protagonists, Bill and Hillary Clinton, are bold and basically decent folks with conspicuous flaws. (Big flaws are a necessary prerequisite for tragic heroes.) And, of course, they have more than their fair share of the requisite *hubris*. They make giant hubristic blunders— called *hamartia* in Greek tragedy. Then, shrilly rebuked by a chorus of braying conservatives, they are forced to confront the error of their ways as their world crumbles around them.

But that's just it. Time and again, over the course of decades, the Clintons are felled by the assorted *hamartias* that arise from their tragic flaws—lust, arrogance, carelessness, whatever. But their world simply refuses to crumble around them—like it's supposed to in a Greek tragedy. Sometimes it comes close—like Bill's impeachment trial or the Gennifer Flowers affair that nearly derailed his first presidential campaign. But in the end, there's never a full-blown *catastrophe*—just a series of incipient and not-so-incipient public embarrassments followed in quick succession by canny maneuvers, narrow escapes, and legalistically parsed words. ("It depends upon what the meaning of the word *is* is.") So the audience—we, the American people—never experience the cleansing *catharsis* that is, after all, the whole damn point of Greek tragedy. And the Clintons, bespattered but unbowed, stride forward once more, making their mark on America and the world—not always, but quite often, for the better.

I'm pretty sure this is not the intended effect of the Clinton Presidential Spaceship. And please don't get me wrong. I respect the Clintons, admire their moxie, and appreciate their generally good intentions. But the whole Greek tragedy thing—that's kind of how I felt before I boarded the spaceship. And that's how I felt when I disembarked. And, besides, they really should have let Simba in out of the hot Arkansas sun because, damn it, that would have been the decent thing to do. I'm talking to you, you big heartless jerk in the blue or possibly gray blazer.

I have a confession to make. I'm a smug New York-slash-San Francisco jackass. And as such, I fully intended to visit Graceland "ironically," as the equally smug Brooklyn-slash-Mission hipsters say. Before I ever set foot in Graceland, I thought I knew all about it. I knew, for example, that Graceland had a ridiculous "Jungle Room," with an appalling green shag rug and a bunch of ersatz tiki nonsense. I knew there was a big gaudy car collection at Graceland, including the famous pink Cadillac that Elvis bought for his mother despite the fact she couldn't drive. And I knew that many of Elvis's weirdly bedazzled jumpsuits from his glitzy Vegas years[13] were on display in Graceland's former racquetball court—along with like a zillion gold and platinum records. So, bottom line, I expected to tour Elvis Presley's tacky mansion and its garish grounds all the while sniggering at the tasteless Tupelo hillbilly who may have been the King of Rock 'n' Roll but, let's face it, had a lot more money than taste.

And, boy, did I get my comeuppance. Because Graceland was… well, Graceland was deeply moving, actually.

Once we designated Hampton Inns as the official hotel provider for the 2014 Simba Cross-Country Death Race, I noticed they were pretty much everywhere. In fact, there were no fewer than twelve Hampton Inns in the greater Memphis area alone. So we picked one that was relatively close to Graceland and spent the night there.

---

[13] Yes, some of Elvis's suits, most notably a $10,000 gold lamé number, were tailored by old Nudie Cohn.

Simba ate most of his dinner and seemed to be rallying across the board. So that was a relief. And the next morning, we drove him to Raines Road Animal Hospital, a small veterinary clinic with a sweet middle-aged Southern lady behind the check-in counter.

After she greeted us warmly, I told her that Simba was nearly fourteen years old and had a paralyzed larynx, that he had been sick to his stomach the night before last, and that his illness was due either to separation anxiety or something much worse, perhaps a recurrence of his snout infection. Finally, I told her that even though Simba seemed to be feeling better now, I was still concerned. So could they please give him a good looking over while Erick and I toured Graceland?

"Don't worry," she said. "We'll take real good care of Simba."

And I have to say that everything about the place suggested they would. A nice young nurse emerged from the back room, knelt beside Simba, and graciously introduced herself. Then she snapped a leash onto his collar and led him away. And Simba, who never really minded going to the vet, was delighted to accompany her.

Erick and I jumped back in the car, drove down Elvis Presley Boulevard, and turned left into the massive parking lot behind the visitor center. We decided not to shell out $77 apiece for the Graceland Elvis Entourage VIP Tour, which would have let us jump the line at the mansion. But we did buy the $45 "Platinum + Airplanes Tour" so we could visit not only the mansion itself, but also Elvis's car collection and both of his jets—the airliner-sized *Lisa Marie* and the *Hound Dog II*, a smaller executive jet that was apparently the King's backup ride.

Oddly, we had to take a small bus from one side of Elvis Presley Boulevard, where the visitor center was, to the other side, where the mansion was. And when we pulled up in front of Graceland—the second-most-visited home in America after the White House—I was surprised to find a relatively staid and tasteful Classical Revival house. Graceland was large but not massive. It was the sort of mansion you might find in an old-money southern suburb. At first I was a bit disappointed because I was expecting a lot more flash. But then I remembered that Elvis didn't actually build this house. He bought it from a local doctor when he first hit the jackpot. "Just wait until we get inside," I thought, "Then we'll see some real hillbilly chic."

But when we did get inside, the entrance hall with its grand staircase and chandelier, its white-on-white living room with stained glass peacock windows, and its formal dining room with gold-trimmed royal blue curtains and elaborate silver and china collections were all quite lovely actually. Sure, there were a few unconventional touches—like, yes, the green shag carpet in the Jungle Room and the multicolored fabric concoction that shrouded the walls and ceiling of the billiards room. And, yes, it was all a bit heavy on the gilt for my particular taste. But first of all, Elvis moved into this posh crib with his parents in 1957 when he was only twenty-two years old. And secondly, he lived there during the course of two decades—the sixties and seventies—that weren't characterized by restrained elegance, particularly where rock stars were concerned. And finally, if you took all the rooms in Graceland and considered them together with the surprisingly comprehensive memorabilia collection laid out in the adjacent "Trophy Building," they told a beautiful only-in-America story about a young man who turned out to be—in composer-conductor Leonard Bernstein's words—"the greatest cultural force in the twentieth century" and, all things considered (and there is much to consider), a remarkably sympathetic character.

Graceland told the story of a poor kid born in a two-room shotgun shack in rural northeast Mississippi. A kid whose twin brother was stillborn and whose dad, Vernon, couldn't hold a job, so the family was always on what used to be called "relief." It told the story of a kid who moved to a public housing project in Memphis when he was thirteen and who wanted to sing so badly that he hung out all day on Beale Street window shopping at Lansky's where all the country music stars bought their elaborately spangled costumes. (Okay, now I get the jumpsuits.)

But the kid couldn't afford fancy costumes. In fact, he couldn't even afford a guitar. And even if he could, he was painfully shy. And pretty much everyone who was supposed to know about such things told him he was a lousy singer. Heck, he even failed his high school music class.

But after years of hard work—driving a truck while he sang on the side—the kid became globally famous. And when he did, he sold millions of records and made zillions of dollars, and teenage girls fainted just at the sight of him. And some called him the King. But others called him the devil. And gangs of teenage boys would try to beat him up after his concerts. And when he finally appeared on the all-important *Ed Sullivan Show*—only after its stone-faced host was forced to book him by popular demand—he was burned in effigy in Nashville and St. Louis. And the Catholic bishop of La Crosse, Wisconsin, sent FBI director J. Edgar Hoover an ominous letter warning him that Elvis Presley was "a definite danger to the security of the United States."

Then in 1958, at the height of his renown, the kid, now twenty-three, was drafted into the army. And even though he was convinced that two years out of the spotlight would end his career, he didn't try to weasel out of it. And he spurned repeated offers to join "Special Services," where he could have done his time performing for the troops. Nope, even though the kid was pretty much the biggest star on the planet, he wanted to serve his country as a run-of-the-mill G.I. (sort of).

And, yes, I know all of that was part of a larger public relations strategy hatched by his wily handler, "Colonel" Tom Parker (né Andreas Cornelis van Kuijk of the Netherlands). And, yes, Elvis didn't actually live in Ray Barracks in Friedberg, Germany, with the rest of his company, which doesn't really help my case here. But he did donate his Army pay to charity. And he used some of his own cash to buy television sets and extra fatigues for the guys in his outfit. And he actually showed up for work every morning at six sharp and drove a jeep all day.

And when the kid was honorably discharged two years later, he seamlessly resumed his career as a rock 'n' roll idol and movie star, billed above the title on more than thirty films. And all the while, he took care of his family and his posse. And all the while, he was remarkably philanthropic, performing free concerts, supporting more than fifty Memphis area charities, and giving away a bunch of cars, including his Rolls Royce Phantom V, to help kids' causes. He even bought FDR's presidential yacht, the *Potomac*, so he could turn around and donate it to Danny Thomas's St. Jude Children's Research Hospital.

Hey, I know Elvis Presley was no saint—not even close. And his manager, Colonel Parker, was just short of a carnival barker, which he literally was at one point. And, yes, Elvis started dating his future wife, Priscilla, in Germany when she was fourteen years old, which is admittedly pretty pervy, even for a guy from northern Mississippi. And, yes, he screwed around prolifically like every other rock star on the planet. And, yes, near the end of his relatively short life, Elvis Presley devolved into a bloated, lyric-slurring, drug-addled caricature of himself.

And when he died face down on the cold tile floor of his Graceland bathroom at age forty-two, Elvis Presley, who once asked for—and received—an authentic federal Bureau of Narcotics badge from President Nixon, had fourteen powerful pharmaceuticals in his system including Seconal, Placidyl, Valmid, Tuinal, and Demerol—a witch's brew of sedatives, barbiturates, and painkillers. But, hey, you try making the treacherous passage from backcountry yokel to global superstar while you're still in your twenties, and let's see how you do.

Anyway, I had these mostly warmhearted thoughts about Elvis Presley—whose music I never particularly loved—after touring what is, at the end of the day, his beautiful family home, a shrine to the King and, yes, a very slick money machine. But when you finish touring the mansion and the vast display of relics in the Trophy

Building, you end up in what's called the Meditation Garden. And buried there next to a lovely fountain surrounded by well-tended plantings are Elvis's dad, Vernon, his beloved mother, Gladys, and, of course, the King himself. And over to the right of the King, just on the other side of Vernon, is a fourth plaque commemorating Elvis's stillborn twin, Jesse, whose body lies in an unmarked grave back in Tupelo, because Vern and Gladys didn't have enough money for a gravesite or a headstone.

And all around the King's grave and continuing down both sides of the path that leads back to the bus stop are literally scores of floral arrangements—some quite elaborate, others mounted on easels with glittery hand-drawn placards, and all sent by ardent fans and loyal fan clubs around the globe. And every one of these folksy heartfelt oblations attest to the boundless joy Elvis gave unto the world—a hunka, hunka burning love that still blazes brightly four decades after his very unpleasant demise. And you know what? When I walked out of Graceland and got back on the bus, I was still a smug New York-slash-San Francisco jackass—but not about Elvis Presley.

15. SICK AS A DOG

Now it was time to make a run for it. After Buck Owens' crystal-less Crystal Palace, the gustatory indignities of Sonic Drive-In, and the exquisitely austere Mojave Desert; after the tallest thermometer in the world (probably) and the tallest cross in the Western Hemisphere (probably not); after scammy Zzyzx and bird-scorching Ivanpah; after Simba's Las Vegas walk of fame and the Venetian Hotel Panic Incident; after the less-than-apocalyptic high-country rainstorm, magnificent Meteor Crater, and standin' on a corner in Winslow, Arizona; after the enchanted Petrified Forest, the El Rancho's faded glory, and sad, boozy little Gallup, New Mexico; after the sublimely absurd Cadillac Ranch and tiny Erick, Oklahoma; after Simba's anxiety-induced illness and paying homage to Slick Willie and the King at their respective Ozymandian shrines—after all of that, a switch clicked in my brain, and I no longer wanted to press my luck when it came to Simba's continued survival—or my mother's. I no longer wanted to stop anywhere else or see anything else or do anything else except get myself to Pittsburgh to see my mother and get Simba to New York to see Laureen and the girls.

I don't know precisely what flipped that switch. The ghastly phone conversation with my dad in Gallup was certainly a factor. As was Simba's upset stomach in Oklahoma City. But most likely it was the Presley family cemetery at the tail end of the Graceland tour. There's nothing like a visit to the graveyard—however small—to remind us of the inevitable mortality that relentlessly stalks both dogs and men. So, like I said, now it was time to make a run for it.

The moment we finished our poignant Graceland tour, Erick and I hopped back in the station wagon and drove back over to Raines Road Animal Hospital. Erick stayed in the car while I went inside to retrieve Simba. The receptionist buzzed the back room. And while I waited for Simba to emerge, I asked the receptionist how he was doing. She told me in her melodic Tennessee accent that Simba was "doin' just fine"—which, of course, came as a relief. But she didn't provide much in the way of detail. And frankly, I should have questioned her more closely. I should have asked her, for example, whether the vet had noticed any lingering effects from Simba's kennel cough. And whether his paralyzed larynx seemed to be getting any worse. But honestly, the receptionist told me exactly what I wanted to hear—Simba was "doin' just fine"—so I didn't dig more deeply.

I did ask for the tab, which came to precisely ten dollars. And I did ask the receptionist why there was no additional charge for examining Simba. To which she replied, "Well, he seemed to be okay, so we didn't really have to do anything." And I guess that, too, should have been a red flag. But again it was exactly what I wanted to hear. So I pulled a ten-dollar bill from my wallet and thanked the nice lady for her kind hospitality. Then we gently loaded Simba into the station wagon and drove back onto I-40 headed east once more toward Nashville. In Nashville, we merged onto I-65 and drove 170 miles north to Louisville, Kentucky. Then we switched over to I-71, which took us the rest of the way across the Bluegrass State.

I don't recall very much about our quick sprint across Kentucky—although I can tell you from previous visits that it's a very beautiful place, at least the parts I've seen. All I remember about our drive that day is that there were lots of billboards along the side of the highway. And some of those billboards invited Erick and me to visit sex shops conveniently located near several exits, while others urged us to accept Jesus Christ as our personal savior. I honestly don't know whether the local porn peddlers and the neighborhood bible thumpers were consciously duking it out for the hearts and souls of Interstate motorists. But the alternating porn and Jesus billboards made for a very yin-yang sort of drive, morally speaking.

And to make that drive even more surreal, Erick and I heard several radio commercials that first spoke in menacing tones about ISIS militants who were beheading people in Iraq and then suggested—apparently as a logical consequence—that we should arm ourselves with the reasonably priced used firearms available at their well-stocked weapons emporium. The connection between ISIS savagery in the far-off Levant and buying a used gun in Kentucky was, of course, tenuous. But the gun store commercials seemed to offer up the same sort of easy-to-grasp, good-versus-evil dichotomy as the billboards. Buy a gun and protect yourself from ISIS. Come to Jesus and protect yourself from porn. Build a big wall and protect yourself from job-stealing Mexican rapists. Oh, wait, that last one's Donald Trump.

At any rate, we were now in a hurry. So we had neither the time nor the inclination to visit any porn shops, however conveniently located. And despite the fair warning, it seemed unlikely that we would encounter any ISIS militants in central Kentucky. So Erick and I let all of the contradictory messaging wash right over us. And after eight hours on the road, we ran out of steam in Cincinnati, Ohio, which was blessed with no fewer than eight Hampton Inns.

Simba had another good night—his second in a row—probably because I ate dinner in the room with him and slept by his side. And the next morning, he was back to his old up-and-at-'em-at-the crack-of-dawn self. In order to get to Pittsburgh that day, we had to drive the 230-mile breadth of Ohio and then cross a 15-mile sliver of West Virginia. But that would only take four hours. And thanks to Simba we got an early start.

By noon, we found ourselves emerging into eye-blinking daylight from Pittsburgh's half-mile long Fort Pitt Tunnel. The tunnel deposited us directly onto the Fort Pitt Bridge. And from there, we had a magnificent view of the Steel City's dozen or so skyscrapers, which occupy a compact triangle of land bounded by two wide rivers—the Monongahela and Allegheny—that merge at that point to form the mighty Ohio. For my money, it's the most beautiful cityscape in America—but I'm a born-and-bred western PA guy, so take that with a grain of salt. At any rate, less than twenty minutes later, I was knocking on my parents' apartment door. And what I found on the other side of that door was deeply disturbing.

In my own defense, I had called my mother every day religiously for the past two years. And I did fly my dad out to San Francisco in April so we could spend ten days together. And of course, I had been super busy jetting back and forth between San Francisco and New York, trying to facilitate our cross-country move. Actually, if I really put my mind to it, I could probably come up with any number of valid excuses for not visiting my ailing eighty-four-year-old mother for the last six months. But the fact of the matter was, I hadn't visited her for six months. And the moment I walked through the door, I knew I should have come sooner.

I was greeted by one of the small cadre of home health-care workers who now took turns trying to keep my very demanding mother as comfortable as possible from noon to eight p.m. each day. And since the agency sent a different young woman every three or four days—likely to keep them from quitting—I had never met the particular young blonde woman in blue hospital scrubs who let me in. So I introduced myself. Then I glanced around the apartment, and my heart sank.

My parents' home, which had always been a warm and welcoming place, was no longer bright and cheerful—even with its rose-colored carpet, sunny yellow sofa, and bold, colorful prints crowding the walls. Now it looked dingy and disorganized—sort of dirty actually—with two walkers, two wheelchairs, and an oxygen tank caddy all jumbled together along one wall of the living room. There were dark, grimy spots on the rose-colored carpet and several long white scrapes across the pink wallpaper in the hallway where the wheelchair had apparently rubbed up against it.

I asked Erick if he wouldn't mind waiting in the living room with Simba for a moment while I went back to my parents' bedroom to let them know I was there. I walked down the long hallway with a distinct sense of dread. And halfway to the bedroom, I heard my father yell from inside the hall bathroom that he would be out in a minute.

"Okay, Dad," I yelled back. "Take your time."

"I won't be long, Dov," he said. (He was the only person who called me that.) "I'm just finishing up in here, so I'll see you in a few minutes."

But I knew that probably wouldn't be true because, over the course of the past two years, my father's Parkinson's disease had progressed to the point where something as simple as brushing his teeth and shaving could take more than thirty minutes, and getting dressed in the morning consumed the better part of an hour.

When I walked into the bedroom—where my mother now spent twenty-two hours in bed every day—it was dark and stuffy, despite the yellow wallpaper and red and yellow drapes. For some reason the drapes were drawn in the middle of the day, so the only light in the room emanated from the forty-watt lamp on my mother's bedside table. As my eyes adjusted to the gloom, I saw my mother lying on her back above the covers in a beige nightgown with her eyes closed and an oxygen tube up her nose. The clear plastic tube led down the side of the bed and across the floor to a mini-fridge-size concentrator that was buzzing and huffing away inside a small walk-in closet. I also noticed that there was now an aluminum railing on my mother's side of the bed to keep her from rolling off onto the floor, which had apparently happened a dozen times. And as usual, the television was blaring C-SPAN, since my mother was one of the fifty or so people in America who were implausibly riveted by hour-long House votes on agricultural appropriation bills.

As I approached my mother's bed, she opened her eyes, looked up, and smiled wanly. "Oh, David. You're here," she said in a soft, happy tone.

But she didn't sit up, probably because she couldn't.

"How was your trip?" she asked.

"So far, it's been great," I replied, as cheerfully as possible under the circumstances. "Simba seems to be doing pretty well—at least for now. And Erick and I visited lots of really interesting places. We went to Graceland yesterday. And I'm going to tell you all about it, but first things first. How are *you* doing?"

My mother looked at me without speaking for a moment. Then her eyes filled with tears, and she started sobbing. She cried a lot these days, nearly every time I spoke to her on the phone. But now that we were face-to-face, I could see that these were tears of pure helplessness… and hopelessness. And without any words, only tears, I knew that the answer to my stupid question, "How are you doing?" was "I'm doing about as badly as possible. And I feel as if I've fallen into a deep pit and that I'll never crawl out of it. And I'm in constant pain from my spinal stenosis, despite the four operations. And I sneak extra OxyContin pills whenever I can badger one of the girls into smuggling them past your father. And if I can get my hands on it, which is difficult, I wash the OxyContin down with vodka, so for a few hours, at least, I can keep the pain and the misery at bay.

"And worst of all, my failing heart can no longer clear enough fluid from my lungs for the oxygen to get in. So I am literally drowning in slow motion. And I'm tethered by a forty-foot hose to that buzzing, wheezing machine in the closet. And once a week or so, the hose gets kinked or I roll over and pull the tube out of the machine. And I don't notice it at first. But after a few minutes I do notice that I can't breathe. So I yell for someone to come and help me. And so far, someone has always come. But now I live in constant fear that, one day, no one will get here in time. And if that happens, I'll slip into death. Because that buzzing, wheezing machine is now all that stands between me and suffocation."

And what can you say to that, except "I love you, Mom," and "I'm sorry you have to live in constant pain. And I'm sorry that you now take powerful narcotics that dim your bright and nimble mind. And I'm sorry that you of all people—our own goddamn force of nature—now have to lie here helplessly in the shadows.

"We always joked, Mom, that you sucked all the oxygen out of the room. But soon all the oxygen in the world won't be enough to keep you alive.

"And you know what, Mom? If the truth be told, I'm also pretty mad at you. I'm angry that you never did your back exercises after your spinal stenosis operations. And that you never did the breathing exercises after your mitral valve replacement. And that you refused to go to rehab like everyone else in the whole goddamn world who has ever had a mitral valve replacement. The doctors told you this would happen if you didn't go to rehab. We begged you to go. So why didn't you do it, Mom? Why did you let this happen to you?

"But in the end, Mom, I am indescribably sorry that this is the way you're going to die—slowly drowning over the course of months. You had a good life, Mom—a husband who proposed to you on your first date and relentlessly adored you every day of your life for the past six decades—even when you weren't easy to adore; two happy, healthy sons; eight beautiful grandchildren; and a coterie of loyal friends.

"You had a good life, Mom. But you will not have a good death. Your death will come down to the incremental turning of a little black plastic knob on the oxygen concentrator—from eight to nine when eight isn't enough, then from nine to ten when nine isn't enough. And then one day, ten won't be enough. And you will die."

But of course I didn't say any of those things. All I said was, "Hey, come on now. What's all this crying? You need to pull yourself together, Mom. Erick and Simba are waiting in the living room. And they want to come in and say hello."

"Oh, that's wonderful," my mother said, wiping the tears from her cheek. "I've always liked Erick."

"Okay, then," I said in a mock stern tone. "You pull yourself together. And I'll go get them."

I walked out of my mother's bedroom and stopped halfway down the hall for a moment so I could shed a few tears myself. Then

I dragged the back of my wrist across my eyes so Erick wouldn't see I'd been crying.

When Erick, Simba, and I went back into the bedroom—after I warned Erick that it wasn't pretty in there—Simba lay at the foot of the bed. And Erick and I stood next to my mother telling her tales from the road. And my mother hung on every word as if we were recounting our journey to Mars or a voyage to Atlantis. And that reminded me—at a moment when I really needed to be reminded—that no one ever will care as much about the minutia of my life as my mother. Nor will anyone ever be as steadfastly loyal, although Laureen comes close.

Fifteen minutes later, my father finally walked into the bedroom and greeted Erick and me in his usual courtly fashion. Actually "walked into the room" isn't really the right description. "Shuffled into the room" would be more accurate. Because since I'd last seen him, my father's Parkinson's had noticeably progressed. And when I saw him drag his feet across the carpet and when I saw his legs freeze up against his will ("C'mon you so-and-so's," he'd say to his legs) I knew that caring for my mother and constantly worrying about her was taking a terrible toll.

I also knew from the way she spoke to him that my mother had decided to simply ignore the whole Parkinson's situation so she could continue to demand my father's unwavering attention. And that, too, was a problem. Because even with a health-care aide in the apartment from noon to eight, that still left sixteen hours a day, every day, when my dad was her sole retainer—the only person who dispensed her pills, fetched her endless glasses of Diet Sprite she didn't drink, brought her snacks she didn't eat, and did the dozens of other random tasks that flitted across my her mind at the rate of three or four per hour.

When my mother wanted to satisfy one of these whims, she had two methods of summoning my father. The most common was simply bellowing, "Norm! Norm!" over and over at the top of her lungs. But if that didn't work, she repeatedly buzzed an intercom system that had recently been installed in every room of the apartment.

During the mere day and a half I was in Pittsburgh, I tried to help my dad as much as I could. And whenever my mother bellowed his name, I would immediately yell, "Don't worry, Dad, I got this." But even then, there were a few tasks that only he could do. And whenever my dad shuffled into the bedroom to find out what it was my mother wanted and then shuffled off again, my mother would turn to me and say, in an exasperated tone, "You have no idea how slow your father is these days. I thought he was slow before, but now it's unbelievable." And she said this as if my father didn't have Parkinson's disease, or if he did, it was certainly no excuse.

And if all that weren't enough to convince me that my parents' daily lives had devolved into a dark mire of pain and dysfunction, their sweet neighbor from down the hall, ninety-year-old Lois O'Conner, made it a point to pull me aside in the hallway and tell me, "David, your father shouldn't be taking care of Hannah anymore. You know he's got the Parkinson's. So someone should be taking care of *him*. And unless you and your brother do something very soon, this is going to kill him."

Then she stared me straight in the eye to let me know that she was serious and that if I failed to act, my father's death would be on me. And, again, I didn't say what I was thinking, which was, "You're talking to me as if I didn't already know that, Mrs. O'Conner. As if I hadn't discussed this endlessly with my brother. As if we hadn't repeatedly told my father, 'You know, Dad, you've really got to get some more help around here. You've got the money, so what's the problem? You're like a frog in water that's been heated so slowly you don't realize it's boiling.'"

And as if my dad hadn't replied every single time, "Well, I'd like to, Dov, but you know your mother doesn't like strangers in the apartment all day."

But, again, I didn't say any of that to sweet old Lois O'Conner, who was, of course, basically right. All I said was, "I understand what you're saying. And, believe me, I'm doing everything I can."

But that too was a lie. Because it was actually my younger brother, Dan, who lived four blocks away with his wife and three children, who was doing, if not everything he could, then certainly more than I did. I did the easy stuff like calling every day and buying my dad thoughtful Parkinson's-related gifts like easy-button shirts and a big motorized recliner that lifted him out of the seat and massaged his back. But whenever my mother or father had to go to the doctor's office—which was at least twice a week—it was my brother who took them. And whenever my mother rolled onto the floor or fell down in the bathroom in the middle of the night, it was my brother who got the call. And when the hotel that was closest to my parents' apartment—alas, not a Hampton Inn—wouldn't admit Simba, it was Dan and his wife, Stacy, who let him stay overnight with their three kids and Brody, their six-year-old cockapoo.

The second evening I was in Pittsburgh, my father decided that all of us—my mother, my brother, his wife, their three children, Erick, and I—should go out to dinner at a fancy steakhouse in downtown Pittsburgh. That meant, of course, that Simba would have to stay at my brother's house, alone with Brody the cockapoo, which wasn't optimal. But I figured having another dog around might tamp down Simba's separation anxiety. And attending what might be my last dinner out with my mother would have to trump Simba's needs, at least for one evening.

It also meant that we had to mount a fairly complex logistical operation to get my parents to the restaurant. In terms of equipment, the mission required a wheelchair for my mother and a walker for my dad, three large oxygen tanks that would hopefully keep my mother alive and breathing for the three hours we would be away from the apartment, a pull cart for the oxygen tanks, two small pillows to make the wheelchair more comfortable, a regulator, and the little wrench that we would use to change out the tanks. The pre-dinner operation alone took several hours, including half an hour to load my parents and all of their equipment into two cars.

In many ways, Pittsburgh is a small town, particularly the Jewish community. And as my mother passed in her wheelchair from the front door to the back of the restaurant, where our table was, she discovered, to her great delight, that she knew several other couples dining there. Most of my mother's close friends had died during the past three or four years. So the people she recognized were more like acquaintances. And they were all a bit younger than she was—maybe in their mid-seventies.

My mother had always been a raging extrovert—an only child who got all the attention at home, then a beautiful young woman who captivated all the high school and college boys. And she had always been the life of the party—sometimes to a fault. Like the time forty years ago when she poured a drink over the head of a guy she didn't like at a cocktail party and then cried out for all to hear, "The devil made me do it!"

The guy, who was a burly six foot three, rose from a now-damp sofa and challenged my father to a fistfight outside. But my father, who trained in hand-to-hand combat and knife fighting in the airborne and was a hardened veteran of more than one barroom brawl, quietly demurred. A few years later, the guy blackballed my parents at the local country club. So I guess, in the end, he won.

Anyway, as I pushed my mother's wheelchair through the restaurant, pulling one of her oxygen tanks behind me, she asked me to wheel her over to three different tables along the way. And since I was standing behind her, I could see the expressions on various diners' faces as my mother rolled up to them in her now shrunken form with an oxygen tube stuck up her nose and the big green metal oxygen tank trailing behind her. These expressions ranged from, "Holy shit! What happened to her?" to "Oh, my God. That could be me in a few years."

So even though my mother was thoroughly enjoying one of her few public appearances in the last two years, her unexpected presence at a fancy downtown eatery wasn't exactly a cause for celebration amongst the still ambulatory, breathing-all-on-their-own set who were roughly a decade behind her on the one-way road to Homewood Cemetery. And to make matters worse, my mother's conversation, which had always been smooth, effortless, even effervescent, now seemed slightly off-kilter. It was sort of like when you talk to someone with a mild mental disability, and you can't quite put your finger on it, but you definitely sense something is wrong. And that, given my mother's once agile mind and lifelong social ease, broke my heart even further.

When we finally got to our table, there were eight chairs and an empty spot at the head of the table for my mother's wheelchair. Initially, I was delighted to see that the restaurant had gotten it right, putting my mom in the place of honor. But then my mother decided that the seating arrangement wasn't exactly to her liking. She wanted to sit, instead, in the middle of the table with her back to the wall, so she could speak to everyone more easily. And perhaps more importantly, so she could see if someone else she knew walked into the restaurant.

This sudden change of plan required two waiters to carefully pull the table out from the wall without disturbing the place settings, then to remove the three chairs from that side of the table, push my mother's wheelchair into the position she wanted, and finally to put everything back together again. When that was accomplished, we all sat down and made ourselves comfortable——at which point my mother immediately announced—quite loudly actually—that she had to go to the bathroom. So the entire process had to be undone and redone again when she returned fifteen minutes later. And even though I knew it was no big deal, particularly under the circumstances, I found myself irritated that my mother seemed completely at ease ordering everyone around in a haughty fashion—particularly the poor waiters—and organizing everything precisely the way she wanted it with no regard for anyone else's preferences.

But then I put that together with her uncharacteristic social clumsiness, and I figured out what was going on. For two years, my mother had been laying in a shadowy room as her once sizable circle of friends slowly contracted—mostly because they died, but also because she couldn't attend social events anymore, and it must be said, because she now tossed off a lot of thoughtless remarks that offended even her closest friends.

So while my mother got to see my brother for an hour or so two or three times a week, and while she talked to me on the phone every day for maybe half an hour, the rest of the time she communicated only with my father and her rotating team of health-care minions. And that interaction consisted, for the most part, of her complaining about her condition, criticizing everyone's performance, and issuing mandates like a petty dictator. So, in effect, my mother had become desocialized, unable to function in polite society anymore. And her strong will—the force of nature that had always been there and had always made her interesting, even fascinating—was no longer buffered by her prodigious intellect and natural charm.

The full extent of my mother's desocialization became clearer when her first oxygen tank ran out of gas after only forty-five minutes. That was fifteen minutes sooner than anyone expected, so we weren't really ready for it. When the oxygen stopped flowing, my mother nodded off at the table. Her eyes closed, and her chin dropped to her chest. And when we woke her up and asked her if she was all right, she realized what was happening and her adrenaline kicked in. She gasped a few times and then shouted loudly, "Norm! Norm! I'm not getting any oxygen! Do something! Do something now!"

My father got a panic-stricken look on his face and hoisted himself out of his chair as quickly as he could, given the Parkinson's. His hands shook as he frantically searched through the little black bag on the oxygen caddy for the wrench to change the tank. But it wasn't there. So after a minute or so—although it seemed much longer—he said to my brother, "Hey, Dan, I don't know what happened to the little tool. Maybe it fell out in the car."

"I'll check," said my brother. And he ran through the restaurant and out the front door to his car, which was in the parking structure next door. Three or four very long minutes later, he came running back to the table with the little wrench in his hand. Then Erick the engineer took over, expertly swapping out the tanks in a matter of seconds—even though he'd never done it before.

By that point, of course, everyone in the restaurant—or at least everyone anywhere near us—was staring at our table in full-blown horror. And under normal circumstances, I would have been morti-fied that my mother had launched into a screaming panic attack in an upscale dining establishment.

But, honestly, what are you going to do? Are you going to get all upset because your mother is screaming for oxygen? Are you going to get embarrassed because she's been a shut-in so long she's forgotten how to talk to people? Are you going to get angry with her because she treats your father like a servant or because most of her problems are entirely of her own making?

No. You don't. You want to, at least at first. But then you re-member that she has always been the most loyal mother on the face of the earth. And that at least until a few years ago, she cared more about your life than her own. You remember that you probably wouldn't have accomplished whatever you did in life without her constant nagging and her lifelong, unstinting, and entirely illogical belief that you and your brother were the smartest boys who ever lived and that the sun rose and set on you. You recognize that this is a truly gruesome chapter in her life, the part at the end. But you also realize that this ghastly interlude between life and death with all of its concomitant horrors—the yelling and screaming, the profound selfishness, the frightening appearance, the self-defeating stubbornness, the utter lack of compassion for your father—you re-alize all of that has to be considered in the context of her entire life. Because even though my mother would likely die very badly very soon, her life was much more than the dreadful run-up to her death. It was decades of love, support, and excitement. It was a constant sense that she was firmly in your corner, that you always had a fierce ally. And it was the constant knowledge that any room she was in would be more interesting simply because she was there.

And this was the time in her life when we, her family, would have to love her without regard to what she did or what she said or how shockingly selfish and self-centered she behaved. This was the time when we would have to love her unconditionally, like… well, you know.

16. DOG RUN

Needless to say, I left Pittsburgh thoroughly depressed and deeply concerned. The whole appalling situation had been much worse than I'd expected—and I'd expected something pretty bad. But for the time being, at least, I had to prioritize my concerns. First I'd reunite Simba with Laureen and the girls. Then I'd figure out what I could do to help my parents during my mother's long slog toward death. Surprisingly, in my late fifties, no one very close to me had ever died—not since my grandparents passed away back when I was a teenager. So for me this was an unknown country.

The last leg of our cross-country journey would be relatively short—a six-hour, 374-mile sprint to the finish line. Erick and I left the Springhill Suites in Pittsburgh's East Liberty neighborhood at eight in the morning. Then we stopped by my parents' apartment to say good-bye.

Even before she was confined to her bed, my mother used to stay up most of the night reading and watching television. Eight in the morning for her was like three in the morning for most people.

And she rarely got up before eleven. So she was still asleep when Erick and I got to the apartment. And I didn't want to wake her. But my dad was up. And he met us at the door in his bathrobe and slippers. When I bent over to hug him, I remembered that he had once been six foot one and a pretty solid guy. But now, at eighty-seven, he was a full three inches shorter, stooped by age, Parkinson's, and chronic anxiety about my mother. I told my father that I loved him. And I begged him yet again to get some more help around the place. But, of course, I knew that wouldn't happen, so I guess that was more for me than for him. And I left feeling like a deserter.

I drove three blocks to my brother's house to pick up Simba. And when my brother's wife, Stacy, brought him to the front door, she said, "I don't know what he's been like the rest of the trip, but you should probably keep an eye on him. He seems really tired or maybe depressed. And he has a lot of trouble getting up and down the steps."

I chalked Simba's melancholy up to the fact that we had been separated overnight. And I knew his trouble with the stairs was arthritis, a long-standing malady. So Stacy's observations didn't particularly alarm me—especially since the alarmed part of my brain was pretty full at the moment.

I took the first shift at the wheel, driving three hours east to Harrisburg on I-76. Then Erick took over when we merged onto I-78. Two hours later, we crossed into New Jersey. When we got as far as the affluent exurb of Summit, less than an hour from Manhattan, we pulled off the interstate to get some gas and walk Simba for a while. I filled the tank while Erick went inside to use the men's room. Then I walked Simba down a small hill to a grassy area with some tall pine trees and bushes. Simba did his business in no time flat. But then, as we started hiking back up the hill toward the filling station, his legs buckled, and he collapsed in a heap on the grass.

"Uh-oh, what's going on, boy?" I said as a wave of panic washed over me.

Simba looked up at me wide-eyed, so I knew he was frightened, too. I tried to calm him by saying, "Come on, buddy, let's get you up. We're only an hour from New York, and Laureen and the girls are waiting to see you. Come on, boy. I know you can do it."

I straddled Simba and pulled up on his torso to take some of the weight off his legs as he tried to regain his footing. He got up on the third try. Then he wobbled back and forth for a moment. But he remained standing. I waited until he fully steadied himself. Then I got behind him, crouched down, and pushed his butt the rest of the way up the hill.

When we reached the gas station, Erick was just emerging from the men's room. When he saw the look on my face he said, "Hey, what's going on?"

"Simba lost his balance and fell over," I replied, "like he did when he got his snout infection last year. He's still pretty shaky, but he made it back to the car under his own steam. So maybe he's okay. But we should probably get moving."

Erick nodded and together we lifted Simba up and gently placed him on his bed in the back of the station wagon. Simba was still breathing hard, but he was also smiling—although I didn't know whether that was because he felt better or because he wanted to ingratiate himself with Erick and me so we wouldn't leave him behind like a dog pack would.

A half hour later, we were approaching Manhattan on I-95, and we had a choice. We could either take the Lincoln Tunnel under the Hudson River—in which case we would have to drive through Midtown traffic to the Upper East Side. Or we could continue twelve miles further north on I-95, cross the George Washington Bridge at the northern tip of Manhattan, and then take the FDR south to the 96th Street exit. Erick was driving, and I was navigating, so he asked me what I thought we should do. I honestly didn't know which way would be faster. And Google Maps was no help, because it showed red lines, indicating heavy traffic, on both routes. But then I recalled from my old days in Manhattan that the approach to the Lincoln Tunnel was always sort of a nightmare. Or at least that's how I remembered it. So I said to Erick, "Why don't we just take the GW? It may be less crowded."

As we drew closer to the George Washington Bridge, we saw signs that required us to make another choice—this time between the upper and the lower decks of the bridge. And again, I didn't know which way would be better. So I opted for the upper deck on the entirely irrelevant theory that it might provide a better view of the city as we triumphantly entered it. But that turned out to be a very bad call. Because once we committed to the upper deck, we saw another flashing sign indicating that there was an accident up ahead. But by that time, it was too late to change course.

I called Laureen on her cell phone. First I gave her the good news: we were only eight miles away. Then the bad news: we were mired in a massive traffic jam. I decided, at least for the time being, not to give her the really bad news—about Simba's collapse at the gas station—because I figured I could do that more sensitively in person.

"So how long do you think it'll take you to get here?" Laureen asked.

"Honestly, I have no idea," I replied. "Right now we're creeping along at one or two miles per hour. But who knows? It could clear up at any minute."

"Well the girls and I are waiting for you at the apartment," she said. "We're sitting on the floor because there's no furniture yet. But we can't wait to see you and Erick and show Simba his new home."

"And guess what?" she continued. "Since we're staying at the hotel for two more weeks while they finish painting the apartment, the staff there got everything ready for Simba's arrival. They put a dog bed in the room and left a big basket full of biscuits and treats. And since I've already been there for six weeks, the doormen all know me, and I've shown them Simba's picture. So they're really excited to meet him. They even put up a sign in the room that says, 'Welcome Simba.' Wasn't that sweet of them?"

"I guess they do that sort of thing when you stay in a hotel for two months," I said. But then I realized that sounded sort of churlish, so I added, "But, yes, that was very nice of them."

"Anyway," I continued, "I'll give you another call when we finally shake loose from this mess."

For the next full hour, we crept along at an infuriatingly sluggish pace, stopping and starting, stopping and starting. And with each passing minute, Simba's breathing seemed to become more labored. And after awhile, he was panting hard as if he couldn't get enough air. Like most people—well, maybe more than most people—I get pretty anxious when I come to a dead stop in heavy traffic and don't know when I'll start moving again. When that happens, Laureen always says she can see my blood pressure rising. But Simba's rapidly declining condition obviously made things much worse. And in my mind, I began to rail against the cruel fates that might allow Simba to travel three thousand miles across the continent to see his family only to let him die a few miles short of the goal. "That would truly suck," I thought.

I looked back over my shoulder and said to Simba, "Are you okay back there, buddy?" And like my mother, he didn't need words to tell me he wasn't. So I tried to rally his spirits with an encouraging halftime-in-the-locker-room sort of speech. And, yes, I realized he couldn't understand one word I was saying, but I thought he might be inspired by the rah-rah tone.

"Don't worry, Simba," I said. "You're not going to die in a traffic jam on the George Washington Bridge. You're going to make it to the apartment. And you're going to see Laureen and the girls. And they're all going to give you a big hug and tell you how much they love you.

"And you know why you're not going to die on this bridge, Simba? Because dying in a Sunday afternoon traffic jam on the George Washington Bridge is a bad way to go. And you're not going have a bad death like my mother. You're going to have a good death—a peaceful death in a comfortable spot with your loving family gathered all around you—because that was the whole goddamn point of this trip, Simba. And in this regard, at least, we will not fail!"

Simba seemed perplexed by my strident tone, and Erick looked slightly uncomfortable, but at least it made me feel better.

When we finally got to the other side of the bridge, we fought our way literally inch-by-inch across three lanes of traffic so we could exit onto Harlem River Drive, which turned into the FDR a few miles south. Thankfully the FDR was wide open. So we zoomed down to 96th Street. And when we got off the highway, I called Laureen again.

"Hey, we're finally in Manhattan!" I exclaimed. "Ten more minutes, honey—maybe less—and we'll be parked outside the building. So grab the girls and come on down to the street."

"We're on our way," said Laureen.

I looked back at Simba, and I said, "You hang in there, buddy. We're almost there."

But Simba didn't look very good at all. And he was panting like he just ran a mile.

Erick negotiated the relatively light traffic on 96th Street, turned left onto Park Avenue and drove seven blocks south. Then he pulled the car up in front of a fire hydrant on the southwest corner of 89th and Park. I jumped out, ran around to the back of the car, and opened the tailgate so I could hug Simba and try to calm his ragged breathing. And right at that moment, Laureen, Angela, and Grace ran out of the building and onto the sidewalk—just as I imagined eight days and three thousand miles earlier. They spotted the car and raced toward us with big smiles on their faces. They took a moment to hug Erick. Then each of them was polite enough to give me a quick hug before they got down to business and welcomed the real star of the show to his new home in Manhattan.

Laureen, Angela, and Grace squealed "Simba! Simba!" over and over again in high-pitched voices. They all hugged him in turn. And they each told him how much they missed him and cherished him. Then they showered him with love and affection as thoroughly as any dog ever has been or will be. And Simba was ecstatic, seeing his family all together again. It was a like a tonic for him. He smiled. His breathing relaxed. And after five or six minutes, he was able to hop out of the station wagon all on his own and jump around a bit with the girls on the sidewalk, his tail wagging furiously. It was clear that the love of his family was exactly the medicine Simba needed.

After the shrieks and the hugs and baby talk all ran their long course, Laureen grabbed Simba's red leash, attached it to his collar and said, "He probably has to pee. I'm going to take him over to see Central Park. It's only two blocks away, and I know he's going to love it."

I told her that Simba had done his business only a few hours earlier, so not to expect much. Then I briefly recounted his collapse at the New Jersey gas station and warned her that he had been panting pretty hard ever since. "Keep an eye on him," I said. "He's still a little wobbly."

"Don't worry," said Laureen. "I just want to show him Central Park so that he gets a good first impression of his new home. There are so many dogs over there for him to play with, especially on the weekend. I think he'll be really excited."

"Sounds good," I said. "But, hey, before you go. Where am I supposed to park?"

"There's a garage on 88th between Park and Madison," she replied. "Just leave the bags in the car. They'll be safe. And when I get back from the park, we'll take Simba up to see the apartment. Then we'll all head down to the hotel. Lisa's waiting for us there," she said, referring to Erick's wife.

"Okay, I should be able to manage that," I replied. "Have a good time with your old buddy, Simba."

"I will," said Laureen. "It's so good to finally see him... and you, of course."

Then she and Simba disappeared around the corner. And I noticed that Simba had a little bit of that old spring in his step. "Mind-body connection," I thought. "He just needed to see Laureen."

Angela and Grace headed upstairs to the empty apartment. And Erick and I got back into the car and drove around the corner to the garage. When we got there, I climbed out of the car and handed the keys to the attendant. Then I turned to Erick.

"Well, I guess we did it," I said. "It was a little hairy at the end, but thanks to you, we got Simba to New York all in one piece. We reunited him with Laureen and the girls. And now that he's seen them he seems to be feeling a lot better. Did you notice how he was jumping around with the girls? He was like a new dog."

"We should get a bottle of champagne at the hotel tonight," said Erick. "We'll drink a toast and celebrate our successful mission."

I was just about to thank Erick again from the bottom of my heart for making all of this possible when my cell phone rang. I pulled it out of my pocket and looked at the screen. It was Laureen.

"Hi, honey," I said. "What's up?"

"Something's wrong with Simba," she replied.

"What is it?"

"Can you just get over here? I'm at something called Engineer's Gate. It's at the corner of 90th and Fifth Avenue."

"Okay," I replied, "I'll get there as fast as I can." Then I hung up.

"What's going on?" asked Erick.

"I'm not sure. It sounds like Simba might be sick again. Laureen wants me to meet her at entrance to the park up on 90th Street. So I'm going to run up there now."

And without waiting for Erick, I took off as fast as I could out of the garage and onto the streets of Manhattan.

17. LUCKY DOG

When I got to the entrance to Central Park—out of breath from my four-block sprint—I found a small group of New Yorkers, maybe ten or so, milling around a long semicircular concrete bench built into one of the impressive baroque piers on either side of Engineer's Gate. I didn't see Laureen. But as I got closer, I spotted Simba. He was lying on the bench on his right side with his legs sticking straight out and his big brown eyes open but unblinking. I knew right away he was gone.

But then Laureen ran up to me. And it was clear that she either didn't realize Simba was dead or, more likely, that she wasn't yet ready to accept the loss. Laureen had two young men with her, both in their mid-twenties.

"I was about a quarter mile up the bridal path," said Laureen, still pretty calm, "and Simba was having a great time playing with all the other dogs. He was like a puppy again, wagging his tail and pulling hard on the leash like he used to in the old days. He was all excited to see the horses and the people and all the action in the park and he wanted to keep going further up the path. But then he stopped to poop. And he fell over. And he couldn't get up again. He howled for fifteen or twenty seconds like he was in terrible pain. It was horrible, David. Then he passed out.

"These guys here were nice enough to carry him all the way back. But now we need to get him to a vet, David, or an animal hospital. And we need to do it right away. And I don't know where to go. Where should we go?"

The two young men who had carried Simba to the bench both looked at me. One of them shook his head discreetly to indicate that it was now too late for a vet. The eight or ten other people gathered around must also have known Simba was dead. But then Laureen walked over to the bench and knelt down to stroke her old buddy—like her child in some ways—and there was fierceness in her eyes.

"Don't worry, Simba," she said. "Everything's going to be all right. We're going to get you the hospital, and the doctors are going to help you and everything's going to be all right."

And all the people in the semicircle around the bench looked at each other and then at me. And without a word, a conspiracy of kindness formed where everyone, including me, would pretend that there was still hope for Simba.

"Well, we better get him to the pet hospital then," said one of the young men who had carried Simba to the bench.

"I'll hail a cab," said another guy in his mid-thirties wearing a plaid shirt.

"I'll help you," said yet another young man with a closely trimmed beard.

Then a middle-aged fellow in jogging clothes with his cell phone out said, "Okay, I googled it, and you should probably take him to the Animal Medical Center at 62nd and York. They're supposed to be pretty good. I'm going to call them now and tell them you're coming. What's the dog's name?"

"His name is Simba," I said.

Then the guy in the plaid shirt yelled from the street, "Hey, I got a cab here."

And without being asked, two other young men—not the ones who carried him to the bench—picked Simba up, all eighty-five pounds of him, and they lugged him over to a yellow taxi that was pulled up to the curb on the corner of Fifth Avenue and 90th Street. Then, with some difficulty, they laid him out across the backseat.

"The first cab I hailed wouldn't take him," said the guy in the plaid shirt. "He said it was against company policy. What an asshole! But this guy's okay. It's probably against his company's policy, too. But he's going to do it anyway because he's a decent human being. Give me your cell number so I can call you later," he said. Then he sidled up to me and said *sotto voce*, "Hey, look, I know the dog's dead. But it's the right thing to do."

"Thanks," I said. "Thanks for everything."

By that point, Laureen was in the backseat of the cab with Simba's head in her lap. And since they took up the entire seat I climbed up front with the driver whose name was Muhammad. I really didn't know whether Muhammad realized Simba was dead or not—and I didn't want to ask him in case Laureen was listening. But he drove very quickly through the streets of Manhattan as if we really did need to get Simba to the pet hospital as quickly as possible.

I heard Laureen call Angela on her cell phone and tell her to grab Grace, hop in a cab and get down to 62nd and York as quickly as possible.

"I'll tell you when you get there," she said.

Since it was a late August weekend, lots of New Yorkers were out of town. So traffic was light, and we got to the Animal Medical Center in less than fifteen minutes. We pulled up to the curb at a pretty good rate of speed. And to my great surprise, two guys in green scrubs literally ran out the front door of the hospital pushing a regular human-sized gurney. It was like something you'd see in a television show or movie. Maybe it was just protocol. Or maybe the jogger in the park told them to act like it was a real emergency. But either way, I knew the perception of urgency would make Laureen feel better.

Once Simba was loaded onto the gurney and whisked inside, I pulled out my wallet and handed Muhammad four twenty-dollar bills. "Hey, thanks," I said. "I know you didn't have to do this. And I realize it might get you into trouble with your company. But, believe me, I really appreciate it."

"No, no, no. It's okay," said Muhammad, waving off the money. "No charge for this ride. I am very sorry about your dog."

"Take it," I said. "You haven't seen the backseat yet. You're going to have some cleaning up to do."

"No, really, sir. I don't want your money," he said. But I took the crumpled bills and thrust them into his hand anyway, which was probably the wrong thing to do, but at that point, I was in a hurry and not really thinking straight.

Then I ran inside.

I passed through two sets of automatic doors into the small first-floor lobby. Laureen was talking to the woman behind the front desk. She sent us up to the third floor, where we checked in at another desk and filled out some forms. After that, we sat in the waiting room, holding hands and not saying much. Ten minutes later, Angela and Grace emerged from the elevator, looking upset, and Angela said, "What's going on, Mommy? Is Simba okay?"

"We don't know yet," said Laureen.

Five more minutes passed, then ten, and I began to envision a miracle. "Okay, he looked dead to me," I thought. "But, hey, I'm not a veterinarian. Maybe they have some way to bring him back to life—like with those electric paddles or something. Maybe there's a chance after all."

Ten more minutes passed. And with every passing minute, I became just a tiny bit more optimistic.

"Do you think there's any chance he might live?" asked Laureen.

"They've been in there an awfully long time," I replied, "so maybe there is."

"I think there is," she said.

A few more minutes passed and a young woman in blue scrubs came in holding a clipboard. I didn't know whether she was a veterinarian or a nurse. She glanced around the waiting room and said, "Simba? Simba?"

Laureen, Angela, Grace, and I all stood up.

"Are you Simba's family?" she asked.

"Yes," I replied. "We're Simba's family."

She paused for a moment. It seemed like a long time. Then she said, in a kind-but-practiced way. "I'm sorry, but Simba passed away. We believe he had a heart attack. We did everything we could to revive him. But it was too late. I'm very sorry for your loss."

Laureen still wasn't crying, but she was close.

"Would you like to see him?" the woman asked. The girls just looked stunned. And Laureen said, "Yes. We want to say good-bye."

The woman ushered us down a hallway and into a small examination room where Simba was laid out on a metal table. His eyes were still open, so he didn't look like he was sleeping. He just looked vacant, empty—like our faithful old buddy in form and substance but without the spark of life.

Laureen approached Simba first. She cradled his head and, for the first time since he collapsed in the park, she let herself break down. For her, Simba was yet another loved one in a long line of family members, close friends, and pets who had died and left her behind—her mother from breast cancer when Laureen was only ten; her beloved stepbrother from colon cancer when she was in college; then Simba the First, again from cancer; and after that, her father and her best friend.

"Thank you, Simba," she said through her tears. "Thank you for being such a good dog. Thank you for being part of our family."

"You were the best dog ever," said Angela, tears streaming down her cheeks.

Some might say that Simba's sudden death was the worst possible welcome to our new home in New York. And most of the time, when I tell people the story, that's their first reaction. But I disagree, because our first encounter with New Yorkers in a time of sorrow and vulnerability was characterized by authentic compassion, subtle discretion, and a wholehearted willingness to help out a couple of complete strangers.

I mean, really, how could any random group of people have been kinder, more sensitive, or more generous of spirit? Two people we never met carried an eighty-five-pound dog a quarter of a mile through Central Park. Two others gently placed him inside a taxi. The cabby, who rushed Simba to the hospital didn't want to be paid for the ride. And craziest of all—I mean really crazy—a group of eight or ten people—none of whom knew each other—resolved without a word, to maintain the fiction that Simba could still be saved in order to spare Laureen's feelings. Even the guy in the plaid shirt called me at the animal hospital like he said he would—just to make sure we were all right.

Once when I told a lifelong New Yorker how a random group of Manhattanites reacted so compassionately when our dog passed away in Central Park, he replied very knowingly, "Yeah, New

Yorkers are great on the little stuff, the stuff that doesn't require any real effort."

But to our family, Simba's death and the compassion we received wasn't little stuff. It was big stuff. So to those of you who say New York is a cold, hard city full of heartless people who only care about themselves, I say fuhgeddaboutit. Because the very first group of New Yorkers we encountered on a hot Sunday afternoon in Central Park, well, they all pitched in when we really needed it. Those are the New York values we saw. And now we couldn't be prouder to call ourselves New Yorkers.

I actually have a theory about the natural kindness of the New Yorkers you meet on the street and in the shops every day. But let me preface it by saying that even though I'm from little Erie, Pennsylvania, I didn't just fall off the turnip truck. And I do realize that not every single citizen of this great metropolis is a kindhearted angel—not by a long shot. Anytime you pack more than eight million people into a relatively small space, you're going to get a fair number of jerks and a smaller group of truly heinous human beings. But that being said, I contend that New Yorkers on whole are a generally kind and friendly people—much more so than when I left dirty, belligerent, crime-plagued Manhattan for supposedly mellow, wear-some-flowers-in-your-hair San Francisco back in 1988.

So what happened over the course of the last three decades to change the basic human nature of a sprawling metropolis? Personally I think this sea change dates back to the World Trade Center attack in 2001. On that horrific autumn morning, New Yorkers—young and old, rich and poor, brown, black, and white—were all united by a common enemy and deeply moved both by the terrible loss of life and by the sacrifice made by more than four-hundred first responders who died in the service of their fellow New Yorkers. Compassion was the silver lining of that unspeakable act. And amazingly, this sense that we're all in this thing together seems to have persisted for well over a decade.

And while I would like to think that a similar small group of super-liberal, affluent Marin County residents or the strutting young techno-lords of Silicon Valley would have reacted to Simba's death in the same spectacularly kind and sensitive manner, it's honestly hard to imagine. It's far more difficult to build and maintain a sense of camaraderie and compassion for your neighbor when you haven't lived through a shared disaster. And it's even more difficult when all of your neighbors live behind high hedges and zoom past each other in Teslas and Priuses all day. As odd as it sounds, my new Manhattan neighborhood, Carnegie Hill, feels more like a small town to me—a place where the kids in their various uniforms and blazers all walk to school in the morning, people in the shops know your name, and the many, many folks walking their dogs early in the morning and late at night readily converse with each other on the sidewalk.

Another reaction I get when I tell people the story of Simba's death is that it's a shame he died only minutes after arriving in his new hometown. But again, I respectfully disagree. Simba got to see his family one more time before he died. He reveled in our warm embrace. And he heard every one of us tell him, from the bottom of our hearts, just how much we loved and cherished him. And I believe from the bottom of my own heart that old Simba, through sheer dint of will, held death at bay until he could say good-bye to Laureen and the girls, but most of all, Laureen. Of course, there's no way to prove that. And it's pretty easy to poke holes in the theory. Like how would Simba even know that Laureen and the girls were waiting for him? Or how far we had to go before he could see them?

So let me put it another way. If you tell me it's a shame Simba died the way he did, I would tell you that when we stopped in Pittsburgh to visit my mother, I saw what a bad death looked like. A bad death is a two-year-long, dread-ridden slide toward oblivion where every day is incrementally worse than the day before it and slightly better than every day to come. A bad death is lying in a shadowy room drugged up and tethered to an oxygen machine in constant fear of suffocation. A bad death is being cut off from the world.

Simba's death wasn't a bad death. It was a good death. In fact, I would go so far as to say that it was a poetic death. Saying good-bye to your beloved family, romping around Central Park on a sunny late-summer afternoon with a bunch of other dogs, and then kicking the bucket in under a minute? I don't think it gets any better than that.

In fact, Simba's death and our journey across America gave me a new way of thinking about death and dying as I bid middle age adieu and look sixty squarely in the eye. It's not a particularly complex or profound theory. But it works for me, and it goes like this: Life is basically a crapshoot. And you never really know how long you will live or what effect your life might have on the lives of others or the world at large.

You might, for example, try to scam the rubes like Reverend Springer of Zzyzx, California, and end up saving a species of fish. You might raise $2 billion to build a solar farm that mitigates the effect of climate change and end up incinerating thousands of birds. You might go broke digging twenty-three years for a giant iron meteorite that was never there and end up advancing humankind's understanding of meteor strikes. You might half bury ten old Cadillacs in a Texas cow pasture as a wry commentary on American culture (or whatever) and end up delighting hundreds of thousands of visitors who neither know nor particularly care about your underlying message. You might write a song that inadvertently saves a town. Or dream of stardom, achieve it beyond your wildest dreams, and still die fat, lonely, and addicted on your cold bathroom floor.

The point is that, even though you should always act with good intentions—because, it's actually the road to heaven, not hell, that's paved with good intentions—you never know what the ultimate effect of those intentions will be. The only thing you know for sure is that someday you will die. You may go sooner or you may go later, but you will die. You can jog, do Pilates, go vegan, and avoid cholesterol, gluten, and dairy, but you will die nonetheless. You can get yourself the best doctors and the best drugs in the world and devote your life to avoiding any sort of physical risk. You can date young girls, buy a Porsche, dye your hair, and get Botoxed, all to forefend the onset of decrepitude. But you will still, most assuredly, die.

So maybe what we should hope and pray for is not the circumvention of death nor its unnatural deferment. Believe me, based on my mother's experience, the few extra months or years you get may not be worth it. Maybe what we should hope and pray for is a good death, a death like Simba's—the warm embrace of our family, a carefree romp in the golden sun, then a nice dump in the park before we shuffle off our mortal coil.

18. A NEW PUPPY, PART 2

On a cold and rainy October evening, two months after Simba passed away, Angela, Grace, and Kara sat on the L-shaped sofa in the family room of our new apartment munching tortilla chips and staring mindlessly at *Law &Order: SVU*. Earlier that day, Laureen and I discreetly told Kara what we were up to. And what we were up to was picking up our brand new eight-week-old, seven-pound, fawn-colored pug puppy.

The new puppy, named Chang by his breeder, had huge black coffee-colored eyes, a black muzzle, black ears, and an adorable inch-wide black stripe around his tightly curled tail. Little Chang trembled on my lap as we drove back to Manhattan. When we got to the garage, Laureen grabbed his crate from the back seat. I wrapped him in a blanket and carried him in my arms around the corner to our apartment building. Then we took the elevator up four floors and entered the apartment as quietly as possible. When we got to the family room, I said, "Hey, Angela, look! I have a new friend for you—just like we promised."

Angela glanced up from her TV program and her jaw dropped. She squealed and yelled, "Oh my god, a pug, a pug! I can't believe there's a pug puppy in the house!

I handed the trembling little ball of fur over to Angela. And she hugged him and kissed him again and again before she reluctantly relinquished him to Grace, who gently stroked his tiny head. When it was Kara's turn to hold the new puppy, she immediately began to weep.

"Hey, why are you crying?" I asked Kara, who has always been quick to tears.

"He's so small and scared," she sobbed. "And he probably misses his family. I just feel sorry for him."

"Don't worry," I said. "He's going to have a pretty good life here."

"What should we name him?" asked Grace.

"Well, first of all, we're not going to name him Simba III," I replied. "So don't even think about it. We're retiring that name once and for all—like they retire the numbers of great ballplayers. Also, the breeder already named him Chang. We don't have to keep that name. He probably doesn't even know it's his name yet. But for some reason, I actually kind of like it."

"Isn't that racist?" asked Grace, who had attended a very politically correct girls' school in San Francisco for eight years and was therefore exquisitely sensitive in matters of gender, race, and sexual orientation.

"I don't know. Maybe." I replied, "Would you think it was racist if a Chinese family got a Labrador puppy and named him Max? Or if we named a French poodle Pierre? The pug is a Chinese breed. So maybe it's appropriate."

Over the course of the next several weeks, we discussed dog names over every family dinner. And we tried out a few to see how they felt. Angela, who loves the study of history and has always had a distinctly pedantic bent, wanted to name the new puppy Zheng He, after a fourteenth-century Chinese explorer who led an expeditionary fleet across the Indian Ocean to the east coast of Africa. Zheng He was a Chinese eunuch—like Chang would be in a few months—so they had that in common. But since no one in the family could pronounce "Zheng He" to Angela's satisfaction, it was a nonstarter—although Angela kept beating that horse for a while.

Grace, on the other hand, wanted to name the puppy something safe and straightforward like Budsy or Spud. But baby Chang seemed far too sweet and sensitive to shoulder such a backslapping sobriquet. So that didn't work.

Kara wanted to name him Gizmo because he looked like a creature with that name in an old eighties movie called *Gremlins*. But my personal favorite—also from Kara—was Voldemort, which seemed both ironic and appropriate because, like Harry Potter's evil nemesis, pugs have tiny smooshed-in noses, which, by the way, is where the term "pug nose" comes from.

But then, we took the puppy out for walks every day, and the various doormen in our building would ask his name, and we would all answer, "We're not sure yet, but for now we're calling him Chang." And since the doormen are trained to address every resident of the building by their formal name, they started calling the little fellow Mister Chang.

I'm not exactly sure why this archaic policy would extend to our dog. They didn't call Louis, the beagle, Mister Louis, or Charlie, the miniature poodle, Miss Charlie, to name just two of the twenty-five dogs that currently reside in our building. I guess it's probably because Chang is generally a surname and therefore requires an honorific. But whatever the reason, Chang became Mister Chang and Mister Chang stuck—although for the first three months we had him, Grace told everyone she met on the street that his name was Spud.

In many ways, Mister Chang was the polar opposite of our dear departed Simba. While Simba was a big strapping hound with a perpetual smile plastered across his gigantic face, Mister Chang was a barrel-shaped little nugget who always looked worried or grumpy—even when he wasn't. (The girls, using contemporary youth parlance, called his facial expression RBF for "Resting Bitch Face.") While Simba was an intrepid beast, more than happy to run off and explore the neighborhood for a few hours, Mister Chang was a sensitive soul who demanded and received constant attention and physical contact. And while Simba's favorite thing in the world was loping around the great outdoors splashing through mud puddles, Mister Chang either had to be forced or bribed with treats to leave the apartment at all—particularly during the frigid New York winter. And when we did finally get him out of the apartment and onto the street, he would prance down the avenue like a miniature dandy in his blue corduroy jacket, carefully avoiding every puddle and patch of snow on the sidewalk so he wouldn't get his precious little feet wet. And finally, while Simba devoted the greater part of his brain to thinking about food, Mister Chang seemed to crave affection above all else. As an older guy on the street once said to me, "Pugs are bred to love you. It's their survival strategy." That seems true, and I now understand why there are so many Crazy Pug People in the world.

Basically, Laureen and I treat Mister Chang more like a grandson than a pet, indulging his every desire. He sleeps in bed with us, or with one of the girls—something we would have never dreamed of letting Simba do. And believe me, I'm in no way proud of this, but after a few months we bowed to Mister Chang's unrelenting demands and added another chair to the dinner table so he could sit with us as an equal. So, yeah, now we're Crazy Pug People, too.

Oh, and one other thing. Although his breed is not particularly noted for this behavior, Mister Chang, bless his tiny Pug heart, absolutely loves to fetch little balls and dog toys—like Simba, the so-called Labrador retriever, never would—provided, of course, that he can do it inside the apartment.

On November 7, 2014, I received a late-night phone call from my mother.

"I'm not going to make it," she said hoarsely.

"What do you mean?" I replied in my groggy two-in-the-morning voice.

"I'm in the hospital," she replied, "and I'm going to die soon. So I wanted to call you and tell you that I love you and that you've always been a good son and that I'm very proud of you."

I told her I loved her, too. Then I assured her, very matter of factly, that she was not going to die, because first of all this wasn't the first time she'd called to say she was going to die. It was maybe the fourth or fifth time. And secondly, she'd already been in and out of the hospital three times in the last year without dying. And third of all, because that's what people always say in these situations, whether it's true or not. But after I hung up I realized that this was the first time my mother had called me in the middle of the night to tell me she was dying. So just in case, I groggily pulled out my iPad and booked a flight to Pittsburgh that would leave LaGuardia at eleven in the morning and arrive a little after noon.

But that turned out to be too late. Because this time my mother was right. And a few hours after she called me, her long-suffering cardiologist, Dr. Kross, bent over her hospital bed and said, "Hannah, there's nothing else I can do for you. I'll see you in heaven."

And my mother, rest her soul, gazed up at Dr. Kross—who had cared for her as if she were his own mother for more than five years—and said, "Dr. Kross, I don't think you're going to heaven."

Given her proclivity in recent years for pissing everyone off, my mother's funeral was surprisingly well attended—by more than a hundred mourners. Even Dr. Kross came. My brother, a Pittsburgh city councilman for twelve years—so very adept at public speaking—delivered a beautiful eulogy. Then I got up and tried to read a parable

I wrote about a mahogany-framed full-length mirror that was in my parent's apartment and in my childhood home before that.

It was an old mirror, and my mother used to admire herself in it back when she was young and beautiful. But very slowly, over the course of three decades—starting at the edges and moving toward the center—my mother covered the mirror with dozens of three-by-five photos of her eight grandchildren. So as her beauty faded, she saw less of herself reflected in the mirror and saw herself instead, as beautiful as ever, reflected in the faces of her grandchildren.

It was a very short eulogy, only a few minutes long, so I thought I could make it all the way through it without choking up. But it turned out I couldn't. So Laureen, who stood next to me at the dais, holding my hand, took over and delivered the last few sentences.

I was touched beyond words that Erick and his wife, Lisa, flew all the way from California on short notice. And they brought our other close friends from Marin, Yury and Zhenya, with them. And being proper Russians, Yury and Zhenya brought a half-gallon of vodka with them to the Shiva—which is sort of like a Jewish wake, only a lot less fun. And the vodka, which we drank in a series of shots over the long course of the mournful evening, allowed us to enjoy a truly bizarre moment that occurred when a female friend of my brother walked up to me at what was essentially my mother's wake and said, "I heard about your dog, and I'm very sorry for your loss."

I mean it was a nice sentiment and all. But it did seem an odd occasion to bring up Simba. And smart aleck that I am, I replied, "Yep. First the dog and now my mother." And while that may not sound funny to you now—probably because you haven't slammed enough vodka shots—it somehow struck Erick, Lisa, Yury, Zhenya, and me as hilarious, particularly when she walked away, and Lucas said, "Can we get a tiny Chinese grandma now?"

On a sunny New Year's Day, at the dawn of 2015, we held our own very small funeral for Simba. There was never any doubt where we would do it. The Sea Ranch on the rocky California coast was always Simba's favorite place on Earth. And anywhere else would have been entirely inappropriate.

Angela, Grace, Laureen, and I drove two-and-a-half hours up the coastal highway to Sea Ranch and pulled into our driveway. Then we walked through the house and straight out the back door to the cliff high above the crashing Pacific breakers. We each spoke for a few minutes about what Simba meant to us as a friend and companion and as an essential member of our family. Erick, who would soon get his own Labrador puppy, emailed a poem, "A Dog on His Master," by Billy Collins, which we read on his behalf. And after I read the poem, I wiggled open the rectangular tin box that held Simba's ashes, knelt down, and carefully poured them over the cliff toward the ocean thirty feet below. The ashes floated momentarily on the breeze and landed in a shallow tide pool. Then a wave rolled in and out again carrying Simba's earthly remains out to sea.

I don't remember exactly what I said during my brief tribute to Simba II, the wrong dog at the beginning of this story but undeniably the right dog at the end. But I now know what I should have said. Because when I got back to New York, I had lunch with my old friend Greenie, who is a terrific photojournalist and a great guy who has faced down a lot of adversity in his life. After lunch, as Greenie and I rode in a cab up Madison Avenue to my apartment, I told him the story of Simba's journey across America and his remarkable demise in Central Park.

And when I finished the story, Greenie turned to me and said, "You know I have a little Yorkie named Brutus. And I love him just as much as you loved Simba. And you know what I realized? I realized that we don't love our dogs because they give us unconditional love—even though that's what everyone says. We love our dogs because they show us that we, ourselves, are capable of loving another being unconditionally."

So yeah, that's what I should have said at Simba's funeral. I should have said, "Simba, you loved us unconditionally. And more importantly, we loved you unconditionally. And how precious is that in this dog-eat-dog world?"

NOTES

Chapter 1

13   "Animal Fighting Case Study: Michael Vick," The Animal Legal Defense Fund, aldf.org, last revised January 2011.

Chapter 4

37   http://dogs.wikia.com/wiki/Labrador_Retriever.

40   "Hunter-Gatherers to Farmers, The Neolithic Revolution: 10,000 years ago," www.historyworld.net.

"Origin of Domestic Dogs," by Ed Yong, *The Scientist*, November 14, 2013.

Geronticide: Killing the Elderly, by Mike Brogden, Jessica Kingsley Publishers, 2001, pp. 60-61.

Chapter 7

76   www.sftodo.com/sanfranciscoweather.

77   *Legendary Route 66: A Journey Through Time Along America's Mother Road,* by Michael Karl Witzel and Gyvel Young-Witzel, 2007, Voyageur Press.

"History of the Bakersfield Sound," by Jeff Nickell, first printed in the Spring 2002 issue of *Historic Kern*, Kern County Historical Society. Reprinted at www.visitbakersfield.com/visitors/attractions/history-bakersfield-sound/

"Bonnie Owens, 76; Singer and Ex-Wife of 2 Country Stars," by Steve Chawkins, *Los Angeles Times*, April 26, 2006.

Chapter 8

88   www.usacitiesonline.com.

"World's largest thermometer repaired in California," *USA Today*, July 11, 2014.

90   *Weird California: Your Travel Guide to California's Local Legends and Best Kept Secrets*, by Greg Bishop, Joe Oesterle, Mike Marinacci, Mark Moran and Mark Sceurman, Sterling, 2006.

Much of this information in this section comes from an article entitled "Quack-Founded Town With Last Name in the Alphabet," at www.roadsideamerica.com.

92   "Curtis Springer's Last Appearance at Zzyzx," KNBC, Los Angeles, 1974, www.youtube.com.

93   "The $2.2 Billion Bird-Scorching Solar Project," by Cassandra Sweet, *The Wall Street Journal*, February, 12, 2014.

"Ivanpah thermal solar power plant produces 'death rays' torching many birds," by Ralph Maughan, *The Wildlife News*, August 24, 2014, and "'Alarming' Rate Of Bird Deaths As New Solar Plants Scorch Animals In Mid-Air," by Ellen Knickmeyer and John Locher, Associated Press, August 18, 2014.

Chapter 9

105   bulletsandburgers.com.

106   www.tripadvisor.com/Attraction_Review-g45963-d3697929-Reviews-Bullets_and_Burgers-Las_Vegas_Nevada.

Chapter 10

114 "Landmark speaks volumes. A few critics aside, residents of Effingham are proud to claim the largest cross in the United States," by Ted Gregory, *Chicago Tribune*, May 21, 2002.

http://www.crossministries.net.

116 "Disaster for Barringer," www.barringercrater.com/about/history_5.php.

118 *Gazetteer of Planetary Nomenclature* by the International Astronomical Union (IAU), Working Group for Planetary System Nomenclature (WGPSN), http://planetarynames.wr.usgs.gov/Feature/616.

"Earth Impact Database," University of New Brunswick.

122 "'Take It Easy' by Eagles," www.songfacts.com/detail.php?id=3067.

standinonthecorner.com/park-history.

124 http://artofjohnpugh.com/murals/

"Standin' on the Corner Park," www.roadsideamerica.com/story/12603.

128 "Geology and the Painted Desert," National Park Service, U.S. Department of the Interior, http://www.nps.gov/pefo/upload/Geology2006.pdf.

"CO_2 as a primary driver of Phanerozoic climate" by Dana L. Royer and Robert A. Berner, Isabel P. Montañez, Neil J. Tabor and David J. Beerling, *GSA Today*, volume 14, number 3, pages 4-10.

"What Is Petrified Wood? How Does It Form?" http://geology.com/stories/13/petrified-wood/

129 "Petrified Forest National Park,"
http://travel.nationalgeographic.com/travel/national-parks/
petrified-forest-national-park/

"Arizona's Petrified Forest Is Stealing Away," by Charles
Hillinger, *The Los Angeles Times*, August 5, 1990.

130 "Petrified Forest Shrinks, One Stolen Piece at a Time," *The
New York Times*, November 28, 1999, and "Rocks with a
conscience pile up at Petrified Forest," by Larry Hendricks,
azdailysun.com, October 27, 2012.

"Civilian Conservation Corps (CCC),"
http://www.nps.gov/pefo/learn/historyculture/ccc.htm.

Chapter 11

135 According to the census bureau, McKinley County's poverty
rate is 35%, which is 2.5 times the national average. From
"McKinley County, New Mexico," quickfacts.census.gov/
qfd/states/35/35031.

http://www.greatamericanstations.com/Stations/GLP.

"History of Gallup," www.gallupnm.gov.

"U.S. to pay Navajo Nation $554 million in largest
settlement with single Indian tribe," by Sari Horowitz, *The
Washington Post*, September 24, 2014.

136-137 "A Town's Showdown With Problem Drinking. Step-By-
Step, Gallup, N.M., Is Mending Its Reputation," by Gwen
Florio, *Philadelphia Inquirer*, February 27, 1999.

Ibid, Florio.

tribalemployee.blogspot.com.

"Health Highlight Report for McKinley County," https://ibis.health.state.nm.us/community/highlight/report/geocnty/31.html.

"New Mexico leads nation in alcohol-related deaths," by Patrick Malone, *The Santa Fe New Mexican*, July 7, 2014.

"Rash of exposure deaths in Gallup, N.M., blamed on an old foe: Alcoholism," by Nigel Duara, *Los Angeles Times*, April 8, 2015.

137   http://blog.credit.com/2013/09/poorest-cities-in-america/

http://www.city-data.com/crime/crime-Gallup-New-Mexico.html.

138   "Gallup named Most Patriotic Small Town," Associated Press, October 11, 2013.

"The Navajo Nation's Own 'Trail Of Tears,'" http://www.npr.org/2005/06/15/4703136/the-navajo-nation's-own-trail-of-tears.

http://www.bosqueredondomemorial.com.

146   "Betty Hutton buried in small ceremony," Associated Press, March 13, 2007.

Chapter 12

151   "Doug Michels, Radical Artist and Architect, Dies at 59," by Ken Johnson, *The New York Times*, June 21, 2003.

"Beilue: Cadillac Ranch turns 40: Ant Farm artists, Marsh make lasting icon," by Jon Mark Beilue, *Amarillo Globe-News*, June 29, 2014.

152   "Stanley Marsh 3's letter to Ant Farm artists on the Cadillac Ranch proposal," by Jon Mark Beilue, *Amarillo Globe-News*, June 29, 2014.

"Stanley Marsh, Cadillac Rancher, Dies at 76, Shadowed by Charges," by Bruce Weber, *The New York Times*, June 23, 2014.

Ibid, Weber.

153 Artist Hudson Marquez: "'Anybody Who Talks About Their Art is Like, Full of Shit'," by Jennifer Swann, *LA Weekly*, January 15, 2013.

http://mediaburn.org/video/media-burn-by-ant-farm-1975-edit/

Chapter 13

157 https://www.grammy.com/photos/roger-miller.

"The Life of Roger Miller (1936-1992)," www.rogermiller.com/bio3.

"Do-Wacka-Do," Roger Miller Museum Newsletter, 33rd Edition, September 2013, http://www.rogermillermuseum.com/newsletter.html.

158 "The Life of Roger Miller (1936-1992)," www.rogermiller.com/bio1.

"Erick, Oklahoma," at Sperling's Best Places, www.bestplaces.net.

160 "McVeigh Chronology, Frontline," www.pbs.org/wgbh/pages/frontline/documents/mcveigh/mcveigh3.

"FAQs about the Memorial Grounds," home.nps.gov/okci/sitefaqs.htm.

"Inside McVeigh's mind," by Robin Aitken, news.bbc.co.uk, June 11, 2001.

161 "The Shadow of Waco," *New York Times* video, July 15, 2015.

"Waco: The Inside Story, Frequently Asked Questions, Janet Reno Statement," www.pbs.org/wgbh/pages/frontline// renoopeningst.

"Sacred and Profane," by Malcolm Gladwell, *The New Yorker*, March 31, 2014.

"Waco: The Inside Story, Chronology of the Siege," www. pbs.org/wgbh/pages/frontline/waco/timeline.

162 "Profile: Timothy McVeigh," news.bbc.co.uk, May 11, 2001.

Ibid, BBC.

163 "Trooper who arrested Timothy McVeigh shares story," by Kim Morava, *The Shawnee News-Star*, February 25, 2009.

"Okla. families can watch McVeigh execution on TV," by Terry Frieden, cnn.com, April 12, 2001.

"Oklahoma City National Memorial," www.nps.gov.

Chapter 14

173 "Building the Center," https://www.clintonfoundation.org.

178 "Elvis Presley jets for sale amid Graceland makeover," by Alan Duke, cnn.com, September 1, 2014.

"Elvis Presley's Graceland: 3764 Elvis Presley Boulevard," graceland.elvis.com.au.

180 "Elvis at Graceland," at www.graceland.com.

Elvis Presley: The Man. The Life. The Legend, by Pamela Clarke Keogh, Simon & Schuster, 2008, page 2.

"7 Fascinating Facts about Elvis Presley," by Elizabeth Nix, www.history.com, July 1, 2014.

181 *Elvis Cinema and Popular Culture* by Douglas Brode, McFarland & Co., 2006, p. 21.

"Elvis Presley in Germany," http://www.german-way.com.

"Elvis Presley's Charitable Acts," elvis.wikia.com.

182 A Rare Chat With Colonel Parker," *The Chicago Tribune*, August 14, 1989.

"When Elvis Met Nixon," by Peter Carlson, *Smithsonian Magazine*, December 2010.

"Elvis uncovered," by Ray Connolly, *Daily Mail*, undated, retrieved July 17, 2015.

ACKNOWLEDGMENTS

My sincere thanks to:

Publishing guru Michael Fragnito for his sage advice and friendship

My smart and faithful agent of twenty-five years, Carol Mann

My wonderful publisher, Lisa McGuinness

My longtime co-designer and digital pre-press genius, Peter Truskier

My brilliant readers: Barbara Berger, Jeff Epstein, Mark Greenberg, Angela Seeger, and Joe Sweeney

My saintly father, Norman Cohen

My steadfast brother and sister-in-law, Dan and Stacey Cohen

… and most of all, my beloved Laureen, Kara, Will, Lucas, Angela, and Grace

… and, of course, the noble Simba (2000–14)

The Wrong Dog is dedicated to my mother,
Hannah M. Cohen
(1930–2014)

Wedding Day:
Laureen and I tie the
knot in Napa Valley
on August 19, 2006.
Doug Menuez

Handsome Boy:
Simba, age six, in
November 2006.
Michael Hornbogen

Once Upon a Time: My mother, Hannah, (above) in the late 1960s; my father, Norm, (above, right) at Fort Bragg in 1945 and with Kara.

Best Friends: Simba and Grace, age seven, October 10, 2006.

Michael Hornbogen

Blended Family: Simba, age 8, with (clockwise) Lucas, 15; Kara, 21; Will, 20; Angela, 12; and Grace, 10 on August 22, 2009. *Michael Hornbogen*

Road Warriors: Erick, Simba, and I pose for a photo in Erick's driveway before leaving on our cross-country journey. *Lisa Miller*

Mojave Heat: According to the "world's tallest thermometer," it was 111° in aptly named Baker, California. *Erick Steinberg*

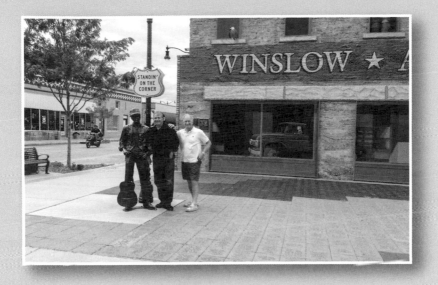

Takin' It Easy: Paying homage to the classic Eagles hit at Standin' on the Corner Park in Winslow, Arizona.

Painted Desert: Erick taking photos at Petrified Forest National Park.
David Elliot Cohen

Painted Cars:
Simba (above)
relaxes at Cadillac
Ranch near
Amarillo, Texas.
Erick Steinberg

Erick in Erick:
Erick fulfills a
childhood dream by
visiting his namesake
town in Oklahoma.
David Elliot Cohen

Ashes to Ashes: Grace holds Simba's ashes at Sea Ranch before I drop them thirty feet off a cliff into the Pacific Ocean on January 1, 2015. *David Elliot Cohen*

Timid Soul:
Simba's successor,
Mister Chang,
hates to go outside.
Tiffany Faulkner

ABOUT THE AUTHOR

For three decades, best-selling author and editor David Elliot Cohen has created books that have sold six million copies worldwide. Most were in the immensely popular *Day in the Life* and *America 24/7* photography book series. A proud graduate of Yale University and Cathedral Preparatory School in Erie, Pennsylvania, Cohen has four *New York Times* bestsellers to his credit along with two other #1 bestsellers—in Australia and Spain. His 1999 memoir, *One Year Off*, was a national bestseller. He lives in Manhattan with his wife, Laureen Seeger, and the youngest of their five children—the other four having flown the nest.